INSIDE THE DANGER ZONES

TRAVELS TO ARRESTING PLACES

INSIDE THE DANGER ZONES

TRAVELS TO ARRESTING PLACES

PAUL MOORCRAFT

Biteback Publishing

First published in Great Britain in 2010 by
Biteback Publishing Ltd
Westminster Tower
3 Albert Embankment
London
SE1 7SP

ISBN 978-1-906447-10-6

10 9 8 7 6 5 4 3 2

A CIP catalogue record for this book is available from the British Library.

Set in Sabon
Printed and bound by
CPI Group (UK) Ltd, Croydon, CR0 4YY

CONTENTS

FOREWORD

I cannot tell you exactly what type of book this is because I don't know. Yes, it is mainly about war zones. Sure, it's about travel in exotic locations. It's also about journalism. And there is, I hope, humour as well as adventure.

Perhaps I can explain *why* I wrote it.

I have spent the best part of the last forty years travelling and talking to really odd – often homicidal – people in unusual places, but these are *not* the war memoirs of a Welsh hack. My initial desire to travel in and write about war came from my frustrations as a Sandhurst instructor and, later, university academic. I didn't want just to talk about or research other countries, I wanted to *feel* them. Another reason was my objection to the type of journalism, especially evident on American TV news, which suggests that reporting and film-making are based on synthetic travels in a bubble. At the other end of the scale, I objected just as vehemently to some TV stars' mock heroics, super-hyped on air. I wanted to explain what went on behind the scenes, particularly the cock-ups. Mostly *my* cock-ups. And my numerous arrests, always in the line of duty of course.

I have struggled hard to be neutral about conflicts, without being afraid to call a spade a bloody shovel when necessary. So if you're looking for political correctness, don't read this book. Although I have sometimes used the dialogue style of a novel, the conversations are based upon my contemporary notes and video or audio recordings. In short, I have tried to make my account as accurate as possible.

I hope readers will identify with my travails (travels comes from the same word) as I walk to Kabul with a camel (and holy warriors) who hated me, get lost on a motorbike ride with psychopaths in central Mozambique, fall down drunk in a shebeen in Soweto, or, like everyone else, become totally confused in Lebanon or former Yugoslavia by the craziness of politicians.

Much of my reporting was done within the cosy intellectual

parameters of the Cold War. Then, post-9/11, came the so-called 'clash of civilisations' and a series of travels in Islamic lands, returning to Afghanistan, despite vowing never to go back, fresh locations in Iraq and Darfur, and indulging in the tragic déjà vu of conflicts in Israel/Palestine. I thought the world had been turned upside down by the assaults on the twin towers, but the economic crash of 2008–9 threatened to do to capitalism what years of communist intrigue had failed to do. Perhaps al-Qaeda had better hurry up, or the Western world will implode before bin Laden *et al.* can aspire to complete their mission.

Looking back, I don't know how I managed to wriggle out of some of the countries I visited, usually with a film, book or radio story in my bag. I am probably one of the world's clumsiest people, so I hope you can sometimes smell not just the cordite but also the fear, usually mine.

I do talk about guns and battles but I am more concerned with colourful characters, the customs, politics, and landscapes. Buildings interest me more than bullets. Sometimes I write about specific events; in other chapters I try to catch the mood of major upheavals, such as the collapse of communism in Eastern Europe, the implosion of former Yugoslavia or the chaos in post-Saddam Iraq. But it's not all depressing, and I sometimes stretch the definition of conflict and write about nice places. Some philosophical themes hover in the distance, but they are very implicit. Journalism is not about 'lectures', it is always about 'stories'. I hope you enjoy reading them.

The photographs are my own, except where indicated otherwise. I have few acknowledgements, mainly because most of the people I met in this line of work did everything they could to hinder, discourage or, occasionally, shoot me. I would, however, like to thank Susan Mears, my agent, Tony Denton for endless computer help, Fran and Liz Ainley for believing in my writing, and my editor Sam Carter. I thank also Caroline Bolton for allowing me to use some of the material from my first foray into autobiography, *What the Hell am I Doing Here?*, published in 1995 by the now sadly defunct Brassey's. Some of the material in this book also comes from my second autobiographical venture, *Guns and Poses: Travels with an Occasional War Correspondent* (2001). I salute Nick della Casa, who was killed in Kurdistan, and Al J. Venter, who survives everything. I also appreciated the good companionship of Irwin Armstrong, a cameraman who was so tolerant of my many technical, and personal, failings. Finally, to Tim Lambon, now deputy foreign editor of Channel 4 News, thanks for so often covering, and kicking, my butt.

Stream Cottage
Gomshall
Surrey
UK
September 2010

LIST OF MAPS

INTRODUCTION

The mountains encircling Kabul are savage, beautiful and sometimes treacherous – like the people who inhabit them. For five years death had stalked their valleys, in the form of Soviet Hind helicopter gunships. These flying tanks were exquisitely armed: 12.7mm cannon protruded from the nose and the stub wings carried bombs and rockets. At first I wasn't too worried about them, as they had been swashbuckling across the clear Afghan skies for days, ignoring us as eagles scorn flies. The mountains seemed to provide protection, the guerrillas were blasé, and I too had become complacent.

That complacency was shattered at 7 a.m. on 21 July 1984 – the gunships came calling. The Russians had launched a major offensive to clear the *mujahedin* rebels from their positions around the capital. I was dozing in a mud hut, along with the rest of our five-man film team, when someone shouted 'Choppers!'

Two fat Mi-24 Hinds were hovering above like expectant vultures. The cameraman, Chris, rushed to set up the equipment to film them. The 'Captain', a richly moustachioed Afghan officer who had defected to the *mujahedin*, screamed at us to take cover. He knew what was coming.

We grabbed our heavy rucksacks and some of the bulky film equipment.

Our translator, 'Doc', shouted, 'Put your equipment in the cave.'

We hastily shoved our kit away as the five-bladed helicopters drew closer.

'Take cover in there,' Doc ordered nervously.

The tiny exposed cave was full of ammunition – it seemed suicidal to hide there if high-explosive bombs started to crash down on us, so Chris and I ran into a small gully. There was no other cover on the stark hillside except a few trees and three decrepit mud huts about 100 yards away. As the only buildings in the area they would presumably be prime targets for the gunships' rockets. Crouching in the gully, we realised it was used as a latrine, but we didn't dare move. Better shit than shrapnel.

Moreover, I had broken a golden rule about never sharing a foxhole with anyone braver than me.

Four sleek MiG-23 aircraft arrived and performed a high-altitude turn above, then swooped down and started to bomb the valley floor half a mile from where we crouched. Two more MiGs joined the party. Framed against the cloudless sky, their deadly grace was almost bewitching.

The helicopters dropped altitude and hovered just above us. A guerrilla opened up with a Dasheka anti-aircraft gun. If by some miracle the Hinds hadn't seen us before, they could hardly ignore us now.

Pointlessly, I shouted 'shut up'.

He was only sixty yards away but he couldn't have heard me above the gunfire, even if he had spoken any English. In vain, I ransacked my severely limited Pushtu vocabulary for a translation.

The MiGs blasted away. As they came out of their bombing runs they sometimes shot out anti-heat-seeking missile flares, which left a mosaic of cloud patterns against the deep blue sky. Chris was cursing like a banshee. Action all around, and from our gully we could not film properly.

'Bend over,' he shouted.

'Is this some last perverted wish, Chris?' I asked, with more bravado in my voice than I felt.

'No, you fool, I haven't got the tripod. Bend over and kiss your arse goodbye.'

'You forget the tripod, I have my face full of crap and my backside napalmed. Great holiday.'

Chris laughed. 'If it was easy everybody would be doing it.'

I bent over, nose into the shit, and Chris put the camera vertically on my back to film the gunships right above us. What a way to go, I thought, acting the human tripod as we filmed – in full colour – our own demise. Each long minute had an acute intensity, a strange purification. Despite the fear, a kind of unreality also intruded. I felt I was the subject, and also the observer, of a surreal Fellini movie.

Above all, I pondered on the psychological role reversal acted out by our film crew. We had seen lots of war recently in southern Africa. The other four members of the TV crew had all been soldiers before becoming film-makers; they were veterans of conflicts in Rhodesia,

Angola, Namibia, and Mozambique. I had covered these wars as a journalist. We had often flown in helicopters, chasing or filming black insurgents on the ground.

Now the tables were turned. We were indistinguishable from our scruffy companions. We, too, were dirty, smelly, frightened guerrillas, caught in the open by government gunships. After years of being on the 'other side' – the mechanised, 'death-from-the-air', safe side – the hunters had become the hunted. I understood a lot about Africa in those Afghan minutes.

Mujahedin tracers flecked past the heavily armoured gunships as they dropped closer, seeming oblivious to the ground fire. Cowering in the gully we might stand a chance if the aircraft bombed us, but the choppers' napalm would devastate the whole mountainside, and us.

Two MiGs flew low along the valley and turned in long, graceful arcs: real Second World War stuff. With the heavy Arriflex camera on my back, I craned my head around to stare straight up at the hovering Hinds. I could see their vast array of weaponry very clearly.

Chris muttered: 'Right, they've finished bombing below us. It's our turn next.'

'What the hell am I doing in Afghanistan?' I asked myself.

I spent decades trying to answer that same question about many other war zones. What was the point in risking so many dangers for so little news coverage? Mere entertainment for couch potatoes back home, or revealing horrors and injustice to make the world a better place? Was it healthy adventure or morbid voyeurism? Merely a personal exploration of the boundaries of my own courage, or lack of it? A version of the old adage 'you haven't lived until you've nearly died'? Or was I following the herd in seeking to topple dictators and uncover unjust wars in the name of professionalism, pride, Pulitzer and personal gain? Though I always considered myself an amateur war correspondent, pride had little place in my war-zone buffoonery, and I won very few prizes, and made precious little money in exchange for sickness, injuries and heartache.

I used to tell myself I was getting shot at for that great video sequence or photograph. But did the pictures make any difference? Or was I in the end just a war tourist, a poseur? This book is my attempt to answer these questions, and the readers may also come to their own conclusions, so long as they sometimes laugh, and even reflect, on the road to reaching their verdicts.

EXPLORING AFRICA

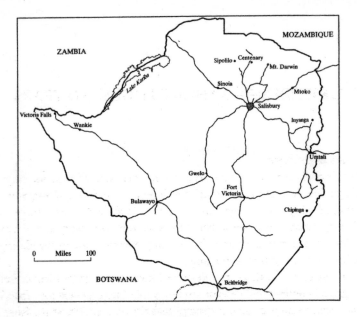

Rhodesia

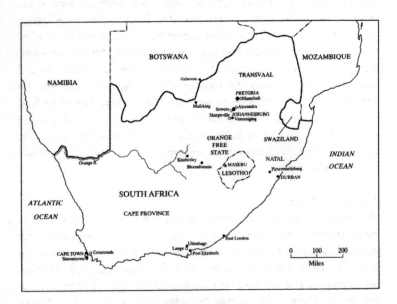

South Africa

1. RHODESIA – A SHORT THOUSAND YEARS

Tours of purgatory

I can't really explain how I started on my long journey without maps. I regarded most of the earlier trips as holidays, not tours of purgatory, although Afghanistan was an exception. Despite my deep roots in Wales, perhaps I became addicted to exile, to always being a foreigner, a lone stranger in an unfamiliar setting. Maybe I found wandering more stimulating than belonging.

I started off with all the keyboard courage of an academic. My degrees in politics and defence studies were of no practical use. True, I had been a senior civilian instructor teaching war studies at the Royal Military Academy, Sandhurst, where I played rugby, rode horses, and did some shooting, all equally badly. I even showed some of the expected macho form by having a row with Princess Anne; I felt sorry for her then husband, my fellow instructor Captain Mark Phillips. But I was the proverbial round peg in a square hole, almost convinced that I was the only sane man in a lunatic asylum. I recalled the old Sandhurst adage: 'From the roof of Old College you can see the panorama of an entire army career – first Sandhurst, then Aldershot, later Staff College, and finally Broadmoor lunatic asylum.' One of the more polite names I was called in the officers' mess was 'rebel'. So moving to a rebel colony seemed appropriate; I wanted to experience war, not talk about it.

The lure of Africa

'Rhodesia is a well-armed suburb masquerading as a country.' The first sentence I ever wrote about the place just about summarised my political views on Rhodesia as I planned my initial trip to southern Africa in 1976. There was more to it than just knee-jerk political correctness: I was intellectually curious about the rebellion against the British Crown. How could the whites, outnumbered by blacks twenty-five to one and ostracised by the world, hang on to power for so long? How could they argue with arithmetic? And because of the political furore, Rhodesia and more especially South Africa had almost ceased to be geographical entities. To the outside world they were more a *condition*, a disease. South Africa was no longer a country but a map of the mind, in which anyone could find his own place. What is more, as a boy I had been seduced by the African tales of writers like Henry Rider Haggard. As a student I had been touched by its apparent mysticism. Armed with conventional wisdom, curiosity and just a touch of romanticism, I set out for Africa in March 1976.

I had a cheap return ticket to Kenya because I couldn't afford the fare to Johannesburg. My only preparation was replying to an ad in *The Guardian* for a job lecturing at the University of Rhodesia – the country's sole university and exempt from UN sanctions because it was multiracial. I saw the ad by chance the week before I left and gave a forwarding address in Grahamstown, South Africa, where a friend of mine was a visiting lecturer. It was a long shot, because I didn't know whether I would even get that far.

My trip to Kenya had been prompted by a friend, Chris, who taught in Nyeri. Over a beer in a dingy Welsh pub he suggested a visit; within a month he was showing me around sunny Kenyan game parks. But despite his expansive hospitality I knew that I would find the white-ruled states more interesting, so I used the last of my money to buy a ticket to Johannesburg.

At Jan Smuts airport I was met by Andy Gancewicz, a big, aggressive, kind-hearted Pole with whom I had worked briefly on the *Western Mail* in Cardiff. Andy thought I was demented when I said I was thinking about travelling to Rhodesia.

'There are lots of jobs here in Jo'burg. Why go to a place where the Afs are knocking the hell out of the whites? There's a war on.'

'That's precisely why I want to go. To find out why.'

Andy showed me around Johannesburg, a downtown concrete jungle alleviated by opulent northern suburbs. It seemed so rich, powerful and organised after decaying, ex-colonial Nairobi, but I didn't like Jo'burg and didn't want to work there. After five weeks I decided to find my Grahamstown friend, Alan Ward, another Sandhurst instructor. But he wasn't in Grahamstown, and the only response to my letter was a cryptic message:

In Lesotho. Get to Maseru. Then travel to Masieneking. Three bus stops due west proceed up a large hill to the left, turn right at the kraal, walk for a mile or so; there you will find me. Gone native.

Alan was one of the most unadventurous and conventional Englishmen I had ever met. It was not the sort of message I expected. Intrigued, I set out to hitchhike to Lesotho. I thought it would take me a day; it took two. I had always found hitchhiking a useful way to meet people and find out about a country, and this long trip taught me a lot about white South African attitudes. On the bus out of Maseru, Lesotho's tiny, dusty capital, I also started learning about rural Africa. A chicken perched on my head and a goat backed on to my lap. I disembarked with relief at Alan's hill and, carrying my small rucksack, started to walk in the blazing midday sun.

My white friends in Africa seemed suspicious and wary of Africans. They didn't travel on African buses or walk around African areas. Whites in Africa didn't walk at all, they drove. Walking through the scrub on a dirt path, I was therefore considered something of an oddity. I was greeted warmly by the locals, who seemed to materialise out of thin air and went out of their way to be helpful when I asked for directions. Their long, convoluted explanations, in sometimes broken but often fluent English, were confusing but more than friendly.

I gleaned the beginnings of two important truths on my brief safari to find Alan. One, African directions are unreliable, as you are always told, out of politeness, what they think you want to hear. If it's ten miles and you look tired, you'll be told it's just a mile or so. As I usually looked exhausted on forays into the bush, over the years I always received the same encouraging directions. It also pays to ask one person; consulting a group produces a long debate in the local language which, when translated into English, ends up as gobbledygook. It was some time before I gave up asking directions and learned instead to request that I be shown the way. With rare exceptions, strangers would make long detours to accompany this oddball white. The tremendous bush skills of rural Africans were impressive, and I later made long journeys with trackers and guerrillas who seemed to have a built-in compass, even when travelling at night through virgin bush.

The second thing I learned was to distrust the white fear of Africans: 'Go in there and you'll get robbed or knifed.' Most whites lived cocooned in their own fears, hatreds, and prejudices. Later, when I witnessed the mayhem in Soweto and the results of massacres in Rhodesia, I sometimes succumbed to the white siege mentality. At times I carried a gun. Experience taught me to be cautious, but my first instincts, based on naive curiosity, mostly prevailed.

I kept walking and asking directions. Yes, some whites were working in a nearby village. Sweat poured from me. I got the inevitable encouragement: 'It's not far from here.' Eventually I came upon a small clearing with a few mud huts scattered around. In the middle of a group of African children was a thin Englishman with baggy shorts and a knotted handkerchief on his head. It had to be Alan.

Alan was as pleased to see me as Dr Livingstone was to encounter another Welshman, Henry Morton Stanley. I spent a week helping him build a schoolhouse, even though he was even less of a handyman than I was. We slept in a mud hut, drank with the tarts in the local beer hall, learned bits of Sesotho and played paternalistic white *bwanas*.

I stayed with Alan for another week in Grahamstown, South Africa. He taught politics at Rhodes University, so I earned my keep by giving a few lectures about a recent trip to Israel.

A letter arrived from the University of Rhodesia offering me an interview for the job I'd applied for, a temporary post teaching politics. They included a return airfare to the capital, Salisbury. For the previous two weeks the road linking Rhodesia with South Africa had been closed because of guerrilla attacks.

'You must be mad to teach politics in the middle of a civil war,' Alan said. 'I hear that the last five white politics lecturers were deported.'

'If they want a lunatic, I have the right qualifications.'

I borrowed some money from Alan, caught an overnight train to Johannesburg, and flew to Salisbury. On the plane I discovered that the man in the next seat was not only a Welshman from Corwen but also a lecturer at the University of Rhodesia.

We landed in Salisbury at 10 p.m., and I asked Hywel, 'Should I adjust my watch?'

'Aye, put it back twenty years,' said my compatriot.

He gave me a lift into the deserted city centre and suggested I stay at the Ambassador Hotel. 'All the journalists go there. Try the Quill Club bar.'

The Quill Club – the press bar – became my regular haunt and the hub of political gossip during the last years of the war. The university interview was for a four-month contract, but Rhodesia, later Zimbabwe, would be my base – my home – for five fascinating years.

After a few drinks in the bar, I returned to my room and switched on the TV. *M.A.S.H.* came on the monochrome single-channel set. It was reassuringly familiar. Next morning I heard bands playing, and scampered into the street to see a parade of young girls, 'drummies', marching with elaborate uniforms, pom-poms and batons flying. It all looked so uncomfortably American, although I was standing next to a very English red-painted box with the Royal Mail insignia.

I went by taxi to the university, about three miles from the city centre. Salisbury seemed orderly, with immaculate gutters and grass verges. Government buildings were cast in the high colonial style, schools in penal Victorian with the occasional Gothic touch, and some of the houses had a Cape Dutch flourish. The city seemed to be hosting a rally for vintage cars; then I realised what sanctions had done to Rhodesian motoring. We drove along wide roads lined with opulent jacarandas and bougainvillaea, through spacious suburbs with giddy mansions and beautifully tended gardens. By contrast the university looked run down: low, cheap buildings in a sea of bush grass.

I found my way to the Department of Political Science and introduced myself to Beryl, the secretary. I was spellbound by her speech – recognisably English, but the clipped delivery and patois made it sound like another language. After a brisk interview with Hasu Patel, the head of department, I was offered a four-month contract teaching political theory and American government, of which I knew little. I would teach whatever I was asked, although I didn't have a book or a note among my meagre luggage. In the administration block, amiable English colonial types sorted out formalities, took me for lunch and lent me ten Rhodesian dollars (R$). Surprisingly, I was given a room in the female hall of residence, and then left to my own devices.

Despite the war, Rhodesia was a very friendly place. In my five years of travelling throughout the country both blacks and whites were almost always courteous and easygoing, with little of the sullen black resentment and white aloofness I had encountered in South Africa. The historian Lord Blake put it well: 'Apartheid south of the Limpopo was a religion, north of it a dubious and impractical expedient.'

I moved into a 'mess', a communal house near the university, bought an ancient Morris Minor and started my classes. About 85 per cent of my students were black, the rest were whites in their early twenties. In one tutorial I had Prime Minister Ian Smith's errant son, Alec, plus two relatives of the black nationalist leaders Joshua Nkomo and Ndabaningi Sithole. Inevitably most academic political discussions reverted to local issues. It was difficult to discuss abstract political theory and engage students with Plato in the middle of a civil war. One student would refer to the guerrillas as 'terrorists', another would term them 'freedom fighters' or the 'boys in the bush'. I was caught in the semantic crossfire and struggled for a terminological compromise. 'Guerrilla' seemed the obvious choice, but some white students objected.

After a week in Rhodesia I had accommodation, a car and a job. I needed to explore the place and, above all, get my head around the political complexities – especially if I were to avoid the fate of my five predecessors, although I didn't think there was much competition for my job. I soon had a pretty good idea why both blacks and whites were fighting, but I could never work out why the Rhodesian whites thought they could actually win. The same applied to South Africa. It just seemed to be delaying the inevitable, and the longer the conflict went on, the more radical and vengeful the black successor regime would be.

The Unilateral Declaration of Independence in 1965 – UDI – was both a bluff and a blunder. Except for a few hotheads, the Rhodesian armed forces would not have resisted a British military intervention, but Harold Wilson, the Labour Premier, didn't have the guts or a big enough parliamentary majority. And it was a blunder because the Rhodesians were essentially independent anyway. If Ian Smith had been half as cynical as some of the British politicians he dealt with, he could have secured Rhodesian independence and then torn up the agreement. So followed sanctions and war. Wilson threw away his best card by renouncing the use of force at the outset and opting for sanctions instead. Threatening to 'throw the book' at the Rhodesians, he simply flicked a few pages . . . one at a time. Sanctions were a gesture, never a concerted policy. Until 1974 they boosted rather than undermined the rebel colony. Britain kept supplying oil, making more than enough money to pay for a useless naval blockade supposedly to stop the oil getting there in the first place. It came via South Africa.

This led to the greatest paradox of the war. Rhodesia broke away from Britain to avoid black rule, but Ian Smith became totally dependent on a South African government that was even more determined than London to establish a moderate black leader in Salisbury. Pretoria wanted to distance itself from Rhodesia's failing white government, but also wanted to show that sanctions didn't work and couldn't be seen publicly to ditch a white ally.

Until 1976 Rhodesia's diplomatic history was a long melodrama punctuated by angry encounters on ships and trains, foolish estimates and silly superlatives. The country's fate would be decided largely on the battlefield. White Rhodesians were sucked into a war they were manifestly losing; had the 1979 Lancaster House talks in London not intervened, military defeat would have been around the corner. I spent most of my five years there trying to understand why the whites couldn't see that they were bound to lose.

I stayed mainly in Salisbury, where roughly half the white population of around 240,000 lived. I did travel around the country in convoys, on board helicopters, occasionally on horseback, and very occasionally on foot, but it was a difficult war to get to grips with. Even when I switched to full-time writing, few journalists were allowed near the actual fighting. There were few 'battles' and most of these were in cross-border raids into Mozambique and Zambia. The war was mainly one of fleeting skirmishes and death from the air by 'Fireforce' helicopters. Short of actually enlisting or accepting conscription, few hacks (as journalists called themselves) witnessed any real action. So I hung around the press bar, falling off the high stools and risking the sandwiches – not entirely ignoble introductions to the Rhodesian art of war. And medals should have been awarded for drinking the local 'wine', said to be the only booze in the world from which you could catch bilharzia.

Salisbury, now renamed Harare, became my favourite city in Africa. Like many writers based there I wrote books and articles full of righteous indignation about racial injustice; like them I lived well and enjoyed myself. Two friends who wrote for the most liberal British newspapers, *The Guardian* and *The Observer*, regularly thundered on about opulent white lifestyles while themselves sitting comfortably surrounded by servants, a pool and a tennis court. Like my more ostentatiously liberal colleagues, I became angry at the stupidity and cruelty of both black and white politicians and soldiers. I grieved at the death of friends and acquaintances. I was incensed by the murder of the white survivors of the Viscount aircraft shot down by Nkomo's guerrillas, the killings of black villagers in alleged 'crossfire' and the massacre of missionaries.

The university was intensely political, partly because some of the most prominent black nationalists taught there. Usually they were not harassed openly by the police. It was a little like Ulster, when Sinn Fein was legal and the IRA was banned. The guerrillas were shot or hanged, but leaders such as Ariston Chambati were normally allowed to teach. I learned a great deal from Ariston, who had an office next to mine. There was one attempt on his life and the university built a big fence around the campus; whether to keep insurgents out or academics in I never decided.

Salisbury – Little white island

You could live in Salisbury and see very little of the war. The city was mesmerised by the killing in the countryside and yet paradoxically seemed entirely untouched by it. Salisbury was simultaneously remote, charming, claustrophobic and seductive. Notices everywhere proclaimed 'Loose talk costs lives' and 'Big Ears is a Terrorist'. But every white dinner party and pub conversation tittle-tattled about the war. Everybody claimed to have inside information about secret deals with the guerrillas, cock-ups in the high command, new South African weapons . . . The second major topic of conversation concerned who was screwing whom.

The conversation was often about the 'situation' – the war – but the ambience was of the colonial heydays of the 1950s: squash at the club, bridge and tennis parties, cocktails at the Reps theatre bar, racing at Borrowdale and endless dinner parties with servants to do the washing-up. Rugby and cricket were important even though South Africa was the only opponent.

Which marriages were breaking up? 'Did you hear what she did when he was on call-up?'

Petrol rationing was always a popular topic.

Who was bringing in olives, pantihose, Smarties, Marmite, whisky, or car parts from South Africa? And all the foreign exchange fiddles. Who was 'taking the gap' (emigrating) next?

Yet the polite 'business as usual' was often a deliberate act of temporary oblivion, especially for the men. By the end of the war the call-up extended to age sixty. Some younger men spent 'six months in, six months out' of the army every year; some were on continuous call-ups. One-man businesses collapsed. Many urban wives concentrated on pottery and bridge, but the women on the farms lived with the everyday reality of mined roads, cattle-maiming, poisoned wells, attacks at night, the Agric-Alert security system warning of a guerrilla raid on the next-door farm, the crash of broken glass, the rattle of AKs, the rush of adrenalin and the dash for weapons beside the bed, shouting at the children to lie down in the corridor between the bedrooms, the smell of fear, cordite . . . and eventually the awful, sickly sweet, overpowering stench of death. It was on isolated farms, half-sleeping, listening, waiting for different sounds amid the drumming of the cicadas, that I learned about bush war.

Sometimes Salisbury did feel the war. A bomb exploded in Woolworth's, killing eleven and maiming dozens. Guerrillas hit the main oil storage depot, destroying a quarter of the country's stocks. The smoke hung over the city for days. Your bags were searched in nearly every shop. At night you watched the TV news about Combined Operations Headquarters' communiqués to find out if any of your friends had been killed.

Whites in Salisbury would say things like 'things will come right' and 'good ol' Smithy knows what he's doing'. Seventy-five per cent of whites voted for Smith both during the UDI years and *after* independence. I spoke informally to him or interviewed him on a number of occasions, but I could never figure out how this sincere, narrow-minded man could generate such a blind following. Maybe he was just a typical Rhodesian; he accurately represented the worst and best of white society. I hesitate to use the word 'culture', but there was a culture of sorts based upon a siege mentality. UN harangues, the war and sanctions galvanised the spirit of white nationalism. Rhodesian propaganda had little effect on blacks but it did work on the whites . . . proof of the old adage that people believe what they want to believe. White society was vitiated with wishful thinking. The majority of white Rhodesians fell hook, line and sinker for the Rhodesian Broadcasting Corporation's view of the world. As in most wars, patriotism displaced perception.

The TV and radio harped hypnotically on a few basic themes: the chaos in black states, disorders elsewhere in the world (especially in countries such as Britain which attracted southern African émigrés) and the monolithic communist threat. Smith claimed to have 'the happiest blacks in the world', bar a few troublemakers misled by professional Moscow-trained agitators. Few whites could put themselves in the shoes of blacks and realise that they would fight too if they were deprived of an effective vote, given inferior schooling, medical services and land, and treated as second- or third-class citizens.

The censorship of news and the pitifully small holiday and emigration allowances made many whites captives rather than supporters of the Rhodesian Front government, although many were also true believers. The negative portrayal of the outside world intensified the cancer of isolation in what was already a parochial society. Rhodesians seemed to understand little of the modern world, and heartily disliked what they did understand. Many whites believed they were sincerely battling against communism to preserve a civilised Christian order, not merely to protect a three servants, two cars, one swimming pool lifestyle. Although the whites did fight long and hard, and despite the ubiquitous weaponry and uniforms, Rhodesia was not a militaristic society. They much preferred beer and *braais* (barbecues) to military parades. Later, as black rule became imminent, the whites looked back with sorrow and resignation rather than anger, and with a bruised pride in having survived so long against the odds.

Most Rhodesians had come from Britain, and were expatriates as much as patriots. Many would have voted Liberal or Labour 'at home'. Crossing the equator did not suddenly turn them into racists. Many had seen the white refugees who fled the carnage in the Congo, Uganda and Mozambique. Once prosperous Zambia, formerly Rhodesia's partner in the Central African Federation, had turned into an economic basket-case after independence. Living conditions in Rhodesia for both whites and blacks were very favourable compared with most of Africa's ramshackle black states. Whites had good reason to fear for 'standards'. Rhodesia, it had to be admitted, was an extremely well-administered state, and not just for whites.

Salisbury seethed with intrigue, much of it concocted in the Quill Club. But there was another Salisbury away from foreign correspondents, sports clubs, broad streets, perfectly cultivated gardens and smart shops. Over 600,000 people lived in 138 suburbs, but the population distribution was very uneven. About 500,000 blacks lived in twelve of these suburbs, known as townships. This was a different world. The little brick houses with tiny gardens were growing more and more overcrowded. Tens of thousands of blacks were fleeing the Tribal Trust Lands (TTLs), refugees from a war that had destroyed their cattle, burnt their huts and killed their children, victims of both guerrillas and security forces. Frightened people huddled with their kinsfolk if they were lucky, or built shanties and scavenged where they could.

As I explored the inequality of life in Rhodesia, I began to understand the reasons for the war. From a liberal perspective in the UK, it was as though a giant local bowls club – Surrey with the lunatic fringe on top – was defying the world. In many ways Rhodesia was unsophisticated and behind the times, a living museum. Rhodesians tended to look back to the days when Britain was Great, before socialism, as they saw it, gutted the bulldog spirit. Like Victorians, white Rhodesia loved to commemorate everything with a monument. The early pioneers conquered the land by force, defeating the indigenous Shona and Ndebele peoples, and all the plaques and statues seemed to shout: 'We fought for this land, and by God we're going to keep it.' This was the kind of fierce patriotism Rider Haggard had written about. I had found what I came for, and began to admire it, despite its wrongheadedness.

I started to understand the Rhodesians' love affair with the land – the rolling hills of Inyanga, the majestic wildlife, the mysterious balancing rocks, the crystal-clear, champagne quality of the air, the invigorating climate, the sense of space, the sensual perfume of jasmine in the suburban gardens, and the rugged wild aromas of the bush – but not with its native people. White Rhodesians paid more attention to their roses, their Currie Cup cricket, horses, dogs, and the level of algae in their pools than to the black people whose land they shared in unequal proportions. Rhodesia may have appeared boundless to the white man because his 5 per cent of the population owned 50 per cent of the land and all the political power. It could not last.

I was befriended by the Rhodesian version of the Kennedys, Senator Sam Whaley and his family, despite their considering me a 'communist' – someone who didn't worship Ian Smith. Sam was a close friend and adviser of Smithy, yet he regularly chatted to me in his study after offering me a Cuban cigar, and allowed his two charming daughters to take me on trips around the country. I couldn't stomach the politics of most white Rhodesians, but it was difficult not to like some of them, especially the Whaleys.

On 24 September 1976, after a splendid meal and some very palatable South African wine, I sat with the whole family to watch Ian Smith. The tired-looking Premier's face seemed even more frozen than usual; half of his face was paralysed by injuries suffered as an RAF pilot in the war. He gave a solemn twenty-one-minute address to the nation, uttering the unutterable. The Whaleys listened with equal solemnity as Smith talked about 'responsible' (not African) majority rule. Trying to pin down Smith was like trying to nail jelly to a wall. A galaxy of British politicians had tried and failed. Only Dr Henry Kissinger, the US Secretary of State, had done it, using meat-axe diplomacy with the utmost charm. British politicians had the colonial albatross around their necks again. Kissinger handed them the management of the Geneva conference on Rhodesia which followed Smith's climb-down.

The best headline came when the Reverend Canaan Banana (the future President) left Bishop Abel Muzorewa to join Robert Mugabe: an irresistible banner reading 'BANANA SPLITS'. Geneva failed and Smith gave up trying to negotiate in a public forum with Mugabe and Joshua Nkomo, who had formed the Patriotic Front to lead the external guerrilla organisations. Instead Smith would forge an 'internal settlement' with more pliant men such as Muzorewa. But the Patriotic Front controlled the guerrilla armies; the Bishop did not.

I left Salisbury to spend some time lecturing at the universities of Cape Town and Natal. On my return I needed to see what was happening out in the countryside. White Rhodesia had largely been a tale of two cities, one of which – Bulawayo – was semi-comatose, while Salisbury was a little white island cut off from the realities of the war.

Battlefield tour
I had already travelled around most of the country but somehow felt I should take in the beauty as well as the tragedies. The South Africans were preparing for a mass exodus of whites from Rhodesia. It might be my last chance to see the sights. As it happened I was completely wrong, but it gave extra impetus to my sightseeing.

I went south from Salisbury to the Zimbabwe Ruins, the impressive dry-stone remains of a great spiritual and trading centre of the twelfth to fourteenth centuries. The Rhodesian Front had always insisted it was built by Arabs or Phoenicians, even that it was the site of King Solomon's mines. It was erected by the indigenous precursors of the Shona people but it was hard for the whites, settled in the country for less than a hundred years, to admit that. I liked nearby Fort Victoria, with its shabby colonial feel. (This is now named Masvingo. I have used Rhodesian titles when describing events before 1980; many towns and streets were renamed after independence.)

The road from Fort Victoria to Chipinga ran through hostile territory. I had three companions in the car, all armed to the teeth. Normally I travelled without a weapon, especially on journalistic assignments, but we had missed the convoy and I knew the guerrillas opened fire without asking about press cards. As dusk approached every bend and *kopje* seemed ominous. Big signs warned against travelling after 3 p.m., especially without armed convoy escorts. We finally reached Chipinga, a mini Dodge City. Racks in the hotel bar were stacked up with FN rifles. The locals seemed pleased that visitors had come to their town, just a few miles from the Mozambique border. The whole eastern border with Mozambique was full of crossing points for Mugabe's guerrillas.

I explored the Chimanimani mountains and the border town of Melsetter. The area had a distinct ecology: lush green slopes dotted with wild figs led to remnants of dense evergreen forests hung with orchids and carpeted with ferns. On the upper slopes grew aloes and proteas. Despite the beauty, the nervousness of the local white farmers became contagious. Many had been driven off their land by Mugabe's men. The rich Eastern Highlands, with their tea and coffee plantations, were suffering the brunt of the war.

The main town in the east was Umtali, nestling in hills right next to the border and once a haunt of retired colonial public servants from India and Kenya. Perhaps the most durable relic of the old colonels and *memsahibs* was the Umtali Club. The juxtaposition of photographs of Cecil Rhodes, the Queen and Ian Smith never failed to amuse me. It was very stuffy and English, but even there the war was beginning to bite. The port had run out for the first time since 1896. Few visitors came to Umtali in those days. I ventured into the Publicity Association office: 'brave, beautiful city' was the last inscription in the visitors' book. Umtali had been mortared recently, and white schoolchildren had marched through the streets singing 'Rhodesians Never Die'.

To the south of Umtali was the Vumba, dangerous and beautiful. It had been the home of many retired folk who dabbled in a little farming. I used to stay regularly at the attractive Leopard's Rock Hotel, rather like a French chateau with its steeply pitched roof capped by turrets, high up in the Vumba overlooking Mozambique, but it was closed after a mortar attack. I had worked in the area, helping to edit a book by a retired British officer, Major Tom Wigglesworth, who had been captured by Mugabe's guerrillas and endured a gruelling time. But he was full of sometimes complimentary insights about the insurgents, and scathing about the Rhodesian Front's propaganda. He was one of a handful of whites taken prisoner and released. The guerrillas made great propaganda play of their humanity in releasing white prisoners while Smith's men hanged captives, but little was said by the insurgents about the many white civilians who were massacred or who simply disappeared.

I had also spent a lot of time in Inyanga, justifiably likened to the Scottish Highlands. The whites enjoyed the cool mountain air, trout fishing and pine forests which reminded some of home. Because Rhodesia was landlocked, the more affluent inhabitants of Salisbury kept boats on Lake Kariba. The lake, a man-made reservoir, was one of the largest in Africa, 169 miles long and 25 miles wide at its broadest. It boasted the closest thing to a beach in Rhodesia. The hotels on the shore and the casino had attracted lots of visitors, until Nkomo's forces ended tourism by shooting down two Viscount passenger aircraft in 1978 and 1979. To be entirely cynical, there is something to be said for wartime travelling in countries which have good hotels. You meet the locals without being pestered by clicking cameras and high prices. The heightened alertness – for a while – is enjoyable and perhaps even therapeutic. I became angry at the deaths and the futility of it all, but it rarely put me off my steak. So I spent a lot of time in excellent hotels and safari lodges in places such as Kariba and Victoria Falls. It was a bit like being in Saigon: you could commute to the war, have a shower and a drink, and then file your story. And the phones worked.

Some of the islands on Kariba, as well as lonely promontories, hosted small bush camps. Bumi was perhaps the best. I planned a trip there at the height of the war with a South African girlfriend, and asked a journalist colleague who knew the place well whether I should take anything special.

'Yes, a pair of trousers in case there's a fire.'

The idea of going to these lonely places was to get away from the war, although there were often 'troopies' (soldiers) on 'R and R' (rest and recreation). On official press tours soldiers and officers rarely talked; in remote locations such as Bumi, or overnighting on farms,

I often dug up the real angst behind the RF propaganda, as well as enjoying the exquisite fauna and flora. There was nothing like sitting on the water's edge watching the lights of the boats fishing for kapenta (a sardine-like fish which, sun-dried, was a popular form of local nutrition), or listening to the eerie cry of the fish eagles which haunt Africa's wetlands. Buffaloes, elephants, impala, hippo, and crocodiles – 'flat dogs' in Rhodesian parlance – were in abundance.

Rhodesia's most famous tourist attraction was the Victoria Falls, which managed to keep up a trickle of visitors during the worst excesses of the conflict. A statue of Livingstone, the first white to encounter this wonder in 1855, stood like some sodden hitchhiker abutting the falls as they cascaded over a massive basalt shelf 1,700 yards wide and 100 yards deep. The spume of spray, 500 yards high, could be seen 30 miles away; the locals called it *mosi oa tunya* – the smoke that thunders. A spectacular steel bridge spanned the gorge into Zambian territory. Trains crossed to take food to Zaire and Zambia, despite sanctions, but access on foot was forbidden during the war.

One of the first buildings in the area was the grand old Victoria Falls Hotel, a classic colonial watering-hole. Monkeys would boldly steal from the tables as guests sat in the courtyard surrounded by the strong, sweet smell of frangipani and syringa trees. Occasional gunfire from the erratic Zambian army did not deter the booze cruises above the falls. Fish eagles, gin and tonic, the roar of the falls, and the incomparable fiery red of an African sunset . . . all this and not an American baseball cap in sight.

South of the Victoria Falls was the Wankie game reserve, as big as Northern Ireland. When the rains came in late October or November the *sandveld* was verdant with grass and foliage; the gemsbok, hartebeest, wildebeest and giraffe of the dry savannah rubbed shoulders with waterbuck, reedbuck, buffalo, elephant and zebra. To the south-east lay Bulawayo, capital of Matabeleland, with streets designed to be wide enough to turn round a wagon with a team of twelve oxen. To the far south-east lay Beitbridge and the Limpopo border with South Africa. On long drives through Matabeleland the granite castle *kopjes* set against the setting sun, the smooth trunks of the upside-down giant baobabs with their coppery sheen, the *mukwa* (bloodwood) trees with their round bristling pods hanging like medals, and colourfully dressed African women trudging along dusty tracks with massive bundles on their heads all convinced me that if I left Africa it would break my heart. Then I would read a newspaper and the idiocies of the politicians would almost convince me to bribe my way on to the first flight out. Africa is about strong passions of love and hate. Europe breeds indifference, everything about Africa evokes emotion – the vibrant colours, the rains on the dry earth, the storms, the spontaneity of its peoples . . . the sheer lack of conformity to nearly everything man-made.

The whites tried to tame Africa in their own image. Wherever the British settled they planted trees and gardens, built churches with neat rows of pews, and ran lending libraries. In Rhodesia, throughout 1977 and early 1978, Ian Smith tried to design a very complicated and tidy constitutional settlement which would establish the kind of majority rule with which whites were prepared to live. In short, tame blacks. In March 1978 Smith signed an agreement with Muzorewa, Reverend Sithole and Chief Chirau. An election based on one person, one vote would be held; meanwhile the leaders would form a transitional government. The Patriotic Front described the agreement as a 'phoney black UDI policed by whites'. In many ways it was. Smith, his security force commander, Peter Walls, and Ken Flower, the intelligence chief, were still running the war. Martial law was extended until, by the end of the fighting, 95 per cent of the country was included. Military aircraft used 'skyshouts' to propagandise the peasantry. Even the spirit mediums were bribed to support the whites. Leaflets were issued on their behalf but the tribesmen were cynical – their departed ancestors had never resorted to printing presses. Whatever the politicians spouted in Salisbury, the military had the final say, although many TTLs could be entered only in strength by the security forces. Thousands of guerrillas roamed the bush, trying to indoctrinate, educate or intimidate the 'masses'.

Rhodesian forces were stretched. Cross-border raids allowed some operational initiative, as did heliborne Fireforce operations inside Rhodesia, but mostly the strategy was containment via the protected villages, equivalents of Vietnam's 'strategic hamlets'. Both Muzorewa and Sithole began to form their own armies, the so-called auxiliaries, supposedly comprising guerrillas who had accepted the internal settlement and come 'on-sides', although very few genuine insurgents joined up. They mainly scooped up supporters from the armies of unemployed in the townships. The auxiliary commanders had great names, such as Comrade Mick Jagger, but their dreadlocks, bandoleers and black power salutes frightened the whites and did little to impress blacks.

Five separate armies now fought for the hearts and minds of the peasantry: Smith, Muzorewa, Sithole, Mugabe, and Nkomo all had large forces. But hearts and minds live in bodies. The body counts escalated as many white officers regarded the transitional government as a convenient Africanisation of the war and got on with straightforward 'culling'. They adopted the Nixonian amendment: once you've got them by the balls, their hearts and minds will follow. One white officer told me: 'If we carry on like this, we'll end up with a white majority.'

Dirty tricks on vultures

A racial Armageddon looked possible, so in trooped the 'vultures' of the foreign press corps. The run-up to the first election in April 1979 brought a wave of hacks. The 'Gang of Four' – Smith and Co. – wanted maximum publicity, so for once it was relatively easy to get press accreditation. It was a time of madness for Rhodesia: wild press parties were the order of the day. The hacks had lots of real money, US dollars and pounds, and liked a good time. Most of the indigenous white males were 'out in the bush slotting gooks', so the press corps attracted hordes of bored local females, many of them tanned, blonde Amazons. This did nothing to improve relations between the soldiers and the press. Special Branch (SB) boosted its surveillance of journalists – and was not always friendly. A distinguished cameraman left his expensive camera gear for a very short time. It was blown up.

'Suspicious package, sir.'

You had to watch the black politicians as well. Jacques Clafin, the United Press International bureau chief in Salisbury, thrust the microphone of his tape recorder deep into a limousine loaded with black delegates leaving the internal settlement talks, hoping to catch a comment or two. When the car drove off, he noticed his gold watch was missing. Nor did he get any comments.

One of the SB regulars in the Quill Club had his expense account increased to cover drinks with friendly journalists. Never had so many journalists been shown so much affection in one place.

Paul Ellman, a prominent British journalist, complained that he couldn't get a phone. 'How can you bug me if I don't have a phone?' he asked the permanent SB attachment to the Quill Club bar.

His phone was installed the next day.

An SB man took me for a slap-up lunch. 'Of course we know who you're working for,' he said with few preliminaries. 'It doesn't matter – we're working with the British too.'

I told the SB man he was barking up the wrong tree.

He asked me to keep an eye on one or two people he assured me were working 'for the other side'. KGB? CIA? Mugabe? I thought it politic not to ask. Then he offered me a temporary military commission so that I could be paid. I told him to bugger off.

Lots of funny things started to happen. I have always subscribed to the cock-up rather than the conspiracy theory of history, so I didn't think they were related at the time, but in retrospect they might have been. First my revolver disappeared from its locker, then reappeared a day later. I questioned my domestic worker – I would have said 'maid' in those days – in case she had noticed anything unusual. I had recently argued in the Quill Club that journalists shouldn't carry weapons on assignment, even though nearly all whites carried guns, especially outside the cities. Lord Richard Cecil, a squash partner, had just been killed, the only white journalist to die in the line of duty in Rhodesia. Ironically, not only was he a Salisbury, after whose forebear the city had been named, but also probably the most militarily experienced journalist in the country. He had been a Guards officer before he became a film-maker.

Then I received my call-up papers. Technically, male residents under thirty-eight could be conscripted if they had lived for two years in the country; as I had become a resident only a few months before, I was not theoretically eligible for call-up. In one respect I was quite keen to see the war from the inside, but on the other hand I could not fight for a lost, and immoral, cause I didn't believe in. Besides, I had just started stringing for *Time* magazine and been elected vice-chairman of the Press Club. Many resident journalists did serve part-time in the police, but I told the call-up board I would leave the country.

They said they would imprison me.

'Try it,' I said. 'Great publicity just before your damn election.'

The next morning I received a letter which said a mistake had been made. I was given a year's deferment.

Then my phone started to play tricks on me. Like most journalists, I felt self-important enough to assume that my phone was tapped. (In

South Africa I picked up my phone and heard one of my conversations played back to me.) Something really strange happened in the week that Smith turned down my request to interview him for *Time*. Normally there were few problems with the phone system, although it was beginning to creak with lack of maintenance due to the war. I picked up the receiver to call a female friend who lived a few doors away from Smithy and, before I dialled, I heard voices. I put it down and tried again. More voices, voices I recognised. I put the phone down; I had been well brought up.

I didn't ring my friend for a day or so, then tried her number again. I heard Janet Smith, the Premier's wife, chatting. This time my journalistic curiosity got the better of my manners. To be fair, I rang my friend only when I wanted to talk to her and, if I got Smith's hotline, fair enough. I could hear a two-way conversation and they presumably couldn't hear me as long as I didn't make a noise. There was no click when I picked up my phone. Mind you, I was always afraid I would cough or someone would bang on my door. I made notes on some fairly inconsequential gossip and used one or two humorous quotes later.

'Where did you get that stuff?' one observant foreign hack asked. 'Have you got access to SB's phone taps on Smithy?'

I couldn't bring myself to admit that I had been eavesdropping. 'Good sources.'

There must have been some stuff-up in the SB, tapping me and Smithy, and the little fish got caught up in the big fish's loop.

The funny things stopped. Good things happened. I started getting all sorts of military clearances and access to the war. I got into Combined Operations (ComOps) HQ regularly, was given lifts on the precious few helicopters, and senior army and intelligence officers started talking to me. I thought it was a late blossoming of my Celtic charm. There were still some hiccups. I spent weeks trying to get the official censors at ComOps to pass a photograph I wanted to put on the front cover of a book. It was a lyrical shot of four distant helicopters flying over a landscape at sundown. They claimed that if the pic were magnified the crude heat-dispersal baffles – to deter heat-seeking missiles – could be seen, and I was given a firm no. That December ComOps sent me a Christmas card with the very same picture on the front. No wonder the Rhodesians lost the war.

Election fever

The 'Gang of Four' – the internal leaders – thought they would win international recognition and thus the war with the first one-man, one-vote election in April 1979. The Patriotic Front refused to take part and vowed to blow the election booths away. Over 70,000 members of the security forces guarded the polls.

I criss-crossed the country on behalf of *Time* with Peter Jordan, a daredevil photographer. Bishop Muzorewa was due to attend a mass rally in Que Que TTL, going by helicopter for security reasons. Peter and I had procured a vehicle that could ford rivers and travel cross-country: a hire car.

About twenty miles from the rally a police roadblock stopped us. 'Hell, man. You can't go down this road. There's terrs [terrorists] all over the place. We wouldn't try it in our [mineproofed] vehicles. Go back.'

I thought that eminently sensible advice. Peter would have none of it. He argued and argued until the police, in exasperation, let us through. My map-reading skills were under par but I navigated along dirt tracks. Armed only with a big Press sign on the dash, we bumbled along until what I had been dreading for years while travelling in the bush finally happened. The barking stutter of AK fire shattered our over-confidence as we careered around a bend. Blue-denim-clad figures with AKs, about twenty men, came out of the bush a few hundred yards ahead. I flicked my eyes to the rear – similar figures were behind us.

'Oh shit,' said Peter, as I started waving the Press sign, not expecting it to do any good.

We had no alternative but to stop the car. Since we couldn't escape, I reckoned it was good tactics to get out. Psychologists argue that you have far less chance of getting a speeding ticket if you chat to the traffic cops outside your own mobile piece of territory. Peter and I walked up to the advancing guerrillas and put on our best affable berk routines. Peter chatted away about working for the foreign press. He was told brusquely to shut up and turn around. To persuade us, AKs were shoved in our backs.

Normally guerrillas would simply open fire, not act like police at roadblocks. After a long search of our documents and gear, I took a chance and explained that we were on our way to speak to the Bishop. It was a hunch because I couldn't work out whether they were on-sides auxiliaries or real guerrillas. They seemed to relax a little when I implied that the good Bishop was practically waiting for us, and eventually let us go after scrounging some foreign cigarettes. I found out later that they were real 'gooks', some of the few who had accepted the amnesty and joined Muzorewa a few weeks before.

When we got to the rally, the Bishop hadn't arrived. Drums pounded; T-shirts bearing Muzorewa's slogan – 'We are the Winners' – were given out free, as were liberal amounts of goat and chicken. This was African-style politicking. Auxiliaries in their teens stood around, festooned in weaponry. As Muzorewa's Rhodesian air force helicopter descended on the overawed villagers, I wondered about the little man who portrayed himself as the black Moses. If he had the support of the masses, why was it too dangerous for him to travel around by road and mix with his people? When I talked to him, he seemed fit and happy despite the long days of campaigning. He led Peter and me on a short jog. A decent man, but not bright or ruthless enough.

The Bishop won fifty-one of the seventy-two seats reserved for blacks in the 100-seat Parliament, becoming the first black Premier of the awkwardly couched Zimbabwe-Rhodesia, a name which reflected the sham of the zebra-like supposed new black state. But the Rhodesian military regarded the April election as its crowning success. Nearly two million people voted in a 64 per cent poll, with little Patriotic Front disruption. It proved that the external guerrillas were nowhere near 'imminent victory'. Never had a ruling minority done so much to hand over (apparent) power to a dominated majority. Few Rhodesians had expected the elections to work at all, thinking it would be like a British league football match of the 1970s: enjoyed only by the foolhardy, the fanatical . . . and the well-armed.

I went to a *braai* in the Prime Minister's mansion. 'Muz', as everyone called him, was holding a house-warming party. The sedate atmosphere of Smith's era had been transformed into a Mad Hatter's tea party. Black Africa was in the white citadel: African women were making pots of *sadza*, scruffy kids scampered around, surly bodyguards lurked with AKs. White advisers, the speechwriters and ad men who had sold their man to the masses, were everywhere.

I sensed the impermanence, and left early to do some shopping. In one department store I fell into conversation with a white housewife who said: 'Before I buy something expensive, I ask myself, "Is it small enough to take with me?"'

The election brought no respite from the war. It escalated savagely, even though Muzorewa became prime minister. No one recognised his government, not even South Africa. The vital factor was British recognition; the country was still technically the British colony of Southern Rhodesia. Despite the fact that a Conservative observer group officially acknowledged the fairness of the April elections, Britain's Prime Minister, Margaret Thatcher, refused to accord diplomatic recognition to Muzorewa. It was his death knell.

The black–white coalition in Salisbury started to self-destruct. The white generals fell out and the Bishop's party split. Some of the middle-aged white police reservists guarding Muzorewa objected to protecting him.

One told me: 'All the whites are called up. Who's protecting our homes? Why don't they call up blacks to look after their own leaders?'

No one wanted to be the last white to die for black Zimbabwe. A very small number of blacks had been conscripted for political reasons, but generally there was no shortage of volunteers for military service in a sea of desperate unemployment. Already about 80 per cent of the Rhodesian armed forces were black.

White morale slumped. One soldier who had been on continual call-up moaned: 'The First and Second World Wars were wars of honour. But what are we fighting for in the Rhodesian war? Just to keep squabbling kaffirs in parliament.'

The constant use of a new phrase in the media upset the whites and prompted one European businessman to quip: '"Comrade" is the Russian word for kaffir.' Muzorewa's failure to end the war exacerbated the poor race relations. Whites had thought 'put up with Muz in exchange for peace'. It just hadn't happened.

The economy was on its beam end. As one prominent businessman observed: 'You're down to the die-hards now. You could call us the intrepid, the loyal or the financial prisoners.'

It was difficult to start a new life in South Africa or Britain with just R\$1,000. Fiddling foreign exchange became a national pastime among the whites. Many foreign correspondents, with ready access to foreign money, made small fortunes on the black market.

Ian Smith was still in the Cabinet, as minister without portfolio, or 'minister with all the portfolios', as Joshua Nkomo dubbed him. Rhodesian Front hardliners still insisted that the war could be won militarily. Under Muz the raids on neighbouring states were intensified, but the war was being lost inside the country. Government infrastructure – schools, clinics, animal dip-tanks and local councils – had been wiped out in the more isolated TTLs, where most of the approximately six million Africans lived. The Marxist government in Mozambique fully backed Mugabe and sent in at least 500 regular troops to help his forces in Zimbabwe-Rhodesia. White power was being swamped by the sheer numbers of the guerrillas.

As one member of the élite Selous Scouts said after a major raid into Mozambique in late 1979: 'We knew then that we could never beat them. They had so much equipment and there were so many of them. They would just keep coming with more and more.'

The security forces could not have survived for more than another year without massive South African military intervention. The 1979 Lancaster House conference in London saved the whites from defeat. White Rhodesia was on its knees, but so were the neighbouring states which harboured the guerrillas. Mozambique and Zambia forced Mugabe and Nkomo to compromise at the peace talks. After endless haggling and a firm hand by Lord Carrington, bolstered by information from MI5 which had bugged the hotel rooms of all the participants, compromise was reached. A new constitution and a ceasefire were agreed. In December 1979 Lord Soames took over as governor: the first time in the long imperial recessional that a white colonial official had replaced an African premier.

New elections were scheduled for February 1980 and over 350 foreign correspondents flocked into Salisbury. As the local Press Club representative I tried to make them welcome, using the opportunity to plug my recent book on Rhodesia. I added an appendix to help foreigners comprehend the patois, military jargon, Shona words, and agit-prop which passed for local political dialogue. One of my best instructors in local patois (and dancing) was Pearl, a mixed-race woman officially designated as 'coloured', or a 'goffel' in crude white slang. The coloureds traditionally defended their small community by erecting a linguistic barrier to exclude honkies from their conversation. They were supposedly honorary whites – they could vote and be conscripted – but were nonetheless treated as second-class citizens.

Their linguistic defence mechanism was transformed into poor man's poetry. 'What's the time?' became 'bowl me the ages'. 'Let's go' translated as 'agitate the gravel'. A garage attendant might be asked to 'throw some sky into my rounds' (put air in my tyres). If a coloured wanted a lift into town he might ask: 'Man, can I have a charity glide into society?'

English-speaking Rhodesians were often scornful of the Afrikaners who made up about 20 per cent of the white population. They would often deploy the rudest (and most racist) insult about them: 'a bloody waste of a white skin'. 'Hairybacks', 'rock-spiders', and 'ropes' (thick, twisted, and hairy) were more polite sobriquets.

Some Afrikaners were very uncomplimentary about blacks, describing them as 'oxygen wasters'.

The PF used colourful terms for whites but reserved their greatest venom for the 'blood-sucking black stooges' in the 'internal, infernal' settlement.

Political correctness was not in vogue.

Besides linguistic hurdles, the 1,300 troops in the British-led Commonwealth monitoring force faced a mountain of problems in maintaining the ceasefire. The well-fleshed British governor, Lord Soames, was sitting on a powder keg. The country was ravaged by five marauding armies. Around 30,000 had been killed, although fewer than 1,000 were white civilians and servicemen. This was, however, a high figure for a small, close-knit community. The whites were bitter, particularly in the security forces, and Soames had to rely upon them to run the country till independence. Soames was like the Pope – he had no divisions. And General Peter Walls, the security forces' commander, knew it. Walls and Soames kept their cool while the country teetered again on the brink of a return to full-scale fighting.

The Rhodesians were convinced that the Brits had cooked up the so-called 'ABM' option – Anybody But Mugabe. Pretoria was also certain that London wanted to patch together a coalition to keep the Marxist Mugabe out in the cold.

From the ceasefire in December until the February election, the country was on edge. Hitching rides on armoured vehicles and helicopters, I zoomed around Goromonzi, Banket, and Sinoia in Mashonaland, little army outposts in Matabeleland, and farms in the eastern districts.

I was glad that I could hitch a lift on helicopters more often than in the past. In the Eastern Highlands, I had an interesting experience in an Alouette chopper. We were about to land at an isolated Christian mission, which hosted a voting station. I was paying full attention to the conversation of a pretty German female journalist, but I wasn't so engrossed to not notice that, about a few hundred feet up, the engine went quiet. I looked at the pilot and he seemed a touch perturbed. The German was too busy talking to observe that I was clenching my teeth, and buttocks. The landing was rather bumpy.

I had understood what the Rhodesian pilot had skilfully managed to do. I later drew him aside and congratulated him on his unpowered landing. He modestly explained a little of the auto-rotation method of landing without engine power. He made it sound like reversing a car, but I know how much skill and judgement it took to avoid a possibly fatal crash. The German and I travelled back to Salisbury in an armoured mineproofed vehicle. She thought it was all part of a normal press facility, and I didn't disabuse her.

(I later crash-landed in an old Dakota, with a faulty undercarriage, on a rough landing strip during another African war. Luckily, the pilot was a South African veteran with lots of bush flying under his belt. And so I developed a somewhat obsessive research interest in the pilots and machines that flew me around Africa. I irritated some of my later companions when I occasionally refused to fly on dodgy carriers. They thought me a wimp but, unusually for me, I kept shtoom about my reasons.)

On the ground in the bush war, the security forces were itching to wipe out the thousands of guerrillas herded together in a dozen or so assembly points, each supervised by a clutch of nervous Commonwealth troops. The dirty-tricks brigades bumbled everywhere, trying to knock off Mugabe or blowing up printing presses and churches. The Rhodesian SAS had arranged for bogus ballot boxes stuffed with pro-Bishop papers. Mugabe's guerrillas, many of whom had remained outside the assembly points, indulged in massive intimidation of the voters.

Most of the British troops showed true grit but some of their senior officers were playing fast and loose with the Rhodesian women. In one case a very senior British officer was foolish enough to seduce the wife of an equally senior Rhodesian officer. If the Rhodesian had shot the Brit, as he intended, God knows what would have happened to the ceasefire.

Lots of whites were preparing for the 'Beitbridge 500', the distance in miles to the South African border, and I was not alone in hoarding petrol. 'Taking the gap' to the south was jokingly referred to as 'defecting to the West'. Rhodesian troops, and tanks, seen for the first time, took up positions around key installations. South African soldiers didn't even bother to pretend they were Rhodesians with thick Afrikaans accents.

Exactly 2,702,275 men and women, under the watchful eyes of 570 British Bobbies standing by the polls, voted in the middle of the rainstorms of February 1980. Everyone waited for the results. Would it be peace, or coup and all-out war in southern Africa?

Before the TV results came in I knew there had been an upset for the whites; I had been up most of the night talking to party organisers. But it was still a shock after years of listening to white propaganda. In a 93 per cent turnout, Muzorewa gained only three seats, fewer than the number of his campaign helicopters paid for by Pretoria. Mugabe won a stunning victory with fifty-seven seats. Nkomo got the twenty seats everyone but Nkomo had predicted.

As one top Nkomo aide told me: 'You give them one man, one vote and look what they do with it.'

Rhodesian whites went into a state of catatonic shock.

We waited for the coup. It didn't come: Walls and the Brits calmed down the hotheads. Walls told his ComOps staff that Rhodesia 'will not copy the rest of Africa'.

A rapid exodus of South African troops and equipment followed. Everyone shredded their files. The white PR manager of the Bishop's campaign was in tears. His shredding machine had jammed after someone tried to destroy some 'We are the Winners' T-shirts in it. Ken Flower's powerful Central Intelligence Organisation (CIO) burnt its files on details of trade with the Eastern bloc (which was larger than commerce with Western sanctions cheats such as the French), and its links with the Vatican and British and French intelligence. Files on the CIO's extensive network of allies throughout black Africa were shoved in the incinerator of the local crematorium. Rhodesia had surprising black allies – most African politicians couldn't be bought but a lot of them were up for rent. Cabinet papers were spirited away to South Africa along with the mess silver from Rhodesia's regiments.

I strolled into ComOps HQ. Guerrillas in dreadlocks were not exactly throwing darts at pictures of Ian Smith, but the mood was as if the Vatican had been taken over by the Mafia. Some whites panicked and drove south with just a few possessions. But after the first tidal waves of shock, many whites responded to Mugabe's calm calls for reconciliation. As one white right-winger observed: 'The war's over and we've got a strong leader.'

The Black Hitler had suddenly become the Great White Hope.

*

On 18 April 1980 Zimbabwe became independent. A right-wing British Conservative prime minister had caused, by accident, the first electoral triumph of a Marxist in Africa.

White Rhodesians had hated Wilson in the 1960s; now their loathing was focused on Thatcher's foreign secretary, Peter Carington. To many Rhodesians, Lancaster House had been a stab in the back, another Munich. They had been cheated, not defeated. My view was they had been saved from themselves and their own folly.

And what did I make of all this turmoil I had lived through? What had UDI brought but death? The Rhodesians had spat into the winds of change but had not been defeated militarily, although they would have been, despite their ingenuity. The history of the security forces was one of tactical and operational brilliance but strategic ineptitude. The initial aim of the war was to prevent the passing of power to any black government, no matter how moderate. An admission of racism, if only within the high command and Cabinet, might have produced a more coherent grand strategy. But no clear political programme – beyond a vague preservation of the status quo – was ever articulated. There was little faith in far-reaching reform as a war-winner; it would have undermined the very reasons for fighting the war at all. White Rhodesians struggled long and hard against the only thing which could have avoided war – African participation in national politics. Faced with the inner weaknesses of their strategies, the Rhodesians resorted to more and more desperate measures. The policy of winning hearts and minds was largely abandoned in the field just as the first moves towards a political strategy of a moderate black regime were coming to fruition. Political warfare gave way to slaughter safaris.

As one senior ComOps officer admitted: 'We relied 90 per cent on force and 10 per cent on psychology, and half of that went off half-cocked. The guerrillas relied 90 per cent on psychology and only 10 per cent on force.'

The insurgents had a clear vision of their purpose: to break the back of white supremacy and establish a black majority government.

This gave them remarkable stamina and their cause the strength to weather numerous political crises and almost consistent military defeat in the field. In the pattern of all colonial wars, the Rhodesian settlers simply gave too little, far too late.

Zimbabwe

I stayed in the new Zimbabwe for just over a year after the colonial war. Salisbury was renamed Harare and became more cosmopolitan. Cuba opened an embassy but the Russians couldn't – they had backed the wrong horse, Joshua Nkomo. The TV was Africanised. Everyone was 'Comrade' this or that. New TV heroes appeared: Yasser Arafat, Gaddafi, and other great thinkers of the time. After an initial improvement with the end of sanctions, the shortages grew worse and more inconvenient. The disappearance of toilet rolls particularly irked my posterior.

Border posts were opened, however. Mozambique was too dangerous because of its civil war, but I journeyed to Lusaka by road. I took lots of cigarettes to help remove gun barrels playfully stuck up my nostrils by Zambian soldiers. It was all part of my learning curve: never irritate, excite, or plead with black soldiers – who in my experience were frequently drunk – when they are carrying brand-new guns which they are itching to use. Grovelling, my natural instinct, could be fatal. A polite, confident offer to share the odd few packets of cigarettes usually worked, but I always resisted the temptation to share my watch or camera.

Zambia depressed me. The long-term expatriates were like zombies, the white-owned farms were like forts, the seediness and corruption of the towns were glaringly evident, and I disliked the regular attempts to mug me in broad daylight in the main streets of the capital.

The Kaunda government screamed for sanctions against apartheid South Africa but the only decent consumer goods in Lusaka's shops were South African. Only the middle-class élite could afford to buy the rows of bottles of Cape wines.

I used to think it was a racist legend that a white expat businessman returns for a brief holiday to Kenya/Zambia/Zimbabwe and meets one of his ex-employees, half-starved, sitting dejectedly outside his former employer's shop/business/farm. The black is overjoyed to see his former 'exploiter'. 'Are you coming back, boss? When's this "independence" going to end?'

Zambia convinced me that the stories were essentially true. Starvation and unemployment are far worse than capitalism. There is one thing worse than being exploited in Africa, and that is the departure of the white exploiters.

Leaving all the massive pot-holes behind, it was a joy to return to Zimbabwe, by comparison a paradigm of good management. But civil war loomed once again. Mugabe's ruling party took its tribal revenge not on the whites but on the Ndebele, who made up about 20 per cent of the population. The integration of Nkomo's and Mugabe's soldiers had been only a superficial success, despite the Herculean efforts of the small British army training mission.

By 1981 full-scale fighting had erupted around Bulawayo. Nkomo's angry guerrillas advanced in tanks and armoured vehicles to wipe out their Shona rivals. The white-officered Rhodesian African Rifles and aircraft flown by white pilots were once more in action against insurgents, as many whites cheered on 'their' side again.

The white exodus increased. Older whites were financial prisoners; they could take just a pittance with them, and had to stay despite the decline in standards of medical care, law and order and education. Younger whites could afford to leave with nothing and start again in Australia or Britain. Many went 'down south', intending to use South Africa as a springboard to America or New Zealand, but got stuck in the cloying déjà vu of apartheid.

There were many initial improvements for the Shona people, especially the fat cats in the ruling party. Schools were reopened, new clinics were built, and some underutilised white land was reapportioned to the peasantry. The schools and clinics had been destroyed by the guerrillas and now white taxes were used to rebuild them, or so many disgruntled 'ex-Rhodies' argued. For most whites the lifestyle and servants remained, despite niggling shortages, high taxes and the impossibly dull TV. Some of the new programmes were so bad that at times I longed for the boy-meets-tractor themes of Soviet drama.

A white architect put it this way: 'The whites are spiralling up on their social life but spiralling down on their business.'

Comrade Mugabe's drive to a one-party Marxist state did little to encourage foreign investment. Nor did destabilisation by the South

Africans, who stirred up the Ndebele dissidents and held up trade at border posts.

One white businesswoman was more fatalistic: 'We had paradise here; now we're becoming part of the normal world.'

At the renamed University of Zimbabwe I agreed to give a short course on guerrilla warfare, unaware that I would be teaching some of Mugabe's seasoned warriors. They quoted huge chunks of Mao to me. I don't know if I passed the course.

I chatted in the comfortable senior common room bar to some of my old colleagues. White liberals who had espoused black rule were the first to leave Zimbabwe; the old colonial hardliners seemed to be taking independence in their stride. Why?, I asked one lecturer, who was Jewish, feminist, pro-Mugabe, forthright and impeccably politically correct on everything.

'The liberals believed that "kaffirs" [marking two inverted commas with her fingers] were human beings, but they're disappointed, while the right-wingers thought they were baboons and are pleasantly surprised.'

The great losers of the Rhodesian war were the Ndebele. A North Korean-trained fifth brigade savagely pioneered a form of 'ethnic cleansing' in Matabeleland. Nkomo, forced out of the government and into temporary exile, said: 'We stand a cursed people. Independence has meant nothing to us.' More than sixty white farmers were also killed in post-war Matabeleland.

The Mugabe Cabinet had more degrees than any other in the world (except West Germany), but it presided over a series of disasters, mainly of its own making. Corruption was rampant. Given preferential treatment and lacking the capacity to use it, African businessmen sold their foreign currency allocations at a 50 per cent mark-up to white businessmen, for whom imports were crucial to survival.

Initially, the cold, austere, intellectual Mugabe seemed untouched personally by corruption, but his half-hearted control of his corrupt cronies and his ruthless manipulation of clan and ideological politics in his central committee suggested he still thought he was running a guerrilla army and not a country. He maintained the tough emergency laws inherited from Smith.

Whites were allowed twenty separate seats in Parliament until 1987, the majority of them filled by supporters of Smithy, perhaps out of habit, nostalgia, or to raise two fingers to Mugabe, or because they thought that in the end Smith was right. He always said the economy, education, law and medical services would collapse under black rule, and that the Ndebeles and Shonas would fall on each other's throats without whites to stop them. (He also said, however, that black rule would take a millennium – it was a short thousand years.) Sadly, most of Smith's prophecies were self-fulfilling because of white intransigence.

At least he had the courage of his convictions and stayed in Zimbabwe.

I didn't. I was taking the gap.

I regarded many black and white Zimbabweans as my friends. I had admired the courage and decency of white Rhodesians but detested their unthinking arrogance towards their voteless compatriots. I had come to love the country but none of its rulers. I had enjoyed an exhilarating five years as a writer and I wanted to keep some good memories. The transition from white to black rule had been spellbinding, but I didn't want to see the country die.

I decided to take up an offer to teach politics at South Africa's most liberal and distinguished university, Wits. Down South was where the action was. The transformation of Rhodesia to Zimbabwe meant the replacement of an efficient, racist, white élite with an inefficient, tribal, black élite. It was inevitable and, ideally, should have happened without bloodshed.

I handed in my police uniform; I had eventually served as a reservist in the dying days of the British South Africa Police, but only after Mugabe won and the police force fell apart. I also found another police uniform in my house as I tidied up to leave. My female housemate admitted she had been in Special Branch. I hadn't known – which speaks volumes for my skills as an investigative journalist. 'I confide in you and you're a spook,' I said testily.

She was not a bit contrite: 'I helped to give you a clean bill of health. You've been such a nosy bastard for the last five years, and they were convinced that your books on the country were a cover, and your Sandhurst background, and your friendship with Ken Flower and his daughters . . . It was me who helped to get your clearance to go everywhere. They were thinking of deporting you.'

We had not been lovers, but I had loved her like the sister I never had. I should have been angry and hurt. I wasn't. Much later, she said she had been joking about my security clearances, but I still wonder.

In June 1981 I tenderly embraced my glamorous long-term companion. With the inevitable sad determination of a traveller, I said goodbye to her and the country I loved.

2. APARTHEID SOUTH AFRICA –
THE GOVERNMENT GOD MADE IN ANGER

It is the dawn of creation and God and Jesus are parcelling out goodies.

God says: 'I'll give Britain lots of fish and coal to make up for all the bad weather. And I'll give Saudi Arabia plenty of oil to compensate for the sand. . .'

God works his way through the countries, balancing bounty and deficiency, until he comes finally to South Africa. 'I'll give the southern part of Africa, beautiful beaches and mountains, an exquisite climate, a vast range of minerals, superb fauna and flora, a wonderful cocktail of peoples. . .' And so he continues until he is interrupted by his son.

'Why are you giving South Africa all these things?'

'Wait till you see the government I'm giving them.'

Every country has its quintessential joke, and this story summed up apartheid South Africa for me. I loved the country but hated the government. The conflict in this strange, fascinating, achingly beautiful land was far more complex than the comfortable stereotypes imposed from thousands of miles away. I never saw it as a straightforward case of good versus evil. South Africa, unlike Rhodesia, was not a case of thwarted decolonisation. The three million or so Afrikaners were a genuine white African tribe. They had nowhere else to go. Africa was home.

South Africa was unique (in sub-Saharan Africa) in having a large poor white population, and apartheid, initially, was the racism of the poor whites. But the ruling National Party enshrined racism in its constitution when it won power in 1948. That was a bad PR move just three years after the fall of Hitler.

Much as I came to despise apartheid and its vicious implementation, I had few doubts about the genuine philosophical, even moral, impulse behind the Afrikaner desire for self-determination. The nineteenth-century history of southern Africa records the savage duplicity of British imperialism, especially during the Boer War. Welshman David Lloyd George had shown sympathy for the Boer struggle and so did I. The Welsh were like the Afrikaners – too near the English and too far from God. I did my best to learn Afrikaans, that feisty derivative of Dutch which was the official language alongside English. Unpopular though it may be now, when I started living in South Africa I was predisposed to understand the Afrikaner, not indulge in knee-jerk moralising. I was wary of the African National Congress not because of their aims – which I supported except for their socialism – but their methods. Yet I knew the ANC would win in the end. And I came to support sanctions and to accept, finally, the armed struggle, although not attacks on civilians. Revolution and war were inevitable as long as the whites, 13 per cent of the population, controlled 87 per cent of the land. If the government were serious about its homelands strategy then the only logical solution was a white homeland approximating the size of the white population. But the apartheid rulers tried to hang on to the lot.

I had first arrived in South Africa in 1976 when the Soweto insurrection was at its peak. The government's political position seemed hopeless: all bullets and no ballot, repression without reform. But reform would have led inexorably to majority rule. There was no halfway house, so I could understand if not agree with the short-term thinking of the ruling National Party. Throughout the 1970s and early 1980s I watched it potter around with half-baked 'new dispensations'. Yet at the same time I would compare the hard-line South African stance with the approach of white Rhodesians – more conciliatory, perhaps, but less successful as a dogma.

When I read Denis Hills's *The Last Days of White Rhodesia*, a sentence stuck in my mind: 'Whatever the rights and wrongs of their cause, it is comforting to be among whites who decline to grovel before blacks. Does it ever pay to grovel?'

Unlike Hills I hadn't been inside one of Idi Amin's prisons. I also disliked the ceremonial angst of the white liberals who patronised selected members of the black middle class. It is just as insulting to fawn upon a man as it is to discriminate against him.

Many Afrikaners were utterly sincere in their belief that the Bible ordained the policy of separate but equal. I thought they were sincerely wrong in believing that God wanted them to keep blacks from the ballot box. Among the wealthy English-speaking liberal community, however, politics was more etiquette than conviction. In South Africa 'liberal' had a special meaning. The terms 'left' and 'right' bore little resemblance to northern European models. Most South African liberals, for example, opposed universal franchise.

There was no doubt about the volcanic impatience of the young blacks in Soweto. South African cities appeared more ripe for revolution than Russia in 1917. For a black radical I could see the attraction of the South African Communist Party. To him, apartheid was synonymous with capitalism. But in the countryside and homelands, where blacks had been shoe-horned into gulags without fences, I found great passivity. In 1976 I didn't think that a successful revolution was imminent because of the sheer efficiency of the security forces. As in most authoritarian systems, the thing that worked best was the secret police.

South Africa, unlike Russia in 1917, had not been defeated in war. It was a regional superpower, a military and economic giant while remaining a moral pygmy. In this sense apartheid worked. It had created a cargo cult on a vast scale for the whites in the 1960s and 1970s. And it had worked psychologically. As intended, it kept the races emotionally apart.

Ken Owen, a South African newspaper editor I came to respect enormously, observed: 'White South Africans tend to profess an undying love for a country they hardly know, whose people often frighten them, and whose stark beauty they constantly change in imitation of Europe.'

Cape Town

My introduction to Afrikanerdom was in the cradle of the culture, Cape Town. My stint at the University of Cape Town was enlivened by elegant vineyards and the finest Cape Dutch architecture. Cape Town was the capital of the Cape province, which is bigger than France, and the republic's summer and legislative capital. About twenty-five miles from the Cape of Good Hope, it was one of the most geographically isolated and yet also one of the most beautiful of the world's great cities. The excellent restaurants and parks, plus the mountains, beaches, and surrounding wine farms, made Cape Town an easy city to live in – provided you were white. Like all South African cities, Europe and Africa, first and third world, mixed uneasily. Parts of Cape Town, such as the cafés in Sea Point, could be found in any cosmopolitan city, but the shanty towns on the bleak sandy flats could be only in Africa.

I had a so-called 'coloured' (mixed-race) girlfriend, whom I met at the university. We both loved eating out, dancing and the cinema. And we enjoyed making love. But the apartheid laws made it illegal for us to do any of these things together. I didn't intend indulging on my own, so we were forced to break the law. I had no problem in contravening this kind of legislation, but – even though Cape Town was more racially tolerant than other South African cities – I knew my friend felt understandably awkward in public places. Because she could almost 'pass for white' – to use the local parlance – we were rarely abused by any rude comments. Only once were we asked to leave a restaurant. We spent much of our time in my flat, where she felt more comfortable. Life in South Africa for 'non-whites' was not a street of joy.

My friend warned me that the security police, who were not above raiding the beds of mixed couples to examine the sheets, might try to plant drugs in the flat. Deporting a foreign journalist and university lecturer in politics on a drugs charge would be more expedient, she explained, than the bad publicity of arraigning me on offences against the Immorality Act. She also explained some of the more arcane mysteries of apartheid: the various grades of 'Coloured' – Cape Coloured, Malay, Griqua, Indian, Chinese, 'other Asiatic', and 'other Coloured'; how the Race Classification Board worked; the sixteen different grades of pigmentation based upon a person's public acceptance as being white, black, Malay, and so on; tests such as whether the hair was crinkly enough to hold a pencil, or the width of the nose . . . Not only was apartheid doomed but it was damned.

When I argued with white reactionaries and white liberals about one person, one vote I would ask a simple question: why should Archbishop Desmond Tutu, a Nobel laureate, be denied the vote when an illiterate, unemployed Afrikaner railway worker was enfranchised?

I found many of my all-white students at the University of Cape Town tediously dogmatic in their supposed progressiveness. I also lectured at the Afrikaans-language university of 'Maties' at Stellenbosch, established in 1918 as the Afrikaner Oxbridge, where I found the students much more open-minded. Simon van der Stel, a stiff Dutch bureaucrat, founded a frontier town on the banks of the Eerste River in 1679. Van der Stel loved oaks, and the graceful boulevards he planted still adorned picturesque Stellenbosch. I spent as much time as possible in the area because of the architecture. The Cape Dutch style contains elements from Dutch architecture but is also influenced by colonial Indonesian traditions and the local environment. The most characteristic feature is the graceful gabled section built around the front door, which is flanked by symmetrical wings, thatched and whitewashed, extending on either side.

I was supposed to be using my visiting lectureship to finish my doctoral research, so I became friendly with Retha, a librarian at Maties. She was a fund of knowledge on Afrikaner culture and offered herself as an intellectual guide. My scholarly investigations soon degenerated into a three-month tour of the local wine farms, for which I am eternally grateful. We drove through the old, beautiful vineyards of the valleys around Paarl, Franshoek and Tulbagh; then returned to eat in splendid eighteenth-century farmhouses converted to hotels.

Afrikaners, although traditionally hospitable to (white) foreigners, tended to be reserved in English-speaking company until they knew you really well. They were especially distant with journalists, whom they sometimes regarded as part of a communist conspiracy. Mixing with Afrikaners in Stellenbosch, or later in army and police camps in South West Africa (now Namibia), and trying hard to follow a conversation in their own language, broke through many of the barriers. I was able to ask why they persecuted people, like my girlfriend in Cape Town, who shared their language, culture, and religion.

'Agh, man. The National Party made a big mistake there. We need the Coloured people on our side. They must get the vote back soon. Good people, you know. . .'

Later in the evening: 'But they drink too much, man, and they're violent. They're OK when they're not on the *dop*.' *Dop* was a tradition of paying farm workers in kind – cheap wine.

Afrikaners also said we foreigners didn't understand their sense of humour. In this they were like the Germans. During one of our wine tours, Retha, my liberal librarian friend, suddenly stopped her Volkswagen on the side of a lake and pointed to a distant blob.

'Race you to that island.'

'But I don't have a swimsuit.'

She just laughed and ran into bushes by the water's edge. The next thing I saw was a statuesque naked form diving into the lake. I had little option but to follow suit. Retha took about fifteen minutes to swim to the island. I arrived there half-dead ten minutes later.

'Agh, shame,' she said in Afrikaans. 'There's bird shit everywhere. Race you back.'

When I eventually got back to the shore, I dived into the bush where my clothes were. *Had been*. Retha had taken them and gone. Maybe I had asked one too many political questions. I never really got to grips with the Afrikaners' sense of humour or their practical jokes. But it might explain why so many South African policemen thought it hugely funny to give flying lessons to black prisoners from the tenth floor of John Vorster Square, the police HQ in Johannesburg. A shocking number of police detainees developed strange illusions that they could fly, and self-inflicted wounds took on epidemic proportions in cells.

Steve Biko was different. The police murder of the black-consciousness leader attracted worldwide attention, as did the incredibly bungled reactions of the minister of police, Jimmy Kruger. Kruger's tactlessness was aptly displayed in Sir Richard Attenborough's moving film on Biko, although the pathos was marred by two facts. Firstly, it was filmed perforce around Harare and too many of the settings were Zimbabwean rather than South African. Some of the local actors were friends and I was distracted by familiarity. Secondly, the film was more about the rapport between Dickie and Donald than the alleged close friendship of Biko and newspaper editor Donald Woods. Although Woods's perhaps hyped heroics were mocked in South Africa, when I later met him in exile I was also seduced by his immense charm.

Durban

I got a fresh perspective on South African politics in Durban, where I taught at the University of Natal. At both Cape Town and Durban I was an academic locum during the sabbaticals of the respective professors of politics. It was a useful financial and intellectual background for my writing.

In December 1497 the Portuguese explorer Vasco da Gama sailed along this coast while pioneering a route to India. As it was Christmas, the Portuguese called the area Natal. In 1824 the Union Jack was flown at Port Natal, which was later renamed Durban after the Cape Governor Sir Benjamin d'Urban. During the nineteenth century Durban witnessed great battles which spawned equally great leaders, such as Shaka, King of the Zulus, and, later, Mahatma Gandhi. After the Boer War (1899–1902) came peace and the union of the two British colonies, Natal and Cape Province, with the two defeated Boer (Afrikaner) republics in the Transvaal and the Orange Free State. A national convention to discuss the merger of the four territories was held in the city hall, later Durban's post office.

Durban became a big subtropical holiday resort, with over a million visitors a year, mainly from the Transvaal. I enjoyed the colonial splendour of classic hotels, such as the Edward, and eating curry in the British Middle East Indian Sporting and Dining Club. Most of the approximately one million South Africans of Indian descent lived around Durban. The old Indian market was burnt down in early 1973, but many of the shops and restaurants had an exotic Asian atmosphere.

One man's shadow, for good and bad, hovered over Natal – Chief Gatsha Buthelezi, the leader of the mainly Zulu Inkatha party. My impression was that Inkatha was essentially a huge protection racket, a ticket for blacks to secure houses, schools, and jobs in the Kwa-Zulu homeland run as a personal fiefdom by the Chief. White businessmen cosied up to the mercurial warrior politician as insurance against their mutual rivals, the ANC.

I travelled around Kwa-Zulu, the successor to Zululand, to satisfy my historical curiosity. Sometimes I went on organised battlefield tours; at other times I strolled around on my own, conjuring up ghosts from my schoolboy imagination. I had seen the brilliant South African TV series *Shaka Zulu* at least twice. Shaka was a black Napoleon in the early nineteenth century. Later conflicts are better known. The Anglo-Zulu war of 1879, for example, created a pattern which became almost compulsory for the later military campaigns of the British empire: the opening tragedy, the heroic redemption, and the final crushing victory. The tragedy was Isandhlwana, the worst British military defeat since the Afghan retreat of 1842. The heroic redemption came at Rorke's Drift, where 110 mainly Welsh troops conducted choirs and battles simultaneously (at least in the film), gallantly warding off waves of charges by 4,000 Zulus. Six months later the crushing victory came at the Zulu capital of Ulundi. The imperial forces formed up in the classic hollow square, four deep with fixed bayonets, with Gatlings and artillery at each corner. There was no digging in, no Boer laager.

'They'll only be satisfied,' said the British commander, Lord Chelmsford, of his critics in London, 'if we beat them fairly in the open.'

The Zulus flung themselves in suicidal waves against walls of disciplined fire. Not a single warrior got within thirty yards of the redcoat square. When the impis faltered, Chelmsford unleashed his cavalry. Zulu power was broken; Zululand was divided up and later incorporated into Natal.

In Durban I gave a talk to a branch of the New Republic Party, a feeble descendant of the United Party which ruled South Africa until 1948. The UP had been led by Jan Smuts, an Afrikaner who fought the British and then became an imperial pro-consul. Most of the senior citizens I addressed there seemed to think that Smuts was still Premier. Some sat knitting in the front row; when I came to the punchline of a longish story, one of knitters had a heart attack and died in front of me.

After the old lady was taken away in an ambulance, I was just about to recommence my talk when a colleague whispered in my ear: 'That's the last time you'll use that joke!'

The NRP ruled in the provincial assembly and even hinted at UDI to escape Pretoria's heavy hand. Natal was the one province where English-speaking whites were in the majority, reversing the normal ratio of 60 per cent Afrikaners to 40 per cent English speakers. Some English speakers, especially in the prosperous farming communities, affected a cut-glass Oxford accent and the foppish mannerisms of upper-class England. These Natalers were patriots of a country that no longer existed.

Durban university, where I was based, was very well-mannered in an English sort of way, although the student protests sometimes got out of hand. Most of the time the white students here seemed rather apathetic (Witwatersrand – 'Wits' – and Cape Town universities were for the activists), and many of Natal's tanned, skimpily dressed females were said to be studying for a BA *Mansoek* – 'man-hunting'. Metaphorically, I tripped over surfboards to reach the lectern to gaze down on a sea of vacant madonnas waiting impatiently for husbands.

City of Gold

Cape Town and Durban were forays from my base in Salisbury, but Johannesburg became my home in June 1981. At first sight, and even after regular visits, Johannesburg was an ugly, scary city. It was the biggest conurbation south of Cairo, with six or seven million inhabitants then, and part of the Vaal triangle, which included Pretoria and interlocking industrial towns. Census figures were very rough guesses. Not much more than 100 years old, its existence had nothing to do with natural beauty, convenience, rivers, or trading routes. It was founded on top of a gold reef. Brash, fast, crime-ridden, well-armed and architecturally a dump, Jo'burg had three redeeming features: wealth, energy, and an excellent climate.

I started teaching international relations at the University of the Witwatersrand (Wits), the largest English-language college in South Africa, and arguably the most distinguished university in Africa. I had secured a year's contract because I needed the money, having been forced to leave Zimbabwe with almost nothing – except three manuscripts. Wits paid me a settling-in allowance and my South African publishers gave me a smallish advance.

Wits was invigorating intellectually, but my international relations department was very conservative and led by a Cold War warrior of Prussian extraction. He waged trench warfare against the politics department, which was of a liberal-Marxist tinge. Much to his disgust, and deliberately fatal to my career advancement, I used to drink with the Marxists. I could not help but recall Kissinger's quip – 'the politics of university are so bitter because the stakes are usually so low'. About the only thing that united Wits were the gripes about a second-rate heating system.

Wits was a springboard for my assault on the local media. I started a weekly political column on *The Star*, the biggest English-language daily in Africa, and later wrote a similar column for the *Sunday Express*, edited by the Cassandra of South Africa, Ken Owen. Three of my books were published inside a year. I started a little political punditry on the radio, and freelance presenting for South African TV. I was extremely wary of its propaganda, so I tried to keep my political distance by researching, writing and presenting my own material. I worked mainly with a distinguished South African film-maker, Marie Bruyns, based in 'Dithering Heights', SATV's HQ in Auckland Park. I ended up presenting on top TV shows, *Special Edition*, *Midweek*, *Network*, serious news programmes, and the glitzy superficial *Prime Time*.

Although I was reluctant to class myself as an advocacy journalist, I genuinely felt that it was possible to address some of the real issues in South Africa even under conditions of censorship. Marie, an Afrikaner intellectual whom I trusted and admired, agreed with me that there were indirect means of skinning a cat. We were probably both wrong and naive, but we did have successes. Some of our best work, however, was canned because of censorship, and our investigation of corruption in horse racing led to my being the first person to be censured by the new Media Council. Some films won awards; one, on black taxis, had a major political impact when reaction to the documentary stopped the government banning so-called 'pirate' black-owned Kombi taxis, which were the safest and most popular transport system for thousands of black commuters. I am sure the minister of transport had never travelled in one.

Although we couldn't tackle apartheid head-on we investigated all sorts of abuses – in transport, housing, education and crime – which had far-reaching political implications. But I grew frustrated with SATV's pig-headed bigotry, especially after Marie was unceremoniously sacked, so I set up on my own as a producer. I tried to cover stories in neighbouring countries, with mixed results because stricter censorship, general mayhem and warfare made investigative reporting more difficult than in the apartheid state. Africa was and is a poor yardstick of press freedom but apartheid South Africa, despite its panoply of media restrictions, was a lot freer than nearly anywhere else on the continent. In some areas you could bitterly attack the government but investigation, especially into anything to do with prisons, the police and the army, was very risky.

The gags on the media were voluminous. You could be fined or imprisoned for even 'embarrassing' the government, an idea which seemed as preposterous as making Genghis Khan blush. I was occasionally harassed by security police, and sometimes films were pulled only hours before transmission by SATV's unofficial internal censors. On one notable occasion I was live on air and the producer, via my earpiece, told me to tone down my questioning of a senior official because the foreign minister, Pik Botha, had just telephoned to complain. I carried on in the same fashion – and my days of live interviewing were over. But, by and large, most of the bad news was reported, especially by the foreign media. In South Africa it was almost impossible to hide a massacre, unlike in most of the countries to the north.

South African journalists were barking dogs who were chained. If you broke the chain you could be imprisoned. Foreign correspondents were deported. Pretoria made the mistake of kicking out the best foreign reporters – such as Peter Sharp, Michael Buerk and Allen Pizzey.

The deportees, usually old Africa hands who had an understanding of South Africa's complex problems, were often replaced by young, inexperienced, and crusading journalists determined to win their Pulitzer by sensationalised but sometimes lopsided reportage.

I became a resident, after a great deal of bureaucratic hassle from the immigration department. Bottom of the list of favoured people were lecturers in politics, journalists and musicians; I scored on two and was as interested in the stupendous local music as in political journalism, so I was lucky to get residence. It made it easier for me to travel in and out of South Africa, but it meant that infringing the censorship laws could now lead to imprisonment, not deportation.

Melville

Johannesburg was a hard city with little soul but, as in all big cities, some of the suburbs were like urban villages. I chose to live in Melville, the 'creative suburb' dubbed 'little Hollywood' by the locals. It was full of writers, artists and actors revelling in the little restaurants and quaint shops. People actually walked around rather than drove. Yuppies had Chelseafied their homes. For three years the reigning Miss South Africas lived next door to my mock Cape Dutch cottage, which made for pretty dinner parties and very light conversation. Melville was spiced with history, laidback kitsch architecture, parklands and 'beautiful people'. A little Bohemia on the Reef. And, of course, all white because of the Group Areas Act. Even the richest black capitalist had to live in a black area.

Beyond occasional forays into the battles in the townships, I lived a comfortable suburban life, along with most of the rest of white South Africa. The Soweto insurrection had been forgotten. Until the townships erupted again in 1984, the white suburbs were immersed in what Nadine Gordimer called a 'dreadful calm'. Most whites regarded politics just as Californians thought about earthquakes; the black townships were out of sight and usually out of mind. The torture chambers of the police HQ at John Vorster Square were just around the corner from the Market Theatre, where white liberals could learn about black suffering from playwrights such as Athol Fugard or Pieter-Dirk Uys, South Africa's version of Dame Edna Everage.

Until the war lapped around their cities in the mid-1970s, Rhodesians didn't want to talk politics or war. In the early 1980s in affluent South Africa it was the same. Sport, the new pool or BMW, Waterford crystal, Gucci shoes, Dunhill belts, Georg Jensen silver, and Balenciaga dresses came before ritual jokes about President P. W. Botha. The war was 'out there', on the border with Angola, a thousand miles to the north. That suited the government, which hadn't even told its own citizens that its army had invaded Angola in 1975.

My talks with government ministers suggested that they too wallowed in wishful thinking. The Afrikaners were desperate to avoid foreign contamination – hence the absurd bans on films such as *Guess Who's Coming to Dinner?* and works by Daniel Defoe, William Faulkner and even *The Book of Common Prayer*. Some of South African Wilbur Smith's books were prohibited. Television – quaintly termed 'the little bioscope' – was not allowed until 1976. I used to keep awake in the cinema by counting the cuts, after exchanging my brain for a packet of popcorn.

Pretoria said it was not only part of the West but was in the vanguard of Western Christendom's battle with Moscow's evil empire. The Afrikaner government had a Ptolemaic view of the world: Pretoria, not Berlin, was the centrepiece of the Cold War. Pretoria therefore had to allow a free press, as integral to its defence of Western values, but it had to curb Moscow's total onslaught, aided wittingly or unwittingly by the local and foreign media. The government wanted to be treated as part of the West and explained that there were similar problems with terrorists elsewhere.

South Africa was third and first world, Australia dumped on Nigeria. You could change worlds by travelling a mile or so from rich white Sandton to the desperate poverty of the black township of Alexandra. The third world analogy permitted a soothing psychic balm. For the comfortable whites the problems were not happening in the next township, which they very rarely visited, or in the dustbowls of the black homelands hundreds of miles away; no, the starvation and turmoil were another *world* away. It was much easier to assuage the conscience by discovering black Africa in the Market Theatre. It boasted a bar and even a multiracial restaurant.

The complacency was shattered when Alexandra went up in flames in the 'unrest' which began in 1984. Ex-Rhodesians in Johannesburg were once again planning to become *uhuru*-hoppers. Most of them could claim British citizenship, but Afrikaners were stuck with their 'green mamba' passports. Dinner parties were full of '*kugel*-speak', the whining tones of wealthy young white females, many of them Jewish.

'So, do you think we can get into Australia? Mannie's over there, you know.'

'Britain's too cold. I fancy California, doll.'

'I'm staying here. It'll come right.'

'What's the difference between an emigrant and a refugee? . . . Timing.'

'Bloody sanctions. Business is so quiet, you can hear the turnover drop.'

'When we Jews leave you know there's a problem. When the Greeks go it's bad. When the Porks [Portuguese] start to leave, it's too late.'

Rich Johannesburgers suddenly started taking a keen interest in portable art. Sydney Kumalo's statues were a bit heavy. John Meyer's hyper-realist paintings sold well in the USA but he painted only twenty or thirty a year. The increased pressure of conscription (the only aspect of apartheid which excluded blacks), sanctions and ungovernable townships shook the whites, but SATV news broadcasts served to reinforce the membership of the Mushroom Club, waging war on truth with a scorched-air policy. Troubles abroad and trivial good news at home were emphasised. It was often so muddled that one was left thinking Lebanon had been invaded by Cabbage Patch dolls led by Brooke Shields wearing a very sexy number.

Second-rate celebrities visiting South Africa were given superstar treatment. I talked to the celebrities too, including the stars of *Dallas*, which became a South African obsession. Some big stars, such as Rod Stewart, risked international opprobrium for big bucks, performing at Sun City in the so-called independent homeland of Bophuthatswana. It was part of the one-person, one-casino, one-vote-once system which allowed petty dictators to run sham countries funded by Pretoria and gambling. Most forms of gambling were forbidden in South Africa. Because of the delayed advent of TV, white South Africans were traditionally big book-buyers. Lots of authors did the circuit. Joanna Trollope was the most elegantly serious; Jeffrey Archer, surprisingly, the most friendly, at least to me. He was almost humble, but South Africa often affected people in odd ways.

My funniest interview was not with an Afrikaner politician but with a comic, Pieter-Dirk Uys. He lived a few doors from me and was most famous for imitating the 'Great Crocodile' – President

P. W. Botha. Uys, who described himself as 'a half-Jewish, half-Afrikaner actor-producer who makes his own dresses', claimed that he made more money pretending to be PW than PW did being himself. And without paying taxes. 'They're royalties, not taxes, because the government writes my scripts.'

'What if you were really PW?'

'I'd get Mike Hoare [who led the abortive South African coup in the Seychelles] to organise a coup on another island – Robben Island – to free Mandela.'

Whites rarely mentioned the imprisoned ANC leader. He could not be quoted in any publication. He was an 'unperson'. But how often did I hear a variation on: 'If Mandela dies in prison, I'm off. I won't even bother to leave the key with the mortgage society.'

My favourite South African collocutor was Denis Beckett, who looked and sometimes behaved like the American actor Gene Wilder. Denis edited *Frontline*, a beacon of irreverent, if eccentric, opposition to apartheid's lunacies. He formed a coterie of writers – whom he usually forgot to pay – which produced some minor triumphs and in one case a major masterpiece, Rian Malan's *My Traitor's Heart*. Denis consumed much of his time, and my beers, in trying unsuccessfully to make me an optimist about South Africa and teaching me South African English, the peculiar and snappy mix of Afrikaans and English street-*taal* (language) which suffused his own and the magazine's prose.

According to Denis, *uitlanders* (outsiders) had great difficulty with South African terms. Very few foreign journalists bothered to penetrate the Afrikaans core of South African politics, depending instead on English-language newspapers. English was the language of commerce but infiltrating politics, the army, the police, and the bloated civil service usually required Afrikaans. In the early 1980s the buzzwords were *verkramptes* (white conservatives) and *verligtes* (those who thought of themselves as enlightened).

In English, traditional *verkramptes* would say things like:

- My Bantus [blacks] look on me as their father.
- We made this country what it is today.
- If you raise their pay they just get drunk.
- You have to show them who's boss, otherwise they'll think you're weak.

In Afrikaans they would say:

– Every white man could take ten kaffirs with him.
– The problem is that our forefathers didn't wipe them out like they did in Australia or America. We were too damn soft.

Verligtes would say in English:

– Apartheid is dead, but the trouble is they've always been given everything.
– What we need to do is create a black middle class.

In Afrikaans they would say: 'Agh, man, they're also people . . . but they're not ready to run a country yet.'

It is wrong to assume that all right-wingers were Afrikaners. The English invented apartheid, the Afrikaners codified it after 1948. Many English-speaking reactionaries looked for a less Afrikaans variant of the neo-Nazi groups which sprang up in the mid-1980s, while English-speaking *verligtes* sniped at the 'hairyback' Afrikaners:

– What I don't like about the hairybacks is that they're so bloody rough on the Afs.
– I'll never forgive them for giving the blacks their own TV channel while we're still expected to share with the Afrikaners. [The original single 'white' channel was divided at 8 p.m. between English and Afrikaans, without subtitles.]

English *verligtes* would tell you that their maid was 'part of the family', but neglected to mention that this 'part' didn't have access to a bath, hot water or a sitting room. I went to dinner parties two or three times a week. They were so common because servants did the washing-up. If I became irritated by the pretentious display of 'progressive' attitudes I would ask two simple and direct questions: 'What is the surname of the maid who has been "part of your family" for so many years?' and 'Have you been to the [black] location/township to which you have lived next door for X number of years?'

Nobody passed with a 100 per cent score. Surprisingly, I was always invited back, and even became a popular hair-shirt for the guilt which swamped white liberals. And it sure beat cooking for myself.

Gangs

I spent the best part of a year chasing stories on various kinds of gangs in South Africa. Marie and I made a forty-minute film on the widespread gang culture. It was no good simply blaming it all on apartheid: that didn't explain the white middle-class gangs in Johannesburg. I started off with the Hell's Angels. The first thing I noticed was the strict hierarchy – many of the gang leaders were mini-Führers. Although some Angels sported swastikas, Joe Pereira, *el supremo*, was a major fundraiser for charity. We might all say no to a little old lady on flag days, but not to a hulking leather-clad warrior.

When I first contacted Joe for a drink to discuss filming he asked: 'Can I bring my wife?' Then he and his wife Joy had to leave early because of babysitting problems.

But Joe, like all the gang leaders, was a male chauvinist. The female members of the 'crew' wore 'Property of Hell's Angels' on the back of their 'colours' or uniform. The lady Angels had to act with propriety: fidelity was in and orgies definitely out. Marie and I were invited to a Hell's Angels rock 'n' roll night. Strict protocol applied. The camera crew had to pile their side-arms alongside the mini-arsenal belonging to the Angels.

'It's rude to dance with guns.'

Protocol also applied on the dance floor. Only one couple danced at a time and the others formed a circle around them.

The Angels story went uneventfully except for one Neanderthal who thumped a cameraman who put a light-meter near his face. But he apologised: 'Hell, I thought it was a breathalyser.'

Next was *West Side Story* revisited. We hung out with Jo'burg's Lebanese and Portuguese gangs, the cutting edge of new immigrant groups trying to prove themselves. They chatted amiably about protection rackets.

Macho, territory, belonging – these were also the themes of the gangs in the coloured townships of the golden city.

Soweto, the sprawling black township, was more difficult. Before the ANC comrades took over the South African townships in 1984–1985, many of the same youngsters were in *tsotsi* (young criminal) gangs. I worked on the gangs in 1982–1983. When I used the trains or black taxis, after initial surprise and suspicion at seeing a sole white man in their domain, I usually got a friendly response. Leaving the 'white' town centre to go underground to catch a train to Soweto, I entered a different, bustling world. I was reminded of the future in H. G. Wells's *The Time Machine* . . . in daylight the polite, idyllic life, then at night the dark underworld.

In order to film in the train the railway police insisted we had a small armed escort. It was a pickpocket's nirvana, so jam-packed no one would know if a train *tsotsi* slipped a sharpened bicycle spoke between your ribs. But I enjoyed the impromptu singing and the train preachers making the most of their captive audience of sardines.

In the beginning it was easier with a film crew; later you had a fifty-fifty chance of being stoned, robbed or worse. House bricks and stones were called 'Soweto confetti'. Mark Peters, a tough ex-Rhodie who had gone through training with the Selous Scouts before he injured his back, worked as a photographer for *Newsweek*. After working in a Durban township during the 'unrest', he said: 'I have spent a lot of time in Africa but I have never before witnessed so much hate in one day. Blacks were killing Indians. Indians were after the blacks and whites. And everyone was trying to kill the press.'

That was not usually my experience in Soweto, but I didn't stick my neck out like Mark. I was nervous of Soweto at first, but I usually had a black companion or knew where to find one if I went in alone. I began the first of many booze tours of the shebeens. In those days liquor outlets were largely controlled by whites. It was very difficult for blacks to sell alcohol legally, hence the 4,000 illegal drinking dens – the shebeens. Lucky Michaels, a liquor king, gave me my first lessons in shebeen lore. He said shebeens were the victims, not the cause, of the gangs. In his pseudo-American accent Lucky told me about the notorious 'wire gangs': a black albino would dress up as a policeman and get people to open their homes at night. The gang would swoop in, tie up their victims with wire, and steal their valuables. This was pretty tame by later standards, when houses were raided by feral youngsters toting AKs.

South Africa's 'super-gangs' were to be found in the Cape. The Cape Town Scorpions and Born Free Kids had branches as far away as Jo'burg and Port Elizabeth. Experts guesstimated that on the Cape Flats about 600 gangs operated with approximately 80,000 members. Although the Cape's coloured gangs portrayed themselves as Robin Hoods, they often fed like parasites on their own people as much as on the rich 'whities'.

Their gang philosophy was straightforward. Them versus us, '*Boer en bandiet*' (Boers versus bandits). Yet, ironically, this rejection of Afrikanerdom was always couched in the most robust Afrikaans. Indeed, the street-*taal*, as much as smoking a white pipe (mandrax mixed with *dagga* – marijuana) and their tattoos, was a cultural bond for the gangsters.

For youngsters in the Cape and Soweto, gangs were a brotherhood for survival in a tough environment where families had been divided by apartheid's 'relocations' (in total three million people) under the harsh dictates of the Group Areas Act. Some gangs included men in their forties. Some grew out of the gangs, especially when they had regular girlfriends. Most gang leaders lamented women as the main cause of gang disruption, not the police. Others stayed in and became professional criminals.

As well as drugs, the professional gangs organised big bank heists, protection rackets, prostitution and contract killing. For white gangsters the price ranged from R3,000 to R5,000 (in 2009 values, £300). One gang leader took a great liking to Marie and offered to bump off, for free, someone she disliked.

I spent a long time talking to Dennis Holmes, an infamous Jo'burg gangster, crippled after a mob shoot-out. He explained that his career started in school: 'It went from marbles to murder.'

'Why?'

'Instinct.'

In the Cape special junior gang branches proliferated, and some joined as young as ten. When the youths had proved themselves – usually in fights with rival mobs – they joined the adult gangs. After further education at the reformatories, gangsters climbed the gang hierarchy. The universities of crime were the prisons. South Africa had the highest prisoner-to-population ratio 'in the Western world' according to the University of Cape Town's Institute of Criminology. Seventy-five per cent of South Africa's convicted prisoners were members of prison gangs, which dated back as far as the nineteenth century. Their nationwide and highly organised structures mirrored the titles and styles of the British colonial administration. In the 1880s a man nicknamed Nongoloza established the *Umkosi wa Ntaba*, the Regiment of the Hills, which operated inside and outside the prisons. The regiment formed the basis for the so-called 'Men of the Number', the main prison gangs called the 26s, 27s and 28s.

Membership was supposedly voluntary. Each gang had distinctive (but mostly imaginary) uniforms, tattoos, salutes and other military paraphernalia. The gangs distinguished themselves by their roles. The 28s pampered and protected their catamites or 'wyfies'. The 26s were the thieves; the 27s were the knife-wielding enforcers of the various codes or 'The Book' of the gangs. Other gangs, such as the Air Force, organised escapes.

The Men of the Number had a school/university relationship with the street gangs, training new recruits and helping them organise outside prison. Once you joined the Men of the Number you were a 28 or 27 for life. And it was difficult to hide the numbered tattoos. The gangs held near absolute sway over the inmates; prisoners feared the gang kangaroo courts, which imposed immediate death sentences much more frequently than did conventional courts. Local Marxists liked to portray these gangs as regiments in a '*lumpenproletariat* army at war with privilege'. When the townships were engulfed in insurrection some of the gangs joined the ANC and others sided with the authorities. Most of the gang leaders were in it for profit, although they might have mouthed revolutionary slogans. Politics initially played a minor role. Poverty, boredom, family break-ups, search for status, all the usual sociological explanations, were part of the cause. Bruce Lee and Mad Max were heroes who transcended race barriers. Many gangsters seemed really to believe that the movies were true-life stories.

Soweto had a homicide rate proportionately six or seven times worse than New York's (*before* the American city cleaned up its act). Apartheid South Africa was often termed a police state, but in comparison with Western countries it was very under-policed. While the white liberals in the relatively well-policed northern suburbs of Jo'burg were demanding that police powers be curtailed, the under-policed inhabitants of the Cape Flats and Soweto said that the police were too soft on crime. Vigilante groups sprang up, the *Makgotla* vigilantes in Soweto insisting, for example, that *tsotsis* were not intimidated by the police. They claimed that their traditional methods, usually a good beating with a *sjambok* (whip), worked better. The *sjambok* was also used in traditional courts to discourage infidelity, hardly a vote winner in the white suburbs.

As the producer, Marie won a number of awards for the gangs documentary. She deserved it. She had shown true grit. Only once did the male camera crew and I force her to remain in the crew minibus.

We were running around back alleys in Soweto with the vigilantes, with stones flying, whips flailing and filming at a fast jog. It was no place for a beautiful woman in designer clothes, and I didn't want her to be thumped, raped or lost. She stood an equal chance, however, of being taken into a tiny, immaculate house and given tea – Soweto was always unpredictable during riots.

The handy thing about apartheid was that I could separate my investigations and smug derring-do in the townships from my sheltered life in the white suburb of Melville. Except for the crime – Johannesburgers became the world's greatest wall builders and razor-wire enthusiasts – you could pretend to forget about the big, bad, black world out there.

There were dangers, of course. Most Johannesburgers never worked out whether to drive on the right or the left. Proportionately more South Africans were killed by cars than in any other country. The death toll was about three times the number killed in political violence. With so much general aggression, people used cars as weapons. Driving within the speed limit was often considered to be an act of provocation. Forty per cent of drivers didn't take tests, they bought licences in the homelands. Good cars, good roads, and bad drivers were a lethal combination. Too much drink and the fatigue of driving in a big country caused lots of minor accidents, which could turn into shoot-outs because so many (white) drivers were armed.

Pretoria

Pretoria was the Afrikaner capital, an uncompromising Boer rejection of both blacks and Brits. Some of the ugly, massive buildings were a manifestation of the most exotic dreams of Stalinist and Nazi architects. The size of the monuments implied a neurotic fear of impermanence. There were attractive structures around Church Square, and in the middle was a statue of Paul Kruger, the arch Boer patriot, covered in pigeon droppings. Compared with hectic Jo'burg it was like a country town, and pretty in October and November when the jacarandas flowered. This is where the embassies were, or at least the remaining ones from enlightened regimes in Chile, Paraguay and Britain.

Nightlife in the Calvinist city was out, unless you liked floodlit putt-putt (mini-golf). But if you were interested in Afrikaner psychology and history it was well worth a visit, if only to enter the holy of holies, the *Voortrekker* monument. To the untrained eye the inside might have seemed like *Wagon Train* carved in stone, but the sixty-four ox-wagons celebrated the Great Trek and in particular the Battle of Blood River on 16 December 1838. Under the brilliant command of Andries Pretorius, 470 Boers defeated 12,000 Zulus. The final score was 3,000 Zulus killed for three Boers. The Boers swore a sacred covenant to God and 16 December became a highly significant date and the calendar opposite of 16 June, Soweto Day, a symbolic day for blacks.

If you hated bureaucrats, Pretoria was hell. If you were a fan of uniforms, it was paradise. Pretoria was where I begged lifts from the military, usually to the Angolan border. You could see lots of interesting places in a Casspir armoured vehicle or a Puma helicopter. The inmates of these machines hated journalists, but I was tolerated partly because I had written a book on the SADF (South African Defence Force). Despite the catcalls from some UN members, many of whose regimes were led by half-crazed officers, in military terms the SADF ran a highly professional show.

My book said just that, while bashing the Afrikaner politicians who used the military to buy time that was wasted. When the book was launched in Pretoria, the generals duly pitched up. Incautiously, I chose to give half of my short speech in what I thought was well-rehearsed Afrikaans. When I switched from my hello in English to Afrikaans, I unintentionally dropped my voice two octaves, clicked my heels, and jerked my back ramrod straight. I thought I had done a good job until some English journalist friends reported on the reactions. An editor of an Afrikaans newspaper was sitting next to Chris Munnion of the London *Telegraph*.

'Tell me, Chris, is this man a friend of yours?' he said in a thick, clipped, Afrikaans accent.

'Yes,' said Chris defensively.

'Is he a violent man?'

'Not that I know of.'

'Then why,' asked the editor, 'has he just murdered my language?'

Gail Adams, a friend from Zimbabwe who was undoubtedly South Africa's best radio journalist, said simply: 'You sounded like Adolf Hitler reading a nursery rhyme in Dutch.'

I gave up, temporarily, my recurring pretensions as a linguist but not as a socialite. My little cottage in Melville became a doss-house for visiting hacks. For all the agonies, journalists – despite their printed indignation – found Johannesburg a comfortable base for a good running story. For a while the 'front-line' states, Zimbabwe, Zambia, Angola, Mozambique *et al.*, warned that foreign correspondents based in Jo'burg would have to move north to Harare. But it didn't work, partly because of the better communications and, frankly, better lifestyles, especially if the kids' schooling or the spouse's medical condition had to be considered. One top correspondent bought a wine farm, another a string of racehorses.

Around the corner from my home in Melville, SATV HQ continued to distil a farrago of idiocy, sheer exasperation and unintended humour. Because I was deemed a security risk my pass was taken away, but as I was still presenting on some of the main programmes, although rarely live, I had to go there regularly. I did interviews never knowing whether they would be broadcast, even if they were highly successful. There was a blacklist of prohibited people, but it was never written down in case someone like me smuggled it out for publication. The list would change from day to day. One minute a union leader and Tutu were in, then they were out. It was Kafkaesque. I did a programme at the beginning of 1984 on Orwell's *Nineteen Eighty-Four*. I knew I was asking for trouble, but I interviewed worthies such as Helen Suzman, Alan Paton, and Pieter-Dirk Uys. Tutu refused, understandably, to take part: he was in and out of the blacklist like a cuckoo clock. Our *Nineteen Eighty-Four* was heavily advertised, then Big Brother pulled the plug just before transmission. Next SATV banned Stevie Wonder's records. I recalled a similar ban, twenty years before, on the coloured South African cricketer Basil D'Oliviera, which had led to the international sporting boycotts. The ruling Afrikaners were like the Bourbons: they never learned anything and never forgot anything.

A topical joke summed up popular feeling about SATV. Bishop Tutu and P. W. Botha met for a pow-wow on a boat in the middle of a river. PW's hat blew off and floated downstream. Tutu jumped out of the boat and walked across the water to retrieve it. That night SATV news ran the headline: TUTU CAN'T SWIM.

A girlfriend gave me an Alsatian puppy, which I called Gelert. 'You need some responsibility in your life,' she said.

She was right and I loved German Shepherds, but such a gift was impractical for someone who was always travelling. Besides, I had a tiny garden, so I said I would keep Gelert for a week; then I moved to a house with a bigger garden and Jenny, a 25-year-old Australian lawyer, moved in to look after me and Gelert. He became the world's most travelled and pampered dog over the next ten years. Jenny, who stayed for nearly two years because she loved my dog, made our house into the unofficial Australian embassy.

In the first week I got an abrupt introduction to Oz culture. I had laryngitis and couldn't make a rehearsal for a programme at SATV.

'Please ring in for me and make my apologies,' I croaked.

Jenny, sweet, innocent and fiercely intelligent, lifted up the phone: 'Sorry, Paul can't make it today. He's crook and in bed with a wog.' (Wog, I learned, is Australian for flu.) If the presumably racist Afrikaner on the other end of the phone had penetrated Jenny's Oz accent, I was apparently a criminal homosexual fornicating across the colour bar. That one sentence breached a whole range of Afrikaner taboos.

'Thanks, Jenny, for ruining my TV career and teaching me Strine in one sentence.'

It was the start of a beautiful friendship. She diverted my growing anger with political life in South Africa by making me share her love for the bush.

'You always want to go where people throw things at you or want to shoot you – can't we go somewhere nice?'

I had been waiting for somebody to say that.

The captive states

As a schoolboy philatelist, I had been intrigued by the stamps from the three British 'protectorates' in southern Africa: they became independent as Lesotho, Botswana, and Swaziland in the 1960s. I resolved to show Jenny some of apartheid's nicer neighbours.

We went to Lesotho first, about the same size as Wales, and also proud of its pony-trekking and choirs. The countries are now twinned. The mountain state is the only country in the world where the entire territory is more than 3,000 feet above sea level. Its dramatic scenery and friendly population of then one and a half million inhabitants attracted a little tourism and a lot of foreign aid. Besides being one of the three remaining African kingdoms, it also had the shortest railway line on the continent – one mile to be precise. Its most distinctive feature, however, is that it is one of only three countries completely surrounded by another state (the other two, by the way, are the Vatican and San Marino). Unfortunately, Lesotho's encircling neighbour was a bully: South Africa. So, although Lesotho's coat of arms proudly proclaimed its aspirations, *Khotso*, *Pula* and *Nala* (peace, rain and prosperity), sadly it had missed out on all three.

Lesotho served as a reservoir for apartheid's industry in both senses: nearly half the workforce toiled in South Africa, and it had major water resources. It also suffered from misrule by its own leaders, especially Chief Leabua Jonathan. The Chief was particularly averse to fair elections, so he declared a 'holiday from politics', perhaps one of the more honest phrases to emerge from Africa. He gained a certain notoriety in Pretoria not just for his bowler hats but also for his flirtation with local communists and his pals in enlightened countries such as North Korea. He arrested Lesotho's king and ignored or banned local parties as well as the College of Chiefs, a rough African equivalent to the House of Lords. The chiefs could rule on matters such as criminality, inefficiency and their own absenteeism. If such a system were adopted in the UK, the Lords might soon find itself empty.

In response, the South Africans sent troops into the country and also set up a puppet army in the hills to keep Jonathan on his toes; I had interviewed some of the insurgents, but Jenny drew the line at my suggestion to mix pony-trekking with a return visit to the mountain rebels. In 1986 the South Africans connived in a military coup which dumped Jonathan and restored the king to his former role. Later, when the end of apartheid restored some sanity to South African politics, tiny Lesotho was still at the receiving end of its neighbour's powerful army: it invaded to squash another coup and inflicted a great deal of damage on Maseru, the dusty capital. The so-called kingdom in the sky had once again been brought down to earth.

Swaziland was much lusher and rather more peaceful. I contrived to spend a lot of time in Africa's second smallest country. For starters, until 1986 it had the only all-steam railway system in the world. Another anorak fascination was the country's philatelic history, and in particular the collection owned by a former RAF pilot and headmaster, Reverend Robert Forrester of Malkerns. He looked like an Old Testament prophet, kind and wise behind a luxuriant beard. I learned much about the former British colony via his explanation of its stamps. And then I was seduced by the game reserves. Mlilwane, the oldest, had charming and cheap wooden accommodation and accessible game for the car-bound. From another wilder resort, at Malolotja, Jenny and I could view thirty waterfalls, rare cycads, and highveld game, including the occasional leopard.

By and large things worked in Swaziland, although they worked a lot more slowly. And the hotels could be excellent, especially around the capital Mbabane. Henry Rider Haggard loved the surrounding mountains, and a little of the mystery remained, despite the rash of hoardings. Many people visited Swaziland, however, for earthier delights: it was considered the brothel of Africa, especially when interracial sex was barred in South Africa. The Why Not Club just outside the capital was perhaps the seediest nightspot in the subcontinent. Topless ladies pranced on pedestals while UK soccer videos were projected on to the back walls; over the snooker tables ladies stretched in micro skirts, despite being totally amnesiac in the lower lingerie department. Naturally, all the hacks congregated at the club during the coronation of the new king in 1986.

The previous monarch, Sobhuza, had ruled for sixty-one years, thus establishing the record for being the longest-reigning but also the most absolute monarch in the world. With a skilful mixture of modern and feudal statecraft he beat the white settlers, imperial bureaucrats, and black radicals at their own game, and brought an authoritarian stability to his country despite its sensitive position locked between the apartheid republic and revolutionary Mozambique. But would this hard-won stability collapse with his demise? Unlike Lesotho there were no political parties for Pretoria to manipulate; the old king had considered them un-African. Not even the most subtle Africanist in the South African foreign ministry could fathom all the nuances of the ever-changing feudal cabals which controlled the interregnum.

Technically, Swaziland was not a monarchy, but a dyarchy. All power was supposed to be shared between the hereditary male ruler – called the Son of the She-Elephant – with his mother, yes, the She-Elephant. This created problems with a king in his eighties. A Queen Regent ruled after Sobhuza, but she was deposed and one of the dead king's many wives took over. The regency was riddled by Byzantine intrigue, tales of witchcraft, massive corruption and various assassination attempts – a model perhaps for the Windsor soap opera. Personality clashes within the remarkable ruling clan, the Dlamini, as well as ideological rivalry between the younger technocrats and the traditionalists inside the royal council threatened the very survival of the conservative monarchy. Eventually the traditionalists triumphed; in April 1986 a nineteen-year-old youth, educated at a public school in England, became King Mswati III.

Thereupon nearly all the bickering stopped and invitations went out worldwide to presidents and monarchs to attend the coronation. The correspondents poured in; they might not have comprehended the complex succession process but they did understand that nearly all the country's single women – black and white – would be dancing topless in front of the king at the capital's football stadium. This would be good TV. P. W. Botha sat alongside Samora Machel and Prince and Princess Michael of Kent (representing the British Queen). Maureen Reagan stood in for her father, a hereditary representative from that most elective of institutions, the US presidency. The Americans got it right, quite by accident: sending a favoured daughter is a mark of respect in the local Nguni culture.

I was covering some of the ceremonies live on SATV. I was supposed to interview the new king but it was cancelled at the last minute, which might have been lucky as protocol required one to crawl out backwards after an audience.

Unfortunately, though, I was left with half an hour of live prime time to cover, after a long report I had produced on the lead-up to the coronation. No king or relative was available, and Pik Botha, the South African foreign minister, hadn't pitched up at the makeshift studio in a Mbabane hotel.

Marie Bruyns, the producer, told me all this seconds before transmission. She said: 'You'll have to suck it and see.'

'Suck what?' I asked in panic.

I bluffed for about fifteen minutes, discoursing on the arcane structure of the royal family with the anchorman in Johannesburg. I was getting desperate; I had run through, twice, all the king's titles: the Great Mountain, the Mouth that Tells No Lies, the Sun, and the Milky Way – the last I think I made up. I was just about to launch into all the chocolate bars when the commercial break gave me a brief respite.

Suddenly, I spied the hotel manager. I grabbed him and proceeded to interrogate him about security arrangements for the VIPs and what special diets they had. Somehow this guff filled a whole live programme.

In Botswana I normally relied not on a TV crew but on my own stills camera, a trusty, idiot-proof Pentax K1000. I did very little political reporting in this big, largely desert country, the size of Texas. Instead I concentrated on 'soft' stories, usually basing myself in safari lodges. Botswana was a country of stark, often unspoilt beauty. In the centre lay the exquisite Okavanga swamps, in the north the nature reserves teeming with wildlife, and to the south and east large cattle ranches. Most of the million or so ethnically homogenous inhabitants lived in the south along the South African border. And yet, for all the poor examples set by its black and white neighbours, and South African raids during the 1980s, Botswana survived as one of the handful of functioning democracies on the continent.

I particularly enjoyed the north. Chobe safari area was the site of Richard Burton's second marriage to Elizabeth Taylor. Here I encountered herds of elephants in their hundreds. Nearby, the northern Tuli game reserve later sponsored the work of Gareth Patterson, the modern-day Tarzan who assisted the famous naturalist George Adamson in Kenya. After Adamson's murder in 1989 Gareth secured permission from Botswana to relocate the Adamson lions to continue their rehabilitation back into the wild. Gareth spent very long periods working alone with lions, and appeared to be able to communicate with them. In 1984 I spent a few days with him and his animals. He was a man who lived his philosophy, often at the extremes of endurance and occasionally danger. It was one of the most refreshingly primeval periods of my life.

Despite occasional South African military incursions, Botswana was politically in a much stronger position than Lesotho or Swaziland – besides owning vast herds of cattle, the country also had lots of diamonds. Like South Africa and its diamonds partner, the USSR, Botswana then produced 30 per cent of the world's supply. Jwaneng, in the southern Kalahari desert, became the world's most valuable diamond mine. This piece of nature's bounty contributed to an amazing 11 per cent national growth rate in the first half of the 1980s.

But there were two problems. Firstly, this new-found wealth seeped into the bank accounts of the élite. Secondly, the South Africans manipulated the mineral windfall. De Beers, the diamond arm of South Africa's giant Anglo-American company, effectively controlled the sale of Botswana's precious stones. Nevertheless, Botswana's economic success story, due to mineral resources and sound political and financial policies, was almost unique in Africa; it was like a diamond in a continental desert of mismanagement. It prudently avoided serious entanglement in the wars that encircled it, and even made an extra profit as a front for apartheid's sanction-busting. Yet even after apartheid all three subordinate states remained in thrall to their giant neighbour. In the 1980s my travels in these three Commonwealth countries, where race relations were so much more relaxed, gave me some hope and respite. For a while I could forget the atrocities of South African politics and succumb to the seduction of the region's scenery and its people. That was Africa: generally great people, usually shit-awful governments. The world could forget, too. Until the revolutionary turmoil of 1984–1986, Western governments tended to cast a Nelsonian eye at apartheid. They were confirming one of the prime directives of journalism: the further away and darker-skinned the victim, the less the interest.

ISLAMIC LANDS

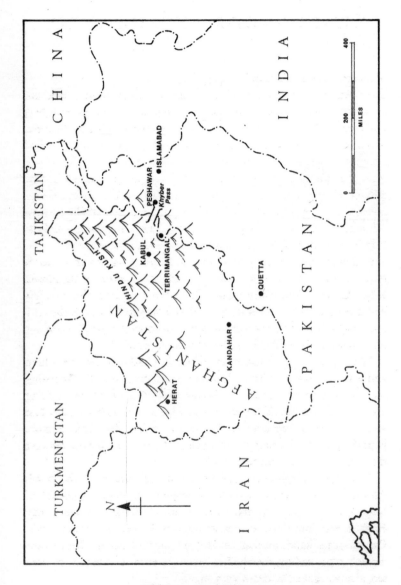

Afghanistan and Pakistan

3. PAKISTAN – CARRY ON UP THE KHYBER

Morocco – Endless souks

There was a brief and intriguing message on my answering machine in Johannesburg: 'Please proceed to Timbuktu as soon as possible', accompanied by an instruction to ring a phone number in Pretoria. The message came from the assistant of an Afrikaner film-maker called Albertus Johannes Venter. A cryptic message relayed by a third person seemed unusual, but I soon learned that such eccentricities were Al's stock in trade. I had met Al, or Big Al as he was sometimes called, once before. I admired his *chutzpah*, but was wary of his reputation for sending people off on crazy and usually dangerous missions. They came back, with little help from Al, and on occasion after a stay in the calaboose.

A day later Big Al rang from the Big Apple. I was to go to north Africa to make a film as a possible prelude to a venture in the Hindu Kush. Al was a Cold War warrior, addicted to conspiracy theories. His had a peculiar South African bent: he was targeted by both the CIA *and* the KGB, as well as other journalists who were trying to steal his film projects. He rambled on about 'mission security'.

Within forty-eight hours of the first call, I had dropped everything and was on my way to Timbuktu via Casablanca. I felt Al was testing me: I had to show form, even though I had lots of TV and writing commitments in South Africa. In Casablanca, I waited for Al. I had seen the film for the umpteenth time just a few days before; more people have heard about the town than the country, maybe because the film is better than the country.

Nevertheless, Morocco was the most welcoming of the north African states. Compared with its neighbours, it was a model of hospitality and stability, and quite permissive by Islamic standards. Hashish was forbidden to tourists but openly smoked by the locals. On the other hand, tourists could drink alcohol but the Moroccans weren't *supposed* to; they had to make do with the ubiquitous mint tea, always choked to death with sugar.

Despite the legends, Bogie never even visited Casablanca. Nor did Al.

After sitting around for a day, I was summoned to the nearby capital, Rabat. As I travelled there by bus, I reflected on my quick cram of Moroccan history – constant invasions, bold exploits and Moorish pirates. Well into the twentieth century Moroccan warlords had dangled the heads of their opponents from their fortress walls. The desert kingdom was never totally pacified by the colonial armies of France and Spain, although it was perhaps the most pro-Western of the Arab League states. European, African, and Oriental cultures blended, modern hotels and Old Testament casbahs, chic bikini-clad women on the beaches and the stern dictates of the Koran.

In Rabat, Al was on form. He insisted that he had a booking for the best (and fullest) hotel in Rabat, although he'd never even heard of the place until he walked in. Al berated the receptionist, a tiny man, for losing the non-existent booking. Towering well over six feet, Al leaned across and, in his inimitably affectionate way, pulled the man across the counter by the scruff of his collar.

'You are a little shit,' Al growled, his voice subsiding to a confidential yell.

The little man had guts. With his feet dangling in the air and his nose three inches from Al's beard, the Moroccan replied with calm dignity, 'And you, sir, are a big shit.'

We got rooms.

Al introduced me to Nick della Casa and Henry Bautista. Nick was a stranger, despite his claims to know me from the Rhodesian war. Henry, one of the best film cameramen around, I knew a little by reputation. Al was excessively vague, rattling on about Henry, Nick, and me travelling for ninety days by camel across the desert to Timbuktu. He implied we would make a film on the Polisario guerrillas in the Spanish Sahara.

Eventually, however, we were instructed to make a normal documentary on Morocco, one of a twelve-part TV series called *Africa in Focus* which won a number of awards and was shown in over thirty countries. Henry was on camera and Nick, ex-British army and ex-Rhodesian Grey's Scouts, was the sound man.

Al said: 'Do a good job here and you're on for the big job I'm planning.' Although he made it sound like the Great Train Robbery, Henry, Nick, and I set out innocently to explore and film Morocco.

Before he left, Al commented on the similarities between his native

South Africa and Morocco: 'They are both misunderstood, surrounded by hostile neighbours, and very pro-Western. And they're both crazy about royalty.'

Rabat was snobbish, conservative and riddled with political intrigue. The king, Hassan II, usually lived there, although he had palaces all over the country. His picture was everywhere, and his eerily familiar gaze transfixed me. Eventually the centime dropped: his features were an amazing amalgam of Frank Sinatra and Herbert Lom. Our official guide, Zakaria, insisted that the king was very popular because of his religious influence. I tactlessly reminded him of the country's least successful garden party: in 1971 over 1,400 military cadets burst into the summer palace and wiped out ninety guests. The king, who had shown a great deal of personal bravery in a number of earlier attempts on his life, escaped unharmed.

We made a forty-minute glossy film in just over three weeks, filming impulsively on the trot. I edited in my head and did the to-camera pieces spontaneously. I had made a hash of one in Tangier, using a radio mike in a crowded bazaar when the camera was out of sight on a balcony. The mike's radio signal kept breaking up when I was jostled; crowds of street urchins stared at me in amazement as I appeared to be talking loudly to myself. The effect was unintentionally hilarious, as were my presentations on a camel.

I had also made an idiot of myself in a mock-up of Rick's Bar in Casablanca, playing the film's famous theme song on a piano. I couldn't play the tune; it was an automatic modern pianola. A child stood alongside in utter delight as I appeared to play 'As Time Goes By', then he asked me to play 'Happy Birthday'. Nick fell about laughing. Later we discovered Nick had accidentally erased the sound from this section. Old film lore relearned: never work alongside animals or kids, especially in a crowded bazaar.

The team had got on well and had made the film relatively quickly and cheaply, but we had all spent enough time in other Arab countries to know Morocco was not typical. We had enjoyed the richness of Morocco's history, although the ghosts of yesterday were being shooed away by package tours and ham-fisted local bureaucracy. I found it a land of extremes, ancient and brashly modern, simultaneously both dazzling and seedy.

'The best war film'

During our enjoyable month in Morocco, Henry, Nick, and I had heard no more about Al's project, which we'd learned was to be filmed in war-torn Afghanistan. Not a gunshot to be heard. And nothing from Al. After the Rabat meeting, he disappeared – his favourite pastime. Henry and I became good friends; we both became fond, and protective, of Nick, an inexperienced and eccentric young journalist. We speculated whether Al was really going to send us to Afghanistan, or perhaps to Cambodia to do a story on the Khmer Rouge's elusive and genocidal Pol Pot. Al tended to clarify his 'missions' at the last minute.

Then, after I had finished producing the Moroccan film, Al rang and asked me to fly to London to make contact with Afghan exiles. After some initial explorations I flew back to Johannesburg to put my affairs in order. Al said I would be away for three months. I flew to Cape Town for a final word with Al. He asked me to bring 'a few things' of his with me, Al-speak for a ton of film equipment plus a briefcase. While I was staggering with this load across the mezzanine floor of Johannesburg's Jan Smuts airport, a high-security area, the unlocked briefcase fell open.

A rifle with a sniper's scope and around 200 rounds of ammunition rolled out. It was like *The Day of the Jackal*. A kind African helped me pick up the ammo and I put it all back in the case. Nobody said anything. I could have been hell-bent on shooting the president.

I had to check in the weapon at security before the flight. 'Do you have a licence for this?'

'No, it belongs to a friend.'

The security man looked suspiciously at the sniper-scope. 'What's all this fancy stuff for?'

'Duck shooting.'

The man didn't believe me, nor did I. But it was South Africa, and I was a respectable-looking white man.

'OK.'

Al met me at Cape Town and immediately resumed his security paranoia. 'You haven't discussed this mission with anyone?'

'No. But you could have told me what was in the damn briefcase.'

Al laughed and said: 'Duck shooting.'

'Like hell. But that's what I told the security check-in.'

He laughed more loudly. Things like mentioning carrying a gun and 200 rounds were not important to Al. He was not a man for details, except when they impinged on his definition of 'security'. At his luxurious mansion he gave me a drink and finally told me what he wanted me to do.

'You will lead three separate expeditions to penetrate Russian lines in Afghanistan. On the first one I want you to march to Kabul from Pakistan, and make contact with the *mujahedin* guerrillas on the outskirts of the city. You might have to dress up in East German army uniform to get in.'

The rest of his briefing consisted of my sitting alone through three hours of videos on the Afghan war. I had never been to that area of the world, and was horrified by the filth, the rugged terrain, the death and suffering. After this televised horror, only partly softened by the best Cape wine, Al rejoined me.

'This is all soft background stuff,' he said casually. 'We need real front-line action. Our film, commemorating the fifth anniversary of the Russian invasion, is going to be the best film ever made on the war. Can you do it?'

'Sure.' That's what I said, but not what I felt.

I spent a few days preparing things in Johannesburg. Henry and I had talked about getting fit for the arduous trip: I was grossly out of shape, despite regular squash, and certainly unprepared for the tasks ahead. Although I had taken the occasional chance when covering unrest in the South African townships, in truth I had hardly heard a shot fired in anger. I was more worried about my fitness than getting shot at. To make things worse, Henry decided not to come because of family pressures. I was thirty-six and had no ties. I made out a will – I didn't own much, but I was a trifle disconcerted to overhear two close friends discussing which pieces of furniture they might get.

I left for London on 18 June 1984. On the long flight I thought of the old adage about fools rushing in, but could I get out? I hoped the experienced Afghan hands in London would provide the answer. I gave myself two weeks in London to develop my initial contacts.

The first Afghan I stumbled on was a Dr Helmandi, an exile who spoke fluent Russian. He said he would help but wanted one or two things in exchange, such as surface-to-air missiles and a return ticket to Pakistan. My main job had to be done in Peshawar, capital of Pakistan's North West Frontier province, where most of the forty or so squabbling guerrilla groups had their headquarters, and I didn't think

I needed the shady Dr Helmandi holding my hand. I took emotional refuge by ringing up a few adventurer friends from my Sandhurst days. Dick Snailham, who had led umpteen expeditions up the Nile and Amazon, went into minute detail about catching scorpions.

'They plague Afghanistan,' he said reassuringly.

A few mates who had been in the British SAS told me about lice, zinc oxide for tender feet and plastic bags for film should the horses drown in the Afghan rivers. They hinted at nastier bits, such as the tactics of the 150,000-strong Soviet army of occupation and the bizarre habits of Afghan tribesmen. Since I was quite open about my ignorance of tribal warfare, I risked some teasing of my freshman status. Inevitably, I was treated to a lengthy discourse on the uncomfortable rearrangement of certain tender parts of the anatomy in which the Afghans indulged with estranged friends and relatives, let alone foreign infidels. I also heard stories about Russian prisoners being flayed alive, tribesmen buggering film crews' horses, and whipping unfit journalists for not keeping up on marches or showing fear under fire. I had the vague feeling that people were trying to discourage me.

Tim Cooper, a man from the London Afghan Support Committee, was helpful. He looked and talked like a dapper, if slightly mad, Hussar, straight out of a Flashman adventure. I explained my elaborate logistical plans in detail. He laughed. 'All you need is a blanket, a couple of pills, and a shell dressing wrapped around your chest in case you get shot somewhere.'

I began to think the British experts were as crazy as the Afghans sounded. Then Al telephoned to suggest I pay a farewell visit to my family in Wales before I left for Pakistan. Another confidence booster.

Dr Helmandi was still tugging at my heels, nagging about his plane ticket and missiles. As I delved deeper into exile politics, it was hinted that he was KGB. Didn't he get his degrees in Moscow? Even if he wasn't a Russian agent, he was aligned to the wrong party, one of the conservatives.

I was told: 'Try the fundamentalists, the ones who support the Ayatollah in Iran.' I was given the address of an Afghan fundamentalist greengrocer on the Clapham Road. Then came an anonymous tip-off: 'He's definitely KGB. He'll warn the Pakistanis and you'll be turned around at Islamabad airport.' I decided I didn't have time to visit the Clapham Road. Journalism is about bashing away even when every contact turns out a lemon. If you try ten times, you'll get there; but if you stop, depressed, on the ninth, you won't. My breakthrough was meeting the Gailani family in a plush Hyde Park apartment, paid for by supportive Saudis. After explaining that I was organising two, maybe three, film crews to enter the war zone to make a big anniversary of the invasion film, the Gailanis offered to help. They promised a whole array of what proved to be useful contacts in Pakistan and Afghanistan.

It was time to leave. Although I now had contacts and knew something of the political problems, I was still worried about the logistics of getting a film team into Pakistan. The military dictatorship covertly helped their co-religionists in Afghanistan, but didn't like foreign journalists. Handled properly, however, and after greasing a few palms, it was possible to send a crew in. The Pakistan government was not averse to lots of money pouring in for the millions of Afghan refugees in Pakistan, some of which could be siphoned off for its own use, so journalists were allowed in to report on the plight of the refugees. Then they could slip illegally across the Afghan border. But to do all this I needed help on the ground in Pakistan.

It came out of the blue. I tracked down Peter Jouvenal, an ex-British army paratrooper turned news cameraman, who had been in Afghanistan more than any other journalist. He was flying out of London the next day; so, unable to meet up with him, I contrived to book a seat next to him.

On the final night a strange apparition materialised at my hotel: Tim Lambon. Short punk haircut, worn-out leather jacket, jeans, big and menacing. I was drinking in the bar with a pretty, friendly blonde (it would be a long, no women, no booze trip).

Tim was direct, a man of few words: 'Al sent me. He said I should come with you. I've just flown from Cape Town.'

I offered him a beer. 'I don't drink alcohol, but I'll have a Coke.' He knocked it back, and I thought he was going to eat the glass as well.

When he went out to get his kit from the lobby, the blonde said urgently: 'He's got that killer look in his eyes.'

Tim came back, looking more relaxed, but I could sense he was thinking: do I have to go into this strange number with that fat little Welshman? Will I have to carry the bugger?

As it happened, he did. His military background (ex-Special Branch of the Rhodesian police, active in an infantry role in the war), his skills as a medic, and his robust humour, wit and shoulders were to prove invaluable on our expedition.

Peter Jouvenal had said he would meet me the next morning at the exclusive Diner's Club bar at Heathrow airport. The Gailani family had also insisted that one of their brigadiers talk to me before we left. I was due to meet both parties at midday, and rushed by taxi to the rendezvous feeling the after-effects of one night's intense preparation for months of no wine, no women, and no kissing on the Pakistani movies. At the Diner's Club reception an irate lady asked how I could invite so many strange-looking people to the exclusive facility when I wasn't even a member. Just as I was about to explain, the phone rang on her desk. It was for me: the blonde from the previous night wanted to say goodbye. Bad timing. The receptionist was furious. I offered to join Diner's Club on the spot, but she said I would need references and so on, implying that my sort wouldn't be wanted anyway. The only member, Peter Jouvenal, had still not arrived.

Inside the club, Tim had been keeping the bald Gailani brigadier happy. Various surly Afghans, not invited by me, mumbled in barely muted hostility across the other side of the lounge. Tim was fondling a long, sheathed knife. It was like a waiting room in a Moscow railway station full of Bolsheviks circa 1917; the air was heavy with conspiracy. The brigadier explained that he knew the Afghans opposite, who had once been friends but were now supporters of rival groups. We discussed our project. Ever security-conscious, Tim became agitated by our loud voices and use of maps – large, difficult-to-obtain satellite maps of Afghanistan. I put the maps away and lowered my tone, trying to be very secretive, then picked up my briefcase. It was not closed properly. All the maps and project plans fell out. Tim glowered at me – another black mark.

Finally, Peter Jouvenal appeared. I introduced myself and apologised for the uninvited Afghan horde. Within a few minutes we scurried off to catch a flight to Islamabad. No one was more pleased than the Diner's Club receptionist, still glaring at me with undiluted loathing.

Tim had to part with his beloved dagger at the check-in, which made him grumpy. I also suggested we sit apart and enter Islamabad airport separately. On the plane I tucked into European food and wine as though I was on my way to a Siberian gulag. Between mouthfuls I swamped Peter and his colleague, Julian Geary, with questions about Afghanistan. Both were amazingly tolerant of my ignorance.

I was particularly concerned about how we should describe ourselves at Islamabad airport, suggesting that Tim should pose as a student and, if asked, say he was planning a walking tour of the mountains. Peter thought Tim should take off his tough-looking biker's jacket. I was wearing a suit and had 'businessman' written on my second, clean, British passport.

Peter and Julian felt I was worrying too much.

'Getting into Pakistan will be no problem,' Julian said, smiling.

Perhaps my two weeks of talking to paranoid Afghans in London had got the better of me. One 'businessman' entering Pakistan was not a real worry, but the rest of the film team's equipment would probably need some smart thinking, or heavy paperwork and bureaucrat-soothing, on my part. I'd bribed my way around Africa and the Middle East, and now speculated on my first encounter with Asia.

The long war

As a historian I had, of course, read Flashman's memoirs of the fighting in the North West Frontier. British policy towards Afghanistan had been shaped by fear of a Russian drive south and the need to contain the turbulent tribesmen. Afghanistan had never been colonised, although the country's survival as an independent state had more to do with the competitive imperialisms of Moscow and London than the diplomatic skills of Kabul. Afghan leaders have always blamed foreigners for their ills, but internal blunders invited foreign meddling. In the early twentieth century Afghanistan tried to play off the predatory empires. Later it squabbled with its neighbours, especially Pakistan, because Kabul claimed large swathes of Pakistani territory.

Various regimes in Kabul tried to modernise the backward kingdom. In the 1960s the king experimented with liberal reform. A parliament, made up of MPs satisfying very minimal standards of sanity and hygiene, was established with limited powers. As all would-be conquerors and local civil servants soon learned, however, Afghans are the most ungovernable of peoples. Fiercely independent, they resented any central authority interfering in their traditional ways even if it was for their own good, such as providing sewerage, running water and schools. Nowhere else in the world did the past live so closely alongside the present. Physical inaccessibility meant that, outside Kabul, the twentieth century had bypassed the country. It had the world's shortest railway, less than half a mile long. Much of the country was passable only on horseback or by camel. It was, above all, a tribal society. Each tribe passionately defended its local customs. In the south the people were mainly Pathans; in the north, Tajiks, Turkomans, Kirghiz and Uzbeks; in the central mountains, unruly Hazaras. The wildlife was pretty wild: wolves, hyenas, jackals, wild dogs, wild cats, leopards, bears and, fittingly, vultures. The tribesmen were like their land: harsh, unpredictable, and brutal. The main unifying factor was Islam: belief in God and country amounted to the same thing.

Then hatred of the Russians was grafted on to raw nationalism, local tribalism, and religious fervour. Soviet intrusion began with Lenin and reached a political climax in the so-called revolution of 1978. Before President Babrak Karmal was installed by Moscow in 1979, three of his predecessors had left office the hard way, variously shot, strangled or poisoned. Russian tanks rolled over the border at Christmas 1979. While the citizens of the West were digesting their turkeys, Russia gobbled up independent Afghanistan.

The *jihad*, holy war, was declared before the Russian tanks rolled in.

Anti-communist guerrillas in the countryside vowed to return Afghanistan to Islamic rule. The tribesmen disliked any government, let alone a communist one backed by foreign infidels. Attempts at land reform and improvements in the medieval condition of women had incensed rural conservatives, both landlords and peasants. The population numbered nineteen million (five million subsequently fled during the war), of whom 90 per cent were illiterate. Local religious leaders believed that communist centralism – even if it brought schools – would deprive them of their authority, so the mullahs whipped up religious passions. And the arrogant behaviour of the Soviet conquerors made matters worse. The Russians soon discovered that defeating and controlling the Afghans were two different feats. The ungovernable tribesmen had simply never learned the habit of submission.

On the other hand, Afghanistan was not exactly Russia's Vietnam.

The Soviets were fighting on their own doorstep. Despite the mounting body bags, press and public opinion were stifled. No 'Hanoi Jane' (Fonda) squawked defiance in Moscow. And although Afghanistan was ideal guerrilla terrain, the tribesmen – despite Hollywood movies and star-struck American reportage – were not natural soldiers. Convinced of their innate martial qualities, they were very reluctant to be trained and spent as much time praying as working out tactics or maintaining their weapons. They hated orders. Their incompetence in technical matters was surpassed only by their faith in technology (and God) to solve all their problems for them.

By sheer doggedness they had managed, however, to keep a superpower at bay for five years. The Red Army controlled the cities, towns, and, crucially, the air. The *mujahedin* (holy warriors) loosely controlled perhaps 80 per cent of the country. But their guerrilla war was undermined by tribal and political feuds, *mujahedin* spending as much time ambushing each other as venting their indignation on the invaders. Their rigid individualism was the guerrillas' main strength, and weakness. No Tito or de Gaulle had emerged to seize overall leadership. The divisions were partly a legacy of traditional social structures in which decisions were taken by village elders, and fighting groups were often hesitant to venture outside their own neighbourhoods. The holy warriors had to work out a fundamental dilemma: to fight a modern war they had to give up their instinctive individualism and tribal ways – the very things they were fighting communism to defend.

Peshawar played host to a wide variety of guerrilla groups in exile, ranging from eccentric royalists to fanatical Maoists. The six most effective groups had formed two rival coalitions: one, the Alliance, composed of Islamic fundamentalists; the other, Islamic Unity, a more (relatively) moderate, middle-of-the-road lot. They spent most of their time intriguing against one another, but they did provide some linkage with the outside world and a channel for funds and arms from friendly countries such as Egypt, Pakistan, China, and America.

By 1984 local commanders fighting inside Afghanistan had grown heartily sick of Peshawar's fat-cat exiles. Able leaders such as the renowned 'Lion of the Panshir', Ahmed Shah Massud, were cooperating with commanders of rival parties who had organised training inside the country and set up full-time combat units. Many of the part-time *mujahedin* – numbering perhaps 150,000 men – regarded military operations as a highly individualistic ritual, performed on a whim or to save face according to their eccentric, if sometimes ferocious, code of honour.

The intensity and tide of the war varied immensely. The conflict in the Tajik-inhabited highlands of northern Afghanistan often bore little resemblance to the fighting in the Pushtun regions of the south-east. A heavy Soviet offensive, tribal feud, or the death of a popular commander could quickly and dramatically alter local conditions, although the news could take weeks or months to trickle back to guerrilla headquarters.

Initially the Soviets concentrated on the proverbial hearts and minds and left the guerrillas to the deserts and mountains, chased by gunships. But the Marxist-Leninist-trained Red Army seemed incapable of fighting a political war, and resorted to crude military power. In 1984 the Russians stepped up the pace of the war, deploying their occupation force more effectively and reducing their over-reliance on armour, which was more applicable to fighting a war on the flat plains of Europe. Crack airborne troops, more attuned to mountain warfare, were deployed. In June and July of 1984 they operated a scorched-earth policy along Afghanistan's border with Pakistan, to wipe out the guerrilla supply columns and force the remaining villagers to flee. Nearly five million refugees were living in squalid camps dotting the border areas of Pakistan and Iran. The guerrillas' backers in the West and the Islamic world realised that without better weapons – such as surface-to-air missiles and the training to use them properly – the *mujahedin* might face defeat.

That's when we arrived on the scene. The information gleaned in London, reading press clippings, and Peter's careful briefing on the plane had given me this much background. Above all, I knew that Afghanistan was not a media war, such as Vietnam. Few American TV teams had reached the heart of the fighting. Covering the war was risky, film crews had to be prepared for days and days of long, hard marches, and walking seemed to be almost an un-American activity. No press helicopters commuted to the battlefields from the plush hotels and massage parlours of Saigon. Inside Afghanistan available women and booze were very rare commodities. It was hardly a popular war for journalists.

Making the right connections
Islamabad loomed below the low cloud. The whole green, low-tiered landscape looked permanently tilted, with rivulets streaming across the red earth. The sky was as blue-black as a day-old bruise. We circled and touched down at 6 a.m. Customs officials were polite and we had

no problems, although the baggage people had lost Tim's dagger. He seemed to have a very sentimental attachment to it, a sort of macho security blanket, so I refrained from commenting that a student on a walking tour probably wouldn't carry a military dagger.

We passed out of the building into the mad, teeming, shouting, smelly welcome of the third world. My first taste of Asia. Everyone dressed almost identically: long, scruffy shirts, baggy pants, and leather sandals. Many of the men had dyed ginger hair (I learned later that they thought this made them look younger).

I was determined not to be ripped off, so I asked an experienced-looking American how much a taxi should cost. Fifty rupees, he said.

Besieged by at least ten Pakistanis clamouring for my custom, I saw a large, new car parked at the edge of the passenger terminal in front of me. An insistent taxi-man kept tugging at my sleeve and pointing to the car.

He agreed to the fifty rupees.

I turned around to check Tim and our luggage. Julian was coming with us, with some light camera equipment; Peter would take the heavier stuff to our destination, the Islamabad Holiday Inn, in the hotel's courtesy bus.

'I've got the taxi fixed up,' I said assertively to Julian and Tim.

'You expect us to travel in *that*?' Tim said, laughing.

A dilapidated 1958 Morris stood where the gleaming new vehicle had been. The ginger-haired Pakistani taxi-driver gave me a toothless grin. He'd already loaded our kit on, and in, the car.

I had been well and truly had.

Despite my anger, the three of us squeezed in with our equipment. I didn't want to make a fuss and perhaps get entangled with the airport police. Julian and Tim thought it was hugely funny. In sanctions-bound Rhodesia I had developed a genuine affection for the reliable old Morrie, but this wasn't of the same ilk. The engine chugged vaguely into life and we jerked through a series of red lights, while the one reluctant windscreen-wiper failed to cope with a heavy downpour of rain. Hooting and weaving from side to side, just missing cyclists, gaily painted lorries and buses that looked like mobile shrines, we coughed along, firing on two or three cylinders. Great puddles swamped the potholed roads, criss-crossed by streams and tinged everywhere with red mud. My window was stuck open; every passing lorry sent a backwash on to the suit I had worn to play the 'businessman'.

Tim, his eyes just visible above a mountain of kit in the back seat, kept chuckling away, as did Julian. They could afford to laugh: I was sitting in the front shielding them from the spray. We navigated through a series of bigger pools – just. Instead of stopping on an unswamped section, the toothless wonder jerked the car to a sudden halt in the middle of a muddy river deluging the road. He braved the torrent and fiddled under the bonnet, but obviously with little hope of resurrecting the drowned engine.

Tim was still convulsed with laughter.

Julian said: 'Well, I must be in Pakistan.'

I just cursed.

The ginger-haired non-mechanic flagged down another taxi, a *slightly* more modern Datsun, painted in the standard taxi livery of black and yellow. We took off our shoes and socks, rolled up our trousers, and waded to the relieving vehicle. The equipment was transferred in sodden haste. My SAS advisers in London had talked about keeping equipment dry in the raging torrents in Afghanistan, but everything was soaked and we were only a few miles from Islamabad airport. I was not doing too well.

For six miles we drove through warm rain along the badly mauled dual carriageway. 'Stop!' I shouted imperiously, suddenly convinced we had left my case on the other vehicle. Nobody remembered loading it.

The taxi-driver carried on. He couldn't speak a word of English. By sign language and Julian's few words of Urdu we turned him around; very reluctantly, he drove back to the marooned Morris. No driver and no case.

In the pouring rain we looked up: my case was on top of the second taxi. Julian and Tim laughed like demented stooges.

We started again, but our driver indicated that he had no petrol. We crawled, eventually, to a petrol station. It had no petrol; same story at the next two garages. Finally, the driver managed to procure a few pints of fuel. Then he got lost; he didn't know his way to the biggest hotel in Islamabad.

Meanwhile, the courtesy bus with Peter in it had long since passed us; Peter had given us a regal wave.

We dragged ourselves barefoot into the sanity of the hotel lobby like shipwrecked mariners, an hour and a half after leaving the airport. It should have taken twenty minutes at the most. After the derelict symbols of the third world we had just endured, the hotel was a marvel of plastic Western efficiency.

The very beginning of our journey to Asia had been a catalogue of blunders, mostly *my* blunders.

We stayed for two days in the hotel. I went to see the political officer at the British embassy – in other words, the intelligence man. He was politely helpful as we drank a colonial-style gin and tonic.

We also had help from other journalists. Normally, international hacks are very cliquey and most reluctant to assist newcomers. Particularly in a war zone such as Rhodesia, Lebanon, or Vietnam, old hands jealously guard information and contacts from the Johnny-come-latelies. It can take months for even the most professional journalist to break into the charmed circle. Afghanistan seemed to be different. There were only a few 'old hands' and they appeared ready to help.

I asked Peter, who was on assignment for CBS, why.

'I'm helping you because you're serious,' he said. 'You're not just nipping over the border, like some American reporters, and standing there saying, "Here I am in Soviet-occupied Afghanistan", and then hopping back a few hours later.'

Hopping sounded fine to me.

Peter was 100 per cent serious about his involvement, and the Afghans responded to him with the warmth of a brother. He always treated them with the greatest respect, and I determined to do the same. Everybody was quite happy to talk about Afghanistan, but none of the hacks would discuss Pakistani politics inside the hotel.

Tim couched matters in his usual Rhodesian war patois: 'It's spooksville, man. I checked this number out. Foreign journalists are always given the same rooms on the same floor.'

Tim and I were very careful about the food we ate, and had been told to clean our teeth with Coke or whisky. But next morning Tim said casually over breakfast, 'The foxtrot has begun.'

So had mine.

After breakfast we met two leaders of rival Afghan guerrilla groups. The first was late: Ahmed Gailani, son of the patriarch of the National Front for the Liberation of Afghanistan. His father was a hereditary saint and the son also acted the holy man.

Tim commented afterwards: 'Too sweet-smelling.'

The Gailanis had rung Ahmed from London and told him to help us. Ahmed was vague about details, but gave us contacts in Peshawar. Because the Gailani group was late, the meeting ran over into the time allocated to their main rivals, the Jamiat-i-Islami. I was worried, knowing of the depths of traditional feuds. Would they pull out knives if they met?

But when Massud Khalini of the Jamiat arrived he greeted Ahmed with a hug, just like rival communist leaders in public. The Gailanis left and Massud, in excellent American-English, sized us up. He suggested we do a three- to four-month trip to Afghanistan's northern border with the Soviet Union; the war needed coverage there as no film crew had gone that far.

'I can arrange that for you,' he said straightforwardly. Was this a serious offer, or a test of our commitment?

I explained that we had two penetrations in mind, one for a few weeks, and a longer one, perhaps two months. The duration of our trips was to prove a major bone of contention. I worried about my stamina on a long trip; Tim was super fit but had to get back to Cape Town to finish his degree thesis. Al had talked about two or three penetrations as though they were trips to the beach. As we were soon to discover, getting in and out was about the hardest part of the journey.

Massud seemed much more organised than the Gailanis and I grew to respect him. The Jamiat people took us to the airport, from where Tim and I flew north to Peshawar in an old Fokker which stank of stale vomit.

Stickily hot, Peshawar was the capital of the infamous North West Frontier, whence soldiers of the Raj had sallied forth to fight the tribesmen. Winston Churchill, soldiering there in 1897, described the locals as 'among the most miserable, brutal creatures of the earth. Their intelligence only enables them to be more cruel, more dangerous, more destructive than wild beasts.'

The troops referred to service on the Frontier as being 'on the grim'. But Peshawar was colourful as well as grim, full of passionate political intrigue as well as drug trafficking, arms smuggling and currency black marketeering. Half-crumbling relics of the Raj lingered everywhere; old steam trains were still working.

Dean's Hotel was named after a former British governor-general, and had sounded a romantic sort of place in my historical reading.

In fact it was filthy, and the dirt bothered Tim a lot. He was always scribbling in his journal (he later gave me a complete copy, even though it was very critical of my leadership of our expedition) and described Dean's thus: 'The colonial charm has definitely been tropically rotting for forty years . . . my room smells like there was a dung fire lit not too long ago here.'

We had been advised to stay there because the dispersed bungalow-style accommodation allowed easy access for visiting '*muj*', as journalists called the guerrillas, and the ubiquitous if invisible Special Branch (like most totalitarian systems, one of the few efficient things in Pakistan) could not monitor our movements so readily.

The first night we met the foreign hacks. Ken Guest had just come out of Afghanistan after a long trip with the *muj*. Three times he had tried to get into the Panshir Valley, but Russian attacks and *muj* ambushes had prevented him. Ken went into some detail about the air attacks and Tim was fascinated. We also noticed how spare Ken's kit was. Peter's was the same. They must have thought our elaborate logistical preparation ridiculous, especially for such relatively short trips, but were too polite to comment.

We had dinner in the Nanking. Peter insisted that Chinese restaurants were the safest place to eat, and Tim and I were still nursing our 'foxtrots'. Other expatriate characters joined us. Ed Girardet, a correspondent for the *Christian Science Monitor* and one of the most charming people I have met, had just finished a book based upon eight trips into Afghanistan. And there was Vladimir Dremlynga, a Russian who had spent six years in jail for protesting in Red Square against the Soviet invasion of Czechoslovakia. 'That was the first political demonstration in Moscow since the revolution,' he said proudly.

He was trying to get hold of Russian prisoners in *muj* jails to take to America as part of his anti-communist crusade. I liked him, even though I was also suspicious of him. Al's paranoia was infectious. I went to bed brooding on the USSR and our forthcoming trip behind Russian lines. It was a night of fever in that ugly, dank room. I didn't know whether it was the beginning of dysentery or malaria. It felt like both. I had terrible dehydration, but the hotel said no room service was available at night.

Tim came in next morning and saw what an awful state I was in. Thank God he was a trained medic. He gave me some suitable pills for my shits and fever. Tim was succumbing to the same thing, so we decided to move to a better hotel, the Khyber Intercontinental, which at least had fridges with cool drinks and in-house videos on the TV. No wonder Julian and Peter had booked in there. We were put in the usual rooms reserved for hacks which we assumed were bugged.

I lay in a daze for two days. Tim was not much better, but at least I was not vomiting as he was. In my waking hours I watched videos, including *The Russians are Coming*, which I hoped wasn't a portent. The films were infuriatingly censored – even a gentle kiss between married couples was cut. Sometimes one had to endure five or ten minutes of snow on the screen; they were not even censored properly.

After two days we both felt better, so Ed and Julian took us on a tour of Peshawar. We ventured into the famous Qissa Khawani, the storytellers' bazaar, with its rows of matchbox-sized shops. Herbert Edwardes, an early British administrator of the area, called it 'the Piccadilly of Central Asia'. Brassware, kids, donkeys looking dead on their feet, heat, smells, and everywhere the multicoloured three-wheeled taxi motor-scooters. In contrast to the bustle of the bazaar we saw quiet relics of the old Raj: run-down St John's Cathedral and the overgrown military graveyard. We took refuge in the famous Peshawar Club, once the home of the Vale of Peshawar Hunt. During the bloodshed and chaos of independence in 1947 a hunt official went around the stables and kennels putting down every horse and hound, unwilling to leave them to whatever fate might spread from the tormented Punjab next door. The club was still and empty, with an almost tangible feeling of ghosts.

The history lesson over, Ed and Peter took us around some of the guerrilla HQs. Tim observed the slackness of the guards and the filthy condition of their new AK-47s. I eventually firmed on two parties, the left-wing Jamiat and the Gailanis on the right. Both began to arrange for our two expeditions.

Tim and I concentrated on getting well and acclimatising to the poor food and heat. Tim gave me an anti-hepatitis injection in the backside, then said I must do the same to him. I certainly trusted him with the big needle, but I was very surprised that he trusted me. We also found an excellent taxi-driver who spoke English well. He said he was a former member of the Indian army during British rule. 'I miss the days of the Raj,' he confessed. 'At least we had food to eat then.'

But the friendly Mr Azar, according to Peter, was probably on the police payroll. Peter explained how we should play the game. Everyone knew that we were heading for Afghanistan, but we had to be a little subtle about it. When we started wearing Pakistani clothes, we said we were dressing to climb in the local hills. I also had to kowtow to the bureaucrats in Peshawar and Islamabad – an endless and thankless task. I visited a Mr Afridi in Peshawar's dark, scruffy press office to get permission to film the refugee camps inside Pakistan. That was allowed, as it showed how humanitarian Pakistan was despite the bad image of its military dictatorship, and, more importantly, it brought in lots of money.

Afridi said I had to go to Islamabad, where I saw a pompous little man called Ismael Patel. 'You are a British team?'

'Yes.' It wouldn't have helped to say that Al had chosen a crew of tough South Africans.

'Then you must get permission from our embassy in London. That will take two months.'

'No. The crew is arriving in a few days.'

'Then tell them not to come.'

'I can't. They're on contract. They've come from all over the world. You see, we're not used to all these permits [a big lie, because South Africa was a very permit-ridden place]. We just follow the news. It's very important that we get this film done before the fifth anniversary of the Russian invasion.'

I had already bribed my way around officials with envelopes full of rupees or, for staunchly religious fundamentalists, a *Playboy* inside a *Time* magazine – more effective than a 1,000-rupee backhander. I felt Patel didn't want to be bribed. He said he would try to help, but with the crew's arrival imminent, we would have to smuggle in the equipment somehow. Getting it out, plus fifty rolls of exposed film, would be much harder.

Back in Peshawar I made final arrangements with the *muj*. The main trip would be with the Gailanis. They would take us through the tribal areas, forbidden to all outsiders, then we would walk for five days to meet Commander Wali Khan, who would arrange for some daylight action, preferably an ambush on a Russian convoy. The cameraman and I, dressed in communist troops' uniforms, would be smuggled into Kabul to film there secretly. Hardly any footage taken in the capital by a Western cameraman had emerged since the invasion. Then we would all walk back. Simple, if we were all lucky and fit. The second trip would be arranged by Jamiat, either in the cold north or in the hostile desert region around Kandahar.

Tim and I flew to Islamabad to make final arrangements for the film crew's arrival. We could not get a film permit for them, as I explained on the phone to Al in London. I asked him to approach the Pakistani embassy in London. 'Get a night-scope, too,' I said. 'That's vital. Most of the fighting is done at night.'

Al mumbled a vague OK, then dropped his customary bombshell: 'Paul, I've had a crew problem. The sound man has dropped out in London. Lost his nerve. And I can't find a second cameraman. There'll only be *one* crew and I want you to organise three trips with that one crew.'

'Al, that's not so easy. It's damn hard getting in and out of there. I haven't even sorted out getting you guys into Pakistan, let alone Afghanistan.'

'That's your job,' he said testily. 'And I'm keen on a trip to the south.'

'Al, it's too dangerous by my reckoning.'

'My contacts here in London say that there's no problem with the south.'

'Look, I'm on the ground with these people here in Peshawar, and the general consensus is that with the Soviet build-up and the lack of cover around Kandahar. . .'

'We'll sort it out when I get there. Bye.'

Then Mr Patel phoned to say there was no chance of receiving a film permit.

'But the crew is arriving in two days.'

'If they try,' said Patel, very curtly, 'their equipment will be impounded.'

Tim and I had done everything we could. We filled in the two days by visiting the famous ruins at Taxila, and then Rawalpindi to find gear such as water bottles. Some of the tiny shops in the bazaar were full of British army surplus, sold or stolen in 1947 or 1948, or so it seemed.

A man followed us through the bazaar, finally approaching us to sell some precious stones. Then he asked if we wanted to buy any heroin. We politely declined.

'Probably a cop testing us,' said Tim, the ex-cop.

We were not being unduly suspicious. That day a letter arrived from the blonde I had met on my last night in London, making all sorts of raunchy comments about my sex life, or absence of it, in Muslim countries. The letter had been clumsily opened and resealed. Dirty fingerprints marred the words, especially on the page making exotic references to camels. At least the police had some idea of what we were up to.

The BA flight to Islamabad arrived on time. I had hired a small bus for the crew and equipment. Four men – Al, Chris Everson, Joe Wilkens, and Ian Robbie – arrived in the customs hall with a mountain of equipment. Six bulky green bags held the camera gear. Besides personal kit, Al had brought in ten boxes of what we later called 'moon food', special pre-dried, packaged edibles used in NASA space flights.

A large customs official stopped Al. 'What are those big boxes for?'

'It's for the expedition,' Al said arrogantly.

'What expedition?'

'Haven't you been told about our famous expedition?'

'Oh,' said the embarrassed customs man. 'All right, but you haven't got any alcohol, have you?'

'No,' said Al assertively, in the full knowledge of whisky and *Playboy*s stashed away.

Another customs man approached Chris and his trolley-loads of film equipment. 'What's inside there?'

'Personal items . . . the odd film magazine and lenses, things like that,' he said with studied vagueness.

'Any drink?'

The official had just started poking around in one of the green bags when Al arrived: 'Hurry, the bus is waiting. Hurry.'

'I'm really sorry, but I've got to go,' Chris blurted out. 'The bus is outside. I'm in a terrible hurry.'

He said afterwards, 'The customs man was like a stunned mullet. We just walked out. That was it.'

Al, big and resplendent in an official-looking blue blazer and tie, had out-bullied the practised bullies in the customs hall. The bluff had worked. No bribes and very little hassle.

We piled into my bus for the three-hour journey to Peshawar. All four newcomers were transfixed by the bad driving and chaotic roads. Gradually we began to size each other up. I vaguely knew Chris from Rhodesia, where he'd had a gung-ho war in the army and been badly wounded in action. After he recovered he was transferred to the mounted Grey's Scouts. Chris was big, strong and difficult, but a first-rate cameraman. Ian had also served in the Rhodesian army. This gentle giant was very close to Chris, for whom he was acting as sound man. Joe Wilkens was the odd man out, an Afrikaner with vague credentials as a freelance journalist. Al, who wasn't going into Afghanistan, had been persuaded to bring him along. Joe could accompany Tim as a 'runner' to bring out after a few weeks any 'bang-bang' news footage (this was in the days before satellite communications gave instant access to journalists' reports) before Chris, Ian and I made our 'long-range penetration', to use Al's phrase.

Our team had been haphazardly shaped by events – the first big mistake. On such trips a definite leader must be selected or elected, and he must choose his own team. Tim was obviously worried about my physical capabilities on the coming operation, but was even more sceptical about Joe. In his diary he confided his thoughts about Joe's intelligence connections, adding: 'He is a granny and will be uphill on the trip.'

Arriving at Dean's (to which we had reverted, as the *muj* preferred to visit us there than in the Intercontinental), we immediately began to organise the finer details of the trip. First we went shopping, kitting ourselves out in local gear: *salwar kamiz* (long shirts and baggy pants), Chitral hats and *patous* (light blankets) to sleep on and act as camouflage during air strikes.

Then I introduced the new boys to the *muj*. Jamiat would arrange our second trip, but the first would be hosted by the Gailanis. The Gailani people insisted on entertaining their guests while briefing us on routes and customs. We were entrusting our lives to what, at least to the newcomers, seemed beturbanned weirdos, all putting on a striking display of nose, beard and whiskers. We must have been raving mad to have volunteered. Given that, the long march and difficult filming seemed logical enough. Julian, Peter and Ed were sceptical of the Gailanis; they preferred working with the more hardline Jamiat. I opted for the Gailanis because they had a good, safe record for working with 'English' journalists and tended to steer away from the heavy fighting zones; Jamiat would be a rougher ride. A safer, shorter expedition seemed preferable for apprentice Afghan hands. Al agreed with my decision, anticipating a series of incursions behind Russian lines, but Chris sniped at the plan.

Peter and Julian gave us a technical briefing, mainly on medical and photographic issues. Tim briefed us on some of our more esoteric medical kit, such as the drips we would carry in big, adapted South African Defence Force rucksacks. We also gave some of our moon food and medical kit to Ed, Julian, and Peter, who were about to leave on the arduous northern route into the Panshir through Nuristan, where little food awaited them. Chris busied himself with meticulous preparations of his camera equipment. He and Tim persuaded tailors in the bazaar to make, almost instantly, straps and bags for our kit, especially the camera and heavy tripod. Joe kept himself to himself, drinking the awful soapy beer and chain-smoking in his room. Al left for Djibouti to supervise another film shoot.

As we sorted out the mass of kit and tried to reduce it to five rucksacks and some long, green canvas bags, we all indulged in the usual, slightly nervous, pre-op camaraderie. We tried the moon food – delicious – played with the gas stoves and checked out our commando knives.

Chris said: 'What are we supposed to do with these? Creep up behind a Russian and stab him to death?'

I had sized them all up pretty well by then. Chris was professional to the core, tough but touchy. Ian would be entirely reliable. Tim was a bit moody but hardy, energetic, and very resourceful. Joe and I would be physical liabilities, I felt sure. I would find out soon enough, for we were leaving early the next morning. The *muj* would collect our gear that night to pack and disguise it.

I went to bed at midnight and lay sleepless. I was apprehensive, but also had a feeling of elation, almost euphoria, that I'd never experienced before. My confident expectations surprised me.

The Wild West

We assembled at 4 a.m. dressed like a cross between Dad's Army and Lawrence of Arabia – Afghan gear and Second World War webbing and pouches. Vladimir, the ebullient Russian who was looking after our remaining equipment, waved us goodbye as we left Dean's in an open truck. Just outside Peshawar we transferred to a Toyota Hiace ambulance with our kit already stuffed under the seats and stretcher. Five of us, plus two *muj*, squeezed into the back. Dr Khalid, our guide, sat up front with the driver. We entered the forbidden tribal areas of the North West Frontier a few miles out of Peshawar.

The tribal areas snaked for nearly 1,800 miles from the deserts of Baluchistan to the mountainous borders with China and Kashmir. No foreigner was allowed to enter, as no formal law prevailed. Officially, Pakistan kept order on the few roads. Beyond a perfunctory police presence, each tribe was ruled and fought according to ancient customs. The tribes were united only by a common aversion to their neighbours.

The British never fully controlled the tribal areas. From the annexation of the Punjab in 1849 to independence in 1947, they tried to maintain a semblance of law and order through an elaborate system of political agents backed by frequent army forays. It was all part of what Kipling called the 'Great Game' to prevent any Russian threat to India. Occasional acts of chivalry and mutual respect for the other's martial prowess encouraged both the British and the tribesmen to treat clashes as a blood sport rather than warfare. Treachery and savagery sometimes turned sport into massacre, however. During the British retreat from Kabul in 1842 the tribesmen wiped out all the women and children after agreeing to allow them safe conduct.

Despite the complicated alliances forged by British political agents, treaties were often dishonoured. A former governor of the Frontier province addressed a tribal *jirga*, or meeting, by saying, 'You are married to us, you can't now go and flirt with the Afghans.'

Hardly had he finished his sentence when a grey-bearded elder interrupted: 'We are Muslims and can have four wives, so why should we worry about sticking to one?'

Much of the mythology of British India grew from tales of exploits on the Frontier. John Masters wrote of the 'sense-sharpening chance of a sudden storm of bullets, a rush of knifemen and bloody hand-to-hand fighting'. *Our* senses were sharpened by roadblocks and trucks full of tribesmen letting off volleys from their AKs. Some were just exuberant, others were celebrating wedding parties with firepower. We passed through five roadblocks, covering our faces with our scarves and moaning like plague victims, not exactly Oscar-winning performances, but luckily the police hardly bothered to peer inside. At two roadblocks the police looked serious. Heavily armed, they tried to seal the road by standing across it. On both occasions the driver started up the ambulance siren and sped through the line of police, who fortunately had the sense to jump out of the way in time; nor did they open fire on an ambulance.

Tim had a cold. Joe kept smoking in the confined space, which annoyed Chris. Ian started to panic as the driver sped along roads that helter-skeltered around mountains on the edges of precipices. I slept.

We reached Darrah, an infamous centre for smuggling heroin and gun running. It was also famous for the Darrahwal Topak – the local rifle, unreliable replicas of the AK family. We peered nervously around the edge of the ambulance's curtained windows. Every tribesman carried a rifle of sorts; some sported old .303s, others nursed real rather than home-made AKs.

We wound tortuously along the banks of the Kurram River past broken-down British cantonments and a Mogul fort, the dramatic backdrop to M. M. Kaye's *The Far Pavilions*. Turning off the so-called road, we bounced and banged across an old glacial scree valley towards the border. Driving cross-country at least meant we encountered no police roadblocks. We passed eerie mud forts; literally, each tribesman's house was his castle. Dr Khalid told us to keep our heads down as we bumped along the stony valley floor beneath the mountains of the Afghan–Pakistan border.

After seven hours of extremely uncomfortable travelling we reached our destination, Terrimangel, a real bandits' nest. No Cecil B. de Mille film could have captured the drama, filth and romance of the place: camels, tents, guns, squalor, rickety wooden houses and Pakistani and Russian spies. Everything was over-decorated, especially the trucks, which looked like gaudy mobile temples, and the rifles, beaded and dangling with charms.

Tim said simply: 'Kitsch is king here.'

The ambulance slithered into a narrow, filthy alleyway and stopped outside a jerry-built, two-storey wooden construction – a Gailani safe house. We were greeted by a band of ruffians, armed to the teeth with RPG-7 rocket-launchers and AKs nonchalantly hanging on their shoulders. Khalid told us to climb a ladder into a top room, where we ate kebabs and rice washed down with Cokes. Full marks to the Coca-Cola company for their marketing and distribution. American capitalist products – admittedly at inflated prices – were available even in the inaccessible foothills of the Afghan border, while overhead Russian communist jets bombed and strafed the enterprising merchants and bandits below.

We relaxed while I pulled out some of the thick wads of afghanis, the Afghan currency, I had obtained on the black market in Peshawar bazaar. Khalid helped me work out how many horses to hire and for how much. We hired three with their handlers, old men with faces rich in character and beards whom we dubbed the Three Wise Men. I doled out some Afghan currency to each team member should we be forced to split up. Chris distributed film cans and batteries in case any supplies were lost or stolen. The rucksacks were loaded on the horses, along with the precious moon food and our medical supplies. The horses also carried the tube containing the heavy wooden tripod, which looked for all the world like a big rocket-launcher and from the air might have enticed a Russian chopper crew to think just that. Ian wore a flak-jacket-style contraption he'd had made in Peshawar for the sound gear. Chris had his Arriflex 16mm camera on a sling over his shoulder. Tim lugged a big black bag with spare film magazines and lenses. Joe and I carried our light personal gear, a still camera each, and medical supplies.

At 8 p.m. we left, joining a procession of *muj* who looked like characters from Chaucer, and started to climb the mountains that towered above Terrimangel. At the top was the Afghan border.

4. AFGHANISTAN – HOLLYWOOD HEROES

Kabul or bust

We climbed, seemingly almost vertically, in mist, darkness, and rain. Almost immediately Joe started to pay for his chain-smoking; he was in a dreadful state. The others had gone off into the night. I tried to encourage Joe, although I needed every bit of encouragement myself. In desperation he hung on to the tail of one of the horses, which upset its handler and the *muj*, who took it as a sign that Joe intended to bugger the horse; not an unusual custom in the area, but hardly a gesture designed to gain respect for us infidels. Already our battle-hardened team was degenerating into extras for *Carry On Up the Khyber*.

A camel suddenly loomed out of the darkness, charging unaccompanied down the mountain, and knocked me over. I picked myself up and continued the nightmare scramble, sometimes on all fours. Somehow Joe and I reached the top, where our colleagues waited impatiently. Khalid – we called him 'Doc' – told us to huddle in the middle of a large group of *muj* to pass the Pakistani border post. In the night, mist, and confusion we sneaked past without detection, as there were no individual security searches. We had made it into Afghanistan.

A few hundred yards over the border we passed a knocked-out Russian armoured personnel carrier lying on its side. Then came another, not quite so terrible, climb. Our group began to take shape out of the amorphous mass of *muj* at the crossing point. Besides ourselves, our guide Doc and the 'Captain', an officer who had defected from the regular army, there were eight *muj*.

We crossed a valley floor, well watered by streams and dotted with fields, but hard going in the dark. Just before midnight the *muj* stopped, reluctantly, at a small village. Already their Christian companions were disappointing them. Our tardiness was laughed at or, worse, treated as an insult to the *muj*, *jihad*, and even Allah himself.

Compressed into a small room in one of the square mud houses, we drank the first of many cups of *chai*, green or black tea, heavily sugared and rarely offered with milk. Like the British, the Afghans' sovereign remedy was to stop for a cup of tea. The householder's grandchildren, timid little waifs, brought us nan, unleavened bread. I grew to like it, but at first it tasted like cardboard. After ten or fifteen minutes the children left with the cups and twelve of us prepared to sleep on the rough quilts. Joe coughed endlessly; the others snored loudly.

Next day we left at 6 a.m. It was Friday 13 July, and the day lived up to its omens. After a few miles we stopped to film a bombed village, where locals proudly showed us a Russian anti-tank gun captured when the *muj* overran a government fort the previous year. It was stuck in a cowshed, as the *muj* had no ammunition and no idea how to use it.

We carried on down the valley until what Tim called a 'glacial re-entrant' opened on our right. On the floor of this vale of stones, the Jagi Valley, we stopped at a *chai-khana*, two rough huts dispensing tea. Two DSHK 12.7mm guns stood at the entrance; the *muj* called them 'Dashekas'. We filmed them clowning around and posing with the guns. Just as they started serving tea in dirty little cups, four MiGs appeared over the crest of the mountain.

'Hello war,' said Tim.

A number of thoughts flashed across my mind. Firstly, I wanted to grab a cup of tea before everything was spilled in the mêlée. Secondly, I spotted a small ridge behind me, a good place to take shots with my still camera of the expected attack and the *muj* firing back (hopefully). But this wasn't a film set, and I would have been totally exposed on the ridge, just a few yards from the gunners. Then I guiltily told myself that I was there to make a movie, not hide or take photos. I tried to help prepare our equipment.

We were not the targets that day, however. We listened tensely to the roar of the jets bombing in the next valley, heavy thumps indicating that someone was catching it. Two planes flipped out of their bombing runs and rolled away out of sight over the mountains. Chris was using a new type of long-life lithium battery, as no electricity was available to charge up conventional camera batteries. Unfortunately the battery hadn't been connected properly to the camera, so we missed this dramatic aerial diversion.

Leaving the huts behind we marched up a desolated valley. It grew hot. After two and a half hours the wide valley became a narrow cleft and we began to climb out over a never-ending series of false summits.

The dry, sparse vegetation provided no shade. Tim was striding out in front with the lead guerrillas. Part of his self-image was founded on his ability to outperform everyone else physically. Joe and I reached the top half-dead, and downhill wasn't much better. After scrambling and tripping for two hours we reached Azara, a hamlet nestling in a pretty valley of apricot trees, flecked with small patches of maize, and watered by an elaborate irrigation system. Asian magpies, mynahs and small hoopoe birds darted here and there. A pine forest bordered on the Gailani house in which we overnighted.

We found a small pool and, assuming it was out of sight, took the chance of stripping off to wash. Out of nowhere a woman, heavily veiled, approached. We had been told to be very careful not to expose any part of our bodies, but now a village woman had seen us. She passed by and nothing was said.

After eleven hours of marching all we wanted to do was sleep, but we had to sit in a large room with the village elders and our small group of *muj*. We were not hungry, but felt obliged to eat some of the sheep just slaughtered in our honour before excusing ourselves from the tea ceremony and climbing on to the roof to sleep under the brilliant stars.

At 4.30 a.m. we awoke and hurried to load up and leave. Doc had hired a fourth horse to accommodate Joe and me, the slowcoaches. I decided to walk first, but after two hours my feet, already badly blistered, began to hurt horribly. Laughing at our heavy going, the *muj* kept up a fast pace; to them it was a Sunday-afternoon stroll. Strings of young *muj* passed us on their way out of the country, pointing and saying something like '*Ax, ax*'. Had they learned the word 'hacks'? I found out that it meant 'camera' or 'photograph'. Every Afghan I met loved posing and having his picture taken.

A *muj* commander who had joined our group earlier in the day insisted on mounting a horse with some of the camera equipment. I asked Doc to explain that this could damage our kit and so perhaps abort the trip. Pretending to misunderstand, Doc loped off, obviously not wanting to confront the senior man. Furious, Chris berated the commander in front of the *muj*, despite my attempts at diplomacy. The commander stayed on the horse, but we had created an enemy and a grudge which would later make our trip more difficult.

As the march grew hotter and dustier, we came to a narrow, steep defile. Joe had been riding the spare horse for hours. Although Chris did not seem to be tired, he asked Joe for a spell on the horse – out of boredom perhaps, or because he loved horses. Passionate expletives followed, and the powerfully built Chris leaned over Joe from the side of the defile, either to pull him off the horse or his head off his shoulders.

The *muj* looked on in amazement: so these infidels fuck horses and fight over them!

Chris subdued his anger, but the incident established a permanent and bitter rift in our team. Although I was probably the weakest physically, I was nominally in charge: a testing paradox. What I lacked in strength I would have to make up for in diplomacy to keep the peace, both within our crew and with the mercurial, heavily armed guerrillas.

A second *muj* doctor, a burly and inevitably bearded fellow, joined our merry band, on his way to set up a small mobile clinic. He was accompanied by a former medical student, a wiry, friendly little *muj* who could speak fractured English. We dubbed him 'Little Doc'. We passed horses and, occasionally, camels loaded with medical supplies in small wooden crates inscribed 'People's Republic of China' in English and Chinese. A camel in one such supply column took a peculiar dislike to me; for some reason – presumably malicious humour – the beast's handler asked me to lead it for a few hours. First it spat at me, then sneezed over me, then spent a good part of an hour trying to bite me. I encountered this animal on several occasions at tea-houses and pit stops; even when tethered, it would try to make my miserable life even more miserable.

I took some consolation in the fact that the horse, which Joe shared with me after a while, seemed to like me. It had no saddle, no proper reins or stirrups. I just sat on the wicker stringing which contained fodder and light equipment, with a bedroll on top. Usually I felt guilty riding, as Tim and Ian steadfastly refused when I offered them my mount. Occasionally Chris took up the offer for a brief change of pace. He walked nearly all the way with the heavy Arriflex camera cradled in his arms or hanging from his shoulder.

We were determined not to be separated from our equipment. An ITN crew under Sandy Gall had been forced to watch in exasperation the dramatic fighting in the Panshir for a whole month without being able to film, having had the bad luck – or lack of caution – to be moved away from their baggage. Sometimes I would wear Ian's bulky flak-jacket-cum-sound-kit if I was riding. Thus burdened, on an extremely uncomfortable seat, riding was only marginally easier than walking. But at least it gave my heavily plastered feet a break. Some of my toenails had already fallen off.

We walked and walked. The Afghans who passed on the track gave us infidels very strange looks, but nearly always issued a hearty greeting. '*Salaam aleikum*' (peace be with you). I learned the reply, '*Aleikum salaam*' (and you), but never quite mastered the string of pleasantries which followed.

I started studying the architecture. A typical house consisted of bricks and dry earth, covered with a kind of stucco made of straw mixed with mud. Many adjoined laboriously constructed irrigation channels and sometimes a village defence system which formed a network of little forts, often with a watchtower.

We marched through exquisite valleys, rich in apricot and mulberry trees; occasionally the *muj* would climb and shake the trees while their companions collected the falling fruit in their *patous*.

At these stops we would ask Doc the inevitable question: 'How much further?' He grew as tired of our enquiries as we did of his vague replies: 'It's a short walk', or 'Only an hour from here'.

We called this 'Afghan time'.

'English time' meant what was said – an hour equalled an hour. In 'Pakistani time' an hour could equal two or three. 'Afghan time' meant that an hour could be a day or even a week.

No wonder American teams, addicted to rigid schedules, found Afghanistan so tough. J. B. Priestley wrote: 'A good holiday is one spent among people whose notions of time are vaguer than yours.' I doubted whether Afghanistan had ever featured in his travels.

From a quasi-alpine valley we moved into a semi-desert plain with no cover apart from thorn bushes. I contemplated the risks of throwing myself into one if we were caught in the open by gunships. The standard, and only safe, tactic was to stay absolutely still, preferably with a brown *patou* over your head. In the Rhodesian bush war the guerrillas nearly always broke this golden rule, although they usually had good cover, especially in the rainy season; if the choppers persisted they broke and ran, hitting the army stop groups or getting shot up by the helicopters.

I was engaged in a purely theoretical discourse on this subject with Chris, a veteran of the Rhodesian war, when two Hind-24 gunships emerged a long way off. They were moving fast and we were completely in the open. I was on horseback, wearing the sound equipment. A few hundred yards away lay good cover of trees and mud buildings, so I urged my horse into a canter and accidentally knocked Joe over. It was mainly fear or instinct, but I shouted an apology, saying I had to protect the sound gear. I made the cover and the choppers flew over, ignoring us.

The village among the trees was derelict: carcasses of dead animals and bomb-holes scarred the tranquillity. My horse sensed death and reared. I controlled it, but it had a mind of its own. '*Shur! Shur!*' was Afghan for 'Move! Move!', but nobody had bothered to inform my horse.

The arid landscape grew hypnotic. Outlandish mud forts occasionally tipped the edge of the horizon. Suddenly we came into a fertile valley with a large stream running through it: Alamkach. About twenty mud houses nestled in the trees and donkeys brayed unbelievably loudly. The stream babbled. Children's voices filled the air. Young boys were working in small fields. Golden patches of wheat contrasted with the green, and a man was winnowing corn. It was like a summer morning in England a long, long time ago.

Gailani's men greeted us in the shade of a big walnut tree, making us feel very welcome. Under the tree, with the sound of the stream lulling us, we relaxed for twenty-four hours, cleaned our equipment, and changed for the first time in three days. We were waiting for a message from Commander Wali Khan.

On Sunday morning, Joe, a staunch member of the Dutch Reformed Church, suggested a prayer meeting. 'We must show these Muslim people that we are devout too.'

In theory it wasn't a bad idea, but to Chris, as he put it, 'it went down like a turd in a punch bowl'. Tim, despite his rough ways, was a devout Christian too, but his faith was more personal. Chris thought a service would be hypocritical, and said so.

Joe gave his commando dagger to the Captain, so all the *muj* started crawling through our kit looking for our knives. We had a hard time being persuasive with our heavily armed hosts, explaining why we didn't want to part with our daggers. It infuriated Chris, who began teasing Joe, mimicking his heavy Afrikaans accent. Tim, Ian and I were also annoyed, but we didn't want to fight the Boer War all over again; we had enough on our plates. Joe was well-meaning, but he seemed to try too hard with the Afghans. Like many Afrikaners, he tended to patronise the natives even while appearing genuinely fond of them.

We were becoming preoccupied with our health, especially our bowel movements. Chris had the runs, but Joe was on the hunt for laxatives. I was the worst, my loose bowels gradually degenerating into dysentery, although I was swallowing eight to ten strong anti-diarrhoea pills a day, and I suffered continual cramps.

We had brought water-purifying tablets but discarded them, either too eager to sip from a mountain stream when totally dehydrated or too reluctant to quibble with our hosts if offered water or tea. We just took our chances, and I had the most vulnerable guts.

I liked the urbane, if occasionally slippery, Doc Khalid. He spoke excellent English and good French. We sat munching apricots as he explained why he had left Kabul to join the *muj*.

'I was living in Kabul when the *Shuravi* [Russians] came. On the day of the invasion I was studying for my final medical exam. I couldn't work properly because of all the aeroplanes waiting to land with the invasion troops. I eventually got to sleep, but I woke up to find Russians and tanks on the corner of every street in Kabul.'

Doc was more interested in the West, especially its social conventions, than talking about Afghan history. He said he understood our Western weaknesses.

'I tell the *mujahedin* that they must not laugh when you cannot walk as fast as them. I tell them you have escalators so that you don't have to move, but they don't really believe me.'

Doc often extolled the virtues of an American ABC team he had worked with previously. Apparently they had been mountaineers and doctors as well as cameramen. 'They kept on walking and carried big rucksacks,' he told us. I grew tired of hearing about these supermen.

'Ah, but they did make one big mistake,' said Doc. 'We were crossing a river and some Russian tanks came around the bend of the road. The man with the sound equipment just dropped down under the water to hide. That ruined their sound gear.' Some consolation at least, but we hadn't been in action yet. We might not fare any better.

Doc and I talked about women, a subject in which he was very interested. Filming Afghan women was a big problem. They rarely appeared, even if they had cooked our food. If a woman approached in the distance, her menfolk would start to bristle and treat us as though we were the vanguard of an advancing army of sex maniacs determined to violate every female under ninety. The women were covered totally in *burqas*, head-to-toe shrouds with a small vent for the eyes. The nomads had a reputation for branding their women with the same irons they used on their animals. We were much too exhausted even to think about sex, and the savage stories told of the *muj* suggested that a bit on the side (in the highly unlikely event that it was offered) was a trifle risky.

Although Doc was a fairly conservative supporter of Afghan customs, he confessed to a secret desire: he desperately wanted to bonk a black woman. He knew roughly of Joe's origins, but could draw no comment on black women from our resident Afrikaner. Doc's quiet but persistent interest in this subject became a standing joke.

'Our men do not see their wives until they are married,' he said sternly. 'Of course, she has seen him in the village and so on. But he has never looked at his wife until they sit back to back on their wedding night. Both hold mirrors and gaze on each other's face in the mirrors.'

'What if she's ugly?' I said, rather obviously.

'No, the parents have made sure that there are no physical problems.'

'And will your parents choose your wife, Doc?'

'That has not been decided yet,' he said vaguely.

We discussed the Muslim tradition of four wives, but Doc had no answer to my question 'Who would want four mothers-in-law?' The conversation drifted on to censorship and Muslim double standards; despite the cuts in videos (even the kissing), and the strict control of booze and girlie magazines, nearly every Afghan we met (when not with any other Muslims) would devour *Playboy* or take a drink.

The day's rest had restored spirits and eased the pain, as well as the blisters we were all developing. Besides resting, we had some beautiful scenic shots in the can plus an interview with the two doctors and the story of the Captain, who had defected after nine years in the regular army.

We started walking with zest. The going was rough at first. We walked through a stony river bed, slipping and cursing all the way. Joe tripped and sprained his ankle. Then we climbed over a steep pass. At the top was an amazing desert panorama: an arid landscape of sandstone, rocks and occasional tufts of grass. After a mercifully short march – just three hours of hard slogging – we climbed up another river valley until we reached a clump of trees in a cleft between three low, steep hills. This was Serracheena – 'the place of the red spring'. We were destined to spend ten days there.

The cesspit

The camp at Serracheena was filthy. Chris summed it up in his usual blunt fashion: 'Meningitis is crawling over this place like that thing in *Alien*.'

The camp consisted of three bombed buildings, one roughly repaired, set among a clump of trees in a small cleft halfway up a bare hill. Some thirty or forty *muj* used it as a base. 'Moustache', the commander whom Chris had tried to eject from our horse, was in charge, and it was clear he didn't like foreign intruders in his eyrie.

Almost immediately two Mi-24 helicopters glided across the sky like big sharks. A Dasheka just above the camp let rip, exposing our position even though the gunships were out of range. Then a machine-gunner in the camp fired a burst accidentally and almost blew off the head of a fellow guerrilla.

I said to Tim: 'They look fierce and can probably do a lot of damage, but more by accident than intent. There's more chance of us getting hit by a *muj*'s AD [accidental discharge] than by the Russians.'

There was no order, no discipline, no training, not even enough organisation to build a latrine: the *muj* just shat in ever-increasing circles round the camp perimeter.

The smell might keep away the Russians, but not the flies.

We camped in the open in a small mud clearing in front of the one usable hut. Beside it was a tiny cave which served as an ammo store. As we sat drinking tea, Chris switched on the BBC World Service. Emlyn Williams, the Welsh playwright, was talking about his boyhood. I started to suffer from what the Welsh call *hiraeth*, but the bleak Kabul mountains mocked my homesickness for the Rhondda valleys. My nostalgia was contagious. The rest of the crew started talking about Rhodesia and comparing it with Afghanistan: 'Now we are the hunted guerrillas – no radio comms [communications], no choppers for a casevac [casualty evacuation], no bath in the officers' mess to return to each night. . .'

The plan was for the chief commander, Wali Khan, to organise an ambush for us. The possibility of a clandestine trip into Kabul would come later. Most attacks were at night but, as we had no night-scopes for our camera, we would have to attempt a risky daylight sortie. We talked about our chances of getting away with it and, as we stayed longer in the cesspit, the chances of being ambushed. Normally it was considered unwise to stay for more than two days in the same place. The KGB and its local equivalent, the Khad, had a countrywide network of informers, and foreign journalists were prize trophies. The Soviets were interested in all Westerners travelling with the guerrillas. Any they managed to capture or kill provided their version of proof for their (accurate) claim that the CIA was backing the *muj*.

If grabbed, we knew we would be in for a rough time. A Frenchman caught previously had had a sympathetic socialist president to exert diplomatic pressure on Moscow. We all had military backgrounds and had been seen with weapons, usually during shooting competitions with the *muj* to humour them. We would surely be branded as mercenaries.

Joe admitted: 'The only thing that worries me is an air strike. The *muj* can say what they like, but an air strike can come in here.'

'I'm more worried about them putting choppers and troops on the hills around here,' interrupted Tim. 'We are very vulnerable.'

'Yeah, but what a position to film from,' Ian said positively.

'But we've got no film if we're caught,' I pitched in more soberly. 'Or if someone gets killed and we're forced to dump our equipment.'

'But we're here to get bombed,' said Chris.

I corrected him. 'We're here to get *nearly* bombed.'

More immediate dangers were to hand in the form of 'Donkey', Doc's nickname for the half-cunning, half-idiotic camp fool. He was the grinning Dasheka gunner and putative mine expert. Right in front of us he primed a Chinese land-mine, then jumped on it to test it. Joe, sitting nearest, did a passable impression of a Superman take-off while the rest of us threw ourselves on our stomachs.

It didn't go off.

We didn't find out whether Donkey was playing the real fool or had deliberately mis-primed the mine.

We spent a couple of days filming intermittently, but the bored *muj* kept horse-playing. It made any filming, even with Doc's assistance, very tedious. We wondered whether the whole valley had interbred to generate a new subspecies of mutton-headed hillbillies. We grew as bored as the guerrillas, playing cards endlessly and trying to read amid the flies. Chris was reading *Scimitar*, Peter Niesewand's novel about a neutron bomb in Afghanistan; I was perusing le Carré's *The Honourable Schoolboy*, about the KGB. In the circumstances it was hardly escapist literature.

In between we cooked our moon food, such a delightful contrast to the perpetual nan and stringy goat. Tim and Joe tried to teach the locals the art of the southern African *braai* (barbecue). The *muj* boiled everything and didn't use any salt, even though they had ample stocks. Eventually the two Africans served up a very acceptable barbecued goat.

Joe was still the odd man out. We tried hard to get him into a team mood, but it was difficult because he had little or no interest in the film. His original purpose, running parts of the film out, had been negated by the problems of getting in and out of Afghanistan. His aims were simpler: he had obtained some good still pictures and enough material for a few articles, and now he wanted to leave. We all despised the filthy conditions and wanted to escape, but we had a film to complete. Besides being reluctant to split up the team, I could not ask Doc to provide an escort back to Peshawar, so Joe would have to wait. But Joe was determined to find his own escort out, further annoying Chris and me. Doc could not really comprehend the differences within the team, nor the absence of a clear leader and our habit of democratically discussing options. Later he developed an astute insight into our differing cultural and psychological make-ups.

We infidels had noticed a world of difference between the small, educated Afghan élite and the illiterate, apparently witless, peasants who made up 90 per cent of the country. It was probably we who were witless; like many journalists in third world countries, we did not know the language.

It was our third night at the cesspit. As usual, we bedded down in our sleeping bags at about 9 p.m. But sleep did not come easily. We squirmed around like a row of huge disgruntled chrysalises, listening very reluctantly to a Donkey serenade. Donkey and his Muppet band were screaming out monotone songs while banging on oil drums for hours on end. Worse, they began pounding old rockets apart and gleefully throwing bits of explosives into the fire.

Tim, our Samuel Pepys, confided in his diary, 'Donkey tried to entertain the troops, but the troops were not amused and contemplated going out there with an AK to fire a few rounds over the natives' heads.'

All of us, including Doc and the Captain, shared his sentiments.

Finally, under the stars, we fell asleep. Then it rained.

'Just our luck,' moaned Chris. 'We're in a bloody desert and it's got to pour with rain.'

We moved into the small mud hut storehouse. Just as we settled in, and had made sure our film kit was dry, the roof started to leak under the torrential downpour. Sleep was out. We busied ourselves keeping the film stock and camera equipment away from the wet.

Then a *muj* started raving at us. We had our shoes on and were told that the hut was also their mosque, all eight square feet of it. Although they could be grossly obnoxious by our standards, spitting and crapping everywhere, Afghans were ultra-sensitive about their religion and women, especially if there was a Muslim audience.

In the morning we witnessed a flash flood: a wave of water a few yards high swept down the dry river bed in the valley below. That was the high point of a day spent eating mulberries, apricots, and grapes. Donkey challenged us to a stone-throwing competition, then duelled against Chris with catapults. The hill man had obviously spent most of his spare hours in such country pursuits, and we were hopelessly outclassed. We were gradually going native. Nervousness and frustration scratched at our boredom. Artillery boomed regularly in the distance; choppers and Antonov reconnaissance planes droned overhead.

On 19 June we walked down the valley towards Jigdalek, the exact spot where a British army retreating from Kabul had been treacherously destroyed in the snows of January 1842. Major General William Elphinstone left the Afghan capital under a truce with 4,500 soldiers and 12,000 camp followers, as well as soldiers' and officers' wives. In one of the most savage defeats in British military history, only one British officer and a few Indian sepoys managed to reach the British garrison at Jalalabad.

A famous Victorian oil painting by Lady Elizabeth Butler, popularly known as 'The Last Survivor from Kabul', depicts the exhausted officer's arrival. The vivid detail of this painting did much to fix in British folk memory the magnitude of the catastrophe that befell Elphinstone's army, and the image of Afghans as two-faced merciless thugs.

Ours was a more leisurely trip. Without blood and snow the valley was idyllic, full of plums, apricots and mulberries. It was well watered but the cultivators had fled from the bombing, leaving only a handful of shepherds and a few groups of Jamiat guerrillas. We looked inside bombed-out houses and examined walls where shrapnel and rockets had left their marks. In one house we discovered a host of shed snake-skins hanging down from the roof like spaghetti. Adding to the sense of death amid such natural beauty, huge 1,000-pound bomb craters were testimony to why the former residents had abandoned their houses to the snakes. Outside, blackened trees bent over to weep, their backs broken by shrapnel.

Returning to Serracheena we found Donkey had brought a message from the Scarlet Pimpernel of the mountains, Wali Khan. We were to wait another two days, as the commander was preparing an attack for us. Having already waited for five days – a major security risk being in one place for so long – we no longer trusted Khan, and speculated whether he was capable of organising an attack.

'I don't think he's capable of even organising an appearance,' said Chris.

We restlessly debated our options, wondering whether we should hide the still photographs showing us with weapons in case we got caught on this promised attack. Out of boredom we climbed a hill to compete in target shooting with an AK-47. The rest of the crew were spot on. I rated pretty much the same as the *muj*, but excused myself because of my short-sighted right (shooting) eye.

We went to bed early, listless, dirty, and with the trots besieging our stomachs. Joe had given up smoking for a while, but he still snored.

The terrible Hind-24 gunships, the scourge of the *muj*, operated from early morning to about 3 p.m., when the pilots returned to scrub up for an early mess dinner at Jalalabad air base, less than 40 miles away. Later on, after the heat of the day, thermal updraughts and swirling winds made contour flying in the mountains hazardous.

At seven the next morning, ugly as sin, two of the squat killers hovered above us, accompanying six MiG fighter-bombers. The Hinds were big battlefield helicopters with five-blade rotors and a total loaded weight of ten tons.

Chris and I bolted for the small latrine gully; crouched there, with Chris resting his camera on my back, we looked up at the titanium armour-plating guarding the gunner's and pilot's cockpits, engines, fuel tanks, gear box, hydraulics and electrical systems. Difficult to knock out of the sky. The Hinds had a maximum speed of 229mph and maximum altitude of 18,000 feet. They were armed with thirty-two rockets and guided missiles, and a traversing four-barrelled 12.7mm machine-gun with drums of 1,000 armour-piercing or HE incendiary rounds.

All *we* had was Donkey blasting away on his pitiful Dasheka.

Anyone firing at a Hind had better be sure of knocking it right out of the heavens – anything less than a fatal shot would normally invite a lethal counter-blow. They dropped lower and lower, ignoring the Dasheka.

One hovered right above us, and we expected napalm.

But we were lucky: the gunships were busy coordinating the fighter-bombers blasting away in the valley below us. Fortunately the Russian or Afghan pilots were trained to stick rigidly to their assault plans; any Western gunship crew would have seized the target of opportunity and taken out the near-defenceless clump of sixty *muj* stuck on an exposed hill below them. This time, however, the Hinds left us alone.

The attack lasted about twenty minutes. Then, a little shaken, we crawled out of the latrine gully. Tim and Joe had been snapping away with their still cameras, but Chris was furious that he had been caught out of position to film the staggeringly dramatic air attack. We were fortunate not to have been hit but unlucky not to have captured on film the bombing runs down the valley.

We felt sure they would come again soon – and next time we would be ready.

All we could do was sit and wait for the Soviets, and the elusive Wali Khan. We constantly harangued Doc for news of Khan, explaining that we had wasted almost a week's filming. Soon we would move on, with or without Wali.

Doc tried to divert us with Afghan-style humour, which was Rabelaisian at the best of times. He told us about Brezhnev's barber – the dead Brezhnev, never Andropov or Chernenko, was always the butt of the jokes. Every time Leonid went to the hairdressers the barber would ask about Afghanistan. Eventually the Soviet leader grew angry. 'You stick to cutting hair and leave politics to me. Anyway, why do you keep asking about that country?'

The barber replied: 'Because every time I mention Afghanistan, your hair stands on end, and it's much easier to cut.'

It seemed a good joke in the hills around Kabul. Doc had a boyish, lavatorial sense of humour, like most Afghans. I couldn't help but like him.

That night we listened again to the BBC World Service, a vital link to civilisation and sanity. A report from Islamabad said the Russians had landed troops to block supply routes. Russian, not Afghan, soldiers were now fighting behind us in the Jagi Valley. Our exit route might be cut off, but at least we hoped to film some action. Although it would be retracing our steps, we resolved to proceed soon to Jagi. We were sure the BBC reports were correct: we had seen large movements of troop-carrying planes and helicopters, as well as hearing increasing artillery barrages emanating from our rear.

We got up at 4 a.m. Nobody wanted to be caught by gunships with their pants down or sleeping bags zipped up. The five of us trekked to a hill on the other side of the valley, a perfect spot to film the expected attack on our own camp. We had taken the precaution of stowing our kit in the cave, despite the ammo. The *muj* didn't seem to care a jot that we were bloodthirstily awaiting gunships which would rain down HE rockets on their flyblown little home.

Our hill had practically no cover. Chris bravely opted to sit on the completely exposed northern slope. Since the camera would look exactly like a weapon from the air, we covered Chris in mosquito nets and pieces of bush and grass to disguise the glinting tripod. Tim and Ian hid nearby. Joe and I prepared rough cover twenty or thirty yards behind Chris just over the ridge, near a gully which could provide a Flashman-style exit if the Soviets turned on us.

The reconnaissance planes droned overhead at 6 a.m., then it grew cloudy. We waited until 10 a.m. Nothing.

Chris was as chirpy as ever: 'Why don't we ring up Kabul and complain?'

Out of sheer boredom, the crew asked me to sing some of my extensive repertoire of rock 'n' roll numbers. The fact that they actually asked for my musical impressions was a sure indication that we were slowly going mad. Donkey had become our mentor.

We gave up at noon. Chris stood up and shook his fist at the sky. 'Come back, you Russian bastards, and fight!'

What he lacked in tact and diplomacy he made up for in strength and courage. Although he had been badly wounded in the Rhodesian war, with five bullets in the lower leg and thigh, he could walk tirelessly carrying the heavy camera. Under fire he appeared fearless.

We repeated our dawn patrol the next day. The weather was fine and the recce plane went over again. Surely, this time, they would come back. We camouflaged Chris and took up our positions. I slept or read le Carré. By late morning, with no show, we grew frustrated and angry; the film needed a good attack sequence.

We returned to the perpetual theme of *muj* inadequacies, all worried about the same thing: the guerrillas couldn't handle their weapons sitting around a camp-fire, so how could they fight in battle?

To be fair, Doc and the Captain were aware of their compatriots' faults, the Captain obviously embarrassed by the *muj*'s lack of soldierly qualities. Doc even asked Tim, who had impressed everyone with his knowledge and handling of weapons, to stay in Afghanistan as an instructor. Tim politely declined, even when Doc offered to put Tim's wife up as well. Katie, a vivacious ex-dancer, would not be at her best covered in a *chador*.

Tim's complex personality intrigued me. Although he spoke the patois of a Rhodesian troopie and had worked as a bouncer, his intellectual versatility constantly surprised me. One minute it would be a comment on Conrad's *The Heart of Darkness*, the next an astute aside on team psychology, or identifying a plant or obscure bird.

From time to time he sported a small white object behind his ear. I assumed it was a hearing aid, although he seemed to hear quite well without it. Because the thing appeared only sometimes, and he never mentioned it, I thought the macho Tim was sensitive about his one physical weakness and never peered too closely to avoid embarrassing him.

Eventually, I saw him pop it in his mouth.

He laughed almost uncontrollably when I told him about my confusion as to where he stored his chewing gum!

For all his sterling qualities Tim was not perfect. He became paranoid when he lost his diary, blaming the *muj* for taking it and remaining absolutely distracted until he found it in a spot where he had tripped over. He was also very fastidious, particularly about security. Mostly he was fully justified. I noticed he had made himself a small survival and get-away-quick kit: a passport, medical pack, exposed film, glucose tablets and lightweight sleeping bag, which he carried in his adapted ammo pouches at all times in case we were ambushed and he had to make his way back alone. I had done the same, though not so thoroughly.

Enough was enough. We had spent nine largely unproductive days in the disease-ridden camp and still no Wali and no film of an air strike.

I told Doc that we would leave at 3 p.m. to film the fighting at Jagi if no definite word had come from Commander Wali.

Suddenly, there was a commotion on the path at the back of the camp. A man led a young boy on horseback into the clearing, his hand swathed in a bloody, makeshift bandage. Nine-year-old Sadat Khan had lost three fingers picking up a Russian anti-personnel device which looked like a plastic butterfly, said Doc.

'The Russians drop them by the thousands to hurt children. This demoralises the parents.' We were a little sceptical: we had seen some anti-personnel devices, but not one of the so-called butterfly bombs. Had the little boy been playing around with spare ammunition, I asked gently. Doc insisted it was the work of the demonic Russians.

The brave young boy sat upright on the floor as Doc looked at his grisly wound. Doc could do little to help or avoid gangrene – all he had were some painkillers. It was immediately decided that we would all march back to Alamkach, where the doctor we had met earlier on the trip had set up his small mobile clinic. Chris filmed my talking with Doc and the child, and we would film his arrival at the clinic. It was very moving material. And we were leaving Serracheena at last.

We set off back to Alamkach at a fast pace. It was hard going over desert and mountainous terrain but – for once – I felt really fit, almost euphoric, as I pushed my legs forward. Also, it was only a three-hour march, and away from our cesspit.

En route I chatted to Doc about the difficulties of treating wounds in the field.

Doc spoke with a mixture of quiet anger and resignation: 'We are educated in twentieth-century medicine but inside Afghanistan, because of the lack of drugs and equipment, we are doing the medicine of the Middle Ages.'

He launched into a long lecture on 'foreign occupiers' and 'ruthless Russians', but many of the problems could be blamed upon Afghan tradition, not Soviet atrocities. Some women, for example, died simply because a male doctor was not allowed to examine the patient. Doc confirmed how it was customary for the husband to describe the symptoms. The doctor had to prescribe at second hand, without ever seeing or speaking to his patient.

Nevertheless, Afghanistan's most recent invaders did not make war by the gentlemanly rules favoured by their imperial predecessors. A doddery seventy-year-old villager told me, via Doc, 'My family fought the British. I had relatives killed by them. But the British did not kill old people, nor hurt women and children intentionally. They never aimed their artillery at innocent people, never.'

Up and down the hill again

Alamkach was jumpy. The Russians were supplying a fort at the end of the valley, less than two miles away, so the *muj* were preparing to evacuate the village if the Russians pushed any further up the valley. We could hear artillery and tank fire. The immediate problem, though, was to attend to Sadat Khan. He was given one of our drips and the two doctors cleaned and dressed his wound. Dusk approached as we filmed this procedure, using some precious battery time for illumination via our 'sungun'.

The doctor said surgery was required; the boy would have to travel to Peshawar. Many wounded Afghans had died on the route by which we had come in. But the lad seemed tough; Doc felt sure he would make it safely to a hospital in Pakistan.

We repacked our film gear ready for a rapid exit from the camp the next morning, and crowded into a small tent, pitched on top of a mud hut for some reason, to avoid an imminent downpour. I slept blissfully unaware of the artillery, but Tim stayed alert to distinguish the various types of ordnance being flung around in the storm.

We got up in wet darkness at 4 a.m. During the night about sixty men had been seen marching along the ridge above us. The slack *muj* hadn't posted any guards, so we didn't know whether they were Russian commandos or nocturnal *muj*. We were jittery: it wasn't like the *muj* to walk around at night in the rain.

We set off immediately to a camp higher up. The river had flooded the previous night but had already subsided, leaving a coating of red mud everywhere, which made it even more difficult to walk over the slippery pebbles.

After a few hours we reached Manay, a more organised camp run by allies of the Gailani faction, who welcomed us with sweet milk tea and killed a calf. We felt honoured, even though they slit the poor animal's throat right in front of us.

Unfortunately, the sweetness of the tea was soured by a letter from the mysterious Wali Khan: the ambush had been set up and we were to return to Serracheena immediately. We'd all suffered enough of both the cesspit and Wali's non-appearing acts; but Doc was under orders and he had to maintain face. And Khan, a man with a reputation in the area, couldn't be seen to chicken out on fixing a hit for some Western hacks.

Very reluctantly, and mainly out of respect for Doc, we decided to go back to the eyrie of flies rather than push on to the fighting in Jagi. In the midday sun, with heavy hearts and heavier boots, we set out to climb back into the desert hills.

I was exhausted and disheartened. The two things I hated most in life, marching and communal living, were beginning to overwhelm me. Tim wrote in his log that I was walking like a dead man. Even had I been fitter, no outsider could walk like an Afghan. They had a distinctive long, flowing step, gliding their sandalled feet over rough stones and scree. The *muj* could walk all day, seven days a week. It was like a sick passion: they would never walk 100 yards if they could walk a mile, usually over the most rugged terrain, preferably the pebbly hell of river beds. Where I stumbled, they walked straight-backed, dancing along trails and desert tracks like scruffy ballet stars. Nor was there a pattern to their marches. At least in a Western army one could expect to rest for a few minutes every hour, even if the route march went on all day. The *muj* walked on a whim as well as on air, stopping twice in an hour, or trekking without a break for six hours across mountains. I kept going with the mirage of a pint of Guinness shimmering in front of me.

Eventually we shuffled back into Serracheena. Donkey greeted us like brothers risen from the dead. Moustache pouted at us with his waxed nostril-piece, like a demon barber in a Victorian melodrama. A gleam of triumphant mischief twinkled in his eyes – the message which had dragged us back was from him, not Wali.

He had made us pay for telling him to get off our horse.

We were told we had to march for another day and a half, then it might be possible to set up an attack. Doc was embarrassed; we were fuming. We paid Donkey, perhaps the only man we could trust in the camp, to ride one of our horses to Wali's camp for a direct response as to why we had waited ten days for nothing. If no message came back we would leave at 3 p.m. the following day. It was another miserable night. Even Tim admitted to feeling unwell. 'My guts are like Niagara,' he put it, poetically.

At 4 a.m. we tried our dawn patrol again, as the hike back would have been worthwhile if we could film a rocket attack on the commander's moustache. Poor Chris was smothered with mosquito nets and grass again, but all to no avail.

Then something interesting turned up. We were invited to a weapons training session at a Jamiat camp a few miles away. Moustache tried to stop us going but we ignored him, trudging off down the valley with one horse. Joe and the rest of the kit would meet up with us later. We passed craters of the 1,000-pound bombs we had seen dropped a few days before. Some of the holes, now full of water, were six to ten yards across and about fifteen feet deep.

The Jamiat camp was extremely well fortified with DSHK gun emplacements. It was commanded by Mohamed Anwar, a well-known Afghan wrestler who had gone over to the guerrillas just before he was due to represent his country in the 1980 Moscow Olympics. Built like an ox, shrewd and intelligent, with a patient face, he was about thirty-eight but exuded the authority and charisma of a much older man. He was a born leader.

Another surprise awaited us here: a big man in blue jeans under his long Afghan shirt, with a double, unshaven chin and Chitral hat sported at a jaunty angle. He shook hands with the insincere firmness of a politician – which he was. Michel de Guillenschmidt, a French Gaullist and the most senior Western elected official to enter guerrilla country, was accompanied by another Frenchman, the unfortunately named George Pons.

I interviewed Michel, who advocated more Western support for the *muj*. They were fighting, he said, for the same noble cause as the French *maquis*. I didn't completely buy into his analogy, as many in the French resistance after 1941 were communists.

Then we filmed the training session, particularly the setting up and firing of a large DSHK Chinese recoilless rifle mounted on a tripod and, unusually, from the shoulder. 'Our' *muj* were clearly outclassed by the discipline and training of the Jamiat men. We were all impressed by Mohamed, who also had a good feel for PR. (Strangely, a Christmas card arrived for me in Johannesburg the following January from the wrestler-warrior.)

This diversion made us some hours late for our rendezvous with Joe, the Captain, and the rest of our kit. The Captain was in a foul mood. It was very dark, so I suggested camping on the trail, dreading the thought of another rapid night march in my weakened condition.

But a trek in the dark it was, across the mountain back to Manay.

In the moonless night we passed ghostly deserted villages, stepping around the carcasses of camels rotting next to bomb craters. After a hard day the treacherous mountain passes took a heavy toll on our tempers. Horses began to slip and stumble, particularly in dangerous passes. The Doc and Little Doc, who was still loyally with us, shone small pen-torches to help our poor night vision. Joe and I had the most difficult time.

The mood grew grim. Doc and the Captain exchanged bitter words, then blows. The Captain marched off into the night towards the border; we never saw him again, so Joe lost a friend and a possible escort out.

Then one of the *muj* thumped Sofi, the gentlest of our three horse handlers. Joe swore at me as I attempted to guide his steps with the tiny torch. I tried to give him the torch and tell him where to stick it, but dropped it. It went out. While I stumbled to find it, a scorpion brushed across my hand. Little Doc quickly kicked it away.

After four hours' unhappy marching we reached Manay. More bad news awaited us: the Manay men had hit a Russian convoy the night before, nailing a tank and an armoured personnel carrier. They had suffered only two wounded, who had been ferried off to the border. The commander showed us his trousers with a neat bullet-hole punched just two inches from his calf. We had missed the whole show, and Chris was hopping mad.

Exhausted, we had a lie-in till 6 a.m. Then another messenger arrived from the literary but never personally ubiquitous Mr Khan. Why had we steadfastly refused to move from Serracheena to his forward base? The letter contained a series of half-truths, misunderstandings and bullshit, and told us to advance to his forward base.

We all said a resolute no, although Joe, who had been so keen to leave the country altogether, curiously voted for finding Wali. Our new plan was to return to Alamkach, lower down the valley, where the *muj* had promised to hit the local garrison for us, then go back to Jagi and finally the border.

En route we filmed some lyrical shots: sheep herded by children, the jingling of goat bells, and, with permission, some workers in a field. Then we were rudely shooed away – apparently some of the distant figures being filmed were women.

Dog-tired, we relaxed at Alamkach with the river tinkling away in the background. We munched wild figs and ate omelette and nan, trying to preserve our moon food in case we had to stay in the country longer than planned.

We indulged in a rarity – a proper wash. Chris tried to wash with the utmost modesty near the camp, but was pelted with stones by village children. Tim, Ian and I walked a long way along the muddy brown river and stripped completely for our first all-over wash in two weeks. I dropped the soap. They roared at my antics as I ran naked downstream trying to retrieve it, expecting to get shot by a tribesman outraged because a female relative was within a ten-mile radius.

That evening we bumped into the two Frenchmen again. They were accompanying a Jamiat group, so protocol indicated that after a brief hello we should be kept apart. We managed to chat later over a communal supper.

Doc discussed various interpretations of the old Afghan story about why Alexander the Great skirted the country in his drive towards India. The Greek conqueror supposedly met six squabbling Afghans; suddenly one put a piece of Afghan soil on the ground, and instinctively they formed a circle to protect it. It was a pleasant little story, although we infidels privately thought the Afghans would strangle each other to grab a piece of the earth.

The next day a *jirga* assembly of village elders in the valley met to discuss the big attack which their foreign guests would witness. It took a long time to arrange because of the issue of who would sit where, indicating deference for this leader or that party.

Chris was quick to add his usual acid comment: 'If they can't even organise seating arrangements, how the hell are they going to organise fighting the Russians?'

While we waited, Doc asked me to write a letter to Wali explaining our point of view, saying he would translate it. I did so, although I suspected the letter was kept for Doc's own defence later. Doc said Wali was an influential man, and we should understand why he kept us waiting ten days. We knew we were exhibiting our own, perhaps narrow, cultural viewpoint, but we tried to explain that Western film crews might grow impatient of waiting for even the American president after a day or two.

Meanwhile, we tried to film equestrian scenes. Certain Afghan tribes had a reputation as horsemen and played a game called *buzkashi*, a very violent cousin to polo, although during the war it was played very little. As actors and horsemen the *muj* in this valley fell far short of expectations. Again we had a great deal of trouble stopping them peering like grinning idiots into the camera at every opportunity.

'*Camera tai magora*,' we kept saying. 'Don't look at the camera.'

We were supposed to film the *jirga* when it eventually began but were told it was inconvenient, so we sat and waited for the verdict. Bored, Chris asked Tim to read from his diary. Tim's prose had a deceptive simplicity and directness that recalled Bunyan's *Pilgrim's Progress*. His religious comments, peppered with psychological and military observations, further enhanced that impression.

Chris also asked me to play some recordings from my daily mini-tape-recorder log. My extract ran: 'The *muj* are so disorganised they deserve to lose this war, because they refuse to think in twentieth-century terms. Maybe the Soviets have a point; maybe they do need to be "socialised". They certainly need something.'

Chris was surprised. 'You're always defending the *muj* when I criticise them. I didn't think you felt like that, or is it for the benefit of the Russians if they catch you?'

I just glared at him.

Into battle

We sat in our tent discussing the action planned for the next day, analysing *muj* strategy, possible Russian responses, and filming technicalities. I wondered about my own grit and, more importantly, my stamina if we had to run far under fire. We had all shown courage, perhaps tinged with stupidity, in volunteering for the trip. Courage may be the grandest of virtues, but for combat journalism experience is every bit as important, both to control fear and to help in anticipating an enemy's behaviour.

The Alamkach commander outlined the rough plan of battle. We would march for an hour and a half to a garrison defended by 400 government troops. The fort also had two outposts of 150 men each. *Muj* forces would comprise about eighty men from the Jamiat and Gailani camps. The return fire was expected to be artillery, 105mm tank guns from dug-in tanks on the perimeter, 120mm mortars, and 12.7mm guns.

Our force would attack one of the garrison outposts. Attacking an entrenched position ideally requires a three-to-one ratio; we had eighty men rather than 2,100. They planned to make the assault in the late afternoon, giving enough light for our filming but also allowing a counter-blow from the air. We questioned the commander in detail on this crucial factor.

There were pro-*muj* Afghan conscripts in the fort and the intelligence was good, he said. In the main garrison two Afghan officers were in charge of liaison with the Russian air base at nearby Jalalabad. Each supported a rival wing of the Afghan communist party, the Khalq and Parcham factions, effectively two separate parties. (Afghanistan was the only communist country ruled by two different and hostile parties. As author John Fullerton put it so succinctly: 'This is not the People's Democratic Republic of Afghanistan but Some People's Divided Republic of Kabul.') Neither officer would want to be the first to lose face by calling up Russian choppers, thus signifying a lack of confidence in their own capabilities, so an air strike was unlikely.

In theory, our attack was clearly suicidal. Our *muj* were half-wits who didn't maintain their weapons and couldn't shoot straight. Jamiat were better trained, but eighty against an entrenched 700 backed by Russian Hinds looked like a one-way street to the Muslim heaven. If a Muslim kills an enemy in battle, he is a *ghazi*, an Islamic warrior. If he is killed, he is *shaheed*, a martyr for Islam and well rewarded in paradise, although we doubted if there was any room for Christian companions. On the other hand, the Muslims fighting with the Red Army were extremely reluctant to sacrifice themselves, as dying for communism was considered a particularly 'dirty' death with no entrance ticket through the pearly gates.

Our instincts and brief experience of the *muj* suggested that no one was in a rush for martyrdom. They were not inclined to perform a Custer's Last Stand for the cameras. We had to play along, cautiously, for it was their war, their battlefield, their rules . . . but our lives at stake.

The thought that goes through everyone's mind at such times, especially in faraway places, is not so much the fear of death but of being maimed, on crutches for life, and all for a battle between tribesmen in an arid valley in a country whose name many people couldn't spell. I was too tired to dwell on such black thoughts, and fell straight into a sound sleep.

In the morning the clans gathered at a leisurely pace. Doc refused to come with us, leaving the major problems of liaison and translation to Little Doc, who spoke very poor English. We filmed the loading of the recoilless rifles, a Dasheka, and ammo on to the horses. By 10 a.m. the sun in the clear sky was already suffusing our bodies as we set off in a long single file, eventually reaching the outskirts of Hesarak village. In front of us lay a huge ridge; on the other side, about a mile away, was the targeted outpost. The crew went up another valley to film the destroyed tank and APC supposedly bagged by the Manay men. I joined a small group of *muj* in a little shady settlement, where we loafed for the rest of the day.

The enchanting rustic idyll contrasted blasphemously with the RPGs stacked against a tree. Children brought grapes and nan, while a bullock threshed corn around and around in time-honoured fashion, sweeping me back to the Middle Ages. I dozed. Erotic memories impinged on my dreams, then I awoke with a start to find a field-mouse climbing up my baggy pants. I jumped up and laughed, as did all the *muj*. The scampering children brought water and more grapes, which tasted like almonds. Obviously the guerrillas had the total support of the countryside. If the government forces had developed a similar rapport with the locals they could easily have swarmed over the ridge to wipe out our small band, which had posted no guards and taken no security measures. So far it was like a picnic, not a killing field.

At 4 p.m. we joined the rest of the force. Chris was fuming: they had been on a wild-goose chase. After a 2½-hour rapid march in searing heat they were led to two old lorries, not a tank or an APC. Was it language problems and cultural difficulties, or were the Manay men who claimed such a big victory deceiving themselves and us? Or was it like Africa, where tribesmen told you what they thought you wanted to hear out of sheer politeness?

The *muj* milled around like boy scouts deciding where to pitch their bell tents. Each group had its own area with prepared positions, with holes and emplacements for the Dasheka, and even little stone walls for the AKs.

This was hardly a surprise attack, more like Saturday night on the town.

We wanted to choose a good spot to film the kick-off; but no, we had to accompany our Gailani troops, who were to initiate the battle by firing a recoilless.

I peered over the top of the ridge from our firing position but could see very little . . . trees, a flag and a crenellated wall. We moved along the ridge. Carrying the tripod and equipment bag, I had trouble keeping up on the slippery, sloping shale. Tim suggested that I pull back down the ridge and take the kit back to the horses, as I would slow everyone down.

He wrote in his log that I resembled 'a bag of the proverbial, tied in the middle with a tea-cosy on its head and a bog brush instead of a chin'.

Staggering all over the place with a cumbersome tripod and bag, he feared I would make an easy target.

That occurred to me, too.

I went down the ridge to find the horses, but our handler had hidden them.

The recoilless boomed off at 7.50 p.m., and the Gailani commander prepared to shoot more shells, which his men had laid out in their carrier tins and primed. As the commander reached out for a new shell, he knocked half of them down the slope.

It was Donkey-jumping-on-a-land-mine time again.

Then the incoming started: 82mm mortars, which went right over the ridge and landed at the bottom of the valley where I sat with the film kit.

Tim, Ian and Chris ducked along the ridge, now under heavy fire, and took cover in a ruined mud house, pulling out a few seconds before it was demolished by an RPG from the outpost.

The large tank cannons started, but their fire was inaccurate as they could not depress enough, or elevate sufficiently, to get a short or flat trajectory. The *muj* responded by letting rip with everything, although much of the AK fire went into the air or out of range. Weapons jammed frequently. There was more sound than fury.

The Afghans matched T. E. Lawrence's description of his Arab Levies: 'They thought weapons destructive in proportion to the noise.'

The *muj* despised the Soviets for hiding in their tanks, calling them 'beardless cowards living in iron tents', but were themselves keeping their heads well down behind their prepared defences. The *muj* had no coordinated plan. This was the real dictatorship of the proletariat, not the tyranny of the few but the total licence of the many. If Afghanistan was a nation of fractious villages, then their combat was an ill-assorted cacophony of squabbling individuals. They were supposed, like medieval crusaders, to be ready, even willing, to die for their God, but it was Tim who stuck his neck out for bravado.

The crew came across a *muj* with a stoppage in his .303. Tim cleared it and fired three shots over the ridge, then cleared another dud in the chamber. Then, head up like an idiot, he told Ian to take a still photo.

As he cocked the rifle an incoming round struck the dust a few inches from his face as he lay in a prone firing position. The *muj* laughed gleefully. Wiping the gravel from his face, Tim kept his head up and let off another three rounds, which impressed the *muj* no end.

Tim later wrote in his log: 'A bit gung-ho, I suppose, but the whole thing was for the cameras anyway.'

A no-weapons neutrality is the golden principle of professional journalism. If we were caught by the Russians, participation in a battle, plus our regular shooting competitions and military backgrounds, would undermine our claims to fair treatment as disinterested film-makers. Tim broke the rules. But this was his first journalistic assignment, and he was still at heart a soldier.

I wasn't thinking much about ethics at the time. In my attempts to get out of harm's way, I was picking up more concentrated incoming fire than my battle-hardened colleagues. Behind me, a mortar shell landed bang in the middle of an inhabited house about 500 yards away. I was half bemused, half fascinated, but it seemed surreal: I was witnessing the event as a journalist, not participating, not feeling. Another shell fell right next to me. I threw myself down, feeling dirt from the blast land on my back and neck. More mortars exploded around me. My half-blind right eye picked up some grit, I hoped, not shrapnel. I crawled into a gully, hoping the valuable extender lens in my equipment bag was undamaged. The Afghan government forces displayed strange mortar discipline, initially sending in only one bomb at random instead of a pattern, so it was impossible to predict which way they were 'walking' on to their targets. Besides the mortars, an occasional tank round screamed overhead.

The *muj* were disengaging, but the government mortars kept on landing beyond them, exploding in their rear around me. I hugged the gully and moved out. Just before dark I bumped into Little Doc and the camp commander who had begun the skirmish by knocking over his shells. We trudged up the valley, meeting the rest of the crew half an hour later. Chris and Tim, believing I had been zapped by mortar fire, were just about to search the gullies for my remains. A *muj* fired three tracers into the air to indicate our group was OK; three tracers were returned from the rest, straggling in the dark further down the valley. In the pitch black we took nearly three hours to stumble back to camp. Just as we reached the outskirts of our base, a tank shell whistled a foot or so in front of Chris and me – the camp was still within the 2–3-mile tank range.

Our battle foray had been something of a damp squib, more set-piece ritual than the real thing. The *muj* didn't seem to have the heart, nor planning, for hard close-quarter night assaults to inflict real damage on the enemy, apparently preferring long-distance sniping to close-range combat. That suited me personally, but it wasn't good for the film.

Doc had already eaten and lay dozing in the open on a rough wooden bed. We cooked some moon food, laughing and complaining about the battle. Nobody on our side had been injured, and we reckoned the other side would have been pretty damn unlucky to have suffered any harm either. It was Saturday night in Afghanistan with a bit of bang-bang. Done in, we fell asleep in our sweat-soaked clothes.

The march home

We awoke to the strangled cry of the camp cockerel at 4 a.m., scheduled for an early start because of the possibility of retaliation from the air. We would have the luxury of a horse each for the return journey, although much of it would be too mountainous actually to ride. I gave a pair of binoculars to the Alamkach commander, and made a pompous little speech thanking him for sharing his battle with us and wishing him luck with the Russians.

We started off at 7 a.m. for a twelve-hour day in the saddle, leading our horses over mountain passes. On a particularly narrow and dangerous pass Joe's gelding mounted Ian's big black stallion. Joe's face was a picture, Ian rapidly debussed and in the pandemonium Chris's horse was almost forced over the edge of the cliff. Chris hugged the camera and quietened his steed. Everything was fine. We had a good laugh about the incident, the only bit of sex we'd witnessed in nearly three long weeks.

At a village market we stopped to buy yellow-green plums and bunches of grapes and film the scene, a peaceful, verdant valley, with narrow paths meandering down between well-watered fields of maize and potatoes opening on to wider avenues enhanced by mulberry and walnut trees.

Within an hour's travel the landscape had changed to arid semi-desert of loose shale and deep red-brown to blue-black dust. We passed another tea-house, swarming with horses weighed down with ammo. Doc became very agitated when we stopped to film as this turned out to be a Jamiat convoy at a Jamiat *chai*-house. Jamiat had suffered numerous raids on their ammo supply columns, mainly from the rival Hezbi group. Doc emphasised our friendly status, but fussed over us to rush our filming.

We soon left, riding on our uncomfortable, stirrupless, wicker-saddled horses for another three hours. Chris and I grew irritated by the accompanying *muj* whacking the horses on narrow high ridges or, occasionally, putting a stick up the horse's rear just to test Chris's – luckily excellent – equestrian skills.

Horses weren't our only animal problem: snarling, vicious dogs often ran out of the mud compounds to threaten us. The *muj* threw stones or, if the dog became very aggressive, raised their rifles just in case. It would be a lousy place to catch rabies.

Despite this, things were now better. We were riding, and were anyway walking much more easily when we had to, even Joe and I. At Azoar, the night stop on our second day in the country, our hosts had yet again killed a sheep for us. We usually paid them via Doc, in an attempt not to offend their strict code of hospitality. The *Pushtunwali* honour code granted total sanctuary to any guest; even if he uttered an unspeakable insult he was safe from retribution, although the host could hunt him down to kill him *outside* the house. On this occasion we knew we would have trouble eating the stringy meat, and allowed our hosts to feast on the sheep themselves. For politeness' sake we usually made a show of participation, but often resorted surreptitiously to moon food cooked on small gas heaters.

The next day we set off before the stars had even paled. It was very cold and mountains loomed ahead of us, each summit presenting another in a desperately frustrating string of false crests. We climbed, leading our horses up the steep paths, for an hour and a half. At the final summit stood a small mud hut with a pot of the ever-welcome *chai*. Anti-communist posters festooned the walls. Tim gorged himself with cookies and experimented – foolishly – with some sheep biltong. Joe complained of a hot-and-cold fever. I felt exhausted. Chris and Ian were fine physically, but Chris was in a foul temper.

Back on the road Tim's stomach had him bent over double in pain until a MiG strike in front of us, at the head of the Jagi Valley, made adrenalin pump out his sickness.

Someone shouted what sounded like 'Choppers' in Pushtu. Joe and I couldn't hear much above the sound of the bombing and dashed into some tree cover. We must have misheard or misunderstood the Pushtu words, as we didn't see any Hinds.

Reaching the tea-house where we had witnessed the air strike on that first morning, we were told the house we were making for had been bombed a few hours earlier. Our host and seven of his family, including small children, had been killed.

Tim recorded the sad news somewhat phlegmatically in his journal: 'That's one for the record . . . a day earlier and we'd probably have lost our kit or something more serious.'

We struck out towards the awaiting carnage. A welcome respite came at a pretty Afghan farmhouse, full of children, laughter, and aromatic country smells. An oxen sled was going around in small circles threshing grain. Chris climbed on to the sled, with the farmer's permission, but it moved just a yard before the rope broke, much to the Afghan family's amusement. They repaired it and around Chris went again, filming an idyllic sequence as the farmer, ever watchful, held a dish behind the oxen to catch droppings before they contaminated the corn.

The little girls were exceptionally pretty, so we filmed them as well. They sat happily posing, very shyly, smiling and covering and uncovering their faces.

Suddenly, they stared hard behind us and ran away.

The bombs landed one second before the sound of the jets reached our ears. Chris swung the camera around to catch the second stick of bombs throwing thick black clouds of dust in the air. The unseen MiGs launched another three bombing runs right in front of us. Previously when we had heard the jets we had had a few seconds to take cover; with supersonic MiGs there was no warning.

We sat in the field next to the house to wait for more Russian visitors, but they didn't oblige. It was a Mad Hatter's tea party in Bomb Alley, the farmer kindly bringing out a pleasant picnic of milk tea, fresh nan and a tray of tasty apricots.

A young man appeared, carrying a 1944 PPSH Russian tommy-gun and sporting a Red Army belt. He chatted and posed for pics, but refused to sell us the belt.

Walking again, one of the *muj* kept asking for my boots. I had given a pair of tennis shoes to a *muj* a few days earlier because his boots had fallen apart. The going was rough, and even Tim's new

Rhodesian army boots were on the point of disintegration. As we had seen with Joe's commando knife, once one present was given, everybody wanted one. I asked the *muj* what he expected me to wear, or did he expect me to go barefoot? This expedition was turning into a mobile cargo cult.

We reached the village of death. The house we had stayed in on our first night in Afghanistan had been totally destroyed: a big crater replaced the room we had slept in. Dead cattle, sheep, donkeys and chickens lay rotting and ballooning with decomposition after less than a day in the summer heat. Women wailed from nearby houses. The eight killed had just been laid to rest, as Muslims traditionally bury their dead almost immediately. Outside the village new scarves were fluttering on sticks marking the fresh graves. Everywhere in Afghanistan we had seen graves, often on mountain-tops, bedecked with scarves as tokens of respect for the martyrs.

We paid off our horsemen from Alamkach and moved to a house on the edge of the village, halfway up a hill. In the background soared a high mountain range. We camped in a large room covered with dirty but comfortable red quilts. A large window provided a panoramic view of the Jagi Valley, although the smell of the decaying animals wafted in waves through the open window.

We started filming. First, I did a to-camera piece standing in the ruins. 'There is no front line in this civil war, it passes through the hearts and hearths of all Afghans,' I intoned, a poor epitaph for the dead family. All that was left of the father was, ironically, his membership card of the Gailani party in his scorched wallet. The rest was vaporised.

Then we trekked for an hour or so to the valley floor to a government garrison overrun by guerrillas the previous year. We trod carefully along a path fringed with live anti-personnel mines, and filmed the stripped hulks of a Russian APC and four tanks. Spent rounds lay everywhere, from 12.7s, AK-47s, AK-74s, and Tokarev 9mm pistols. Russian and Afghan ration packs, peppered with holes, littered the battlefield.

We returned to a vegetarian supper, as in the mourning period no meat, except chicken, was eaten. We were relieved; we'd had enough of stringy dead goat. Early next morning we climbed up the hill behind the house, having slept badly because of all the bugs crawling over the red quilts. The local *muj* commander assured us no jets would arrive before 8.30 a.m., but we knew that Russian pilots were not inclined to sleep in and reckoned on a 6.30 a.m. visitation.

Spot on time, the MiGs, subsonic on this occasion, rolled into the Jagi Valley. A wall of fire came from the far side of the valley; the fundamentalist Alliance had installed nests of Dashekas, apparently supervised by Arab instructors, although we were not allowed to go across to see. (I later speculated whether Osama bin Laden was in this base – of this gentleman, much more later.)

For the next hour squadrons of MiG-21s and MiG-27s bombed four different sites.

After the excitement we settled down to scrambled eggs and coffee, but our breakfast was interrupted by a MiG-27 dropping two bombs on a village just half a mile away. They didn't explode.

The next MiG swept in. We saw the bombs fall, open their corrective parachutes, and explode with a thunderous roar right in front of us. We couldn't ask for a better show. Chris got the actual explosions on film, but the MiGs' speed eluded the camera.

Better still, we found out later that no one had been killed in the village just for the benefit of a one minute or less film sequence for bored couch potatoes in the West.

We were called down from the hill for lunch in the house. With so many MiGs wasting the area we all felt a bit fidgety sitting around relaxing, and the stench of dead animals put us off even a vegetarian meal. We asked Doc why, as a medical man, he hadn't suggested that the villagers remove the carcasses for hygienic reasons, let alone the smell. He gave a very vague answer.

We wanted to go to the adjacent village to film the results of the morning's bombings, but this started a long palaver. Visiting that village was a very delicate matter, said Doc, translating for the local commander. He could not take us there, as courtesy demanded, as both villages were involved in a long feud in which thirteen villagers had been killed, five of them recently.

Doc led a convoluted debate on the *Pushtunwali*, the Pathan code of honour, which operated alongside the stern dictates of the Koran. The code included a number of observances, of which *melmastia* (hospitality), *badal* (revenge), *teega* (truce), and *nang* (honour) were crucial components. The *jirga* decided on all important issues, peace, war and matters of honour. Most important of all, quarrels had to be settled honourably. Disputes arose frequently over *zar*, *zan*, and *zamin* (gold, women, and land), and each tribe or clan maintained an account of profit and loss, as it were, in matters of *ghairat* (self-respect). Traditionally blood had to be paid for in blood, and the killings would go on for generations of enmity which made even the Irish look forgiving and forgetful of slights. The harshest penalties were frequently reserved for fellow clansmen or relatives. More recently, blood feuds were often settled by cash payments. 'Not all the roubles in Russia could compensate for the Afghan national *badal* against Moscow,' said the local commander.

We discussed the fact that the blood feud was alien to Christian beliefs of turning the other cheek and forgiving neighbours, citing the parable of the Good Samaritan. Doc said that in tribal society the victim would evoke no sympathy, but rather tribesmen would ask whether the robber had made a successful getaway. He felt the Bible was full of tales of vengeance, not least by God; Allah was much more merciful.

Doc thoroughly enjoyed relating a series of old Pathan stories about asylum and truces, and modern ramifications, *Nanawatey*. 'In the past a man seeking a truce would go before his enemy with a rope around his neck as a mark of humility. In very serious cases, women wearing the Koran on their heads would go to the enemy's house to plead their family member's case.'

The tribesmen did not accept *Nanawatey* when it involved female modesty, for a woman's good name was regarded as a sacred trust. Even tribal elders refrained from pleading the case of a woman who had infringed the strict sexual code. If an unmarried woman became pregnant usually through the advances of a cousin or brother, since females were kept away from everyone else, she could expect no mercy. Her own brother or father would kill her, and the man too if they could find him. The previous year a woman who had killed her illegitimate baby was sentenced to death by a court in the tribal areas. Before death she was to suffer twenty lashes, serve seven years in prison, and pay a $200 fine. On appeal to the High Court she was acquitted of the infanticide but found guilty of giving birth to an illegitimate child; her punishment was reduced to two years' hard labour and a fine of $100. Apparently she had been made pregnant by her cousin, who refused to marry her. In past cases of marital infidelity, if a husband didn't shoot his wife outright she could expect to have her nose cut off and sometimes her upper lip too, to mar her beauty and be a lasting mark of Cain whether or not she was guilty of the accusation.

The female role was not always passive: grandmothers frequently acted as guardians of the standards of the *Pushtunwali*. If *badal* was exacted, it was often the matriarch who knew the precise history of the dispute. For honour's sake she would expect her sons to avenge a killing, even if she knew that they in turn would be killed.

The commander was genuinely intrigued by our Western ways, asking about our codes of honour. 'What would happen if your woman was unfaithful? Would you kill the man?' he persisted.

'Well, some European countries recognise what are termed "crimes of passion", which allow more lenient treatment for a man who kills an unfaithful wife or her lover. But murder is certainly the exception. Often there are blows, but usually divorce follows or it is accepted and forgiven,' I said defensively.

The commander could not hide his disgust at our wishy-washy ethics.

Doc was well versed in the lore and traditions of his land, often referring to the warrior-poet Khushal Khan Khattak. I did not tell him that I knew his favourite poet had addressed most of his love poetry to a young man. It was the wrong time for a cultural discussion. Chris was understandably itching to start filming. I was always the amateur anthropologist, and knew from long experience that in traditional societies these matters took time.

The commander was stalling us, repeating his strong reluctance to visit the next-door village. If he went there he might have to kill someone, so Doc would accompany us. Even the fight against the Russians could not take precedence over this little war.

The 'enemy' village was less than a mile away, and we found the locals slaughtering a bull in thanks to Allah for saving his followers from harm. Our welcome was warm. They showed us the bomb craters, and we filmed the unexploded blockbusters. One had embedded itself a few feet from the entrance to an underground bunker – if it had gone off it would have killed forty women and children sheltering there. We debated why the bombs hadn't detonated: faulty Russian workmanship, or, far less likely, sabotage by loyal Afghan ground crews?

The welcome changed dramatically to hostility when a villager arrived to tell our hosts that we were from the rival settlement. Before a third front opened up, we departed gingerly along a path lined with sullen faces. Doc said we had come within a whisker of getting our camera equipment destroyed.

As we crossed the two big fields separating the warring villages, an elderly man with a rifle blocked our way. Two women were working in the distance and our path went through their field, so he led us on a half-mile detour around the fields along a muddy brook. In the stream lay the cow and donkey carcasses which had been rotting under our window: either a total disregard for health measures or a shocking piece of deliberate bad neighbourliness, since the polluted stream flowed into the rival village and was its main water supply. No wonder we all had gut-rot. Mine was becoming exhaustingly acute, with attacks every five minutes or so. Joe also felt rough, so we returned to the bedbugs to rest while the others went to film another village.

Chris tried to shoot some of the interesting stone houses, but our local commander stopped him because women were in the far background, even though Chris assured him they were not in frame. Admittedly, as Doc explained, the men were obsessive about their women's modesty in these border tribal areas, but Chris was irate and frustrated by his inability to film.

Tim wrote in his diary:

Chris, rather unnecessarily I thought, lost his rag completely, adopting the attitude that he was making a film that would help them so why the hell didn't they want to help him to do it. Not correct. These people don't see the benefits from a film and couldn't give a fig whether it is made or how good it is. If it crosses their social structures then they won't make allowances but will get hosed off.

*

Things were going sour. The fact that the border and our ambulance lay a few hours' walk away over the mountains tempted us all. Joe was more than keen to get out, I was sick, and Tim and Chris had fallen out. Chris was generally very touchy, not least with my suggestion that we should leave because we had overstayed our welcome. The commander was already upset by the death of eight kinsfolk. To the peasant mind the suspicion that the Russians had bombed the exact positions where we foreigners had slept might have turned into more than a coincidence. Then Chris and the commander had argued about filming near the women. Ian agreed that our hosts had had enough of our less than delightful company.

We still needed some shots of MiGs, having filmed the bombing and explosions but not the delivery vehicles. Early the next day we positioned ourselves on the hill hoping for more aerial antics. Up in the sky aircraft, with the latest computer-guided technology, roared in the far distance as we stared blankly down on a medieval landscape. For three weeks we had not seen even a chair. No roads, no electricity, no machines, only weapons and destroyed military vehicles. The single exception was a bright red tractor working just a mile from the border.

Waiting for the bombers, we discussed the film. We had captured some lyrical evocations of the countryside, as well as dramatic and moving footage of the injured boy, but precious little action. We had intended to stay in for at least six weeks, but events and Joe and Tim's limited timetables foreshortened our adventure. Chris, Ian and I dreaded the thought of coming back soon, and I doubted whether I was in good enough shape to go anywhere. Nor was I keen to split the team, as Chris suggested, to let him and Ian camp on the hill for a week after we left. Besides my determination on principle that we should all leave together as a team, I was worried that Chris might antagonise the locals into violence without Doc to smooth things over and my occasional diplomacy.

Chris thought he could stay there without *muj* protection for a week or so, but I pointed out that this was a complex tribal society into which we were allowed to intrude – just – on great sufferance. Already, we were more than pushing our luck. Chris refused to accept this, saying I wanted to leave only because I was ill. If the MiGs had provided some more action for us, and Chris had managed to get their attack on film, we might have left the country without a row. The Russians, however, wouldn't fight exactly when we wanted them to. So, unforgivably in front of our hosts, we had a rip-roaring verbal punch-up which left Chris ranting, the commander embarrassed and Doc grievously offended. Ian, always the gentleman, remained aloof. We should have sorted out our problems privately instead of swapping insults in the commander's house. It was difficult for me to keep a lid on things because I was nipping outside every five minutes with diarrhoea. Thank goodness for the *Pushtunwali*.

We left at 3 p.m. and trudged gloomily through the alpine forest, reaching the unpoliced summit border crossing after an hour or so. We looked back to Afghanistan. Our last sight was a martyr's grave, freshly adorned with scarves and pieces of coloured cloth hanging from sticks. We clattered down the foothills into Pakistan.

Entering the bandit town of Terrimangel in daylight, we were told to disguise our kit, wear *muj* head-dress and speak no English, to avoid detection by Pakistani police. Tim wrote: 'The cover-up made Paul look like Rumpelstiltskin, Ian like one of Snow White's dwarfs after a dose of steroids, and Chris a foreigner with a *patou* wrapped around himself. Joe just looked cranked and I hate to think what I looked like.' With his very short hair and faintly Mongol appearance, Doc thought Tim could have passed as an Uzbek. But if Tim looked the part and walked almost as well as an Afghan, the rest of us had no choice but to brazen it out and hurry through, eyed suspiciously by local ruffians as we wove around tents, camels, chickens, donkeys and mess on the ground.

Doc said to me quietly, 'If you put your bag down there, a man could say, "It's mine," if he had a gun. What matters is force. There is no law here. You might film a man and he could shoot you because he thought you were taking a picture of his wife. They fight tribal battles here still – it used to be with old rifles, but since the war they use RPGs and mortars.'

We passed through unhindered. I hadn't washed properly for weeks, wore filthy clothes and was tanned and bearded. I smelt rotten, so maybe I could pass for a local – provided I spat now and again.

At the Gailani safe house we climbed up the rickety wooden stairs almost exactly three weeks after leaving. Outside about fifty *muj* were loading up a big ammunition convoy, but we were told it was too risky to film. Peter Jouvenal had said that returning from the Afghan countryside would make Peshawar look like New York, and certainly the mud hut's filthy loo seemed like the Hilton. Kebabs which three weeks before we had treated with grave misgivings we now munched like caviar, accompanied by seven or eight Cokes each.

When the British army soldiered on the Frontier a column reckoned to march about ten miles a day in rough terrain. We had walked or ridden for hundreds of miles behind Russian lines over rugged ground and sometimes under fire. Although the film was not complete, I treated myself to a cigar that had miraculously survived all the pounding. I lay back, puffed on the rich tobacco and said a silent prayer of thanks.

Red tape

Although we had got out safely, our mood deteriorated. Peter had warned that even the fittest adventurers often fell apart once they got out, as though one relaxed one's guard after the sheer effort of will to keep the body going on gruelling Afghan journeys. It was time to say goodbye to the remaining horsemen. We paid the loyal Sofi well, plus a tip (he, like the others, went afterwards to Doc for more *baksheesh*), and the persistent *muj* eventually got my boots.

The others bedded down while Tim and I joined some Gailani leaders for tea. The conversation turned to chemical warfare, a pet theme of Afghan guerrillas in conversation with Westerners. Doc told a story of when he worked in the main hospital in Kabul: 'Some Afghan villagers came in with minor wounds. Thirteen out of twenty-five died and we couldn't work it out. Eventually, we decided it was poison bullets.'

Tim and I were very sceptical of 'poison bullets'. Tim thought it was probably poor hygiene.

Next morning, before boarding the Toyota ambulance, we tried to film the incredible squalor of the little street outside. Next to the rickety steps of our wood-and-mud house, at the side of a kitchen, stood a long-drop loo. Beneath this 'thunderbox' were other thunderboxes – crates of ammo. In the street chickens and children traipsed over open drains. On the corner stood a junkyard with an amazing pot-pourri of militaria: rocket fins, artillery and tank shells, bits of armoured vehicles and helicopters. A schoolboy's paradise and bomb squad's nightmare. A butcher walked casually by, carrying a large shoulder of meat swarming with flies. The village blacksmith hammered away, shoeing a horse. Donkeys brayed.

Chris tried one last time to film some *muj* standing around or loading our vehicle. For the millionth time, '*Camera tai magora!*' (don't look at the camera), but, as usual, they stared inanely into the lens. Chris cursed and climbed into the ambulance. Doc had forbidden us to film beyond our little street, which was a great pity because Terrimangel was an Ali Baba wonderland for the photographer, and Chris was reluctant to film through the curtains of the ambulance after we left the bandit hideout.

We departed at first light, glad to be on our way back to baths and civilisation, which in our filthy condition amounted to the same thing. Chris and Ian fretted about achieving the right psychological mood to return to Afghanistan. I'd had enough, but realised I would have to go back if necessary. Joe and Tim would take the next available plane out of Pakistan. Sadly, as Tim put it, the team was one in name but not in spirit.

Inside the van we made two piles of film, with the unexposed stock on top for any policemen who tried to seize the fruits of our labour. Exposed film was hidden, coyly marked 'Refugees'. We toyed with the idea of sending some of the stock separately with trusted *muj*, but it seemed safer to keep everything in our sight.

The bumpy cross-country marathon began. At a little town called Sadda rival *muj* had let off several bombs in the market, so the place was crawling with Pakistani police. Going through the roadblock we covered our faces with scarves and pretended to sleep. If the police had looked inside, we wouldn't have fooled a soul.

We dropped from dry hills into valleys with strips of lush vegetation – heavy rains made the return journey much greener. Travelling on something approximating real roads, the Toyota picked up speed until we hit a massive traffic jam. Klaxoning our way to the front, the cause of the hold-up was immediately apparent: a bridge had been washed away by the rain. Twenty yards of the span had disappeared into the foaming muddy swell, and the bridge would obviously be down for days. Our excellent *muj* driver vaguely remembered an old British Raj military road; after three hours of cross-country travel which would have worried a four-wheel drive and fording two wide rivers, he found the old track. An hour later we were back on the road on the right side of the broken bridge.

Chris and Ian were looking understandably forlorn, knowing they would probably have to repeat this awful roller-coaster ride. Joe was very quiet. Tim nodded away through the back-breaking bumps. I was intrigued by the remnants of the Raj: old forts, classic Victorian railway bridges, 'dragons' teeth' cement tank-traps, perhaps from the Second World War, and occasional decaying cantonments, relics of grandeur. Joe grew interested too.

'Sad how this place has fallen apart ever since the Brits left,' he commented sombrely.

'Yeah, just like South Africa,' I said, to tease the Afrikaner. It was the only time Chris smiled that day.

A roadblock loomed ahead. The police came forward to stop us, so the driver put the klaxon on, increased speed, and the policemen jumped out of the way. A few miles on lay another block and more policemen. This time they were alert, with rifles at the ready.

We slowed down as the officer put his hand out to stop us. Pretending it was a salute, Doc gave a smart salute back, and we slipped over the chain across the road before the surprised police officer could do anything. Our cheek worked.

After twelve hours in the ambulance we reached Peshawar and switched to a truck to take us to Dean's Hotel. Vlad the Russian gave Tim a mighty hug and welcomed us as if we had escaped a Soviet prison. All our kit was safe.

The hotel manager, looking at our filthy condition, said knowingly, 'You've been to Afghanistan, haven't you?'

'No, we've been walking in the hills,' I replied unconvincingly.

The run-down hotel was full, so we happily switched to the more luxurious Khyber Intercontinental. I dreamed of a beer and a bath, but in usual Pakistani style the hotel could not serve any beer for some obscure reason. I kicked up a fuss. It isn't the badness of bad hotels which is so annoying, but the badness of so-called good hotels.

Even without a beer, a bath was a primeval joy after stripping off my lice-ridden clothes. I was clean and lean, the trip having cost me 40lbs in weight.

Tim and Joe flew off, and Doc helped us organise a second trip into the north. Nick della Casa was asked to fly out; he would be a useful replacement, despite his occasional vagueness and habit of disappearing on his own private walkabouts. If Nick couldn't come, I would have to go back again. It wasn't a thought I embraced willingly: I was still sick, but I kept busy trying to get permits to film in Peshawar and set up a third penetration of southern Afghanistan. Fortunately, however, Nick was able to join us.

I tried to read and think myself into Pakistani politics as part of my total onslaught on the local and national authorities. We couldn't even begin to film street scenes, let alone the sensitive refugee camps, without permits, which in turn would allow the export of the 'refugee' films.

The Pakistani media reflected paranoia inspired by the fragility of the unpopular military regime. Externally, the crucial Washington axis was under fire because of Pakistan's lack of democracy, poor human rights record, heroin smuggling and nuclear weapons aspirations. Internally, the suppression of political parties and regional nationalism prevented stability. The answer usually was to blame India. I formed the impression that Pakistanis were so wrapped up in anti-Indian paranoia and Byzantine bureaucracy, and so busy shuffling permits and papers, that they wouldn't notice if they were invaded by the Russians.

It was decided that Chris would go into Afghanistan again. John Rubython was coming from Cape Town to attempt the hazardous trip to Kandahar. Although a well-known and highly competent stills photographer, John did not have Chris's experience with movie cameras. Chris was worried – rightly – about the overall quality of such a patchwork assignment. Al flew in and out again, having confirmed that my main job was to look after the new team.

'And get those permits,' he said, just before departing.

After further visits to Islamabad and the Peshawar press office, and much waiting, bribery, and bullshit, I got them.

We could now make a 'tourist' film about Peshawar, and film in one designated refugee camp. An authoritarian regime suits the film-maker better than the anarchy which often precedes and follows it, so long as your documents are in order.

While we waited for our stage-managed visit to a government show camp, we set out to explore Peshawar on film. We walked and walked the ancient city until we stopped getting lost; our forays before the first Afghan trip had been quite superficial. Peshawar derived its name from a Sanskrit word meaning 'city of flowers'. The old part of this Pathan city was dark, with tall houses, narrow lanes and overhanging balconies, redolent with the smell of meat, fruit, tobacco and drains. The air was full of the raucous sounds of chickens, putt-putt motors of three-wheeled taxis, the tapping of hammers and the occasional shot in the air, usually to celebrate a wedding rather than a feud. Kebab and *tikka* meat sizzled on hot coals outside dirty tea-shops. In and around the Qissa Khawani bazaar, tiny shops sold *chappals* (sandals), and striking bandoleers and holsters. Gun shops proliferated. Here a shop sold lapis lazuli and there, sadly, the skin of a snow leopard.

A journey's end or long halt for caravans of antiquity from all over the Middle East and Central Asia, the seedy capital lay in the lush

Peshawar Valley, well watered by the Kabul River winding its way down to the mighty Indus. Vital, bustling and intriguing, every turning was a film-maker's delight. The locals were not so camera-conscious or vain as their Afghan kinsmen, and even policemen were helpful, rushing to beat anyone who obstructed us or blocked our way. After all, we had permits.

The British had built their own cantonment when Peshawar was their Frontier headquarters, full of gracious avenues and flaming bougainvillaea. The sandwiches at the Peshawar Club were still good, but came with soft drinks rather than punch (the Marathi word for 'five', named after its ingredients: sugar, lime juice, spice, water and arak).

An old retainer who had worked at the club since 1945 mused about the changes. 'In 1945 many people were happy. Many gentlemen and officers and their ladies . . . much dancing, many beers, much whisky, now nothing. Ah,' he sighed, 'the local politicians came and now no dancing, no beer, no people . . . very sad.'

Indeed it was. The billiard tables were ripped. The ballroom had burnt down and had been roughly rebuilt, and the chandeliers were missing. Yellowing photographs of colonels, huntsmen, and drama societies were stacked in a mouldering, stuffy office. In Peshawar cricket was still played – perhaps the most lasting legacy of empire – but the polo ground was closed.

The most poignant relic of the Raj was the military cemetery near St John's Cathedral, filled with graves of young soldiers, mainly aged nineteen to twenty-five, from once-proud regiments now merged, restyled, rationalised and disbanded. We filmed some of the arresting epitaphs on the headstones: 'killed by assassins', 'murdered by Afridi tribesmen', 'died bravely during the siege of. . .' We wanted to contrast the quiet relics of the Raj with the bustle of modern Peshawar, and compare the sound and fury of the Afghanistan war with the *muj* political leadership safely ensconced in a city far removed from the battles. We also wanted to examine the fall-out of the war in the refugee camps and hospitals.

The Red Cross had set up hospitals and rehabilitation centres around Peshawar, where we filmed amputation operations on war-wounded patients. Worse were the limbless children learning to walk with their stumps. A little girl, aged five, had lost one leg to a bomb. As she hobbled around with crutches, I noticed that the toes on her remaining foot were painted with red nail varnish. A boy of about seven, with both legs taken above the knees by an anti-personnel mine, smiled bravely as he talked to the Swiss doctor in charge. This was the real tragedy of the war: not Soviet imperialism or injured Afghan pride, but the carnage thrust on the innocent.

We had seen enough of the agony of the refugees; it was time to talk to their squabbling political leaders. Faisal Akbar, a spokesman for all the *muj* groups, admitted that the main problem was lack of unity and the need for a single leader.

'Why not the Panshir's Ahmed Shah Massud?' I asked.

'Ah, he is a good fighter but he is young.' Faisal gave a convoluted explanation of why Massud had been criticised for his various tactical truces with the Russians. What he didn't say was that the brilliant guerrilla commander came from the wrong minority tribe. As in Africa, it was never polite to discuss with Westerners the crucial issue of tribe. In turn, most journalists and academics refrained from mentioning the indelicate subject.

I did ask him how long he thought the war would go on.

'Thirty or forty years. We are indifferent to time. We will fight on.'

That the *muj* were setting up attacks partly for the film led to a debate about 'creating facts'. Where do you draw the line between passively filming activity and actually encouraging it? Do you carry on filming a self-immolating Buddhist monk or do you try to douse the flames? In a sense, all journalists – by their very presence – are instigators. We discussed our recent experiences during the rioting in Soweto. Cameras definitely triggered off mob activity; it was theatre in the street. But we did not over-moralise, and the ever-energetic Chris was keen to get a good battle scene in the can.

We had to wait a day or two before departure, so Doc took us around the carpet shops. Chris and Ian bought two exquisite silk Afghan carpets, $800 cash each. I purchased a cheaper woollen Baluch from Herat. Doc wangled a good price after explaining our contribution to the *jihad*.

Nick's boyish amiability and Old Etonian-style charm had recharged our spirits. It was once again a real team. Peshawar also was in festive mood, with pennants fluttering everywhere to celebrate Independence Day. The taxi-scooters, with their coloured dangling tapes and crudely painted visuals, often of movie heroes or kung-fu action, looked even more garish.

'Set up a tinsel factory here and you'd make a fortune,' said Ian.

The last day was spent sorting out kit in the hotel. As usual, hotel staff kept barging into the room. It happened fifteen times in one day, including an alleged cleaning man at 10.30 p.m. when I was asleep. Special Branch activities plus incompetent rudeness, we assumed. In the evening we had a drink in the so-called bar. No Afghan friend could join us, we were told severely, as the bar was reserved for drinkers – that is Christians, implying that 'criminal' was an equal description.

Ian, Nick and Chris left at 7 a.m. next day for their long journey in the ambulance, all in fine fettle as I wished them good luck.

The southern front

John Rubython and Mark Stucke were also in good spirits, despite their 6 a.m. arrival at Islamabad airport. After an hour's row with PIA about tickets, we caught a plane for Quetta. I'd met John a few times in Cape Town; now he seemed tense, even though he had managed to slip his well-hidden camera through customs without any problems. Mark, a New Zealander working in London, was twenty-two and dead keen.

Eventually we circled over Quetta, the arid capital of Baluchistan. This old British garrison was still a military centre and fighter aircraft, mainly of Chinese origin, stood in concrete pens around the landing field. Hamid Nasser Zia, of the Gailani family, was waiting for us with a jeep. I had met him before. Then, as now, he was cool, aloof, elegant and dressed all in white. We loaded up and set off for the best of the bad hotels, the Blue Star.

I asked Hamid whether the jet fighters were facing north against the Russians or west to the Iranians.

'Neither. They're just for show.'

Despite using Pakistan as a sanctuary, the Afghans here and in Peshawar had little respect for their hosts.

We arranged to meet the *muj* later and decided to explore Quetta, the main town in the sparsely populated semi-desert region of Baluchistan. It was cruel and merciless country, worthy of its sons. The Baluchi tribesmen were divided – on maps only – by the borders of Afghanistan, Iran, and Pakistan. In the 1970s, backed by the Russians, they had fought a long war against the Pakistanis for

Baluchistan's autonomy. Situated in northern Baluchistan, Quetta marked the southernmost point of Britain's North West Frontier defence line. In the nineteenth century Kabul's potentates regarded all the province up to the sea as Afghan territory. If the Russians could control it, the coastline would give them a choke point to threaten the West's umbilical oil supplies. That, at least, was the Cold War warriors' angle.

Like Peshawar, four roads led to Quetta. To the south-west lay old Persia and the lost kingdom of the Shah. To the east and south-east were two routes to and from India. North-west the road led directly to Kandahar, the base for the Afghan guerrillas' southern front and the target of our operation, whence Russian convoys ran through hostile territory to the ancient city of Herat.

I took John and Mark around the bazaar to kit them out in local gear. I liked Quetta. It was cleaner, prettier and more orderly than Peshawar. Much of the town was destroyed in an earthquake in 1935 which killed over 20,000 of its inhabitants. The British military rebuilt it, which perhaps explained the more disciplined pattern of the streets.

Back in the Blue Star I briefed the new team. Al, I felt, had been too sanguine in his instructions. They would have no cover from Hinds in the open desert, and the route had been ambushed frequently by crack Russian airborne commandos. On the other hand, in the hotel we met a number of journalists who were about to go in. This obviously made the cameramen feel more at ease. We made friends with Hugo Delatude, who was with a French TV team from Antenne 2 scheduled to go in on the same day as John and Mark. What worried me about the pack of journalists was the ease with which we could be targeted by the local Special Branch and, worse, the KGB, who had infiltrated Quetta as thoroughly as Peshawar.

My suspicions were later justified: Jacques Abouchar, a well-known correspondent for Antenne 2, travelling with the rest of his team and guided by our Quetta acquaintance Hugo, was ambushed fourteen miles from the Pakistani border. They were surprised by tanks firing heavy machine-guns. The 52-year-old Abouchar was shot and captured after being wounded, then led off like a trophy on top of a tank. (He was eventually released after a show trial.) The French crew and the rest of us at the Blue Star had been under close scrutiny by Afghan and KGB agents. The French team was ambushed by a combined Russian-Afghan unit with specific orders to capture Abouchar alive. This operation was directed at one audience: Western journalists trying to report on occupied Afghanistan.

This happened a few days after I flew out of Quetta without even photographing the steam engines which had teased my ears for three days.

In Islamabad I received a surprise phone call from Ian in Peshawar. I knew he had returned with the ambulance after making the journey into the tribal areas, knocked out by diarrhoea, but had gamely made a second attempt to rejoin the team.

Full of anxiety about the two teams, I left for London, where I had to set up some political interviews. The customs officials had got to know me, after my raucous attempts to stop them opening cans of film in broad daylight, or retrieve lost daggers and cases. They had obviously decided that, for the sake of peace and quiet, for once discretion was the better part of bureaucracy. The film cans were not opened as I had my permit to export film of the 'refugees', and were loaded safely on board the BA jet. I relaxed with an English beer, even though it was early morning. I had suffered nothing worse than a massive dose of culture (and stomach) shock, but had probably failed a number of tests. Despite ten years of travelling, mostly in the third world, I had viewed my brief experience of the Afghan war through the narrow prism of my Western European prejudices. In three weeks I had endured a little of what the Afghan people had stoically withstood for over five years, and had made some friends among the *muj*. By Peter Jouvenal's criterion, however, I had failed the ultimate test. He told me that there were two types of journalists who covered Afghanistan: those who came once, and those who came again.

I swore I would never touch Afghan soil again. In the end I did go back, but not for a long time.

New maps
Both teams I had reluctantly left managed to get some extra footage for our film, but the Kandahar two had a very torrid time and were almost shot up and captured. So in the end we all survived and I edited the film in Johannesburg.

Decades later I still find it hard to forget the suffering I saw in

Afghanistan: the deliberate Soviet policy of what has been called 'rubblisation' and 'migratory genocide', destroying everything to make peasants become internal or external refugees. The tragedy is the Russians have long gone, but the Afghans are still killing each other with much better weapons than they had before the Russian invasion. Afghanistan, never a nation, became a cluster of fortress towns surrounded by tribes warring among themselves. When they were not fighting they were busy growing opium (after Burma, Afghanistan was the world's biggest producer). Anarchy and plunder returned as natural pastimes.

Nick Danziger, an experienced traveller, put his finger on it: 'The civil war was more about tribal and sexual apartheid than about the defeat of a foreign invader.'

Eventually, the harsh Taliban regime unified most of the country, although Ahmed Shah Massud still fought on in the north, but this time he was backed by the Russians. But his 2001 assassination was to lead to dramatic events culminating in the almost unbelievable: British armies sent for the fourth time to fight on the Afghan plains. That story is recounted later.

Despite the briefness of my first visit, Afghanistan taught me a lot about combat and filming. Like Evelyn Waugh's famous greenhorn in *Scoop*, we blundered into a war like ignorant fools, and we came out, surprisingly, intact and with a film. Although most of the team found the physical conditions less arduous than I did, the trip had a profound effect on us all. The disabled children, exquisite valleys, Hind gunships, Chris's humour, Donkey grinning inanely, Tim's *braai* . . . These instants in the Afghan wind sweep back when people asked me the obvious question – would I do it again?

I would prevaricate and recall Chris's constant quip: 'If you can't take a joke, you shouldn't be in Afghanistan.'

It was not my first combat assignment, but my first team effort. I learned the hard way that such an expedition requires a clearly defined leader who is fit to lead and who has carefully chosen his own team. The next time, if I were asked to be the leader, I certainly wouldn't choose me.

The most important personal insight came from reading Tim's log. It was largely unflattering and entirely truthful. To have an acute observer write in detail about you – when you're under fire, sick with dysentery, and trying to lead a team of fractious individuals in a primitive environment where people have a habit of poking a stick up the backside of the horse you're riding – was bound to draw a new psychological map.

And all for half an hour on TV or, in some countries, just a few minutes of bang-bang.

AFRICA II

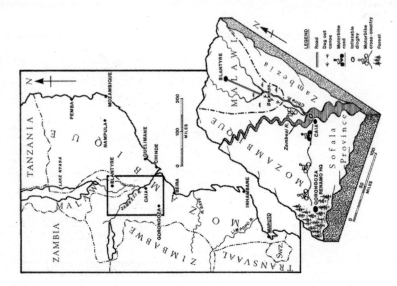

Mozambique

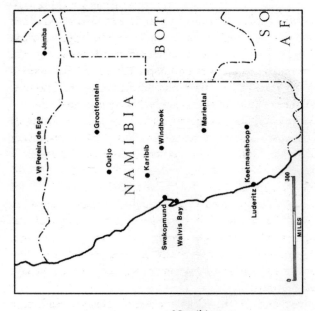

Namibia

5. ANGOLA AND MOZAMBIQUE –
GUERRILLA CHIEFTAINS

Angola's Patton

He looked about thirteen but he was a soldier. His bush hat was much too big for him, as was the AK he cradled. His tattered uniform hung on his small, spindly frame. He sat on a captured Russian truck, which stood in the shimmering heat of the Angolan-Namibian border. A fresh-faced South African soldier, only a few years older than the boy, offered him a cigarette.

'He's too young to smoke,' said a fellow South African gruffly.

'If he's old enough to carry a gun, he's old enough to smoke,' replied the fresh-faced youth.

I was sitting on the back of an adjacent Russian truck waiting to be driven to the rebel capital of Jamba to interview Dr Jonas Savimbi. It was August 1986 and the scene was being set for the biggest African tank battles since Rommel. The passing exchange between the two teenage smokers made me reflect on the tragedy of war in southern Africa – not only its almost total embrace of the young, but also how the fate of all the countries in the region had become enmeshed.

Until the outbreak of the war against the Portuguese in 1961, Angola was one of the least reported territories on earth. After independence in 1975 the conflict became a sadistic civil war, mainly between a pro-Marxist government in Luanda, the capital, and Savimbi, the bush warrior. Russia and Cuba backed the MPLA (Movement for the Popular Liberation of Angola) government in Luanda; Savimbi's Unita (National Union for the Total Independence of Angola) was helped a little by the Chinese and a lot by the Americans and South Africans. Angola, twice the size of France or Texas, was churned into one huge devastated battleground, when its oil and fertility could have made it a second Brazil.

Savimbi was one of the most interesting African leaders, a charismatic political chameleon. The former Maoist, trained in

China, had been dubbed the 'Mrs Thatcher of Africa' – presumably a compliment. He was certainly tough, touchy, vain, intelligent and determined. And he liked yes-men around him. Whether his military qualities matched his PR genius is debatable, although he certainly led one of the best-trained and best-disciplined guerrilla armies Africa has ever seen. After nearly forty years of fighting the 68-year-old Unita chief continued campaigning, despite losing an election and his Western allies. He was eventually shot on 22 February 2002 in a gunfight allegedly orchestrated by his erstwhile South African, Israeli and American friends. In his last years his political and military skills had curdled into a brutal and paranoid dictatorship.

In 1986, however, Savimbi was Pretoria's key player in the wars of destabilisation raging throughout the region. South Africa was fuelling big wars in Angola and Mozambique and smaller ones in Zimbabwe and Zambia. These proxy wars disrupted the front-line states' support for the ANC and the transport systems required to make anti-apartheid sanctions work.

A pilgrimage to Savimbi's HQ was expected of foreign reporters on any serious fact-finding trip to southern Africa. There were two routes. One, courtesy of the CIA and Zaire, took longer and could be uncomfortable, partly because Zaire's army was dangerously and drunkenly unpredictable. I took the easier route via Wonderboom airport near Pretoria. Old Daks, lovingly termed 'vomit comets' by troopies, flew over South African-occupied Namibia (then South West Africa), dropping to treetop level in the final stages of the journey to avoid stray SAM-7 missiles. I had a romantic attachment to Daks; in Rhodesia I had flown in some which had taken part in the 1944 Arnhem campaign. Durable and reliable. Mine landed at Jamba at night. It was a full moon and the rough strip was lit by hurricane lamps. Guests were met by extremely well-turned-out Unita officers, searched, and offered the unique opportunity to have their passports stamped with 'Free Angola'. Most declined, as it would have invalidated their passports to travel elsewhere in Africa.

Sometimes journalists spent five or six sixteen-hour days bumping along flat forest tracks or stuck in endless quagmires if Savimbi wanted to demonstrate his latest advance on the capital, Luanda. Access to Jamba, however, was much easier because it hugged the south-eastern border with Namibia. The Portuguese called this area 'the end of the world' – with good reason. Savimbi's well-camouflaged fifty-mile-wide capital was very isolated. Pretoria poured in massive amounts of military hardware from bases in the Caprivi Strip, while South African and Portuguese businessmen traded in contraband: smuggled diamonds, poached ivory and rare wood.

Savimbi had summoned a small group of hacks because he wanted to announce his latest victories. It would be hype, but we were always afraid of missing out in case he really did have something important to say. We drove in trucks along empty dirt roads, signalled forward at deserted intersections by immaculate military policemen wearing spotless white gloves. We were taken to an officers' mess and regaled with South African wines and beers.

I chatted to an amiable group called Black Americans for Free Angola: 'If the US gives aid, there's less need for reliance on South Africa.'

This was a comfortable war to cover for the majority of newshounds who avoided, or were kept away from, the front. Savimbi, an inveterate self-publicist, garnered acres of favourable news coverage despite being an African nationalist who supped with the devil in Pretoria. The message, though, eventually palled. It was always 'next year in Luanda', but he never reached the Luanda Station.

On the other hand, people had written off Savimbi so many times. He was a great survivor, an African Houdini. In 1975 his forces took part in the South African invasion which stopped just short of Luanda. When his allies retreated, Savimbi led 300 of his surviving troops on his own version of Mao's Long March. By the mid-1980s Unita was rampaging all over the country, running rings around crack regiments of Cuban troops. (But South African tanks and jets were usually in the background when Unita stopped running.)

At this press conference on 21 August 1986 Savimbi was ebullient about repelling the latest offensive which some experts had predicted would overwhelm his forces. There was an extra Patton-like swagger to the bearded warlord, who also sported a pearl-handled Colt revolver slung low over one hip.

Savimbi did not openly admit that the latest American Stinger missiles had turned the tide of battle for him, but said: 'We have got all we asked President Reagan to give us and it has arrived in a very quick manner.' Artistic appreciation of that generosity was displayed in a massive mural of Savimbi and Reagan which dominated the central parade ground.

Savimbi, with characteristic rhetoric, dismissed the threat of an attack from his old friend, the ever-lachrymose Kenneth Kaunda: 'There is a difference in having soldiers for parade and having soldiers for fighting. Mine are seasoned soldiers for fighting; those in Zambia are for parade.'

Actually, Savimbi was being kind. Zambian troops couldn't even manage a proper parade.

Savimbi droned on about the enemy's use of chemical weapons which had blinded some of his troops. A Unita colonel gave an eye-witness account: 'The leaves of some trees became totally dark, the sand became very, very dark as well . . . The smoke was yellow and green.'

Observers of other wars, such as Afghanistan, will have noted how often guerrilla spokesmen harp on the theme of chemical and biological weapons. They know it is the type of story Western journalists want to hear.

My favourite Unita story concerns a small, pilotless Seeker drone which the South Africans used for spying. Unita soldiers observed the plane being shot down. A South African colonel with a sense of humour told a search party to hunt for it, as the matter was politically sensitive: 'The pilot is a very small Japanese.'

Unita liaison officers with the South African Defence Force were more tactful. The South Africans spent a small fortune dropping tons of propaganda leaflets on the rival MPLA forces before Unita officers gently informed their allies that very few of the MPLA troops could read. Other South African propaganda ploys were equally disastrous. They used 'skyshouts', loudspeakers in aircraft and on the ground, to amplify sounds of hyenas. But this gimmick also unnerved the superstitious black troops in the South African forces.

The South Africans fought with great skill and bravery in Angola, although they were always outnumbered and often outclassed by modern Soviet equipment, but they never mastered psychological warfare or press relations. During and after Pretoria's first big lunge into Angola, Afrikaner troops were instructed to tell journalists they were American or English mercenaries to disguise the extent of South African involvement. Blacks might all look the same to some foreign correspondents but Afrikaners – with very thick and often broken English – couldn't really pass for Texans or Geordies. From then on South African troops talked about 'going to the States' when they crossed into Angola.

Before I left Jamba I asked Savimbi about his relations with the anti-Marxist Renamo guerrillas in the other big Portuguese-speaking ex-colony, Mozambique. He was quite dismissive, implying they were in an altogether different junior league. I was interested because I was about to interview Savimbi's approximate counterpart in Mozambique, General Afonso Dhlakama. Jamba was the Las Vegas of guerrilla HQs; next I would visit the seediest of bandit hideaways. Mozambique made even the Afghan camps look plush.

Mozambique's Black Pimpernel

The challenge was: 'Make a professional film about Renamo.' No one had ever done it before; few were crazy enough to try. Their reputation made the Khmer Rouge look almost polite. One or two journalists had managed to wriggle into Renamo-controlled areas, but no one had been deranged enough to attempt a long-range penetration with modern, heavy, professional video equipment. It was all Tim Lambon's idea. After our trip to Kabul, I knew he was the Rambo type. He had, however, a fatal flaw: he was prepared to work with me again.

The civil war in Mozambique was definitely not a media event. The (then) Marxist Frelimo (Front for the Liberation of Mozambique) government in the capital, Maputo, did not allow Western press much access to the fighting in the interior. (Much of the time the government didn't even know what was happening in the bush, except that it wasn't nice.) So the international media largely fed on government disinformation. Like all communist dictatorships, Frelimo was efficient in two areas – propaganda and the secret police. In contrast with both Savimbi and Frelimo, Renamo – the Mozambique National Resistance – had the worst PR of any guerrilla organisation. Even Pol Pot could have given them lessons in how to win friends and influence people. Part of the reason was the complexity of the story. Another was the almost total inaccessibility of the guerrillas. And also, to be frank, Renamo was in the massacre business.

Portugal's grip on its 400-year-old colony had always been tenuous outside the few coastal cities. The entire white population, concentrated largely in Beira and the colonial capital, Lourenço Marques, numbered only 27,000 in 1940, although subsidised waves of poor immigrants pushed the total to 200,000 by 1970. A handful settled in military-style kibbutzim in the rural areas, but most preferred the sheltered employment and racial privileges of the urban fleshpots. This sudden surge of white settlers made Mozambique the largest white 'tribe' in sub-Saharan Africa after South Africa, Angola and Rhodesia. The neo-fascist thugs who ran Lisbon were not the type to dabble with democratic experiments, especially in the colonies. Forced black labour continued until 1973. The secret police, animals officered by intellectuals, ran a tight ship. But Mozambique was one of the poorest colonies of the poorest state in Europe (after Albania), and survived largely by servicing its richer neighbours, Rhodesia and South Africa. Trade, transport fees, tourism and black miners working in South Africa made Mozambique tick . . . albeit with typically Iberian *mañana*.

In 1964 Frelimo began a guerrilla war against the Portuguese. Mozambique had a black population of about seven million, made up of nineteen tribes from nine major ethnic groups speaking about seventeen different languages. It was a war won mainly by default, although by 1975 Frelimo claimed 10,000 men under arms. Frelimo squabbled endlessly and murderously, encouraged by the colonial police's manipulation of tribal rancour.

The first guerrilla supremo was Eduardo Mondlane, who was the country's first PhD and also the first Mozambican recipient of a CIA donation ($10,000 in 1963). Frelimo argued over the correct roles of chiefs, churches, and socialism; unresolved disputes which resurfaced as causes of the post-independence civil war. In 1969 Mondlane was assassinated in his Dar es Salaam office by a letter bomb, probably planted by internal rivals but with a little help from the secret police. It was briefly and bizarrely mooted that his American wife, Janet, should take over as interim leader. A white American female guerrilla leader might have done wonders for Frelimo's image in the salons of the West, but little to induce conservative black peasants to join the cause. Instead, a diminutive former hospital orderly, Samora Machel, succeeded Mondlane.

As with France in Algeria, Portugal was not making a profit by holding on to its African possessions, especially when the insurgencies expanded. The colonies were an anachronism of Europe's oldest empire led by its oldest dictatorship. Something had to give. After many years and with very little bloodshed, the dictatorship and empire collapsed in the 1974 military coup in Portugal. Flowers and optimism filled the streets of Lisbon, but chaos and a brief counter-coup erupted in

Lourenço Marques. The feeble but bitter UDI lasted about as long as the generals' *putsch* in Algeria. The Portuguese army, helped by Frelimo, put down the white coup. A Portuguese exodus began. By June 1975 half the whites had fled; within a year only 10 per cent remained. The towns were full of scavenging stray dogs, abandoned pampered pets. White farmers killed their cattle rather than leave them. Mechanics sabotaged their machinery. Some blacks looted and raped. The few skilled whites who remained – either financial prisoners or committed socialists – were desperately needed. Few blacks had been trained to take over the reins at any level. Of the 350 train drivers, only one was black.

While few South Africans visited Angola, Mozambique was a popular holiday resort, with glorious beaches just an hour's drive from the Transvaal border. Gambling, cheap prawns, wine and sex, especially the multiracial variety banned in South Africa, attracted many whites, including the conservatives who needed to taste sin before they could adequately condemn it at home. The colony's LM radio was a youth cult for young white South Africans. LM played the Beatles, banned by the half-wit censors in the South African Broadcasting Corporation. But suddenly the 'Yeah, yeah, yeahs' were replaced by martial music, then African voices attacking neo-colonialism. Overnight the lucrative tourist trade evaporated. Over 30,000 prostitutes were suddenly out of work in the renamed capital, Maputo.

Mozambique was free from Portugal but not from war. The new president was sucked into the rebellion in next-door Rhodesia. Frelimo had cooperated closely with the guerrillas fighting Ian Smith, so the Rhodesian Central Intelligence Organisation, headed by genial Cornishman Ken Flower, started recruiting dissident Mozambicans to form an anti-Marxist army: Renamo. It became a Frankenstein's monster. In March 1976 Machel closed the border with Rhodesia. Direct Rhodesian army raids and Renamo sabotage were bringing Mozambique to its knees. When Mugabe was victorious in Rhodesia, Renamo shifted to Pretoria for its patronage and arms supplies. Mozambique entered the very heart of darkness.

Renamo was born in double original sin, the bastard offspring of Flower and apartheid, but it was not simply a puppet of white racists. Patriotism intruded. Much of the original political rhetoric was cooked up by Rhodesian intelligence officers and, by the style of it, late at night after too many whiskies. But initially Renamo attracted much genuine support among the peasantry: those who objected to attacks on the Catholic Church and the mosques, farmers hostile to Marxist land collectivisation, traditionalists who resented the downgrading of the chiefs, youngsters looking for adventure and food . . . During the carnage of the 1980s most of the *povo* – the masses – came to detest both sides in a war that killed tens of thousands and created more than three million refugees. The South African military backed Renamo for the same reasons it aided Savimbi. But the doves in Pretoria's foreign affairs department, led by Pik Botha, realised that destabilisation in the neighbouring states was destroying Pretoria's image abroad.

It had become apartheid's second front. And the violence was contagious. Guns were flooding back into the eastern Transvaal from Mozambique. In 1984 Botha doubted whether 'Renamo had the capacity to run anything more than a Mercedes and a few atrocities'. But to army hardliners the Renamo boss, Afonso Dhlakama, was an anti-Marxist who was beating the Russians at their own game. Renamo deployed classical guerrilla warfare to undermine Soviet satellites whose Eastern-bloc military advisers had been transformed into defenders of the status quo. The Red Army's revolutionary ardour had dimmed. And many in the CIA agreed. The Contras, the *mujahedin*, Unita and, maybe, Renamo were the vanguard freedom fighters in the war against what Reagan dubbed the 'Evil Empire'.

But Renamo's alleged passion for cutting off ears, noses and lips relegated Dhlakama to a horror chamber with a million-dollar price-tag on his head. The Black Pimpernel was hunted by over 60,000 Frelimo troops backed by Cuban advisers, East German intelligence officers, 2,000 Tanzanian soldiers and over 20,000 reasonably effective Zimbabwean troops, whose officers were trained by the British army.

Ex-British SAS men were sniffing around as well. Dhlakama was a difficult man to pin down for an appointment.

When Pretoria made half-hearted peace with Frelimo in 1984, some South Africans were keen to get rid of Dhlakama, although Renamo still had friends in military intelligence. Amid the ballyhoo of the Nkomati agreement, Pretoria said it would stop helping Renamo if Frelimo kicked out the ANC guerrillas. South Africa gave Frelimo £1 million in vehicles and radio equipment. Playing both sides against the centre was not the deal struck at Nkomati, however. Soon Machel realised that some Afrikaners were acting in bad faith. The resurgent

Renamo was, to quote a senior Frelimo official, 'unpicking the social fabric'. Frelimo held the cities but, throughout the country, Renamo owned the night.

Some Mozambicans were Frelimo by day and Renamo at night. Renamo held – or ran riot in – vast swathes of territory, while Frelimo reinforced the towns. And even the few major cities were more scrap-heaps than modern conurbations. Renamo, adopting classic Maoist tenets, hoped that once the rural areas were fully consolidated, the Frelimo-held cities would fall like ripe plums. The economic collapse and Frelimo's military performance were so dire that by 1986 Mozambique could hardly be called a state any more. This beautiful Eden became a fertile wasteland.

Over 60 per cent of the people lived in absolute poverty. Over 70 per cent of the gross national product came from aid. As one cynical aid worker put it: 'The People's Republic of Mozambique has become the Donors' Republic.'

The abiding images, for me, were lushness and fear. Two punch-drunk armies trampled the famished peasantry like bull elephants locked in mortal combat. So when Tim Lambon suggested a little trip to find Dhlakama's HQ in central Mozambique, I didn't expect much of a holiday.

With much effort Tim made contact with a Renamo man in Malawi. We would try to cross the border illegally from southern Malawi. It was fairly easy to hide in the swamps along the Shire River, but the main difficulty was getting a professional camera through Malawi's main airport. Hastings Banda, the paranoid geriatric who ran Malawi, didn't like journalists and wouldn't even let them holiday there, let alone work. With six months' notice he would occasionally make exceptions for the SATV and BBC. Everything in Malawi revolved around Ngwazi, the conqueror. Like General Pinochet in Chile, Ngwazi claimed to know where every leaf fell in his domain.

Malawi was conservative because Banda was ultra-conservative. Malawi was Banda squared: small, disciplined and notably intolerant. He ruled as a modern African monarch, dressed in a black homburg, three-piece suit and thick spectacles. Photographs of the highly eccentric autocrat were everywhere. Dr Hastings Kamuzu Banda, LRCP and LRCS (Edin.), LRFPS (Glasgow), Life President (Paramount Chief) of Malawi, Minister of External Affairs, Defence, Justice,

Agriculture, Works, Women and Children's Affairs, and Community Services, was a busy man for his ninety-plus years. He was also a puritanical bigot. The most respectable female visitors might have their mini-skirts or bell-bottomed trousers confiscated; males without a short back and sides could expect compulsory haircuts at the airport. When his people displeased him Banda would go into fits of terrible temper tantrums, shrieking that they should 'rot, rot, rot' in prison. And they did. Lucky ones were hunted down by the secret police and covertly murdered. Killers in Malawi's police specialised in staging car accidents; opponents would be 'accidentalised'.

Malawi was also a beautiful, green, mountainous land adorned by the thin, blue Lake Malawi. Banda was good at PR and there were no riots or wars, so Malawi was sold to white tourists as the 'warm heart of Africa'. His refusal to indulge in racial politics meant good business with South Africa and the encouragement of expat skills. Malawi initially prospered because it retained white expertise and, a rarity in Africa, an efficient and honest civil service, modelled on the British system. Provided you avoided politics, Malawi was a safe and pleasant little country; Banda kept out journalists in case they found out the really nasty political downside of his benevolent dictatorship.

Malawian customs officials were industrious and difficult to bribe. The only way to pass through the airport without physically going through customs was in a wheelchair, because the space between the customs desks was very narrow. So Tim would go to Malawi in a wheelchair, recovering from a bad accident (although not as bad as the one he might have if he were caught by the Malawians). The dismantled camera would be in a bag hanging on the back of the wheelchair. The trouble was, even in such an apparently disabled state, Tim's military bearing and haircut advertised that he was still capable of launching a successful one-man assault on the presidential palace. I suggested a wig and a cosmetic grey facial pallor. In the end we decided on a distraction: an attractive blonde with lots of silk underwear. It would have to work first time. Unlike other TV performances, boogieing through borders brooked no rehearsals.

At Jan Smuts international airport, Johannesburg, South African Airways staff rolled Tim on to the plane. In Malawi another SAA air hostess wheeled him safely past the customs hall while his blonde companion's collection of exotic underwear caused maximum embarrassment to the most puritanical customs men in Africa. She was ushered through, the video tapes under the knickers. Tim kept up his act and limped for a week, despite the discomfort of a thick plaster cast in the sweltering October heat and rains. After finally contacting the Renamo liaison man, he rang me in Johannesburg with orders to bring more tapes and a battery-charger.

I hollowed out some books and made them look terribly suspicious, especially the wires from the charger. An educational publishing conference was being held in Blantyre, Malawi's old capital. I flew there via Harare loaded with books and video equipment, plus some camping gear 'for a walking tour'.

Heading into customs, I met a Zimbabwean publisher I knew. 'You are loaded down; going to the conference, are you?'

'Of course.' He knew I wasn't, but he didn't let on. Ex-Rhodie white solidarity and all that.

One has to tell lots of porkies in the line of duty, but I always hated this part of the job. Digging at truths attracted me to journalism; paradoxically, my stock in trade was dissimulation. I even became good at it. Putting piety aside, I managed to persuade customs that my funny mix of dismembered books, tapes, electronic equipment, and camping gear all made sense on a walking tour. My small Pentax camera fitted the story, as did my luminous orange rucksack.

Tim met me in a bar in Blantyre and took me straight to a Renamo safe house. He took off his cast and we set to work on the wheelchair, cannibalising parts to make frames for our rucksacks and using the foam to stop shoulder straps chafing. We spray-painted the orange rucksacks olive green. Tim converted one of the crutches into a monopod for the camera, which also had its own green carry-pack. Besides the video camera gear, two still cameras and a medical kit, we each carried one change of clothes, a sleeping bag made out of light parachute material and some emergency rations. We also adapted one rucksack to carry a solar panel to make electricity for charging camera batteries.

We worked through the night, finally leaving at 3 a.m. with two missionaries. Carrying Bibles for passports we were waved through three roadblocks of disciplined (and sober) Malawian troops. On the edge of the Shire River we contacted the local headman, who helped us negotiate a lift in a very crude dug-out canoe. We paddled and poled our way across the river and through swamps for an hour and a half. Halfway across we realised we had forgotten our monopod, but it was too late to go back. Wobbling against fast currents, with hippos grunting alongside, pushing through croc-infested swamps, we fretted over our four heavy packs and the sensitive, expensive and uninsured equipment.

The canoe dropped us on a small island. This was Mozambique. The fisherman pointed to a mountain for our bearings and left. We kitted up with rucksacks on our backs and fronts. Tim, much the stronger, also carried the camera. We trudged forward, sometimes waist-deep, through the swamps. I admired a kingfisher darting down to seize a fish. Lily-trotters hopped dementedly. We reached drier land, where soldier ants started biting like small piranhas.

We found a track and headed due south towards the mountain, about twenty miles away. I was never a great walker and after an hour or so my shoulders and back began to ache with the load. But it was not like climbing an Afghan mountain on all fours, and I was at home in the familiar smells and sounds of the African bush. I felt good about the trip.

The ever-resourceful Tim, who had spent nearly two years sneaking around Mozambique during the Rhodesian war, was unusually negative. He had domestic troubles at home in London. This trip taught me that mind over matter was not just a myth. My head was in the right place so I kept my spirits high, despite my physical weaknesses. Tim was physically a very hard man but his mind was elsewhere. For once in our many adventures I was psychologically the motivator. I carried the mental load, even while he was piled up like a pack donkey.

We passed small mud-hut villages. A woman, with one breast like a dried pea and the other dangling down to her waist, stopped and stared in utter disbelief. The villagers didn't wave, nor were they hostile. They were just stunned. Perhaps the younger ones hadn't seen whites before – certainly possible in this utterly remote area.

I started thinking about David Livingstone, grateful that we had a modern first-aid kit and, above all, anti-malaria tablets to protect us against the constantly aggressive mosquitoes. Soon we could not place a finger on an unbitten, unswollen piece of flesh.

Tim, an experienced army medic, reminded me not to scratch, despite the constant itching. 'It can go septic in hours in this place,' he warned.

Three unarmed men stood waiting for us on the edge of some bush; our contact man in Malawi had got a message across the border before us. We greeted them with a traditional African handshake and Tim went into the accepted series of Shona formal exchanges. This wasn't exactly Shona-speaking country but we were understood to be friendly. We didn't say we were looking for the Renamo warlord; we did not mention Renamo at all. After the greeting we did not speak. They were there to guide us.

They certainly weren't porters, dancing along unladen, while I started to stagger. They didn't offer to help, unlike Unita soldiers, who were wonderful about carrying equipment for journalists.

Tim knew me of old; he didn't have to read my thoughts. 'Don't ask them to help with the kit. They are testing us. And we are being watched from the bush. Ignore them and try to march properly, you old Welsh bastard. If you fall over now, I'll kick your arse.'

I pointed to the far distance. 'Race you to that tree?'

He smiled. That set a pattern. No matter what shit came down on our heads, it was my job to make Tim laugh. It's funny how on dangerous trips your subconscious pops up with psychological maps to guide you.

A strange apparition wheeled an old black Rudge bicycle from behind a tree, reminding me simultaneously of *Easy Rider* and *Macbeth*. I had expected a Khmer Rouge-style ruffian bandoleered up to the eyeballs, not a genial-looking bespectacled figure in blue jeans (tucked into his socks) wearing a clean checked shirt and a purple mohair tea-cosy as a hat. He was carrying a symbol of Renamo rank, a transistor radio in a gaudy bag made of curtain material. Unlike the smartly dressed officers in Savimbi's 'Free Angola', he didn't want to stamp our passports. Our three silent guides drifted off.

We talked to the unarmed tea-cosy with great politeness in a mix of broken Shona and Portuguese to establish our *bona fides*, although we were circumspect. Blacks thought whites in Africa were always in a hurry; Tim knew from long experience that taking time with the greeting rituals was vital. Everything mattered, from the handshake to the eye contact to the sitting position. The Renamo man avoided eye contact initially as a form of deference. He was not being shifty. If I had offered him a gift (which I didn't), he would have accepted it with both hands upturned, as in supplication.

It was established that he would take us to a nearby Renamo forward base. He loaded two of the rucksacks on his bike and walked ahead of us. Suddenly two ragged, barefoot teenage sentries materialised out of the bush alongside us. One carried a PPSH tommy gun and the other a 5.56mm commercial hunting rifle. At the sight of each new weapon Tim, a walking encyclopaedia of armaments, would launch into a detailed history of its make and history. More usefully, he was just as adept at using them. Two more ragged soldiers joined us carrying folding-butt AKMs.

Tea-cosy indicated that we should stop. The seven of us sat in a circle and smiled at each other. The four soldiers dared not speak in front of Tea-cosy, who seemed reluctant or incapable of answering our questions. Two cowboys in denim jackets arrived on 100cc trail bikes. The sentries carried our kit as we were whisked off on the back of the bikes to be shown off on a circuitous roar around the camp. The Renamo base was an exact replica of the type Mugabe's guerrillas had built in the hundreds in Mozambique during the Rhodesian war. We dismounted and went through the greeting ritual with a Commander Zimba.

Not much more than twelve hours after I disembarked from the plane, we were in a Renamo base; arrogantly, I thought I had done more in twelve hours than most London commuters would do in twelve years. Tim had organised well and everything was going to plan. We had been lucky. So far.

In Afghanistan we had been hostages to the whims of the unpredictable *mujahedin*. Both Tim and I felt at ease in Africa, the old Africa, where the white man was treated as boss, or at least with respect. We knew something of the languages and cultures. We thought we knew how to treat Africans.

I also had a niggling suspicion that this confidence might be misplaced: we were in the middle of one of the biggest wars in the world, with tens of thousands of casualties every year. And the polite and friendly African troops around us spent a lot of their time cutting people up.

Commander Zimba produced a large hunting knife and gave it to one of his sidekicks. Zimba led us in prayer, then we were fed with chicken and *sadza* (ground corn). We ate this for three weeks, three times a day. I grew sick of the scrawny chickens but fortunately I had already developed a taste for *sadza*, although Tim and I took vitamin supplements to keep our strength up. Sometimes we were given rice and occasionally captured Frelimo tinned food, usually Russian fish or Australian cheese.

Our first meal was accompanied by raucous Shona music from a transistor radio. Night was falling. The guerrillas were mainly in T-shirts but we put on all our clothes and waterproof ponchos with the hoods up, despite the overpowering and sticky heat, to guard against mosquitoes. It was an eerie gathering in the light of home-made candles. We popped purifying tablets into the water and gratefully drank two bottles of Fanta orange smuggled over the border.

Zimba described his heroic experiences which Never, his translator, relayed in adequate English. Never was patently pleased to be sitting at the officers' table. Tim entertained the troops with his Polaroid camera – I used my torch to show the pictures materialising from the black. Our hosts oohed and aahed at the magic. Everyone wanted a pic, laughing long and heartily at the poses, especially Never scratching himself under both armpits like a monkey.

I pulled out my Portuguese phrasebook, as most Renamo officers could understand something of the still official language of the country. Tim thought I had gone around the bend as I persisted in reading out lines such as: 'Would anyone care to partner me in a waltz?' I fell about laughing and the guerrillas appeared mildly amused, albeit also confused, by my antics. I was already bush-crazy and thoroughly enjoying it.

We retired to our mud-walled thatched hut to sleep. We were in swampland and the air was clouded with malarial mosquitoes. Tim constructed an elaborate cage of bamboo and gauze to cover his upper body. I took the lazy sauna route and pulled my plastic poncho over my head with a small airhole. I was soaked in sweat. Music blared outside the hut and the locals kept popping their heads around the door to examine the new monkeys in the zoo. I fell instantly asleep.

We awoke with the dawn, eager to continue our journey. Zimba had promised to take us to the main camp on the back of the bikes. The guerrillas had been given a week's notice of our arrival, but thought about petrol only at the last minute.

'Why didn't they plan to get petrol before?' I asked Tim.

'Stop thinking like a white man,' he replied. 'This is army life – hurry up and wait.'

We tried to film their radio hut containing a hand-cranked generator for communications, probably an old Mortley-Sprague, according to Tim. But the guerrillas were understandably hostile to our snooping around the communications equipment.

We eventually left the base in mid-afternoon on two small Hondas and a Yamaha. With so much gear on our backs and chests it was an uncomfortable back-seat ride, but I would do anything to avoid walking.

The *vleis* were full of yellow flowers, just like the Burmah Valley in Zimbabwe. We passed deserted Portuguese trading posts, and I wondered why the locals didn't live in them and repair the roofs. Was this forbidden by the guerrillas for security reasons, or was it some kind of superstition? There were no white survivors in the whole hinterland of Zambézia province.

The Renamo HQ in Zambézia was thirty-five miles from the Shire outpost. We went across country on rough tracks, sometimes crossing streams with crude bamboo bridges and ditches traversed on single railway sleepers. With so much weight on our backs the constant jolts made Tim and me wince with pain after a few hours. For a while we drove along roads, once intended for four-wheel drives but turned into narrow tunnels in the undergrowth by encroaching nature. We had to duck constantly to avoid low branches.

The HQ, well hidden among mountains and forest, held about 500 rag-tag troops and perhaps two or three thousand camp followers (as well as a much bigger army of rats). The camp was made of wood, mud and thatch, with bits of looted furniture indecorously adorning the primitive style. After Jamba, this was very crude. Fortunately it had one generator providing occasional electricity, as our solar panel experiment was not working properly and we needed to charge the batteries.

We were taken immediately to meet the camp boss, Commander General Calistu Matade Meque, whose mad bloodshot eyes made it clear that we were at the mercy of a dangerous eccentric. He was continuously waltzing on the edge of schizophrenia, or worse. Our translator, Roberto, had worked in Rhodesia and, when sober, did a good job of interpreting the general's rapid staccato speech. We had decided to use translators where available or speak Portuguese, keeping Tim's command of Shona in reserve.

Meque invited us into his mess, a tiny European wooden

construction. It was like a surreal re-creation of what the locals thought the Portuguese would inhabit; a dark, dank, frilly doll's house. Curtains were draped all around the room, except for the weird triangular windows, which actually had glass in them. The tablecloth boasted napkins which no one except Meque and whites dared use.

The general offered us each a brown Malawian beer. Tim was a teetotal, non-smoking fitness fanatic, so it always fell to me to drink the booze. Imported beer was OK but rare; some of the camp moonshine was tough going. Meque knocked over the second bottle, but everybody pretended not to notice. I think he was too drunk to notice himself.

After an hour's pleasantries we came to the point. Would Meque please provide us with a guide and, if possible, bikes to take us to central Mozambique to visit the President at his Gorongosa 'capital'?

The general went into a long explanation about the President's absence in the Beira area. In a radio communication with the Shire base the President had agreed to meet us within the week at or near Gorongosa, about 150 miles south. But Meque was not keen on us carrying on to central Mozambique, wanting us to film his planned attacks in the north. We were happy to video some bang-bang, even with these crazies, but both Tim and I felt that finding the President and filming him for the first time was the essential core of our trip. If we managed any action en route, fine. Tim had pressing reasons to return to London within a month. Once we started wandering around the country we could be delayed for ages. Guerrilla promises of attacks were always to be treated with caution. The longer we stayed, the greater the risk of being wounded, falling sick, or, worse, being captured by the opposing forces. We reckoned Frelimo had to be monitoring Renamo's signals, and two Western journalists visiting Mozambique's most wanted man would be a very tempting target.

It was clear that the general was an egomaniac who wanted us to film his great victories. We had become his hostages as much as his guests, and would have to be very careful if we were to be able to proceed into the interior. Initially, his whimsically autocratic manners were reminiscent of Shaka Zulu's not-so-gentle court. When he was half sober and in a good mood he would allow long discussions about Renamo's struggle. He complained about the harassment of religion and traditional chiefs and the forced communisation of land, and talked wistfully of free elections and the end of Marxist tyranny. This was partly Shona territory, so the old ways, spirit mediums, the need for polygamy and *lobola* (bride price) were also discussed.

Meque was first and foremost a soldier, not a politician. He might also have been a homicidal maniac. Our meals were always strained affairs, especially if he became drunk.

After one difficult dinner, as we stood outside his mess hut, the general (shaking somewhat with intoxication) drew his revolver, looked me in the eyes, aimed at me, and fired at a range of about six feet.

I didn't throw myself to the ground because I saw him move his hand slightly to the right. It was a bloody good shot. He took the head off a puff-adder in a branch hanging close to me.

The general enjoyed his little joke, having made it clear that our lives were in his hands. It was the only time he smiled.

We lived in a small wooden hut furnished with two old beds. It was on much higher ground, making 'mozzies' less of a problem, but both the hut and camp were plagued with rats. It was difficult keeping them out of our survival rations, and we could do little about their scampering over and around us as we tried to sleep. The generator flickered on occasionally, so we could sometimes read at night and charge the batteries.

Meque, who always put a very polite veneer on his dictatorial ways, allowed us to use his toilet and crude shower facilities. Unfortunately they were close together, and I managed to drop the general's treasured bar of soap down the black hole. Wisely, Tim suggested I replace it with my only bar.

We were woken by sirens in the middle of the night. Tim was always anxious about an air strike, partly because he had been in Maputo a few weeks before and had noticed numerous Soviet gunships lined up at the airport. We slept in our clothes with our kit handy for a quick exit. We shot out of the hut ready to scramble into the surrounding bush, but the guerrillas were calmly sitting around a camp-fire. It was a 'training exercise'.

We went back to our rats. And creepy crawlies: I didn't realise it was possible to have so much natural history in just one bed. We couldn't sleep so we listened to the sanest thing in Africa – the BBC World Service – on Tim's small radio.

*

The insurgents were clearly under formal discipline, and not the disorganised 'bandits' painted by Frelimo. The worst infringement of discipline was to intimidate the *povo*, the peasantry. The Renamo code was similar to that of Mugabe's Zimbabwean guerrillas, which was breached as much as it was observed. Male soldiers were not supposed to fraternise with the numerous female cadres in the camp. Both sexes volunteered, or were shanghaied, for the duration of the war. Morale appeared high, but the camp's inmates were all understandably terrified of Meque. Military standards were low. Ordinary soldiers wore rags; officers dressed in a bizarre array of Rhodesian, East German, Tanzanian, Zimbabwean, Portuguese and Frelimo camouflage. Weapons were in a terrible condition. They were never cleaned, except with soap and water! There was sometimes Malawian or home-made beer for the officers, but no oil for weapons. They could have used petrol or some of the lamp paraffin. A minority of the officers kept their AKs in good condition.

Renamo officers were second-generation guerrillas. Frelimo had absorbed perhaps 30 per cent of the expertise of their Eastern bloc or Chinese instructors during the 1960s. In turn Renamo soldiers, many of whose officers were ex-Frelimo, adopted a percentage of that original training, beefed up by Rhodesian and South African advisers. During the whole journey of hundreds of miles we did not see any direct evidence of South African involvement, however, except the radio network, apparently donated before the 1984 Nkomati agreement.

Meque decided to put on a weapons and training exhibition for us. Like many African guerrillas they tended to shoot up in the air with their eyes closed. It was all automatic fire: nobody seemed to have heard of a target and firing on single rounds. Then the general rolled out a galaxy of ill-assorted hardware, ranging from old German Mausers to Russian AGS-17 grenade-launchers which, according to Tim, were very rare in Africa. They also had Russian SAM-7 surface-to-air missiles which Meque modestly said he didn't know how to operate. Tim did, and was itching to have a go. But we thought better of it and politely refused Meque's kind offer. The Frelimo air force (when it managed to fly) and Zimbabwean gunships were a major problem for the rebels, who had no effective defence against air attacks.

Otherwise, Meque boasted, 'Zimbabwean troops run away just like Frelimo when we attack them. They always call for air support.'

Renamo claimed that it captured all its weapons; Frelimo said the rebels' arsenal was largely comprised of Russian weapons seized in Angola and donated by South Africa.

We filmed a flag-raising ceremony, but whenever we started to film something interesting the camera would pack up, the tape run out, or the battery go flat. On the roller-coaster ride in, part of the lens had been damaged. Tim had great difficulty focusing properly. Then Meque announced a football match. Armchairs were pulled out for us on the edge of a dusty field. The general sat in the centre wearing Ray-Bans and listening to a ghetto-blaster at full volume. The shooting on the football pitch was as bad as their weapons-handling.

We had been in the camp three days and were heartily sick of this pirates' den. We kept nagging the general to let us proceed with our mission, but got nowhere until Meque mentioned his stomach ailment. Tim listened carefully and made a concoction from our medical kit. After a few hours the general was mightily pleased with his miracle cure, and proceeded to thank us with a two-day drinking spree. Looted beer had just arrived. The officers went through that in a day and then turned to palm wine. They had also found, traded or pillaged some fresh batteries for what Tim called 'wog-boxes': ghetto-blasters which boomed around the camp. The party got into full swing, enlivened by the occasional playful burst of rifle fire.

I felt it my duty to join in the fun, but the abstemious Tim was becoming more and more irritated and stayed in the hut while I danced and drank with the guerrillas. Meque kept asking where Tim was, so I felt obliged to drag him out. There were rumblings of bad vibes: some officers might have thought Tim a racist. I explained that 'Tim's religion won't let him drink' but he could hardly refuse to dance. He did so, but he was not a happy man. Tim had led African soldiers and lived with them at close hand, but his Rhodesian upbringing made him wary of partying with African women. I encouraged him by pointing out how attractive some of the women were, especially one who could have strutted on a Paris catwalk.

Tim was always frank and, to me, he could be racist. 'You've been in the bush too long, Paul. You know what they say, "In the bush absence makes the blacks grow blonder."'

I looked again at the guerrilla-model.

'Don't even think about it, boyo. They'll cut your balls off,' said Tim.

Instead I did something crazier. There was always great anger and violence burning inside Tim that sometimes he only just managed to suppress. Despite my often exasperating habits it had never been turned on me; Tim seemed to have almost endless patience for my manifold inadequacies in the field. Now he was reaching the end of his limited racial tolerance. I had to get him out of what he called a 'chamber of horrors party' without insulting Meque, who was fired up on brandy.

I asked the general to stop the music because I wanted to say something. Clearly annoyed, Meque stood up – all the seventy or eighty followers jumped up like Muppets – and clicked his fingers for silence.

With alarm on his face, Tim muttered: 'Whatever you've got in mind, this had better be good, or we're in real shit street. The general's totally out of his skull.'

I cleared my throat. The group of officers and their ladies sat down in the dust. Meque's eyes were rolling around the back of his head; only the red-inflamed whites were visible. Roberto had long passed the stage where he could understand his native tongue, let alone translate anything. All the senior officers had their mouths and eyes gaping wide; no one had dared to stop one of the general's parties before.

I groped for phrases in Portuguese and sought words in Shona from Tim. This was clearly an emergency. 'We are very honoured by the general's great feast. I wish to thank him by showing our gratitude in my own language and culture. As we have no proper gifts worthy of the general, I would like to sing a song praising him.'

Tim looked at the ground, hoping it would swallow him up. The guerrilla band sat mute and immobile, like a row of extremely well-armed tailor's dummies. This would be a tough audience. Perhaps some of my words were understood through the drunken haze.

I started with a spirited version of 'Sospan Fach', then led into 'Swing Low, Sweet Chariot' with lots of rugby club actions, and finished with the Welsh national anthem sung at the top of my voice. I think I was in good form that day, and the canopy of trees and huts made my voice bounce around a little.

When I had completed my party piece I was met with utter silence.

My audience was confused, bemused and perhaps amused, but it had defused the tension with Tim, who slunk away. No one would show any response until Meque reacted.

Concerned, I saw him reach for his gun.

This was not good.

The general let off a few rounds in the air, which seemed to indicate approval, for the odd clap and cheer emanated from the dummies. The ghetto-blasters were turned back on and the cultural standards were once more elevated to the camp norm. I staggered off to the hut. That night my guts were ripped apart by the palm wine.

I awoke with the worst hangover of my life. Chickens stamped into our hut like storm-troopers, or that's what my delicate ears told me. I had still not opened my eyes. I did so carefully and slightly moved my eyeballs. I resolved never to move them again and clamped my eyes shut. Smugly teetotal Tim had little sympathy with my self-indulgence. We were left alone while the officers nursed their hangovers too.

The heavens opened and, once I had recovered sufficiently, Tim and I played mindless games of battleships on bits of paper. When the rains stopped he went out to forage for bananas. I watched two giant chameleons mate. Utterly bored and feeling dreadful, I lolled in the damp heat gazing at massive snails sliming their way across the floor, too tired to chase away the chickens which regarded our hut as their roost.

Meque relented the next day and said we could leave that afternoon. We spent the morning filming the clinic, a mud hut which dispensed only aspirin. The chief motorbike mechanic doubled as the doctor. In the nearby school the teenage teacher had one book, a Frelimo textbook, with the pages containing Marxist propaganda torn out. The children sang beautifully.

Tim thought we had a fifty-fifty chance of getting to Gorongosa and back to Johannesburg with our lives and film intact. I wasn't so pessimistic, but knew we could be picked up by Frelimo and jailed as apartheid mercenaries for our military and South African connections. Jail in Maputo would be very bad news indeed. I recorded a short to-camera piece explaining my British background and our serious endeavour as disinterested journalists. I wrote a brief note to my father in Wales. I already had a will taking care of my German Shepherd; my Australian girlfriend had just left for the UK. I had no responsibilities, which made it easier. I felt more lightheaded than alone. Tim, though, fretted and wrote a long letter to his wife. We packed these letters with our used tapes and still film, wrote a covering note to the British High Commissioner in Malawi, and asked Meque to send these to Blantyre if we didn't return within a set time.

We were ready.

Of course the guerrillas were not.

If they had only spent less time drinking . . . Eventually three men were designated to accompany us on two decrepit Honda 50ccs and another, better, 100cc bike. Hardly suitable for bundu-bashing across very rough country with five men and lots of kit, plus weapons. But that's all Renamo had scrounged from South Africa or stolen from Frelimo. They treated them roughly so they were always breaking down. Alberto, the doctor-mechanic, was a genius with all things technical. He also looked like a good soldier. Pedro was a pleasant duffer. Zacharias was certifiable and arrogant. After a series of mishaps, punctures, major repairs and false starts, plus two farewell drunken bouts from the general, we left the next morning.

We were making for the great Zambezi River about 120 miles south, travelling through virgin and primitive forest. It was hard, however, to enjoy the scenery. Either the going was rough and we had to carry the bikes and kit, or on barely discernible tracks the three rebels drove with great speed and little skill. Alberto was OK; Zacharias kept forgetting he had no brakes; Pedro was obviously a frustrated speedway driver. Tim was on the best bike with the safest driver because he carried the camera. I took the spills with the other two.

Often when we stopped – or crashed – villagers would come to greet us, sometimes bringing *sadza* and water. We passed a religious college; people waved Bibles at us. They did not seem starved, although the peasants were dressed in rags or bits of sacks and occasionally bark. Long columns of porters passed heading north, carrying bags of ground corn on their heads for sale or barter in Malawi. I didn't feel this was any PR fix. We stopped where we (or the bikes) wanted. The peasants did not appear cowed. In that raw, primitive, regressive society there appeared, on the surface, to be few local problems with hearts and minds.

We hopped from base to base in what Renamo called liberated zones, passing abandoned Portuguese stores, farms and once-pretty little colonial towns painted in light pastel shades, faded now, but their gardens ran riot with the colour of flame trees and poinsettia.

Everything was deserted.

Locusts had picked one large area clean.

A beautiful, isolated, desecrated cathedral arched towards the heavens, as if crying for help. Blasphemous graffiti despoiled its walls.

On a desiccated tarmac road, a bright red tractor stood forlorn and gutted.

A train was strewn across an embankment, its carriages overgrown by fast-devouring bush.

Once this part of Mozambique had teemed with wildlife. We saw just four deer, a few monkeys and some tree snakes during the entire journey.

Tim fell sick after two days of non-stop travel. At one small camp where we stopped to scrounge petrol, I called a halt. Tim had lots of old war wounds, his back was in agony and he would have to lie down for at least eight hours. He even accepted some brandy from my hip flask. I foraged for food and managed to make some soup. It was a change for me to look after him.

We camped in an abandoned Portuguese store which had a little wooden structure outside, a real long-drop with a seat. What luxury, especially as I was still suffering from the palm wine. Just as I sat down a great big hairy thing lashed at my naked posterior. Fearing Africa's biggest spider, I flew out through the door. It was just a large bat.

Tim had bad news. 'I've been listening to their conversation and something's wrong. I'm not sure what – I get the impression that Alberto has been ordered not to take us to Dhlakama. Meque is up to something. We might have to disarm them and make our own way south.'

'What do you mean, "disarm them"?'

'Take their guns.'

'And what if they resist?'

'Then we'll have to shoot them.'

I went into some detail about the bad PR, lack of guides, and the simple fact that I had no experience in taking on some of the world's fiercest guerrillas.

'Alberto's the one to watch. He's one tough son of a bitch. The other two are berks. And anyway, they might shoot us, if the general ordered them to.'

'It doesn't make sense, Tim. Renamo want us to make a film about them. Dhlakama knows he needs the publicity.'

'You keep saying they know bugger-all about PR.' Tim thought for a while and added: 'I think the general is his own man. He may not be as mad as he makes out. He has his own agenda. Act in your normal amiable-buffoon way and I'll try to get to the bottom of what's going on. They haven't cottoned on to the fact that I can handle their lingo.'

I had become fond of Alberto, admiring his expertise and stoic endurance. I didn't fancy shooting him. Besides, I had just watched him making a clutch plate out of tin cans. Without him, I might have to walk.

'What you could do, Paul, is flatter Alberto and ask to see his AK. Tell him what great condition he keeps it in. And I'll sort out the other two, if I have to. I'll give you the word if I think the crunch is coming. You remember how to use an AK?'

I mumbled a reluctant yes.

Tim gave me one of his long looks. 'If you're in trouble, don't panic and don't leave the safety catch on.'

This gung-ho stuff just wasn't me at all. I had trusted Tim with my life on a number of occasions and would do so willingly again, but I wondered how sick he was. He definitely had a fever.

I did ask Alberto if I could see his gun and he gave it to me proudly and trustingly. I felt awful. But I had to see if I could do it. The crunch never came. We got the impression that Alberto later confided in the President, and some action was taken against the wayward general.

Tim got better. And the gun thing seemed nonsense, because in the inevitable unloading, bike-carrying and crashes, the AKs were often piled on us anyway. It was against all journalism ethics to be armed and technically we deserved to be shot as combatants, but it was impossible to play by the rules when you had five people on three bikes in the middle of one massive madhouse.

The bike I usually rode had no mudguard. It was raining hard, and we churned through mud in a long, hellish descent to the Zambezi. Then the sun came out. I reached the river happy but covered in stiff, dried mud.

A half-finished bridge stood guard on either side of the river. A large substation for the Cabora Bassa hydro-electric scheme – one of southern Africa's biggest disasters – mourned its own crippled and useless state. Bits of transformers decorated the roofs of the villagers' huts, although hardly any of Mozambique had regular electricity.

Petrol was king – for the Renamo élite's motorbikes and for boats to cross the wide surging river. Everything was cannibalised to keep the few machines and motors running.

'This is something out of *Mad Max*,' noted Tim.

A Russian Antonov reconnaissance plane droned overhead as an unpleasant reminder that some things still worked properly. On the other side of the fast-running river, crossed in a captured Frelimo inflatable, bikes and all, were millions of pounds worth of heavy plant. Massive cranes bent, as if in pain, marooned like dead Martian machines from H. G. Wells's *The War of the Worlds*.

Not far from the southern bank lay Caia, a largish small town in Sofala province recently captured from Frelimo. It had a big, empty airstrip. Caia was absolutely deserted, as though vultures had picked clean its carcass. A child's tin rocking horse and a 1930s typewriter were the only artefacts left behind after the flight or pillage. It was as if a neutron bomb had been dropped. Indeed, all I had seen of Mozambique seemed to irradiate a dread, post-apocalypse feeling. Renamo troops were camped *outside* the town. Was this a Khmer Rouge addiction to the ideological purity of the countryside or prudent fear of Zimbabwean gunships?

We were shown hundreds of Frelimo prisoners, whom Renamo said would be freed after a time. Those who wanted to enlist could. None would be kept against their wishes. That seemed dubious, as did the Renamo officers' explanation that Caia had been ravaged by retreating Frelimo troops, not advancing Renamo. The prisoners were lined up and we filmed them: it seemed a mere propaganda opportunity, especially as Renamo were reluctant to let us talk to the prisoners.

No one speaks English, we were told.

We slipped away from the Renamo officers and managed to snatch brief conversations with the POWs. One had worked in Bulawayo for twenty years and spoke excellent English. He confirmed the bullshit about not being kept against their wishes. They were not beaten, but food was very scarce. Our conversation was disrupted by a sudden charge to a nearby river, where a hippo had been caught. They were all desperate for meat.

In broad daylight, for the first time the bikes raced along good tarmac roads. Pedro was in his element, going flat out with no brakes. He pretended to misunderstand my instructions to slow down. We reached the edge of the Gorongosa forest and camped at a satellite of the main HQ. The Gorongosa 'capital' was, I realised later, something of a movable feast if not sometimes a mirage. Zimbabwean paratroopers had destroyed big bases in the area on a number of occasions. But Renamo clung to the Gorongosa vicinity for political and strategic reasons. It was a convenient place to disrupt Zimbabwe's vital Beira corridor, the road, rail, and (Lonrho-owned) oil pipeline link with Beira harbour.

A smartly dressed aide told us that the President would see us that night. Was Afonso Dhlakama a nationalist committed to an African variant of social democracy, as Renamo propagandists implied, or the most vicious mass murderer since Hitler, as Frelimo insisted? Was he a super-patriot or a crude puppet of Pretoria?

We were led into a small clearing with one freshly made thatched hut. Two young bodyguards patrolled nearby. Dhlakama sat quietly and alone in the hut, an unprepossessing, chubby young man dressed simply in a blue shirt and dark slacks. No Savimbi-like posturing with fancy six-guns. With his glasses on he looked for all the world like a timid bank clerk, but no doubt Genghis Khan had his good days.

He was thirty-three, he told us, and looked like a younger version of his arch enemy, Mugabe. Dhlakama, too, was Catholic trained. He said he was a family man with two children. He was confident, quietly spoken, and relaxed. Obviously intelligent, he spoke a very precise Portuguese, although he understood English. Unlike most politicians and generals he was prepared to listen. He discussed international affairs, and asked why everybody rated his movement as the most cut-throat of the international mafia of insurgencies. He offered us a Coke, the most common capitalist symbol in Africa (although not in Mozambique), and a suitable counterpoint to the Russian AKs that surrounded us.

Dhlakama had not had much to do with journalists. That was obvious because he was (apparently) open and trusting. We were invited to dinner, where we politely devoured fresh bread rolls, Australian cheddar, and, what luxury, some Nescafé. The other guest was Vincent Ululu, the President's amanuensis, who was an excellent linguist and something of an expert on Charles Dickens. After the meal he showed due deference in the imperial court by asking permission to smoke. As Ululu lit up, a boomslang slithered across the tree above his head.

Dhlakama gave his first-ever TV interview next morning, mainly speaking Portuguese. We needed some sound-bites in English, and Ululu helped the President with his pronunciation. Dhlakama was a bit hesitant so we suggested cue cards – not telling him what to say, but advising on technical delivery.

Tim then referred to an 'idiot board', a common term for a large cue behind the camera.

The warlord showed some displeasure at this phrase. It was a bit like mentioning a favourite Jewish grandmother to the Führer, I suppose. I explained hastily to Ululu, who luckily saw the funny side and translated the correct nuance in Portuguese.

After the interview, we talked for two whole days. Dhlakama was open but not stupid, and predictably denied that he relied on South Africa. He emphasised in almost Maoist terms his self-sufficiency.

'We have no complex theory. Our strategy is simple, and based upon the support of the people.'

He claimed to control 85 per cent of the country, denying any part in the grand scheme to destabilise southern Africa. He had no contact with Savimbi, he said, and proceeded to attack Unita's overtures to Frelimo following Savimbi's condolences on the recent death in a plane crash of Samora Machel, the Frelimo President. On the way to Malawi, on my stopover in Harare, I had witnessed the riots and protests against South Africa, which was blamed for Machel's death. The presidential plane came down just inside the apartheid republic.

I told Dhlakama that South Africa's deputy foreign minister, Louis Nel (who had met Dhlakama several times), also sent a letter of condolence to Machel's widow.

'That was kind of him,' said Dhlakama.

I couldn't stop now. 'Ah, but, Mr President, the letter arrived a week before the crash.'

Dhlakama didn't laugh.

Tim was always telling me off for trying to tell jokes and stories in languages I could hardly speak. They always went off half-cocked but I couldn't help myself. Most of the conversation was serious. How could it not be in the midst of so much death?

In breaks between the long dialogues, Tim and I sought light relief by using a paraffin lamp to project shadow figures with our hands against the white walls of our tent.

I enjoyed talking to one of the world's most dangerous and secluded men. I'd like to think that he also enjoyed talking to me about international affairs, despite my limited Portuguese. He was so eager to learn about the outside world. The West, particularly America, he said, had no idea of what was really happening in Mozambique.

The people of Mozambique are now independent, but they are not free. Everything is done by force. People are taken by force to live in communal villages; children are sent to Cuba without their parents' consent. We believe independence has nothing to do with this sort of thing. The ideals which drove us to take up arms against Portuguese rule haven't yet been fulfilled.

Dhlakama launched into a tirade against the US State Department, 'who have been doing a good job of promoting the cause of Marxist Frelimo'. He also accused Pretoria of betraying him. As he had spent ten years being hunted by thousands of troops, I couldn't really blame him for being a touch paranoid.

He insisted:

Renamo is winning. We are not the desperadoes, it's Frelimo that's desperate . . . All the aid money is being used to buy weapons to keep them in power, not given to those who are dying of hunger . . . They spend their days watching the ports along the coast, hiding and waiting in Maputo for the arrival of a boat from the USA bringing food and everything else that's necessary for the survival of Frelimo which is surrounded in the city of Maputo. In fact, Frelimo survives only in the big cities.

I asked why, if he was doing so well on the ground, did he have such an atrocious external image.

'The Marxists have traditionally been brilliant at propaganda,' he conceded.

'You could do better at PR and propaganda,' I said, 'by releasing the Western hostages you are holding.'

Renamo held three: a Brit, a German and a Portuguese. Because Dhlakama had an obsessive interest in Britain and a much-inflated view of the UK's influence in Africa, I spent hours explaining how the release of the Briton, especially just before Christmas, would help his cause. It might even help procure a visa for his much-cherished plan to visit London. Dhlakama subsequently released all three but nobody thanked me, not even the British Foreign Office. Sir Robin Day later interviewed me for the BBC and asked how I did it, so it wasn't a secret. And the freed Brit could at least have sent me a Christmas card.

We parted on good terms.

Dhlakama said: 'You were the first TV journalists to come all this way. You will be the first to be given a TV interview when I enter the presidential palace in Maputo.'

I'll keep him to that, I thought.

Dhlakama's off-the-record remarks confirmed his naivety if not his integrity. Tim and I were utterly cynical about some of his claims, but the fact remained that we saw no evidence of current South African involvement.

And we looked hard.

Tim used all his extensive military expertise to examine radios and weapons. Some of the trade marks and registration numbers could have been interpreted, with just a bit of licence, as apartheid stock. Our film would have made a small fortune if we had done so. But we played it absolutely straight. After travelling for over 300 miles we did see a basic and nationwide indigenous organisation. We saw food being grown. We witnessed no cruelty to the peasantry, although Renamo was hardly likely to stage a quick atrocity for the benefit of our cameras.

On the harsh return journey we stayed at camps where no sentries were posted, lacking even basic defence perimeters.

'The Viet Cong would make mincemeat of this lot,' said Tim.

We concluded that Renamo guerrillas were doing so well militarily not because they were any good, but because Frelimo was so bad. The journey to 'Free Mozambique' had been instructive but we left as sceptics, still wondering about the amazingly coincidental congruence of Renamo's and Pretoria's strategies.

We almost didn't make it out. Three miles before the final Shire River base, Pedro drove us straight into a low branch. The bike motored on, on its own, and stopped in one piece. To be fair, we had been driving cross-country for days, it was pitch black and the lights didn't work. Pedro was at last too dazed to drive, so I piled all the kit and his weapons on to myself, let him flop on the back seat, and drove the last stretch into camp.

Tim was some way behind. I saw a hut with a light on and walked in cursing: 'Where's the fucking Dettol?'

I must have looked strange: a Rambo headband and bandage over my head, three weeks' growth of beard, covered in cuts, bites, bruises, an AK, and ammo belts.

'You look like you need some whisky, not Dettol,' said a deep American voice.

The hut was dimly lit by a candle and the tall American was covered with what looked like a beekeeper's helmet. It was Holger Jensen, a massive Vietnam veteran working for *Newsweek*. I knew him from drunken binges in Salisbury.

'Whisky? Yes, please . . . I like your hat.'

'Yeah, it keeps the bugs out,' said another American, Tom, a chain-smoking acquaintance not too far removed from friendly relations with the CIA.

Holger was also on his way to Gorongosa; we had started a stampede of hacks. I wondered how his bulky frame would survive on the back of a tiny bike and whether it would even move with his weight, although he didn't have any cameras. Seeing Holger was a bit like thinking you were climbing Everest for the first time and finding a can of Heinz baked beans at the summit.

Renamo had asked us not to disclose the very tenuous route via Malawi. We didn't, both to keep other hacks out and to ensure we could get back in later. And we had given a promise. Nick della Casa, who was a near neighbour in Johannesburg, decided to try our route a month later. Although I saw him nearly every day, he never asked my advice. He was caught up a tree stealing paw-paws near the border: Renamo locked him up for eighteen months, thinking he was a spy. Others were arrested in Malawi and deported. One or two unfortunates were handed over to Frelimo.

Nick was treated well, according to his own account when he returned to London. I tried to use my Renamo and British contacts to speed his release, even though he had done very little to help a mutual friend imprisoned in Botswana, despite being directly responsible for the man's arrest. Nick was a born troublemaker, for all his immense personal charm. He led an amazing life, right out of Kipling. His early death (at the hands of Kurdish bandits) was sad, but almost biblically inevitable.

Tim joined us for five minutes of war-and-mosquito stories, then we had to move on. Surprisingly, I had kept a cool head the whole time, but on this very last stage I panicked in the dug-out canoe when Tim offered the boatman double the normal fee to go faster. He reckoned we had a chance of catching a bus on the other side of the river. We started to wobble almost uncontrollably in the fast current. I quietly offered our excited sailor four times the amount to disregard Tim's offer.

'We've gone through all this shit, and there's no way I want all this film to tip over into the river.'

I knew how to balance in a single kayak, but this was like trying to juggle on a highly unstable hollow log in the middle of a massive stretch of fast-flowing deep water full of crocs.

'Relax, Paul. He's knows what he's doing. Nobody would hire him if he tipped this thing over. He makes his living from it.' As if in rebuttal the young fisherman gave Tim a toothless idiot smile. I closed my eyes, concentrated on balancing, and wished I could levitate.

There was no bus, but a government Land Rover eventually picked us up, unconvinced by our walking-tour story. It was obvious we had been in a battle zone. I was keen to get away from the government man, who dropped us off at a ramshackle bar. It was a brothel, and we persuaded the madam to hire us a truck. We diluted our whiteness by picking up two black hitchhikers, Anglophile teachers both desperate for pen-friends in the UK. On that premise they befriended us immediately. Very fortunately they had relatives on the first three roadblocks, where we were introduced as bosom buddies. That's one of the good things about Africa, the ability to bond quickly. And I replied to all the letters from my new Malawian pen-pals.

We arrived at the Mount Soche Hotel in Blantyre after picking up our 'civilian' gear from the safe house. I wondered what the person cleaning our hotel room would think of the abandoned crutches, medicines, and bits of wheelchair.

'Miracle cure. The Soche Lourdes,' said Tim. He restrapped his leg cast and limped all the way to the Johannesburg plane.

We had made it.

The film didn't sell too well, despite our pioneering efforts. TV networks that were interested in Africa – and there weren't many – wanted anti-apartheid stuff. The dogma of conventional wisdom reigned in most Western newsrooms. Some didn't believe our film; those that did, didn't care. I became irritated by London executives pontificating on guerrilla warfare with all the embattled *savoir-faire* of the Northern Line. In Johannesburg some of the better journalists, such as ITN's Peter Sharp and Mike Nicholson, took the trouble to ask me how we did it. They had tried and failed. Allen Pizzey, a good friend from CBS, thought we had been duped. Others said we had flown into Gorongosa in a South African helicopter, just as Louis Nel had done. As it happened, the South African security people tried to stop us, not help us.

I made enough money from the limited film sales and photo-stories to more than cover my expenses, but the trip did untold damage to my academic reputation (such as it was). At a seminar at Oxford, for example, I argued the opposing viewpoint when worthy dons talked in detail about Renamo bandits. Because Frelimo was on the side of the angels, *ipso facto* Renamo had to be bandits with no organisation or goals; mere starving wolf-packs scavenging for food. Just as happily I would have made a film about the other side (Frelimo in fact asked me to make one later). And I would have made more money. In my opinion, each was just as bad as the other.

What irritated me most was the self-righteous omniscience of my Oxford-type friends. They knew everything about Renamo and wrote books based on their long-distance learning. But they refused to visit or at least try to visit the areas they described, relying almost entirely on Maputo's government news service. Seldom has such a big civil war been analysed so often from just one side. They refused to sully their prejudices with experience. This was the kind of intellectual Stalinism that encouraged me to switch from ivory-tower academia to the real world of journalism. A kind of Gresham's Law applied: the further you are away from experiencing first hand, the greater the sum of intellectual knowledge. Coward that I am, I came to believe that there is nothing like being shot at occasionally to sharpen your wits, and prose.

Perversely, I resolved to return. I had actually enjoyed myself in Mozambique, not least because, despite being the continent's worst walker, I liked the bush. And it was partly psychological. Other arduous trips had amply displayed my physical limitations very quickly; on the Renamo foray I had largely transcended them. I wasn't suicidal but I didn't care what happened to me. I had no job, no debts, no family to worry about, and no particular woman nestled in my life. All that mattered was what was happening that minute in that place. And there had been a goal, not just aimless adventure. I also had Tim. Once again, I played Danny DeVito to his Schwarzenegger.

The next time, Tim wouldn't come.

Hotel California

I planned to spend Christmas 1991 in Wales. It would be a chance to be with my Welsh family for the festivities for the first time in many years.

Then I received a call from David Hoile, a Renamo contact in London. The war was playing havoc with the Malawian economy; settlement talks between Frelimo and Renamo had been stumbling along for months. Publicity about a possible total end to the war was OK with the Malawians. Peace was breaking out all over southern Africa. Or so it seemed.

'President Dhlakama will give you an interview. He wants to discuss the ceasefire and a settlement. Can you fly in next week?'

'Fly in? You mean, no bikes?'

'No, a light plane, low under the radar, straight to Gorongosa.'

'Sounds good, but it's Christmas soon.'

'I will get you in and out before Christmas Day. . .'

Tim was busy, and also negative about the sales possibilities. I just wanted to get back there and hope to cover my expenses; Tim was in the big league now. Most of the bang-bang stuff was done by freelancers, often at great risk and usually without insurance. Tim was still adventurous but the bottom line had become more important. He made a lot more money than me. But he was a highly skilled cameraman, and I was nothing special: I could organise, write, research, present and produce, but network staffers could do all that, and often better. Combat cameramen were an élite breed, and rightly so.

J. J. Swart said he would come. We had worked together in South Africa but now he was based in London. He was fit, young, adventurous and used to the bush, having done national service in the South African army. Not that I expected much action on this trip.

David was coming too, with a female journalist, Fiona, who had never covered a war or been to Africa. It was David's show, he having made the arrangements with the Malawian Special Branch to get us through without hassles. We were met at the airport by two top security men and escorted through customs. I had remembered the dress code and made JJ wear a hat with his pony-tail rolled up inside. But Fiona had slacks on. JJ was quick. He dragged out a long cloth he had in his bag, then asked an Indian woman to make it into a formal sarong for Fiona to satisfy the officials.

We resorted again to the Mount Soche. I sat by the pool and listened to the early-evening crickets while a waiter in a fez brought me a drink on a tray. Fiona was immediately dubbed a female Indiana Jones when she came out in safari gear. She seemed good fun, and David was the one of wittiest people I have ever met. Back in shorts and in Africa after a three-year break, I felt alive again.

The next morning we flew out in a Piper Aztec with 'Pilots for Christ' emblazoned on the side. Sitting beside the missionary pilot was Domingos Adgira, a Mozambican living in Canada. We flew very low to slide under the radar, looking down at almost the same route I had endured on foot, canoes and cannibalised bikes. It took a few minutes to pass over the Zambezi. In 1986 getting the inflatable pumped up, the engine working and the bikes loaded had taken hours, despite the chanting of a witchdoctor.

I thought: bugger all the anthropological stuff, the bites and mad generals, this is the way to go.

I chatted to the pilot, who had been flying for only nine months. Then we circled where we were supposed to land. The strip had been made between very tall trees to disguise its role. It certainly fooled me.

'That's a footpath, not an airstrip.'

The pilot didn't help much by saying a quiet prayer, but it was the niftiest bit of bush flying I had ever seen. Domingos was very emotional, perhaps from relief after a very tight landing or simply his return to Mozambican soil after twenty years of exile.

Renamo's bikes were now bigger and better. They had graduated to 200cc engines and proper trail bikes, not lawnmowers with seats. They ferried us to a very well-organised camp. The rags had gone; the troops were wearing smart olive-green boiler suits. JJ and I were allocated a large hut with Domingos and three others. The beds even had sheets. Amazing.

David said: 'Welcome to Hotel California.'

Rats were still in evidence, one of which persistently raided our little food store, so I dubbed our mansion 'Casa del Raton Mickey'.

About twenty foreign Renamo representatives, mainly from North America, Germany, Portugal and Kenya, were scheduled to meet with local Mozambican bigwigs for the second national congress to discuss the internationally brokered settlement talks and planned election.

Meanwhile the war went on but there had been ceasefires in

some areas. Frelimo had ditched Marxism. Since the independence of Namibia, the winding down of the war in Angola and the release of Mandela, hopes were high for the end of twenty-seven years of war in Mozambique. Pretoria had actively aided Maputo, so Renamo had called Frelimo 'a South African-backed Soviet surrogate state'. With the collapse of the Soviet Union, Frelimo had nowhere else to go but talks with Dhlakama. The rebel president would discuss these changes with his main henchmen before the congress of 1,500 people at Gorongosa.

Dhlakama was due in a day or two, so we took it easy. The food in the camp was good and orderlies brought hot water for the showers. Either Renamo had got its act together or this was a very convincing Potemkin village. JJ was obsessively interested in filming fauna and flora, which was a problem because I was producing a political film. He got bored easily. As we weren't short of tapes and the camp had electricity for the batteries, I didn't stop him filming ants mating and flowers growing.

He also liked climbing trees at any opportunity. After drinking half a bottle of duty-free whisky he swung around the camp like a chimpanzee on speed. Fiona, who had consumed the other half, did the same with almost as much athleticism. Both redheads, they looked and acted like twins. Suddenly a boomslang slithered in front of Fiona and both dropped out of the tree at the same time. She didn't go near a tree again. She was given the greenhorn treatment, suffering patiently our long lectures on forest animals, many of them invented; but, except for one large spider in the loo, she behaved like a pukka memsahib. She had even brought an elaborate, mobile, folding, all-dancing contraption that transformed itself into a sort of four-poster bed with mosquito netting on all sides. I had never seen such a thing in Africa before.

I *had* seen the old British army training films screened by Renamo, of the Biggles meets *Carry On Up the Khyber* type, full of majors with clipped accents and obliging Scouse sergeants, made for national servicemen in the late 1950s. If such films had contributed to the Renamo resurgence then Frelimo must have been in a lot worse shape than I imagined.

JJ and I filmed the local clinic (aspirin the only drug on offer), village scenes of women grinding millets and amputees, alleged victims of Frelimo. In one village I was delegated to maintain the visitors' honour by drinking the *skokian*, which tasted like boot polish, turps and semolina, but the old chief seemed pleased. He gave me two live chickens to take home. We also filmed an excellent sequence of tribal dancing which the soldiers were practising for the congress. It was the best and most authentic I had ever seen: horns, drums, animal skins, dust, colours . . . Later the dancers enacted various rituals and mini-morality plays which owed a little to Mao but more to ancient paganism. Not a single tourist in a thousand miles and it felt good.

I interviewed some of the delegates while we waited for Dhlakama. Adelino, one of the last great white hunters, had lost everything to Frelimo's nationalisation and been tortured by Frelimo. He now lived in Madrid. The delegates from Kenya were shifty; the man from the USA was brash and wore a baseball hat; the man from Frankfurt acted Germanic. It was interesting to see how exiled Mozambicans had exaggerated the customs of their adopted lands, as many forced migrants do. That was better than huddling in ethnic ghettos and celebrating old rituals as the British tend to do.

I spent time with Domingos, the Mozambican on the plane and the most humane man I met in Africa. I would have liked to round up all the Frelimo and Renamo politicians, put them on one of the beautiful islands off Mozambique and keep them there, in comfort, to argue for the rest of their natural lives. I would make Domingos president, and let the people have a yearly referendum to see whether he should stay or go. If you share a mud hut with a man, you get to know him quickly.

I had a long chat with Almeida, the Renamo minister of information. He had spent a lot of time with Nick della Casa when Nick was imprisoned by Renamo. Almeida told me that they were desperate to get rid of Nick but the British – who had repatriated Nick on a number of previous occasions – had had enough of him. I asked about my old friend, the mad general. 'Ah, yes, he is a character but a fine soldier,' Almeida said warily. A number of journalists had lately suffered his hospitality. 'He has been reported killed many times, but he is still there.' I could see why so many people would want him out of the way, including – from the look in their eyes – some of his own officers.

Almeida did a lot of running round for us, so I gave him a small present of a spare Swiss army knife; he had frequently asked to borrow my own well-worn one. After I finished grilling him about

Renamo's continued reputation for mutilations, JJ whispered in my ear: 'Great present . . . now he can cut off ears, noses and lips with Swiss precision.'

Dhlakama arrived in a smart blue suit on a red bike. His female bodyguards were riding shotgun. Much podgier, the general had become a fat-cat politician. He greeted me by name like a long-lost brother and asked after Tim. I suspect that the faithful Ululu had refreshed his memory. (I gave Ululu a copy of *Great Expectations*; he had asked me to bring him a book by Dickens when I last met him.) Dhlakama did seem genuinely pleased to see me. Despite being busy with the delegates, he gave generously of his time. He had now travelled widely and his English had expanded as dramatically as his girth. The Portuguese were grooming his family for big things. His wife was taking an extended etiquette course in Lisbon.

We chatted alone about world politics. He still had a touching faith in British power.

'London has the key to peace.'

He asked why a Conservative government was spending so much training a still-Marxist Frelimo army in Zimbabwe while it couldn't afford to maintain some of its own famous regiments. A good question. He queried my reply that British support for the front-line states had been the Thatcherite alternative to full sanctions. But Thatcher – 'Machel's pal' – had gone, he said. Britain no longer needed to shop on both sides of the street, as Mandela was free. Dhlakama also thought the British were prolonging the war. He wanted Britain to use its leverage on Mugabe to pull out Zimbabwean troops from Mozambique, and all British military aid to Frelimo to end.

'Because of Lonrho's investment in my country, Britain should want peace. Along with the Americans, Britain could bring peace tomorrow.' Dhlakama's political education had been good, but I didn't have the heart to dissect his misplaced confidence in British flexibility when it came to foreign policy.

He then took me shooting. That was still vintage Renamo. His female sharpshooters did only marginally better than Fiona, who almost wiped out the Renamo Cabinet with an accidental burst of automatic fire. On the way back he stopped for some electioneering with the masses, doing a number with a little kid which was an exact replay of Saddam Hussein's PR debacle on CNN. But the light was poor for the camera. We rode back through the forested camp. Lights twinkled around camp-fires. It was like Disney's version of Sherwood Forest.

We filmed the pre-congress cabal of Renamo delegates. Dhlakama in a dress uniform looked like the chief scout. Around him were old chiefs in 1930s demob suits, the white hunter in safari gear, tense academics, some hoods, some *mestiços* . . . an apparent attempt to balance the classes and tribes of the old Mozambique. Fiona, JJ and I were the only journalists there. I didn't know if we were witnessing a historic milestone in southern African history or a remake of *Al Capone*.

I did a long interview with Dhlakama on the atrocities, all but accusing him of being a mass murderer. Asking someone whom 99 per cent of the international media thought was a paranoid genocidal maniac, in the middle of his army, whether he killed people seems a little bold, in retrospect. I didn't think so at the time, because he struck me as open-minded. I had warmed to him. I still had doubts, however, even though our missionary pilot was totally disdainful of all politicians except Dhlakama. 'I trust him completely; he cares about the faith and fears of his people.'

Everything was in the can and we could go. Renamo arranged for the missionary plane to return for us. Dhlakama insisted on personally giving me a lift on his own bike back to the landing strip, reminding me that he would give me the first interview in the presidential palace.

The whole trip had taken a week, and there had been no mishaps. JJ and I edited the film in record time and it was screened internationally. It even made some money for the Christmas I managed to spend at home in Wales.

6. SOUTH AFRICA – THE ENDGAME

Crossing the Rubicon

In 1984 the Orwellian nightmare began to assume a tangible form in South Africa: from the blasphemy of the 'necklace' (a burning, petrol-filled tyre around the neck of an alleged collaborator) to the frenzied doublespeak of government propaganda. At the beginning of that ominous year the armed struggle was just over twenty-two years old. ANC guerrillas had proved remarkably inept, even by African standards. White power looked more entrenched than ever. From the Sharpeville massacre to the June Soweto uprising sixteen years had elapsed. On the cusp of each crisis capital and whites had fled. They had panicked, but the security forces had not. Each wave of resistance was absorbed, diluted, pushed back, pumped underground. From Soweto 1976 the cycle of revolt had been reduced to eight years. But no ANC master plan existed, the exiled leadership in Lusaka always slow in keeping up with, let alone controlling, events forged in the crucible of black anger in the townships. From 1984 to 1986 blacks in both urban areas and countryside would rise up once more, hyped by foreign media as the beginning of another 1917 revolution. It was not to be.

For the first half of 1984 P. W. Botha's imperial presidency was riding high. He had humbled Marxist Mozambique into signing a peace agreement, and won a referendum at home to proceed with his new 'dispensation', the tri-cameral parliament for whites, Indians and coloureds. There was precious little wrong with the old Westminster system: perhaps all it needed was the extension of the franchise, equally, to blacks. Botha gathered up the business community in his drive against the Bolshevik menace. After all, this was 'a step in the right direction'. It was not – it was a declaration of war on 75 per cent of the population, who were arrogantly excluded from the new system.

The 'unrest', in Pretoria's parlance, began to snowball. The cycle of insurrection fed on itself as one area emulated the tactics of another. It was all recorded, faithfully and otherwise, on TV, thus stimulating further pressure, especially from the USA. There Bishop Tutu whipped up the sometimes prefabricated moral fervour of the chattering classes. American pressures on South Africa duly encouraged the 'young lions' in the townships. The South African government believed that TV cameras, ravenous for blood and guts, sometimes created rather than merely recorded the grim events. Pretoria's almost total ban on non-SATV coverage of the unrest was thus unsurprising; more remarkable was the year or so it took to implement. It was a cynical gesture which seemed to work. Perhaps Pretoria had adequately sized up the attention span of Joe Public in America. But in 1985 being an anti-apartheid groupie was the moral fad in the USA. Even Ronald Reagan noticed.

The vicious pantomime of death was endlessly recycled – boycotts, stay-aways, rent strikes, demonstrations, riots, police retaliation or provocation, single shots, tear-gas, panic, confusion, concentrated automatic fire . . . funerals and more funerals. At the burial services – one of the few legal outlets for the outpouring of political and personal grief (before funerals were also restricted) – ANC and Russian flags were openly displayed, along with wooden replicas of AKs. The cutting edge of the insurrection was arson and murder of suspected informers, black councillors and policemen, perceived to be the main, and available, local representatives of apartheid. The 'necklace' became a trade mark of the young comrades in their war on collaborators. In the compressed, often breathless, reportage on TV screens in Europe and America, South Africa was going up in flames.

I attended a meeting of 'concerned citizens' in Johannesburg city hall, sitting by chance next to Harry Oppenheimer, the richest man in South Africa. We exchanged a few pleasantries and I looked around for any heavies minding the ageing boss of Anglo-American. There were none that I could see. Crazy violence was everywhere in South Africa, but he couldn't have gone solo like this in the USA. Worthies such as Beyers Naudé and Helen Suzman sat alongside empty chairs for proscribed organisations. Suzman claimed that if only the locals could see just a little of the barbarous police behaviour shown on foreign networks, 'tens of thousands of decent white South Africans' would raise their voices in protest.

I wasn't so sure. Some whites wouldn't believe the pics even if they saw them. One of Pretoria's prime weapons against its own electorate was ignorance. Blacks in the closely knit townships relied upon a very effective news grapevine; whites had a less effective gossip machine which, in the twilight world of censorship, produced epidemics of alarmist rumour-mongering. For blacks the regime's aim, if not the result, was intimidation along the lines, though not the extent, of Orwell's *Nineteen Eighty-Four*. It was ironic that, as in Rhodesia, government propaganda was internalised by the whites but usually scoffed at by blacks, presumably the most important target. The Angolan war, with real-live Cubans and Russians involved and captured, added flesh to the abstraction of a communist onslaught.

South Africa's 'alternative' press, like the *Weekly Mail*, and sometimes the more establishment-oriented English-language papers such as *The Star*, the *Cape Times*, and Ken Owen's blistering editorial and columns in the *Business Day*, played Russian roulette with the censorship laws. According to opinion polls most whites relied upon, and trusted, SATV for their news information; but only bits of truth escaped the mindless censorship of local television. Liberals beat their breasts or emigrated, while the silent majority of whites adopted hard-line stances on security.

As one Afrikaner farmer's wife said: 'We will never give up. We will fight to the last Afrikaner. We did not accept English rule and we will never accept Bantu rule. We don't mind sanctions. We will go back to ox-wagons if they cut off our petrol.'

Another woman, from a Jewish, liberal, business background, was ruthlessly candid: 'Let's be completely logical. We can hand over peacefully now, fight and lose, or we kill the lot of them.'

On 21 July 1985 Botha declared a state of emergency in some areas, the first in twenty-five years. The security forces already possessed extensive powers of arrest and detention, exempting them from potential prosecution for any act carried out in 'good faith'. To the comrades, this seemed a licence to kill. By the end of the year over 1,000 blacks had indeed been killed, many by police action. Over 7,000 people had been detained, usually without trial.

On 31 July 1985 William Butcher, the conservative chairman of Chase Manhattan, refused to roll over further loans to South African borrowers. The republic's most serious financial crisis ensued. Despite its fundamentally sound economy, Pretoria's credit rating was now lower than even that of chronically mismanaged Zaire. To restore confidence government officials hinted strongly that the President would deliver an epoch-making speech at the National Party congress in Durban on 15 August. As the crisis mounted, so did the expectation that P. W. Botha would finally break the political deadlock. The least that was expected was the freeing of Mandela. It was billed as the Rubicon speech.

Jenny, my Australian girlfriend, and I watched the televised version of the speech with growing amazement, then disappointment, and finally cold rage. PW dug in his Achilles' heel. During a bleak performance watched on TV around the globe, Botha wagged his finger and contemptuously dismissed his critics. He offered little beyond threats. Some of his backwoods Afrikaner faithful might have shivered with wicked delight when their man once more gave two fingers to the world, but the Rubicon fiasco finally switched off the English-speaking business magnates in South Africa. The influential *Business Day* called the president a 'hick politician'. Not only was the content diabolical, but so was the exaggerated and bellicose presentation. Botha was obviously totally oblivious to the PR disaster he was inflicting on his country.

'I am too embarrassed to live in a country which is ruled by such people,' Jenny said.

I agreed, and we both made plans to leave.

Botha's speech was the final straw after ten years of watching racist *folie de grandeur*. But what really did it for me was a conversation an hour after the speech with some top SATV officials, who told me how wonderful they thought PW's performance was. I searched in vain for a hint of irony. It was hopeless.

Money talks loudest: the rand fell to an all-time low against the dollar. Foreign investors deserted in droves. With a performance like Botha's Rubicon, market-led sanctions became much more important than official government-sponsored pressures. Once again, Pretoria had shot itself in both feet. Desperate top white businessmen started to talk officially to the ANC in Zambia.

Pretoria blamed nearly all the violence on the ANC, and more particularly the South African Communist Party. The ANC had not instigated the revolt that began in 1984, and was taken by surprise by its outbreak and enduring scale. And the SACP was an important *restraint* on the *Umkhonto*, the ANC's military wing, which wanted to hit soft white targets. In June 1985, however, the ANC adopted

183

a strategy of 'people's war', intended to take the struggle into the comfortable and almost untouched white suburbs.

Botha would not talk to ANC 'terrorists' and looked for elusive 'moderates'. No one stepped forward, not even Chief Buthelezi, who insisted that Mandela's freedom was a precondition for serious talks. The roller-coaster of often savage repression and occasional wilted carrots of reform had become mutually exclusive. As veteran journalist Stanley Uys noted: 'Botha's reformism in South Africa today is like a lift going up in a building that is coming down.'

The major reform of 1986 was the scrapping of the hated pass laws and influx controls. More than eighteen million Africans had been arrested for infringing these laws. In March 1986 the partial state of emergency was lifted. The violence was endemic but appearances mattered: keep the violence off foreign TVs, tell them apartheid is dead often enough, play with doublespeak at home, rule by loud semantics and the quiet sword. The ending of pass laws was a real reform, but Pretoria obfuscated the central issue of political power for blacks.

The comrades struggled to make South Africa ungovernable. 'People's courts' were set up to establish their often arbitrary rule. Sometimes adults were terrorised by bands of feral youngsters, especially for breaking consumer boycotts. Often victims were forced to consume all their 'illegal' purchases on the spot, sometimes fatally in the case of cooking oil, washing powder, soap and paraffin. Parents grew frustrated with the long school boycotts and self-defeating demands for 'liberation before education'. During 1986 the liberation mania began to dissipate. After two years the severity of the repression, sheer physical exhaustion, and frustration with the excesses of both disciplined comrades and roving bands of *tsotsis* and psychopathic elements had taken their toll. Chaos in the townships was not the same as people's power.

But black–white polarisation escalated. In June 1986 George De'Ath, a friend who worked as a freelance cameraman for the BBC, died from head wounds received from axes and pangas deployed in the fighting between *witdoeke* vigilantes, the police and the comrades in Cape Town. He was the first foreign correspondent to be killed while covering the civil war.

The *Cape Argus* newspaper described the mood in the black communities: 'You can reach out in front of you . . . clench your fist and squeeze fear out of the air.'

In June 1986 the state of emergency, lifted in March, was re-imposed. By the end of 1986 more than 23,000 people, including 9,000 children, had been jailed under the June decrees. The South African Defence Force smashed the pretensions of the liberated zones in the townships. Pretoria was back in charge.

Jenny's cousin came over from Australia. He was a fire chief in Perth, not one of nature's radicals. In a Melville restaurant, over sensual local wines, he said: 'I love the countryside but socially the place is like a prison. And those bars,' pointing to bars on all the restaurant windows. 'I don't feel they're keeping the other fellow *out* but me *in*. I feel caged.'

South Africa's main trading partners were lining up against it. The logical, economic arguments against sanctions, and there were many, no longer mattered. Imposing sanctions was a question of standing on the side of the angels; you were either for or against apartheid. The tide of opinion swept up even stonewallers such as Reagan and Thatcher.

I asked the boss of a once highly profitable small business how things were.

'Oh, wrist-slashingly normal,' he sighed.

Despite the military defeat of the comrades, a psychological corner had been turned. It would take time, but belief in ultimate victory had been implanted in the popular psyche. The Great Crocodile led his followers into the May 1987 election with all his customary Teutonic charm. The emasculation of the liberal opposition and the increase in seats of the right-wing Conservative Party – the first time since 1948 that the official opposition had been on the right – indicated that the voters, especially English speakers, had moved to the right, attracted by the security ticket. With this new reliance on English speakers, the Nats probably no longer represented even the majority of the Afrikaners. Botha now led a minority of a minority tribe.

The wind-down of the unrest brought renewed confidence to the whites. Except for the liberal minority, South African whites seemed naturally (or desperately) inclined to be optimistic. Their peculiar political environment demanded constant psychological reassurance.

'There's nothing wrong with us, the world just doesn't understand us.'

Hence the importance of rebel sports tours and bimbo starlets. Few people bothered to pay to watch them perform, but that didn't matter. The important thing was that foreigners 'come to see for themselves'. Township violence was off the world's TV. Tourists started to trickle back, as did a handful of the whites who had taken the 'chicken run' to Australia and Britain.

The ANC kept up its bombing campaign. In July 1987, sixty-eight people were injured in a bomb attack in central Jo'burg. As long as the ANC waged war and the white right wing bayed for tougher action, Botha found it difficult to move ahead with his stalled, if not moribund, reform programme. The rise of the Afrikaner Resistance Movement, the AWB, mesmerised Pretoria. Pretoria hoped that given enough rope the AWB leader Eugene Terreblanche, a spell-binding orator, might hang himself.

In April 1987 I attended an AWB mass rally in Jo'burg city hall. I was chilled to my marrow . . . and, sitting at the front-row press table, sprinkled by Terreblanche's spittle. In an action replay of 1930s Germany, long swastika banners adorned the hall, jackbooted storm-troopers raised a Hitler salute, little blond children waved flags and powerful rhetoric raged against liberals and communists, anyone who questioned the Afrikaners' divine right to rule. The gleam in the eyes of the wildly enthusiastic audience boded ill for the future. After a series of antics, including the habit of falling off his horse in public, Terreblanche became a music hall Hitler for some. The conspicuously armed right wing grew, however, and so did underground cells. Terreblanche, the dark messiah, bided his time.

In 1989 President Botha, enfeebled by a stroke, had reached a political dead end: Rubicon, the curt dismissal of a Commonwealth peace mission and the public humiliation of his coloured and Indian allies lit up his tri-cameral parliament as a ship of fools. His successor was F. W. de Klerk, a brighter and more sophisticated figure. But the political log-jam remained: no credible black leader could talk to Pretoria until the ANC was legitimised. P. W. Botha had once warned that the whites had to 'adapt or die'.

Comedian Pieter-Dirk Uys responded: 'People have adapted a little . . . and died a lot. And we have swapped a laager for a bunker.'

On 2 February 1990 de Klerk finally dragged his party out of the bunker and across the Rubicon. The ANC and the Pan-Africanist

Congress were unbanned. On 11 February Nelson Mandela was finally freed after twenty-seven years in jail. De Klerk and Mandela haggled long and dangerously over the details of a transitional government and the elections scheduled for April 1994.

I didn't see the whole endgame. I had stopped presenting on local TV, because of my frustration with the censorship. I had opposed sanctions in Rhodesia because of the massive pious hypocrisy oozing from the sanctioneers, and had a certain sympathy and occasional involvement with the swashbuckling sanctions-busters. But in South Africa I thought sanctions might save lives by bringing the Afrikaner government to its knees, or senses, that little bit earlier. My own small business ventures suffered, because of the extra costs of film for example. Non-comprehensive sanctions prolonged the war in Rhodesia but shortened it, I believe, in South Africa. And I was angry in a way that I hadn't been in Rhodesia. I became aggressively argumentative at dinner parties, wanting to shake people by the throat and make them see sense. It was bad journalism. I had become a talker not a listener.

In late 1986 Jenny went to study at Cambridge. It was time for my dog, Gelert, and I to leave too. Little things in the last few months confirmed my decision. Partly it was the crime. A shot went off nearby and some of my friends drew guns in a Hillbrow restaurant as though it were the Wild West. Jane, a dashing extrovert, pitched up at my house and insisted on showing me her new derringer and garter holster.

A hundred yards from my house I saw two coloureds kicking a black who was lying semi-conscious on the pavement clutching two apples. It was outside a grocery shop but I had no idea whether the prone figure was a thief or not. Whatever the cause, I feel you shouldn't kick a man when he's down. Armed only with a squash racket – I was on my way to my squash club – I managed to persuade the attackers to desist and told the dazed black to run away if he could. Just as I was helping him up, two burly, scruffy whites started shouting at me in Afrikaans. One drew a gun and pointed it at the black while the other kicked him in the head.

I told them to back off as I advanced, wielding my squash racket.

If I had thought about it, I wouldn't have been so damn stupid. But I was indignant and also white enough to persuade the assailants to desist. They drove off cursing me in Afrikaans. The black man disappeared, seemingly unfazed by it all; perhaps he was in a state of shock or drunk. Five minutes later a group of black and white children was playing soccer on the same spot.

In my last week in South Africa, May 1987, I revisited my old campus at Wits and stumbled on a student protest and riot police charge. I knew enough to decide where to stand – behind the police lines and a little to the side, downwind. I followed the line as it lunged, whipped, and launched tear-gas grenades. When I stopped to help a student (who was not part of the protest but had accidentally walked into it) I, too, was gassed. In a confined space you have to vomit immediately; in the open you can get away with feeling nauseous and headachy, especially if you put a wet handkerchief over your face early enough.

As I was packing up the house, a coloured knocked on my door and said he was canvassing for the National Party.

'I support the ANC,' I said briskly (and illegally).

'Right on brother, so do I.'

'But why are you canvassing for the Nats?'

'Agh, man, I needed a job.'

He pushed a leaflet into my hand and walked out of my gate. South Africa was a funny place.

I left Melville with sadness, but Johannesburg with relief. I was going to write in Spain. A year or so after Mandela was released I thought that sanctions should have ended immediately. Apartheid had been totally and irreversibly scrapped. De Klerk had shown courage and gone the whole way, unlike that other reforming lawyer, Gorbachev. South Africa needed help quickly. After forty years of anti-apartheid campaigning, a host of vested interests had mushroomed. Sanctions were almost the *raison d'être* of the Commonwealth and thousands of anti-apartheid groups in Europe and America. For too long, belief in sanctions had been seen as a litmus test of morality. It took nearly two centuries for the American constitution to reach the black underclass. South Africa looked like it had a few years before it exploded, unless economic and political conditions improved rapidly. Sanctions withered, de Klerk and Mandela maintained an uneasy rapport and the killings went on during the four years of constitutional haggling.

The international media were less interested now, unless a big massacre, preferably involving whites, popped up. The Inkatha/PAC/ ANC conflicts were 'black on black', too confusing to explain to America. But calling Inkatha versus ANC 'black on black' was about as helpful as describing the Second World War as white on white. South Africa had been a microcosm of every conflict known to man: black versus white, terrorism versus militarism, socialism versus capitalism, tribalism versus nationalism, federalism versus centralism, group identity versus individual rights . . . Once the constitutional issues were properly resolved, the real post-bellum problems would start: land and wealth redistribution, nationalisation, education reform, mass unemployment, AIDS, drought, soil erosion, overpopulation. The bitter anti-apartheid campaigns had been rich in slogans but poor in offering solutions.

Much of the rest of Africa had slid off the political and economic maps. Once attractive capital cities looked like they had been carpet-bombed. Parts of former Portuguese Africa had reverted almost to the Stone Age. Mozambique was trying to woo back Portuguese businessmen. Zambia was desperately trying to persuade white farmers from Zimbabwe and South Africa to travel north to restore agriculture in that fertile land. Africa had already been partially recolonised by the World Bank and the International Monetary Fund. Some liberal African experts were talking of formally recolonising areas such as Somalia, where government had effectively collapsed. Programmes could be set up to seduce back ex-colonial powers and settlers who knew Africa and could speak the local languages. Such schemes would of course have to adopt a politically correct name, say 'government restructuring'. They would operate under the UN, supported by the European Union's former colonial states, and, once some order had been restored, with the popular consent of the African people expressed in a referendum.

After all, black Africa had been nagging the world for decades to enforce one person, one vote in South Africa. Now they could start introducing it into their own countries. While the vast majority of African politicians who had specialised in ripping off their own subjects and banking foreign aid money in Switzerland could be expected to howl, millions of African peasants would undoubtedly have welcomed the return of the colonial powers.

'When will independence end, boss?' had a core of truth.

As the millennium approached, such a solution was highly unlikely, however. Africans could rightly point out that Austria or Turkey would be better advised to recolonise the Balkans. But Africa was dying, Europe (post the 1990s Balkans) was not. The colonial era might come to be regarded as the zenith of African development.

(It was also responsible for the crazy patchwork quilt of colonial boundaries which sliced through tribes and geographical logic. Many of Africa's territorial wars could be ended if the sacred cow of maintaining artificial imperial borders was sacrificed, as happened in Eritrea.) If the whites return they may be able to rebuild roads, hospitals, schools, and clinics. And they could earn the plaudits of the Greens by perhaps saving what remains of the big game. So long as whites could survive in black-ruled South Africa, the new state could become the breadbasket of Africa, not another basket-case; the engine for continental renaissance, not its holocaust.

South Africa had been a difficult conflict to cover. Some journalists felt it was a special case, apartheid a special evil. After witnessing a massacre or two it was easy to take sides. No wonder Pretoria accused foreign journalists of incitement. Most journalists did not crusade against Pretoria. Nevertheless the vast majority, even the crusty old Africa hands, were frequently appalled by Pretoria's ham-fisted manipulation of the media.

It was always difficult in Africa to balance moral convictions with professional standards. Just giving a rough balance, say 50 per cent blame to Mugabe and 50 per cent to Smith, sometimes created a legitimacy by default. Maybe neither man deserved 50 per cent of the moral argument. Yet it was better to make this kind of mistake than give in to advocacy journalism and crusade against apartheid.

I certainly felt like putting on shining armour at times. Once you started accepting apartheid as a special case, where did you stop? You could make the argument for a whole series of special cases. Professional detachment is blown out of the water. Those journalists who did take up cudgels for the ANC should remember that revolutions tend to devour their own children. Were partisan foreign journalists prepared to stay in South Africa and accept personal responsibility for what followed? The Shah gave way to the Ayatollah, Obote to Amin. Were conditions better after those revolutions? Mandela became a secular saint but what happens if he inadvertently played Kerensky to a future despot? Should we judge Africa by Western standards? Or should we patronisingly make allowances? Who should decide what these universal standards are? I do not know the answers. In my experience, independence in most African countries seemed to mean a lot less press and personal freedoms and, more importantly, less food. But what do I know? I'm only a white man.

7. ZIMBABWE – A RETURN

Zimbabwe revisited

It was February 1987 and I had just returned from Mozambique. Mugabe was at war with Renamo and two film-makers, namely Tim Lambon and myself. I had got up Smithy's nose with my books and now I was in trouble with Mugabe. He had taken grave personal exception to the film I had made on Renamo, and I was banned from the country. I was thinking of quitting Africa and wanted to see old friends in Zimbabwe before leaving. The British High Commission in Harare and the embassy in Pretoria left me in no doubt that the Zimbabweans would throw away the key and the Brits wouldn't help me at all if I chose to ignore their advice.

That made me even more determined to go and I thought of someone who might help me. Ken Flower had remained as Mugabe's security chief for a year or so after independence and was still a consultant to the Marxist government. I couldn't contact him directly but I got a message to him. His reply said, in essence, that I was stupid but he dared me: 'If you can get a bottle of Chivas Regal to my house, I will cover your arse for two weeks, provided you don't cross any borders illegally and keep your word that you are just visiting friends. No politics, journalism, or monkey business.'

Covering my arse was the right phrase – I knew from first-hand accounts that white political opponents of Mugabe had been sodomised in his jails, risking AIDS on top of the pain and degradation.

Just before I left I met Susan, a very attractive, blonde ex-Rhodesian, at a party. She insisted on coming with me, despite the risks. She wanted to see her sister and she liked adventure. 'Besides,' she said, 'a couple looks less suspicious.'

I knew my name was on the computerised wanted list at Beitbridge. I headed through Botswana to the Plumtree border, which had a reputation for being slack. With luck there might be no electricity, let alone computers. I ran out of petrol en route, forgetting the prime axiom on long-distance travel in black Africa: if you see a gas station, fill up. I boasted to Susan that I was a world authority on crossing African borders. I had traversed a few recently without passports, by paying small bribes to locals to take me on foot around any border posts. This time I was in a car. I explained my affable-berk routine: pretend to be stupid; it removes the racial tension and hostility to arrogant white men. I had added the (partly true) refinement of posing as deaf, which stopped the long harangues and request for bribes and sometimes evoked compassion. Underneath my glibness I was really nervous.

Despite her South African papers, Susan skipped through immigration at Plumtree. I didn't, although I had an elaborate British identity (I had a fairly wide selection of completely genuine passports and documents by this stage).

Grilled for an hour, I tried to explain and was told: 'Shut up. I can kick you out of here. I'm trying to help you.'

Like hell. The tough-looking official, clearly an ex-soldier and a party man, was the political type. No chance of bribing him. When I was allowed to speak, I said I was a British tourist travelling through South Africa, Botswana and Zimbabwe, which was essentially true. It was just a very long tour.

'Where's your return air ticket to London?'

'I don't have one. I am not sure from where or when I shall travel back. I have more than adequate funds.'

I showed him my traveller's cheques and credit cards. He wasn't interested.

I changed tack and showed my South African papers. He seemed most happy with my gun licence. So, I was a kaffir-shooting Boer. No longer confused, he had proved some kind of point and let me through.

Sue said: 'It's so nice to be back in Rho—'

I gave her a sharp tap on the ankles.

She recovered quickly. 'It's so nice to be in *Zimbabwe*.'

He hesitated, then stamped the forms. We passed a queue that snaked around the building. Next the vehicle and luggage were searched. Then I was asked to drive the car over an inspection pit. It was Sue's car so I didn't think she had stacked explosives under the vehicle. We drove off.

It wasn't until we had a puncture that I realised Sue's car had its spare wheel under, not in, the boot. Of course, it had been whipped at the inspection pit. Happy to have passed through border patrols, I wasn't on my guard. Having overcome that tricky problem, we negotiated a series of police roadblocks en route to Bulawayo. The first one made a fuss about my British driving licence, which had no photograph on it. The soldiers passed it around with great suspicion. I had given them a licence issued in Wales, in Welsh (with an English translation, admittedly). This caused great consternation. I shared some cigarettes and we were on our way.

At the next roadblock I stopped and got out of the car. 'Stay inside,' I was told threateningly. 'Where are you from in South Africa?' South African plates, of course. I should have hired a car in Botswana.

'Johannesburg.'

'Why aren't you wearing your safety belt?'

'I was until I stopped.'

'But you are not wearing it now.'

'I was getting out of the car. . .'

'I didn't tell you to get out.'

'Would you like a cigarette?'

'No. Have you got any beers?'

I hesitated. Would he get me for drunken driving? I had beer in the boot and in a coolbox on the back seat.

'May I get out to remove some beers from the boot?'

He grunted, and let us pass after a few alcoholic presents. I wondered how closely these fellows liaised with Zimbabwe's tourist board. We stopped at Bulawayo to visit Sue's aunt, who was delighted with our gift of a rare item – toothpaste.

Eventually reaching Harare, I knocked on Ken Flower's door. He seemed pleased to see me, even before I gave him the Chivas Regal. We chatted about old times, although Ken lowered his voice, like all white Zimbabweans, when we broached politics. Some place, I thought, where the intelligence boss has to speak in whispers. He stopped talking when his cook walked into the room.

'Don't go into the Quill Club,' he said. 'See your friends unobtrusively and then get away somewhere quiet. Why not try Kariba?'

Glenda, an old friend, drove down from Lusaka to meet us in Kariba and show me her latest baby. She always got straight to the point: 'Hell, you've put on weight. Why are you wearing that *moffie* [homosexual] pink shirt? When are you getting married?' She winked at Sue.

'Give up, Glenda. You know I'm a professional bachelor. Besides, I've only known Sue a few weeks.'

I loafed around Kariba, which was still full of very old-fashioned colonial characters. Some seemed lively, while a few appeared to have had all their vital juices squeezed out of them. Slightly open-mouthed I sat in a pub listening to a very loud racist conversation that could have escaped from Karen Blixen's time. Two farmers were discussing the driving habits of *munts*, the traditional derogatory Rhodesian term for blacks.

'I wouldn't let one of my *munts* drive my Merc. Are you mad?'

'How come you trust a *munt* with your $150,000 tractor or your $300,000 Scania truck but not your $30,000 bashed-up old Merc?'

The next day Sue and I crossed the lake to Spurwing Island. We were put in a small bungalow where a few years before her close friends had been trampled to death by buffaloes. Not a good omen. I walked around to find Rob, the game ranger.

'Herpes is a good omen,' he said cheerily.

'I beg your pardon?'

'Herpes, there,' he said pointing. 'That giant heron means good luck.' The handsome bird stood nonchalantly on the jetty.

I fished, canoed and drank. Mostly drank. The island was isolated and romantic. I felt lucky to be alive after the rigours of my recent adventures in Mozambique. I was in my favourite place in my favourite country. Over dinner I got drunk and proposed. I had done this once or twice before but luckily no one had ever taken me seriously.

Sue said yes.

Only eight people were on the island and they were all in the little dining room. Rob thought an immediate wedding was a wonderful idea; it would be useful publicity for his safari camp. The rest was a haze. The next day I tried to suggest to Sue that perhaps a pause for thought might be a good idea. Didn't she want to have her friends and family at her wedding?

But by this time Rob had organised a special licence with a magistrate.

We crossed the lake and drove for hours to Karoi, then back with Mr Chigagora, a chubby, genial man. He had been a political commissar in Mugabe's army and was now the local magistrate. He was most affable even when I mentioned the war.

By the time we reached the lake it was dark, and a storm was whipping up three-foot waves on the water. It was quite dangerous. I suggested we stay at a hotel on the water's edge. I was stalling. But Rob was keen to get back; his wife would be worried. On calm waters in daylight the trip took about fifteen minutes. An hour later we were still on the lake. The engine packed in; somehow Rob restarted it. I sat on the prow trying with a torch to find our way around sandbanks and the forest of petrified trees which rose from the water like shimmering ghostly scarecrows. The storm and rain grew worse, and the waves grew more robust. It was pitch black. Then we hit a sandbank and I jumped out to push the boat off.

'Get back. *Now*!' shouted Rob.

I did, and a croc slithered across the bank from which I had just leaped. The magistrate seemed quite unperturbed, despite his seasickness, assuming that the two white men were experienced sailors who knew what they were doing.

Rob and I knew that what we were doing was stupid.

In the maze of half-submerged forest we eventually spotted Rob's wife waving a lantern to guide us home. Aching all over from sitting on the buffeting prow, I dragged myself into the bar. I was in double shock from my recent and forthcoming traumas, and sank three beers straight off.

An hour later I was married, in the open air, surrounded by buffaloes and elephants. I had scrounged a pair of socks to go with my khaki shorts and borrowed a ring. The magistrate gave a wonderful little speech about this being 'God's own place'. I could hardly disagree with him.

When I got back to Johannesburg I rang my mother in Wales and described events.

'Where did you get all the animals from?'

'They're not from the zoo,' I said. 'They live there.'

I took my honeymoon on my own. I had booked a seat on the famous Blue Train six months before. It had been given to me as part of a journalism award; I had to write a story about the train, and the next vacancy was six months hence. The wedding had been most dramatic and so, incidentally, was the divorce.

8. NAMIBIA – THE SOUTH AFRICAN REICH

South West Africa – now Namibia – was German in the late nineteenth century. After the Great War, the League of Nations asked the South Africans, who lived next door, to look after it for a while. The South Africans refused to give it back. So there was a war. All the unrepentant ex-German Nazis in South West Africa could now comfortably switch Reichs. The 90,000 whites appeared to be an endangered species there, so to make sure they didn't become extinct the people who ran the country (who just happened to be whites too) gave them a specially protected reservation which also happened to be nearly all the land with good grazing and water. The blacks had the deserts but the whites did not consider them an endangered species. The whites controlled what was under the land too – lots of minerals. Apartheid, itself a first cousin of Hitler's racist laws, was applied in South West Africa, although less rigorously than in the southern republic. What mattered was equal opportunity. Blacks, if they were bright enough, could get on. But the white 20 per cent of the school population got 80 per cent of the education budget. Blacks were largely taught in Afrikaans but many of the important exams were held in English or German. The blacks had a low pass rate, thus justifying the whites' low opinion of black abilities.

I sat in a cramped Hercules aircraft pondering these conundrums, surrounded by South African soldiers devouring comics. I had hitched a lift on an air force plane to Windhoek, the spotlessly clean capital of South West Africa. Then I cadged a ride in my favourite war-horse, the Dakota, which flew very low as it approached the Omega base. It was hot, hot, hot in the Caprivi Strip in the suicide month of October. It was 1985, and the tangled mess of war between Angola, South Africa, the Cubans, Unita and various other hangers-on was in full swing. I wanted to travel along the length of the 960-mile Angola–South West Africa border, sometimes accompanied by a film crew, sometimes by troops. When I could slip away from military escorts, I would snoop around on my own.

I had covered the war there on and off for years, but I was more interested in 'South West' for its angry, beautiful landscapes. It was the last great wilderness in southern Africa, the same size as France, Belgium and West Germany combined and, with fewer than 1½ million inhabitants, it boasted one of the world's lowest population densities. Much of the land was untouched desert. In some places no rain had fallen for a century. Yet the wild symphony of harsh desert, lunar landscapes, pastoral serenity and almost unmolested wildlife was also the reluctant requiem for twenty-five years of bush war, most of it unreported.

South West was arguably the final unresolved legacy of the German defeat in 1918. If any metropolitan country – besides Belgium – deserved to lose its colonies it was the Second Reich. In the late nineteenth century Berlin sent out hard men to colonise in the furnace heat that blasted the burnt-out badlands. Namibia, like the Namib Desert, implies 'the place where there is nothing'. The badlands, however, held lots of something – diamonds. The first commissioner, almost prophetically, was Dr H. E. Göring, father of the Nazi leader, who set about exterminating the local tribes, especially the Herero. In museums and old history books I came across early pictures of the few surviving Hereros. Beyond the minor difference of colour they were identical to the starved and enslaved inmates of Belsen. The South Africans did a bit of massacring, too, using bombs from aircraft. They started in 1922 and kept going until the late 1980s.

The UN complained, to no avail. In 1958 the leading black nationalist, Herman Toivo ja Toivo, sent a recorded petition to the UN hidden in an old copy of *Treasure Island*. He also wrote to Queen Elizabeth and the Pope. There were even demands for the territory to be designated a US protectorate. Clearly, the nationalists were desperate. South West became *de facto* a fifth province of South Africa, set to take the same route as its minder: both black and white nationalists talked past each other. The diminishing band of 'moderates' staggered in the middle of nowhere. Many Namibian nationalists had worked in South Africa alongside ANC activists. The same pattern emerged: petitions, passive disobedience, strikes, and finally armed struggle. In 1961 Sam Nujoma and other leaders of the South West African People's Organisation (SWAPO) set up their HQ in Dar es Salaam, Africa's revolutionary oasis.

Guerrillas began to infiltrate South West in 1965 to establish bases in Ovamboland along the central section of the border with Angola. The terrain was well suited to partisan warfare. With the exception of a small section in the north-west, along the Cunene River, the Angola–South West border was a straight cartographic line. In the centre the Ovamboland–Angola border ran for 270 miles, theoretically dividing the Angolan Ovambo people from their kinsfolk on the other side. Ovamboland was exceptionally flat, covered in the west by often dense *mopani* bush and in the east by forest. In the subtropical climate, the rainy season (usually October to April) provided ample water and luxuriant foliage for guerrilla penetration. There were anthills everywhere, all for some reason pointing north. Everywhere, too, were *cuca* shops, tiny general stores with very little on sale but sporting grandiose titles such as 'California Inn', 'Los Angeles', and 'Country Club'. The Ovambo were said to be born capitalists, 'black Jews', but most supported the Marxist-leaning SWAPO.

The war began properly in 1966 and became more acute after Portugal quit Angola in 1975. Pretoria always danced to two tunes, dealing with the UN over independence but simultaneously promoting a local UDI. Meanwhile, real power was gathered in the hands of the South African Defence Force, which initially regarded SWAPO more as a public nuisance than a military threat. South African intelligence agents stirred up the usual cocktail – tribal, ideological, and personality clashes – to weaken SWAPO, which didn't need much prodding to tear itself apart. Then both SWAPO and South Africa became sucked into the Angolan civil war.

The result? A dirty little war in the last, almost forgotten colony became South Africa's very own Vietnam. It was a bizarre war in an almost surreal place, with images of the Tet offensive, old Rhodesia and the savage Congo of the 1960s. To the north the South African military conducted brilliant conventional campaigns in Angola, and almost textbook counter-insurgency inside northern South West. But they lost the 'hearts and minds' battles, the only ones that mattered. Meanwhile, in the south, almost quarantined, a kind of peace reigned among the big farms, rich diamond mines, and fishing fleets working out of picturesque ports.

South West once made a profit, but then became a proverbial colonial millstone. It was not formally an Afrikaner colony, rather a territory illegally occupied. Pretoria not only kept a large army there, in contravention of the original League mandate, but also used it as a forward base to send legions into Angola, Zambia and Botswana. Originally South Africa planned to integrate the territory formally into the republic, then it decided to boost its local allies, centred around Dirk Mudge. In a free election SWAPO would have won, so there followed ten years of chicanery, of Mudge-style Namibianisation as futile as America's Vietnamisation, because Pretoria adamantly rejected what it termed 'the red flag in Windhoek'. But the massive Angolan land battles in the late 1980s made even Pretoria realise that the game was up. South Africa would pull out of South West if the Cubans quit Angola. Pretoria was afraid of more sanctions, and wanted to denude South West's large deposits of uranium, diamonds, phosphates, and other minerals. Hence the great filibuster. South African diplomats, often the clumsiest representatives of an unsaleable regime, became Machiavellian princes over Namibia.

Occasionally the puppets would roar; Mudge balked at Pretoria's imperialism and tried to build up his own army. But after Mugabe won in Zimbabwe, the question was clear: how could Mudge, a white former National Party leader, do what Muzorewa, once an internationally accepted black nationalist, could not? The monotonous rhythm of South African diplomacy jangled the nerves: bash SWAPO, boost Mudge, and then talk to the UN. Buying time, losing ground. It became a cliché of southern African politics: to avoid total sanctions, Pretoria would have to free either Mandela or Namibia. The scale of the battles in Angola would eventually force the apartheid regime to do both.

But, in 1985, to the casual foreign visitor, the territory was a country that worked. Unusually for Africa, the roads were as good as the beer. Game parks were well run, as were the hotels, with their alluring mixture of German efficiency, Afrikaner hospitality and African good manners. The clarity of the light made it a photographer's dream. An overwhelming sense of grandeur and space harmonised with the Moët et Chandon quality of the air. Because of the war and its isolation it was almost untouched by that great abomination of the late twentieth century, package tourists. Below the narrow northern war zone, South West was usually the quintessence of primeval tranquillity. Enchanting classical German buildings looked as though they had been plucked from Rhenish forests and planted in the desert. Brechtian characters strolled along the sand-scoured, melancholic streets of quaint little towns such as Lüderitz and Swakopmund.

The Caprivi Strip, named after General Count Georg Leo von Caprivi di Caprara di Montecuccoli, Chancellor of Germany when the territory was acquired from Britain, was a finger of land which the Second Reich tried to stretch to touch German East Africa (Tanganyika). This strategic crossroads bordered on Angola and Zambia in the north and Botswana in the south, while Kasangula, at its extreme eastern tip, was the point where Zambia, Botswana, and Zimbabwe intersected. This was perhaps the shortest border in the world: Botswana and Zambia touched for just forty-five yards.

Omega was the HQ of 201 Battalion, made up of Bushmen troops officered by whites. I had been there on several occasions to interview SWAPO prisoners. Journalists were often given the PR treatment about South Africa preserving the ancient Bushman culture. I was fascinated by what remained of the subcontinent's oldest inhabitants. Like all those interested in military affairs, I marvelled at their almost supernatural field skills, especially their unerring tracking abilities. Their fathers had been hunted almost like beasts by southern Angolan tribes. Many Bushmen now regarded the South African military as their protectors and only source of employment.

Their officers confirmed their reliability under fire. Off duty they could be a trifle erratic, explained the camp doctor, as he pointed to a corporal nursing a wound in his backside.

'He was shot with an arrow by a Bushman who refused to work after drinking too much.'

A discussion followed on the cultural survival of the San (Bushmen). A South African lieutenant, who could speak one of the seventeen highly complex local San dialects, was defensive: 'The army is not turning the Bushmen into a war machine; it is preventing their extinction.'

Another officer added: 'We are not trying to Westernise the vulnerable Bushman culture. We just want to make him a better Bushman.' The army, he said, encouraged Bushman troops to spend a day each week with their children teaching them old customs and fieldcraft.

I wasn't sure an urban Afrikaner could show a Bushman much about bushcraft. And I wondered what would happen to these wonderful little people when South Africa pulled out. A good deal under SWAPO would be as likely as the Chinese Communist Party fêting the Gurkhas in Hong Kong.

In mineproofed armoured vehicles we travelled to small army towns such as Oshivello and Ondangwa, where the white civilians and soldiers' families lived in stockaded areas with a trim little sandbagged bomb shelter in front of each bungalow. At the adjoining air bases, the occasional artistic touch was evident. An Alouette gunship had 'I'm Noddy' painted on its Browning; 'Boswell Wilkie Circus' adorned the sides of a Buffel armoured personnel carrier. 'Road Runner' topped the logo list.

Oshakati had the best collection of propaganda posters to inspire bored white troopies: 'Think: it might be a new experience'; 'Winners Never Quit'. Warnings about mines abounded, with good reason: SWAPO guerrillas were experts at mine warfare, but the majority of victims were black civilians. And everywhere the unofficial scrawl: *Min Dae*, indicating just a few days left of national service. But it was not *Apocalypse Now* revisited. There was no 'fragging' that I could discover. Morale was generally high. And, although posters warned of the dangers of drugs, this army was not 'dropping out' in large numbers.

Ovamboland's flatness was monotonous. The rains, however, were beginning to brighten up the bush; the sandy soil smelt rich and fecund. I would call into *cuca* shops to find a Coke. Often little was on sale except information. Some informers bought shops but were killed by SWAPO. A BMW might be parked outside some conspicuous shopkeeper's *cuca*. The cleverer ones professed poverty and purchased property in Windhoek.

The huts and villages were often poor and scruffy compared with the regimented tidiness of the army bases. On the bases the ordinary soldiers were suspicious of foreigners and had been told not to talk to journalists. But in the mess they would relax quickly over a beer or two with my Afrikaans-speaking film crew. The bored white conscripts moaned like young soldiers everywhere. The army didn't give them jobs that matched their skills, a comment echoed by many graduate soldiers.

The officers in the regular permanent force were also suspicious, but border duty was often boring for them, too. They liked meeting strangers, especially if the conversation was in Afrikaans. South African forces were officially bilingual but English was the language of formality, of reserve. Slangy Afrikaans was the language of combat, fear, orders, prayer and laughter. The talk was of war, sex and sport, the universal clichés of men at war. Above all, the war.

'SWAPO is good, so we have to be, too,' said a keen Citizen Force 'camper' (reservist).

More beers.

A graduate officer admitted: 'We might be winning the war here but we are losing it at home.'

Someone wore a T-shirt advertising *Koevoet* (Crowbar), an élite and ruthless police unit: 'Our business is killing and business is good.'

We filmed as we drove along the road that ran beside the 'cutline', the border with Angola. The troops rode up and down in Buffels like cowboys checking range fences. I went up in a Puma helicopter to get aerial shots. Dust was the real enemy of choppers, not SAM missiles. Then a change of pace: a motorbike patrol with hardy cross-country scramblers. The motorcyclists acted as outriders for our small convoy. The enemy here was camel thorn – punctures, not mines. Next a horseback patrol: 'SWAPO doesn't hear us coming until it's too late. The terrorists are dead scared of horses, you know.'

I always tried to avoid walking too far, especially with heavy film equipment, but we needed some foot patrols for the documentary. I disliked violating homes in kraals, although the soldiers were polite in front of a camera.

Suddenly I heard shouting and two shots half a mile ahead.

Four SWAPO insurgents had been captured with just a whisper of resistance. I thought it might be a set-up but I sat in on the interrogations. They were genuine. The guerrillas were not terrified. They were not mistreated (in front of me). They knew they were destined for a long captivity, unless they opted to be 'turned' and join Windhoek's army. They would have better training, food, proper pay – for the first time – medical attention, entertainment . . . Why not? They could later say they were infiltrating the enemy to learn further skills before defecting back. Two of the captives, however, quietly explained that they were committed to SWAPO ideology and would never fight for 'the puppets in Windhoek'.

Ruacana was the furthest settlement on the western end of the border, overlooking a big hydro-electric project on the Cunene River. Because of the war less than 10 per cent of the potential electricity was being produced, even though the full amount was needed to boost attempts to cure chronic unemployment in the region. Perhaps 50 per cent of existing local jobs depended upon servicing the South African armed forces.

The commander of the Ruacana base drove me around in his pickup truck. Elvis Presley blared from his on-board stereo. He chewed a pipe and addressed his wife as 'Corporal'. The main interest in Corporal's life was the new 'tourist wing' she'd had built near the tiny wooden hut that was the officers' mess. The 'tourist wing' was also a wooden hut with four rooms with bunk beds. There weren't any tourists in this military zone, a mile from the Angolan border, so she was glad to accommodate the film crew. We would christen the building.

The commander moaned about the recent ceasefire. 'Now we have to wait for the bastards to come and hit us first.'

We were supposed to stay for two nights, but decided to go to another small base at the last minute. On the second night SWAPO obliged the commander with a stand-off bombardment, hitting the Ruacana base with 122mm rockets, mortars and a recoilless rifle. The new tourist wing was partially destroyed. Our room was demolished entirely and two officers in the next room were wounded. The commander was angry and embarrassed; Corporal was mortified, especially when we returned to film the damage they were trying to conceal. An angry reaction force pursued the attackers and claimed to have killed eight SWAPO guerrillas about ten miles across the border.

In the mess afterwards one of the officers in this retaliatory group admitted: 'I'm here in the operational area because this is the one place I can kill kaffirs legally.'

South West seemed like a surreal dream. Elsewhere, in dirt and muck – say in Afghanistan or Mozambique – there were highs and lows of fear, panic, and exhilaration. That was the way with guerrillas. Here death was sanitised, casual, organised by a very professional army which had mess waiters, hot showers, and air conditioning. . .

The next day the commander put on a powerful artillery display. Thirty high-explosive shells rained down on Angola. It looked good on film but I wondered how many Angolans had been killed.

We drove south in a Buffel to Opuwa, the midget capital of Kaokoland, stopping en route at a small Ovahimba village. Only a few thousand of these 'cattle people' had survived in the deserts of Kaokoland. They were a primitive, handsome tribe who daubed themselves in animal fat and ochre. The women plaited their hair and looked like red Bo Dereks. The soldiers gave them water and tobacco. The camera assistant had saved all his army ration packs and bargained some food for two carved bone bracelets. Most Ovahimba were almost untouched by civilisation, although a few less noble savage ladies were to be found drinking beer and smoking pipes outside a tiny store next to the army base.

At the Opuwa base I met a black major in the South West African Territory Force who wanted to show me the sights. We walked for a mile through flat, bare desert to a corrugated-iron box. It belonged to the major's lady, Dorcas. Although the inside was immaculately tidy, the tiny metal hut had no windows.

Over some beers, she explained slowly in broken Afrikaans: 'I want no windows. SWAPO come and shoot me otherwise.'

The discussion in the Opuwa officers' mess was hearty and sophisticated. More conservative officers spouted the 'Africans are generally happy here, we only need to kill the small number of communist troublemakers' philosophy.

A law graduate from Stellenbosch, however, led an opposing faction: 'You are talking about South West, but presumably the same applies to South Africa. If the blacks are so happy, why not give them the vote and let them happily vote for the National Party?'

The variety of opinion expressed – from brutal racism to liberal concern – suggested that this was not the brainwashed killing machine depicted by anti-apartheid activists. Morale seemed high. But coloured troops in the area had recently refused their home leave in the Cape, fearing reprisals in their own community because they were serving in the army.

In mid-1985 an appointed multiracial government was set up in Windhoek, the equivalent of the internal settlement in Rhodesia. Some blacks had voted for an earlier version of this government. This was the fundamental paradox of the war in South West: young white South African conscripts were fighting and dying to defend one sort of black majority rule in Namibia while fighting to prevent the same principle being applied at home. It made no sense. I didn't expect to find any answers when I sought out the leaders of the new government in Windhoek.

You can tell a lot about a country from its main airport, particularly in a developing country. Windhoek's main airport was clean, efficient and ultra-modern, with international signs ready for independence. Outside, visitors were not assaulted by armies of hustlers and hawkers, garishly painted broken-down buses, peeling paint or hand-painted signs saying 'Do not urinate here'. It was not Africa. This airport was named after J. G. Strydom, the Afrikaner apostle of apartheid, a typical example of Pretoria's hamfisted PR. Another misnomer was Windhoek's grandiloquently titled Government of National Unity, which couldn't even agree on what to call the country. Whites wouldn't accept the hated word 'Namibia'.

The new administration reeked of Muzorewa's defeat. Their rationale was to buy the time the Bishop never had. The same white Rhodesian clichés permeated the conversations. The new black ministers had a taste for blonde secretaries and black Mercedes.

Many whites in Windhoek felt that their country was being used as a social laboratory, a litmus test for the fainthearted in the south.

A restaurateur who still refused, illegally, to serve blacks said bluntly in Afrikaans: 'The *huigelaar* [two-faced] Botha clan is using South West as a playground to see if it [multiracialism] works. If it doesn't they will shoot the kaffirs.'

Social engineering clearly had its limits in Windhoek.

So did fashion sense. I took false refuge in an *Oktoberfest*, full of fat local Germans in *lederhosen* guzzling quarts of beer.

A briefing by intelligence officers at the defence HQ was almost a relief. I was told that just before the rainy season offensive 'only forty SWAPO terrorists are active in the operational area'. They conceded that the rains would make the numbers grow. Instinctively I looked through the barred windows to see if the rains, and my exit, were about to begin.

I asked what I thought was an intelligent question: 'Is it cost-effective to have such a massive and expensive military machine running around after forty guerrillas on the northern border of South West, when South Africa itself is said to be infiltrated by hundreds of ANC insurgents?'

'No comment. I was not briefed to reply to such a question.'

The cameraman and myself were escorted out quickly. Another glorious piece of Afrikaner diplomacy.

On a tour of Windhoek bars I bumped into one of the tough military escorts I had met on the border. He wore a beautiful pink silk shirt, a touch of rouge and a delicate gold earring. I politely declined his kind offer to take me to a gay club.

Windhoek, however, was seductive; solid colonial buildings injected grace into its dusty, small-town charm. The city centre was dominated by a German Lutheran church and a Teutonically well-preserved German fort. Surrounding hills were outlandishly adorned with imitation Rhenish castles. Some roofs were steeply tilted to stop the accumulation of desert snow.

The splendid architecture put me in a good mood and I was more inclined to be polite when I received an invitation to take afternoon tea with the Afrikaner governor-general. (South Africa wasn't quite that obvious; Louis Pienaar's real title was 'administrator-general'.) Louis and his wife treated me with an olde-worlde courtesy I had not encountered outside Jane Austen.

'South Africa,' he said, 'could leave like a thief in the night.'

Pretoria was sick of the shenanigans of Windhoek politicians.

The feeling was reciprocated. Windhoek's most famous character, Johannes Martin Smith ('Smitty' to admirers), was venomous about the Boers. Smitty, a one-man slum who ran the *Windhoek Observer* almost single-handedly, was the scourge of the local establishment. People read his paper, sometimes banned for carrying nudes, for his column 'The People Hear'. My friend Denis Beckett, no mean scourger himself, dubbed Smitty's weekly diatribe 'one of the most libellous gossip columns of modern times'.

A highly articulate lawyer, Anton Lubowski, a more conventional, pro-SWAPO white nationalist, summed up his political views: 'Namibia is a land of internal exile where individual worth is colour-coded, law and order means a state of emergency, and Christianity is a mask for inhumanity.'

Pretoria took Lubowski more seriously than Smitty's barbs. The lawyer was later assassinated.

After war and politics, I wanted to see South West's four-footed inhabitants. Windhoek was a good base from which to tour the country. To the north was Etosha Pan nature reserve. Our camera assistant, overcome by the abundant wildlife, exclaimed: 'Christ, if you look hard enough you'll even see a smurf.'

We did see everything but a smurf. Above all, I marvelled again at how giraffes always seem to move in slow motion.

In Africa, the best of the day is dawn and evening, when the game is most abundant. At the Namutoni fort I watched the thin sliver of the moon hang behind the battlements. Scops owls called, and in the distance I could hear the strangled war-cry of a hyena.

Swakopmund, on the coast, had a distinctly European air. The clean, cool oasis of palm trees and sturdy Teutonic buildings still dreamed of Kaiser Bill's Germany. With presumably unintended appropriateness, vehicle licence plates for the area bore the abbreviation SS (for South West Swakopmund). Local whites seemed to have trouble distinguishing apartheid from Nazism, although there was some contention as to whether the Kaiser's or Hitler's birthday was more important.

In the central Rehoboth region I encountered one of the distinct South West coloured communities. I was told they took great pride in being called 'bastards'. 'Coloured' was a tremendous insult, apparently. Actually the Rehoboth Basters were a mixed-race, mainly Afrikaans-speaking people originally from Namaqualand in the south. In a number of long conversations I managed to avoid the awkward nomenclature.

Keetmanshoop, to the south, the centre of the prosperous karakul farming region, maintained the South West tradition of good hotels with even better, if occasionally stodgy, food. The town was ninety minutes' drive from the Fish River Canyon, one of the natural wonders of Africa. Travelling west through Ai-Ais, a springs resort, I ventured into the Namib Desert. As a travel writer I always tell people to carry water in desert regions; naturally I broke down without any spare water, having not seen another car for hours. Out of the heat haze emerged a police patrol car. The two policemen fixed my car and dispensed free cold beers. This was a long way from Soweto.

At the end of the desert road lay Lüderitz, a run-down port with heart-sick German buildings. In English, I asked a black for directions to a hotel; he replied in perfect nineteenth-century High German. I explored some of the nearby ghost towns such as Kolmanskop, villages besieged by sand and time. Much of the coastal region was *verboten* because vast tracts were owned by diamond concessionaires. Some of the coast was accessible. Sailors called it the Skeleton Coast because of the many wrecks littering the area. To reach them required a four-wheel drive. The secret of driving through dune-fields was to let the tyres down until they were like squashed balloons. Then, once four-wheel drive was engaged, you could move fast. It was like hover-crafting across powdered snow. I was amazed to discover how slow the desert was to heal itself: tyre tracks could last for decades.

I left South West by train from Windhoek to Keetmanshoop. It took thirteen hours. A goat joined the train; some AWOL soldiers, accompanied by military policemen, left. In the compartment was a scholarly South African colonel researching ethnology who tried, unsuccessfully, to explain the differences between the many Namibian tribes.

South Africa had the military power but SWAPO had the popular support. Battlefield attrition and the convergence of superpower self-interest in Angola eventually levered Pretoria out of Windhoek. On the first day of the UN-supervised transition in 1989 – ominously 1 April – SWAPO started to invade, a stupid thing to do when they were about to win the forthcoming election. Whatever the reasons, with UN blessing the South African forces remobilised. A world-class busybody was also to hand: Margaret Thatcher flew into Windhoek on the same day. The 'African Queen', as she was dubbed, was touring southern Africa. This was a replay of Lord Soames's use of Rhodesian troops in January 1980 to counter guerrilla excesses. It was a strange twist of fate, South African troops hunting SWAPO guerrillas with UN consent.

'It feels strange to be in the right for once,' said a senior South African officer. 'I'm not sure we can handle it.'

In a week of savage fighting over 260 guerrillas were killed. Nonetheless Sam Nujoma won the most seats in the following elections and, in March 1990, South West Africa finally became Namibia. During the election campaign good ol' Sam was accused of some pretty nasty politicking.

After independence a sticker on a Windhoek car bumper read: 'Fuck the rhino, save the WHITES.'

THE MIDDLE EAST

The Middle East

9. MIDDLE EAST – THE JERUSALEM SYNDROME

Ever since God gave Charlton Heston the Ten Commandments Israel has been in the news. After 1948 too much in the news: 'We may be a chosen race but I wish God would choose someone else,' was the gut feeling of many Israelis I met.

Since those tablets of stone, the world – and now the media – have expected Israelis to behave better than other tribes in the region. That's what you get for having a hotline to God.

When I was a student I spent time on various kibbutzim. On one in the Negev Desert I was a lifeguard for six weeks, monitoring a quiet swimming pool, disturbed only by an occasional bikini. I sat and read in the sun. So I initially had a good impression, particularly of Israeli soldiers in their short skirts – though these gun-toting Lolitas could be very feisty.

And I was interested in how the Hebrew language had been revived by Eliezer Ben-Yehuda in the 1870s. He said to his infant son: 'I am going to speak just Hebrew to you. You will be the first native speaker of Hebrew for nearly 2,000 years.'

I used to wonder how the kid ordered a pizza or bought a paper when nobody could understand him.

I studied Hebrew, especially using the rapid-immersion method called 'Ulpan' used by the waves of new immigrants to Israel. Along with other Welsh Nationalists, I was keen to apply some of these lessons to the revival of Welsh.

The revival of Hebrew had been a success. Maybe God had taken an overlong lunch during the Holocaust but now he was back on the job. I shared some of the guilt by default of the previous generation which had caused or allowed the Nazi abominations to happen. I could see, however, the obvious objections to the largely Muslim Palestinians paying for the guilt of the Christian West.

*

I spent a while at the Hebrew University, Jerusalem, on a scholarship to study the effects of the Yom Kippur War. I was stuck in a military hospital in England during that conflict, watching it on television, and was taken aback by Israel's unexpected fragility and the suddenness of the Arab attack in October 1973.

In the words of one Israeli poet, 'When I heard the sirens of Yom Kippur, I heard the cries of Auschwitz.'

My research was on the war's psychological and political aftermath. The scholarship was meagre so I lived in a cheap hotel in Jerusalem's Arab quarter. After making a few Arab friends and being roughed up once by Israeli police when I was in Arab company, I began to see another side of Zionism.

Perhaps the best way of summing up the Israeli-Palestinian dispute is to call it a confusing tale of two peoples with justice on each side in conflict over the same land. It was not a case of right and wrong but right versus right. Historically, I could see both sides of the argument. Emotionally, I empathised with the Jewish people but personally found most Israelis disgustingly arrogant, especially towards Arabs.

No matter how much I disliked Israeli bigotry, I couldn't resolve the simple dilemma couched by Israel's most distinguished political scientist, Yehoshafat Harkabi: 'Israel's problem is that with the best will in the world it cannot meet the Arabs' demand, because it is unlimited and cannot be satisfied as long as Israel exists.'

In Europe and southern Africa, I taught university courses on the Middle East and acted as an examiner. Levels of ignorance about the history of the region appalled me. Some students seemed stuck in the biblical era and never managed to reach the twentieth century.

One said that Noah's wife was Joan of Arc, and that 'Solomon had 300 wives and 700 cucumbers'.

I also liked 'the Mediterranean and the Red Sea are connected by the Sewage Canal' and 'after 1973 the oil slicks [sheikhs?] raised the price of oil'.

And 'during the Final Solution Hitler tried to kill all the semantics, or Jews, in conservation camps'.

'The lost diatribes of Israel' lost me too.

These comments came from senior schoolchildren or history undergraduates.

I'm not sure whether the Western media have done that much to remedy popular ignorance about the growth of Islam, especially in the Middle East. The pack journalism of the Gulf War or the parachute hackery of the media stars often enforced the stereotyping of the region. The fall of the Shah was the classic example. The pruning of foreign desks in major newspapers had almost destroyed the old specialists, leaving only generalists, men with built-in universal bullshit-detectors.

But if you didn't speak the languages how could you tell what was bullshit and what was not? Only one in 300 foreign hacks in Iran spoke Farsi. The comfort of the monoglot pack was too tempting. No wonder the Shah's downfall came as such a shock to them, and their editors. But then the Cold War was still in business.

The opponents of the Shah were dubbed, interestingly, 'Islamic Marxists'. Wasn't the Shah a moderniser and all-popular, except for the few fanatics – beturbanned, black-robed, self-flagellating. . .? (At the time, I used to wonder, if the Shah was so damn popular, why did he need such a large and viciously omnipresent secret police.) Next door the same beturbanned weirdos were on the right side in the holy war against communism. Afghan fundamentalists were freedom fighters, Muslim militiamen; at worst noble savages and at best plucky anti-Soviet heroes.

TV depends upon pictures. No pictures, no story. The best stories involve drama, action, and often bang-bang. That is the nature of the beast. It is hard to record trends rather than events. But the decades-long misreading of the Islamic revival will continue to have a very major impact on the security of Western Europe. TV portrays many Islamic groups as history's slow learners, anti-modern fanatics, and their terrorism as a form of madness without roots. Some are certainly nasty, vicious primitives who would benefit from enforced lobotomies, but the majority are not. TV images of heroes and villains are still conditioned by the deceased Cold War: a mission to deliver foreigners from communism, poverty or religious fanatics. George Bush Junior could have found much worse poverty and fanaticism in the inner cities of America. I remember once confusing two bits of film showing ruins in Sarajevo and Los Angeles.

On domestic news TV stations tend to play it down the middle. The press councils and Joe Public have lots of ideas on what is fair in their own backyard. Abroad, journalists like to act tough, but whether in the Falklands or the Gulf the machismo usually toes the government line. The press watchdog rarely leaves the kennel when it comes to challenging conventional wisdom on foreign policy.

Precisely because nearly all Western journalists believe they are above and beyond ideology, they are most susceptible to its effects. I did not believe there was a wide-ranging media conspiracy to sanitise – to Americanise – the 1991 Gulf War, but many Western correspondents switched off their brains as they put on desert camouflage. From the numbers of Iraqi troops to the percentage of smart bombs, the official line was swallowed. It was later realised that only 7 per cent of the bombs were smart, laser-guided weapons; the vast majority were free-fall, old-fashioned gravity bombs. And they usually missed. The carnage of the Iraqi retreat was severely sanitised on Western screens. Gory footage and splatter shots had no place in TV spectaculars which looked more like arcade games than military massacres.

The American and British defence establishments learned from the Falklands and the invasions of Grenada and Panama: control of the media was paramount, especially in the initial stages of fighting. But satellites had perhaps become as powerful as politicians. The era of laptops, Marisat telephones, and portable dishes threatened the military control of the news from the Gulf. Despite all the years of trying to improve military relations with the media, especially the development of 'pools', the Pentagon cracked down hard on the hacks.

'The pools were a prison which the news establishment in America willingly conspired to build, with the Pentagon as architect-in-chief. To some extent the same thing happened in Britain.'

Such was the opinion of Alex Thomson, a UK Channel 4 correspondent. Far from the battle-cry of 'CNN rules, OK', the hacks had been emasculated. Finally, the US military had avenged themselves for the perceived misreportage of Vietnam; in Saudi Arabia, never had so many hacks been kept so sober for so long. Or, in another adaptation of Churchill, never in the field of human conflict had so little been disclosed by so few to so many. At the time many of the hacks had little idea they were being hoodwinked. As Colonel David Hackworth, a much-decorated veteran before he turned journalist, put it: 'Most didn't know a tank from a turd.'

At great risk maverick journalists, usually those who did know shit from shrapnel, broke away from the defence pools to cross into Kuwait. The freelancers were part of the reason Stormin' Norman stopped short of advancing on Baghdad. President Bush Senior did not want a second Vietnam live on cable. My old mate Tim Lambon – still teetotal – was naturally among the mavericks, conning a US army uniform and official pass to escape the pools and escort officers. He had a tough war, although the problem was more working with prima donnas such as Kate Adie than being bombed by Saddam Hussein.

I had a terrible war – I had to watch the build-up on TV. It took so long. And I thought Saddam would back down, not believing it would come to the crunch. When it did I tried to scramble out of my lecturing schedule at Cardiff University and persuade TV stations to buy my promised film in advance. Tim was already in Saudi Arabia, hired by a British network. And you needed big network muscle to get a TV team through the very restrictive Saudi authorities. J. J. Swart, my old South African cameraman-colleague, joined me on a plane to Israel; Tim said it might be possible to cross from Jordan into Saudi and come across the desert. The trouble was JJ had a South African passport, then unacceptable in most Arab countries.

With my usual immaculate timing, I arrived in Jerusalem the day the war ended. To be fair, it had lasted only 100 hours and I had moved fast. There was no point in trying to join the thousands of hacks in Kuwait. I had to do something different and I had to make some kind of film. I couldn't rely upon the standard phrase – 'calm but tense' – used by war correspondents who had arrived just after the fighting and needed to justify their expenses.

JJ had organised for us to stay at the Tel Aviv Hilton – fortunately, because the Israelis had set up the major press centre there. Compared with the bribe-burdened, paranoid Arab states, Israel's smooth PR made life easy for foreign journalists. The high literacy rate, an urbanised, multilingual population, often fluent in English, a democratic government and a vigorous press – plus the influence of the US Jewish lobby – had prompted many news organisations to set up bureaux in Israel. At the press centre I bumped into a CNN cameraman who knew me from South Africa. He was friendly with the Israeli officials and told them I was a very distinguished journalist – it's nice when friends are prepared to lie for you. In less than fifteen minutes we obtained our work permits, more than I got in three years while living in Spain.

Ramming my brain into overdrive, I checked into the hotel at 7 p.m., fixed up accreditation, attended and filmed a press conference and did a one-on-one TV interview with the charismatic deputy foreign minister, Bibi Netanyahu, and another with Ra'anan Gissin, the equally telegenic army spokesman. I sorted out editing facilities, did a brief voice report for the BBC, then walked around Tel Aviv for two hours to film the ceasefire celebrations. Most people were not sure that the war had ended but Israelis were jubilant that their greatest enemy, Saddam Hussein, had been defeated. Teenagers waving gas masks shouted 'Saddam is a maniac'.

I had forgotten how scruffy Tel Aviv was; one suburb gave the impression of a seedy oriental bazaar filled with dusky Israelis. As we filmed in (Ze'ev) Jabotinsky Square, I recalled the words of the old Zionist in the 1920s: 'We won't really be a country until we have Jewish policemen and Jewish prostitutes.' I saw lots of both.

JJ and I returned to the hotel to attend a press party, where we bumped into more old friends. We also met a Dutch army captain manning a Patriot missile system. The Patriots hadn't knocked out any Scud missiles – or not more than one or two – but had played a vital part in the propaganda war. The captain said we could film the battery the next morning during the visit of Teddy Kollek, the celebrity mayor of Jerusalem. After viewing some of the footage on our monitor, we crawled into bed about 2.30 a.m. We had done an awful lot in less than eight hours.

Early the next morning we filmed the Patriots and did an interview with an irascible Kollek. He went straight into a tourist pitch with the ambiguous line: 'Why is it that every time someone gets killed in Jerusalem it's blamed on politics? There's a hell of a lot of "ordinary" crime.'

Right on, Teddy, that's sure gonna make people rush out and buy an airline ticket to Jerusalem.

Then I nipped out to buy an Israeli bank.

Actually all I wanted to do was cash a traveller's cheque, but the amount of papers I had to sign, phone calls that were made, and close scrutiny of my passport by the manager and the office cat made me realise that Israel was the Middle East, not a bit of Yankeeland in the Levant. In my naivety I had thought that Israel would welcome foreign exchange on principle, even if in practice it was just a few pounds.

We filmed some of the damage done by Scuds in Tel Aviv. The Israeli government claimed 20,000 homes damaged but this seemed a tremendous exaggeration.

I bumped again into my CNN mate, who said that Shimon Peres, the leader of the opposition, was attending a wedding at our hotel. I had a soft spot for Shimon and risked the intrusion of grabbing him as he kissed the bride. The old pro gave me ten minutes of canned wisdom.

I always liked his ponderous Kissinger-style delivery, oozing gravitas: 'History is like a galloping horse. When it passes near your home you must mount it or miss it. Now is the time to negotiate with the Palestinians.'

A military censor, ironically a colonel of Iraqi origin, came to check our pictures in the comfort of our own hotel room. He was particularly keen to examine the Patriot stuff, explaining that a wide shot could give away the battery's position. 'We are protecting our allies, in this case the Dutch, not just Israelis.'

He explained carefully and reasonably the security reasons for erasing certain sections. I could see the military rationale and wiped the offending shots in his presence.

We hired time in an editing suite and packaged some of the material we had collected after twenty-four hours in Israel. I did a short news item on the end-of-war celebrations and sent the Peres and Netanyahu interviews whole via satellite. Bibi Netanyahu, destined soon for the premiership, was a good performer, looking good and sounding wise, despite his far-right position:

'It took twenty-eight countries with armies and air forces much bigger than ours to control one Arab country. Living here on a sliver of land, on a pin-head, we have been fighting twenty Arab countries alone. Do they really expect us to reward the PLO with an Arab state in the West Bank which will be one mile from the Knesset, our Parliament?'

I retired for a drink and bumped into an arms dealer from New York, who demanded: 'Where has the hardware Saddam bought gone? All those Stingers, those big artillery guns from South Africa, a million mines. It's all bullshit. Everybody believed Saddam's bluff.'

He said the Israeli security men on duty at the Patriot batteries stopped the Americans from countering the Scuds, for deliberate political reasons. The Israelis, he insisted, wanted one or two Scuds to hit Israeli cities and the West Bank.

After one (soft) drink I had to do a live satellite interview to

Johannesburg, one of the rooftop, skyline, potential-Scuds-in-the-background shots from a high building which became the vogue in the Gulf War. I struck up a rapport with Colonel Gissin – fortunately, as I had to reschedule the interview after confusing the times between local, UK, South African, and GMT, forgetting that satellites operate on GMT.

JJ was shouting on the phone to Jo'burg in Afrikaans while I tried to make sense of the Hebrew around me. I had an earpiece to listen to the anchor in Jo'burg, and my mike to talk to them and the interviewee. When we started live, with no floor manager to tell me how I was doing, I realised my fly was open. I couldn't adjust my dress on air, and prayed that the camera went quickly into a medium close-up of my chest. The interview, in English, went well but was too long, as thinking of angles, questions and my fly undermined my already severely limited capacity to count, so I ran way over time. But the anchor didn't say anything in my ear. Maybe she was transfixed by my dress sense.

I tried to get some sleep despite worrying about the interview. You feel self-conscious if millions of people watch you making a cock-up.

There was a tremendous explosion and I rushed out on to the balcony: not a Scud, but a crack of lightning and a mighty storm. Shivering in my underwear, I sought the warmth of my bed, but somehow the balcony door had slammed and locked. It had not been a great evening; a night on a rain-swept balcony did nothing to add to its appeal.

The next morning I was grumpy. Frustrated attempts to secure a visa to film in Jordan did not improve my mood. Then I did an interview in Afrikaans with the South African ambassador to Israel. I had not done any work for SATV for some years, partly because of my (late) conversion to sanctions. After Mandela's release I had sold documentaries and did a little work for them as a foreign correspondent, and SATV paid quite well and promptly, unlike many other TV stations.

We hired a car and drove north. I planned a short documentary about the security position in Israel in the immediate aftermath of the war, which meant travelling around all the sensitive spots: the Lebanese border, the Golan Heights, the West Bank and Gaza. En route we would collect some pretty visuals which I could massage into a short tourism piece. What was lacking was bang-bang, especially if the war was really over.

I had picked up a bit of gossip that Terry Waite and perhaps John McCarthy, two well-publicised British hostages, were being held in southern Lebanon. It was an extremely long shot but worth a go. I used one or two old Israeli military contacts to speed my access to the Lebanese badlands.

I visited some acquaintances in the north who lived in settlements next to Arab villages. 'Relations between Arab and Jew are on a knife's edge,' I was told. The Israelis were incensed by the Palestinians' passionate support of Saddam and stories of West Bank Arabs cheering from the rooftops as Scuds rocketed over them to hit Tel Aviv. 'There are two problems with the Russians: their Scuds and their immigrants.'

We stayed the night in Nahariya while I made arrangements with the Israeli army and UN peacekeepers to proceed into Lebanon. Leaving the car at the closed border crossing of Rosh Hanikra, we passed through army and police checks.

At the end stood a white UN car manned by a black woman with a wonderful smile: Sarah, a Ugandan. Zig-zagging through big cement blocks Sarah and I discovered a mutual friend who had been in a convent school in Uganda. Some ex-convent girls, I've found, treat the world as one huge pub, and thus sometimes make it big in journalism, although they are forever plagued with inbred, inescapable guilt. Actually our mutual friend didn't drink, but she was a bloody good journalist.

Sarah was immediately on-side and did her best to ease my way with the various UN contingents from whom I scrounged accommodation and armoured lifts. The main UN base was staffed with French troops, who had erected a mini Eiffel Tower to make them feel at home. Sarah introduced me to her boss, a loquacious Indian, Timur Göksel.

In his office a notice read: 'If you think you understand Lebanon, you've not been properly briefed.'

After we had swapped Al J. Venter stories and established other mutual contacts, Göksel arranged UN passes for us. Our first escorts were large Fijians driving Finnish armoured personnel carriers.

JJ had boundless energy. In Africa he would climb any tree or vantage point for his shots. In Lebanon we rode on top of the APCs, but he kept moving around to get travelling shots. I couldn't be in view, and spent bumpy hours clambering around trying to stay behind JJ's camera. I fell off on one tight corner. I soon recovered my position, but I am pretty sure the slight limp I have to this day was caused by that incident.

We passed through a series of roadblocks manned by the surly South Lebanese army, who were in the pay of the Israelis. The landscape was initially dry bush and hilly country.

'Zia' (not his real name) was a burly Fijian lieutenant who soon befriended us. For some odd reason he thought that I was an expert on mercenaries; to become one was his main ambition in life. He sorted out our accommodation in the Fijian camp up in the hills. The Fijian army was sloppily based on the British model, but the officers' mess was strictly dry.

Zia said: 'Some people drink to socialise; we drink to get drunk.'

These big, tough Fijians were very amiable when sober but I could see they would be a handful on the grog, so the no-alcohol rule made sense. Life in their mess was boring, however. The food was awful and the only outlet was watching TV. After watching *Bonanza* and *Zorro* in Arabic I nagged Zia to take us on a tour of Palestinian camps.

We drove to a heavily armed PLO camp on the coast. On the outskirts two Palestinians invited me into the camp to 'take some tea'. I accepted out of curiosity but Zia pulled me aside and explained that the spot we were in was exactly the one where an American, Colonel Richard Higgins, had been captured by Hezbollah; he was later hanged.

We moved on through territory controlled by the Lebanese army. Zia left the negotiations to my fractured French, little knowing that letting me tell shaggy-dog stories in French to jumpy Lebanese soldiers was more dangerous than wandering around a PLO camp. Still, we managed to talk our way through five roadblocks on the pretext that I needed to speak to the Lebanese army commander in Tyre. We were not supposed to film, but JJ put the camera on his lap and let it roll.

Few Western journalists had been into Tyre since the Israeli invasion ten years before. I expected chaos but found instead a thriving pirate economy. Mercedes proliferated, many apparently stolen in Europe and smuggled into ports such as Tyre. Banks and shops operated in the biblical but now high-rise city. Wrecked cars and houses littered the landscape, although many new cars and buildings were also to be seen. How the Lebanese economy had survived sixteen years of civil war was a minor miracle.

Lebanon was once called the 'Switzerland of the Middle East'. After 1975 the civil war killed at least 150,000 people, a quarter of its 3.5 million population had fled the country. It struck me as paradoxical that the Lebanese, famed abroad as great fixers and organisers, had succumbed to domestic chaos. I suppose a bad political system will always swamp positive national characteristics. I had just been reporting on the collapse of communism and wondered how the Soviets had managed, in East Germany, to impoverish a state chock-a-block with energetic Germans.

The origins of the Lebanese wars are so complex as almost to defy classification. Internal religious rivalries (Muslim versus Christian), allied with ideological and class hostilities and old tribal feuds, had been exploited by outside powers. In this international battlefield Syria, the PLO, Israel and Iran had been major contenders; America, Saudi Arabia, Russia, France, and Iraq also had stirred the pot.

The 1991 Gulf War brought changes to Lebanon. First the Americans cosied up to Syria, once called a 'terrorist state' by Washington. Next came the termination of foreign subsidies to the numerous warlords, cutting off the PLO from its Gulf funds. Supplies to Iraq's Christian allies were also strangled. Even Iran, keen to rejoin the world community, was encouraged to rein in Islamic fundamentalists. And Syria, with its 40,000 troops in Lebanon, could no longer rely upon a destitute Russia to bankroll its military machine, which ran on Soviet technology shown to be very inferior in the Gulf War. Most important, though, was the utter war-weariness of the Lebanese.

As warlord Walid Jumblatt admitted: 'We are all just fed up with this war.'

Certainly ordinary Lebanese were sick of the militias and their Mafia-like protection taxes. On the other hand, they did provide a rough-and-ready sort of order in their military statelets. The Syrian army had helped the weak Lebanese army recapture much of the country, although the southern region was still a hotchpotch of UN troops, militias, PLO and Israeli-backed Lebanese proxies.

The black market thrived, despite triple-figure inflation. Lebanese were starting to return from abroad. But those who had stayed, especially the drug smugglers, would suffer if the pirate economy was curbed. Nevertheless, Lebanon was allowing itself the luxury of hope. Some of the 5,000 UN contingent began to feel that in a few years they might be able to pack up and go home.

When we reached the Lebanese army HQ in Tyre I spoke to a deeply suspicious and very charming general who explained in immaculate French that we could not film. He was a civilised man who shared my interest in the Roman ruins in the area, so provided our cameras did not leave our vehicle we could indulge in some sightseeing. Urbanely, over mint tea, he gave us two hours to get out of town.

We filmed discreetly from the vehicle and visited the market near the bustling harbour. I wanted to send some 'Wish you were here' postcards to Europe. Postcards proliferated but apparently stamps were unavailable. Since tourists were an endangered species, JJ, a compulsive shopper, managed to haggle some real bargains; it remains the only time and place in the Middle East where I saw a foreigner get the better of an Arab trader.

Zia, however, was keen to get us out of Tyre. He became very shifty. We had switched from an armoured vehicle to a UN Land Rover. He drove down some back streets, just the three of us, until we reached a small shop. He asked us to wait outside for him.

'Don't leave the UN vehicle. It's your only protection. I'll be back in an hour.'

Of course, we wandered off to film, though keeping the Land Rover in sight. When Zia came back he confided that he had just visited the relative of a Lebanese Muslim widow, and told us a poignant love story. He had seen her in a little shop. For months he visited on various pretexts, bringing flowers regularly. She had two children; her husband, a militiaman, had been killed two years after their marriage.

Zia was a large black man, under strict military orders not to fraternise with local women. He was also already married. She was surrounded by fanatical Muslim extremists who would happily take pot-shots at any UN officer, let alone a black married Christian carrying on an adulterous relationship. . .

She told Zia: 'Our love will get us killed if we are caught.'

'I know. But I don't care.'

'Nor do I,' she replied, sealing their dangerous pact.

Zia wanted to take her to Cyprus and then France, where he planned to join the Foreign Legion. (This is a true story; not even Mills and Boon would mix a forbidden love with the Foreign Legion.) The plot was complicated by the fact that her relatives had whisked her off to Beirut where she was practically imprisoned. Zia told me how he planned to spring her.

'I will marry her,' he said, pulling out some of his poetry for me to read. I could see that he was desperate, completely crazy, and about to ask my advice and practical help. Before I could become actively involved in his suicidal venture, JJ and I decided to join some nearby Irish troops. The dry Fijian mess, and the mosque outside our bedroom which wailed us awake at 5 a.m., were getting to us. We filmed the Fijians playing rugby, then Zia drove us to the Irish battalion. He had time, he said, to take us to an interesting place. JJ was wary until Zia said it was a shopping trip.

About ten miles from Tyre, way up in the hills, was one of the world's greatest army surplus stores. The Lebanese owner had spent years amassing stolen weapons and equipment. JJ was in seventh heaven, and we immediately bought two UN caps.

Suddenly Zia started shouting and raving, clutching a flak jacket with the name of a close friend on it, he explained, stolen a few weeks before from their HQ. This was a massive affront to the honour of his country, his army and himself.

The shopkeeper said he could have it for $20.

Zia said he would take it for free. It belonged to him.

Zia drew his pistol.

The shopkeeper, with great speed, pulled out a brand-new AK-74, cocked it, and aimed it at Zia's chest.

In Lebanon the customer is not always right.

While they cursed each other, JJ took cover. I sneaked out to tell the Fijian private guarding the Land Rover to get in there with his rifle.

The two Fijians, with rifle and pistol, faced the determined shopkeeper, who had been joined by another man armed with an AK-47. Four weapons a few feet apart and lots of angry words. What would all those shots going off do in a shop full of ammunition?

Luckily, I spotted an Amal militia officer sitting in a jeep across the road, and quickly explained the situation. He rushed in to defuse what was about to become, literally, an international incident. The guns were lowered and half an hour later Zia came out with the flak jacket. He didn't pay anything. He had made his point.

Unfortunately we were late for our rendezvous with the Irish troops. I had been dreaming of Guinness, but the Irish captain displayed a strict regard for punctuality which I had not before encountered in the Celtic personality. I tried hard to persuade him to accommodate us, applying my own Celtic charm, and attempting to evoke pity for the limp caused by a twisted knee ligament acquired when I had fallen off the APC. But the captain didn't like journalists.

'Without UN escorts, you will have to quit Lebanon.'

I rang Göksel, who arranged for us to join the Finns. I had given up any idea of even asking about hostages. Southern Lebanon was one dangerous place.

The Finns ran a luxurious mess compared with the Fijians, and we wallowed in pizza, lager and saunas. This was a war for journalists. The officers, who spoke excellent English, treated us with great courtesy. In exchange we listened to endless bad jokes. The Finns must have learned a lot from their alliances with Germany. Their briefings were equally Teutonic: I took endless notes about the precise calibres of every rifle in the hands of the local militia. The frustrated PLO guerrillas, I was told, paid the local Lebanese $100 per rocket to fire Katyushas into Israel.

The Finns gave us a lift back to the UN camp at the border, and we crossed back to Israel to pick up our hire car. Lebanon had depressed me; I wanted to find some gleam of hope in the promised land, even though it is strictly against union rules to say nice things about a war zone. I visited a few of the Israeli peaceniks to search for a good news story for a change. The war had polarised most Arabs and Jews in Israel, even those who were active in the peace movement. In Kfar Yassif, in Galilee, I came across a different story.

The Arab mayor, a communist leader called Nimur Murkus, had invited Tel Aviv Jews to stay in his village, an unlikely target for Saddam's Scuds. Mayor Murkus opposed Scud attacks on civilians. His invitation, ignored in the international media, was echoed by a number of other Israeli Arab mayors. We spent an enjoyable day with Murkus and his family, getting the perspective of 'moderate' Arabs who were Israeli citizens.

Later JJ and I sought out the Jews who actually took up the offer. We contacted a wonderful 76-year-old lady from Tel Aviv, who spent some days in Kfar Yassif with her son and her dog while the rockets rained down on heavily populated Tel Aviv. 'After sixty years of hatred,' she said, 'it was marvellous to stay with Arab people who treated me so kindly.'

Elsewhere, behind the scenes, tiny groups of Jews and Arabs were working together. I interviewed a rabbi who held small religious gatherings with Arab Muslims and Christians. The same rabbi organised trucks of food to be taken into the West Bank just after the 24-hour curfew was imposed at the beginning of the Gulf War.

JJ and I drove north again – it is easy to get around Israel, it's the same size as Wales – to stay the night at a kibbutz hotel at Kfar Blum. A number of South African Jews had settled there and I wanted to do a quick documentary on how they had gone through the war. We arrived late in the evening but a group of ten ex-South Africans and former Rhodesians were more than happy to be interviewed around a large table. They talked about the difficulties of adapting to gas masks and the special problems with children's protection. You always get somebody who wants to play the clown, so one did a brief filmed chat through a mask.

They complained that they had no masks for their pets. I did point out that initially the Palestinians in the West Bank had no masks at all.

In the morning we filmed some visuals and cutaway shots around the kibbutz, a pleasant agricultural settlement in the shadow of the Golan Heights. The ex-South Africans joked about life without cars and maids; capitalist businessmen from Jo'burg and Cape Town, not without difficulties, had accepted the socialist ideals of the kibbutz movement. About 3 per cent of Israelis lived in kibbutzim.

Zionism was always a paradox. Jews in the affluent West were encouraged to give up their comfortable lifestyles to accept the bracing austerity of nationalism in Israel, while Palestinians in the West Bank were told to forget their national ideals in exchange for the economic advantages of the Israeli connection.

We left early to drive through the Golan to film Mount Hermon, shrouded in mist and rain, then cut back across the West Bank in late afternoon. The West Bank seemed empty, dry, dusty and run down. In Israel there was crowded bustle, set amid a greening landscape. Over 190 million trees had been planted since 1948.

In Jerusalem we stayed at the American Colony, a beautiful hotel. It was the press watering-hole and the best place to make contact with the PLO, although everybody was watched by alert Israeli intelligence men with bulges under their jackets and strong American accents. The old city was largely closed because of a strike called by the PLO, but

I found an Arab restaurant open and chatted to the locals. They all expressed support for Yasser Arafat and Saddam Hussein.

I made contact with the PLO and arranged for a guide to take us through the West Bank, even though it was still officially closed to journalists. Our guide, Suheir, was a brave and pretty eighteen-year-old student. We needed a hire car with Israeli plates to get through the Israeli army roadblocks, with our camera equipment stowed in the boot. Many journalists had had their cars stoned and burnt by Palestinian youths, so we needed an official PLO guide in case we came to unofficial PLO roadblocks.

When we saw a group of youths carrying stones, Suheir told us to put an Arab head-dress across the top of the dash. Around the next bend was an Israeli roadblock, so she whipped it away.

We drove into a forty-year-old refugee camp at Ramallah. The conditions were wretched. The camp's elders told me how thousands of new Russian immigrants were taking Arab jobs: 'The curfews keep us at home and then they hand out our jobs to people who have been here a few weeks. We were born here.'

They also complained about the Israeli army's practice of bulldozing and dynamiting the homes of activists. The older generation in the camp clearly supported Arafat and Saddam Hussein, although the younger elements were backers of Hamas, the fundamentalist opposition to the PLO.

As I was interviewing the camp elders, a messenger came to tell us that Israeli soldiers were looking for foreign journalists. Suddenly there were soldiers everywhere, partly because an Israeli woman had just been stabbed about a mile away. We drove the car into the large backyard of an old UN refugee building on the edge of the camp and sat tight. We might have our film confiscated and suffer deportation, but Suheir told us that she would be jailed.

Six nervous young Israeli soldiers sauntered into the yard. The only way out was past them, so JJ and I put on the UN caps we had bought in Lebanon. Our cameras were hidden in the back seat. I drove towards the soldiers, slowing down just enough to say quickly that we were UN workers.

They shouted at us to stop and raised their rifles, but didn't open fire. We got out of the camp as rapidly as possible.

In Jericho, the biblical oasis 750 feet below sea level, I interviewed

Rhodesian blitzkrieg: a Soviet BTR-152 armoured car, used by Frelimo, destroyed by Rhodesian forces at Chimoio, Mozambique, September 1978. (Rhodesian government)

The Great Fire of Salisbury: Prime Minister Ian Smith, 11 December 1978. Guerrillas blew up the central oil depot in Salisbury, Rhodesia. (Author's collection)

'Tame terr': a security force auxiliary, loyal to Bishop Muzorewa, 1979, Rhodesia. Five separate armies operated in the last days of the war. (Courtesy of Allen Pizzey)

Metal dreadlocks: marching with the *mujahedin* near Kabul, summer 1984. (Author's photo)

Above God is great: extensive prayers before battle against Soviet-backed troops, Afghanistan, summer 1984. (Author)

Left 'Butterfly' bomb: Sadat Khan, a young boy injured by a Soviet anti-personnel device, being treated by 'Doc' Khalid, the translator. Afghanistan, 1984. (Author)

Bombed out: film crew (Chris Everson, in front, and Ian Robbie) arrive to find their temporary home blown up by Russian aerial bombardment. Afghanistan, 1984. (Author)

Putting on a brave face: Ian Robbie and Chris Everson prepare author for to-camera piece. Afghanistan, 1984. (Author's collection)

Boy soldiers: Renamo guerrillas in central Mozambique, 1986. (Author)

Planning to be a fat-cat politician: Afonso Dhlakama in his final, podgier, days as a guerrilla chieftain. Mozambique, 1991. (Author)

'Red Bo Dereks': Ovahimba women getting supplies from a Southern African Defence Force patrol. South-west Africa/Namibia, 1986. (Author)

Once the Gold Coast: young
entrepeneur, Elmina Castle. Ghana,
1992. (Author)

Salami tactics: a young woman sits
outside her house which had been
sliced in half by Israeli bulldozers.
Jenin, West Bank, 2002. (Author)

Fallen idols: the ghosts of colonialism and Marxism. Cacheu fort, Guinea-
Bissau, 1992. (Author)

All tanked up: author during MoD visit to British forces in Gornji Vakuf, Bosnia, 1998. (Author's collection)

Not the Brigade of Guards: rebels of the Sudan Liberation Army. Darfur, 2004. (Author)

Teaching people how to vote? Policeman of the Sudan People's Liberation Army, Bentiu, South Sudan, during the 2010 election. (Tony Denton)

Winning hearts and minds: schoolchildren and orphans queue up to get goodies from British troops in Kabul, 2002. (Author)

'You sort it out now.' Locals complain to a British major about lack of electricity, water and jobs. Basra, Iraq, May 2003. (Author)

Keeping his head down: Tim Lambon shooting with a mini-cam while in US Marine Corps Amtrack. Fallujah, Iraq, 2004. (Lambon collection)

a prominent PLO official, Professor Sa'eb Erakat. He was one of the Palestinians negotiating with US Secretary of State James Baker, who was in Jerusalem at the time. We filmed the interview and JJ surreptitiously shot some scenes from a roof. It was too risky to film openly. Six PLO guerrillas had just been killed in the West Bank and unrest was growing in Gaza. The Israelis were unlikely to swallow our blue-cap routine a second time.

Returning to Jerusalem we filmed secretly in an Arab hospital. We were allowed to interview young patients wounded, they said, by Israeli troops. The wounds were real but I had a problem with the boys' repetition that they were 'on their way to the mosque to pray', that they had not thrown any stones . . . Whatever the real reason for their injuries, the tragedy of teenage paraplegics lay heavily on me. I would have liked to check each Arab claim with the Israeli authorities, but that was impossible. We weren't supposed to be filming in the West Bank at all. I had to rely upon my own balance when it came to editing the film.

We also interviewed Major-General Shlomo Gazit, the former head of military intelligence, who arrogantly derided the idea of a Palestinian homeland in the near future. Either he was not up on the latest intelligence or he wasn't sharing any contrary data with us. But why should he?

We took a day off to film some of the old city of Jerusalem, which enchanted me no matter how often I visited it. You could see, smell, touch history here. In many streets you could pretend to be in any time of the last two millennia. Many shops were still closed and few tourists were evident. Nonetheless, storekeepers whispered to us to come in and buy behind closed shutters. Business was business, and JJ was still a shopaholic. Again, he managed to beat down the best hagglers in the world.

Israelis, it must be said, were not exactly backward when it came to business either. Jewish friends delighted in telling me stereotyping stories. I loved the one about the Jewish primary school:

TEACHER: Hymie, what's two and two?
HYMIE: Depends. Are we buying or selling?

We wandered for hours through narrow medieval streets, full

of twisting lanes, oriental souks, steep stairways and dark, covered passages. We felt no threat, just wonderment. I could almost understand the Jerusalem Syndrome, which hospitalises forty or fifty visitors each year. The spiritual overload of the old city causes people suddenly to think they are the messiah or his mum, with the odd sprinkling of John the Baptists and the occasional King David. Most of the nutters come from Europe or America, and they are usually Protestants rather than Catholics or Jews. The psychiatric literature abounds with analysis of the syndrome which is divided into various stages. Stage four, for example, involves preparation of a long, ankle-length, white, toga-like gown, often, I presume, with the aid of hotel bed-linen. Then sufferers march about and sing (popular in the locality anyway, though not in togas) and one of the final stages is preaching a sermon.

An Israeli psychiatrist told me that he once had two Jewish messiahs in his care at the same time. Apparently they got on very well with each other, even though they both said it was a pity they had to chat to an impostor.

Most patients recover after four or five days and recall their crisis as a pleasant experience before flying off home to resume their normal lives. But going back to selling insurance or fixing radiators after being the Son of God must be tough.

Jerusalem must have affected JJ and me because we ended up in the desert filming and visiting St George's Monastery. Both of us were attracted to the place and the long walk there, though neither of us succumbed to wearing togas.

On the journey to Eilat we swam in the Dead Sea; I took the obligatory picture of JJ sitting reading a newspaper in the super-buoyant salty water. At Eilat, a friend from Cape Town ran a diving school. We hired equipment and dived with the dolphins.

On previous visits I had driven deep into the Sinai to visit Sharm El Sheikh and the intriguing ossuary at St Catherine's Monastery. St Catherine's, at the foot of Mount Sinai, was supposed to be the site of Moses's burning bush. The Greek Orthodox settlement is the oldest working Christian monastery in the world, with a world-renowned collection of ancient texts and icons.

I remembered the monastery from a first trip shortly after Israel conquered the Sinai. I had driven cross-country on virgin sands to reach it. After days of travel, we were very thirsty. At the bottom of the hill up to the monastery stood a little white-and-pink striped tent, where a Bedouin was selling ice-cold Cokes from a paraffin fridge, at justifiably inflated prices. Our small group slurped down the drinks with relish.

An Australian colleague said: 'All I need now in the whole wide world is a Mars bar to go with the Coke.'

The Bedouin, who apparently spoke no English, suddenly beamed when he heard the phrase 'Mars bar'.

'Ah-haaa,' he said excitedly, and definitively, 'Marianne Faithfull'.

Again this is absolutely true, though a dinner much later in London with Marianne Faithfull's former manager elicited the information that the Mars bar and the Rolling Stones story was a media confection, so to speak. That would surely have disappointed the Bedouin trader.

That was just after the 1973 war. Now Sinai was back in Egyptian hands.

After the rare, relaxing break at Eilat we headed north to film around Gaza, where the mood was very tense. It had always been a complete dump – Samson probably didn't miss much by being eyeless in Gaza. You could reach out and touch the Palestinian anger.

We also filmed in the picturesque port of Jaffa to beef up the short travel documentary I had in mind. In less than three weeks we had made a political documentary, sent off news footage by satellite, and made a soft travel film plus some short pieces in Afrikaans. We had enough in the can.

I went to Israeli defence HQ to buy some aerial library shots and used the opportunity to get customs security clearance. It would be more troublesome at the airport, where they might insist on viewing all the tapes.

We were interrogated for four hours by security personnel at the airport. Two men questioned us separately and in detail on our contacts with Palestinians, then swapped around to see if there were any discrepancies. They didn't check the already security-tagged film. We missed our plane but eventually caught another and arrived back safely in London. The rudest people we met on the whole trip were the customs officials at Heathrow.

I left the Middle East feeling again just a little optimistic (though that feeling was always soon shattered). The proverbial window of opportunity was opening just a mite, perhaps, perhaps. The basic issue was still straightforward: land for peace. Jewish survival versus rights for the Palestinians. Cynics would say swapping Jews for oil. Nevertheless, the Palestinians had lost everything, and had turned to Saddam Hussein in utter despair. Equally, the return of the possibility of death by gas traumatised the Israelis. Israel had a population full of worriers, as well as would-be generals. But one of the main lessons of the war was that the old argument about strategic depth (the need for land to buy time in case of an Arab invasion) was seriously flawed in the missile age.

Once Israel could rely on the almost unconditional support of Washington, but now American public opinion was changing. The image of a tiny democratic state of brave Holocaust survivors had been tarnished by the arrogant military occupation of the West Bank and Gaza. The power of the once-mighty Jewish lobby had declined. With the collapse of the Soviet Union, no longer was Israel seen as the only reliable ally in the region. Instead, it was arguably a strategic liability costing the US $3 billion a year in military aid. In the longer term, utterly dependent on its American life-support machine, Israel's position had to weaken. Syria had lost its Soviet patron, Iraq was humbled and America was top dog in the Middle East. Except for the Palestinians, the Arabs – cowed by American weapons' wizardry in the Gulf – had lost interest in fighting Israel.

In one sense Saddam won, by accident. He put the Palestinian uprising, the *intifada*, back on the centre of the world stage. The 1993 Israeli–Palestinian accords could have led to a Palestinian state, of sorts. But Yasser Arafat seemed unable or unwilling to control endemic corruption and contain Islamic radicals. The Israelis withdrew from southern Lebanon but found no peace. The Middle East became more unstable, especially as the *intifada* was taken up by the inhabitants of the new Palestinian Authority. The Israelis reacted with reprisal raids; then the zealots sent in suicide bombers to the centre of Jewish towns. Another Arab–Israeli war looked inevitable as the new millennium dawned. Israel was still the only real democracy in the area, the Arab states all more or less dictatorships. And, as the former Soviet empire further crumbled, forty-five million ex-Soviet Muslims were in danger of being swept up by Islamic fervour.

And Jerusalem? How do you divide that ancient and holy citadel? Perhaps, just perhaps, the city should be shared under UN supervision. Jerusalem is the toughest nut to crack, but nobody said a Middle East solution was going to be easy. Maybe Steven Spielberg could make a film called *The Jerusalem Syndrome*. In it Charlton Heston Mark II would star as a deranged messiah who comes up with an answer to the city of three great world religions. But Spielberg knows that his co-religionists would be unlikely willingly to deliver Jerusalem to the UN or anybody else. By the turn of the millennium fickle Western sympathy had swung back to the perception of Israel as an underdog. Bogeymen such as Saddam Hussein and Osama bin Laden had evoked fresh empathy for the Zionists, despite the provocative behaviour of the settlers in the West Bank. Yet Israel's very existence seemed imperilled by the firestorm of Arab anger symbolised by Islamic suicide bombers.

For decades the received wisdom had been that there could never be a military solution to the Arab–Israeli problem. But right-wing opinion in the USA and in Israeli security circles was suggesting a radical solution to the chronic sense of insecurity. Israel would launch a lightning attack on the leadership of the PLO's security apparatus, and those of Hamas and Islamic Jihad. Israeli troops would stay long enough to decapitate the *intifada*, evacuate the more far-flung Jewish settlements, and then build – right along the border, including Jerusalem – a dirty great big high-security wall; one stronger than Jericho's and longer-lasting than Berlin's. Gaza had been cordoned thus already. The PLO had been given a chance for peace but now Palestinians would also have lost their chance to swamp the Israelis by demography or a war of gradual attrition. Draconian as this might have seemed in 2000, it might have been better than another all-out war between Arabs and Jews. Such a conflict could have sparked an Armageddon in the arc of Islamic instability from Kosovo to Saudi Arabia and Egypt.

For believers, that would fulfil biblical prophecy. But if mankind has free will, then presumably he (or she) can reject what God has prophesied. Perhaps Moses, and Charlton Heston, should have declined the invitation to climb that mountain.

AFRICA III

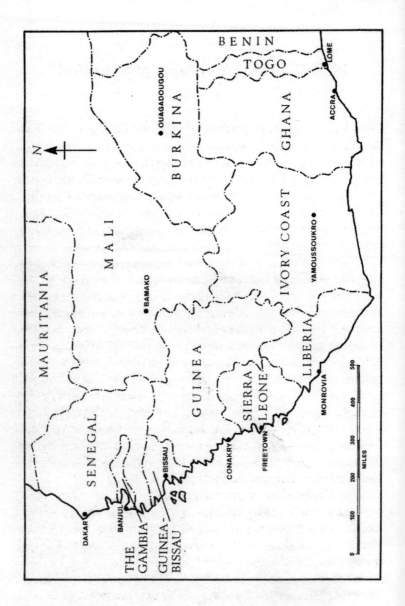

West Africa

10. WEST AFRICA – FORTS AND CASTLES

West Africa is where the whites went to harvest blacks. But before the black gold they hunted for yellow gold. For three centuries nine European states built, fought over, and ransacked hundreds of forts and castles along the steamy, disease-ridden West African coast. The African continent has thousands of fascinating fortifications, ranging from the small Beau Geste forts of North Africa to the dry-stone masterpieces of Great Zimbabwe in the south. In the east Arab traders built Islamic citadels. West Africa, however, has the best collection of European-built fortresses.

The fortresses originated with the Portuguese, who started exploring this coastline in the late fifteenth century. Driven by favourable winds and currents, early explorers sought gold, glory, and a southern maritime route to the riches of the east. A strategic impulse also intruded: Portugal wanted to find the legendary Christian kingdom of Prester John. Feeling threatened by advancing Muslim armies in south-eastern Europe, they thought a Christian thrust from the rear could undermine the march of Islam. Some of their castles were built with massive walls, similar to the great Crusader forts. Perhaps the Portuguese were mindful of the successful Muslim onslaught on the bastion of Constantinople. Instead, the African forts became prizes in a long series of colonial mini-wars waged mainly between the Portuguese, Dutch, British, and French. Sometimes African armies would pitch in to tilt the local white balance of power.

West Africa was not my normal stamping ground, so when I received a phone call from Al J. Venter about making a film in the region I was keen. It was early 1992 and I was bored and frustrated in my native Wales. Any adventure would do, even a crazy one arranged by Big Al. I liked Al so I had a very low learning curve about saying no to one of his 'missions'. He always worked a double, or even triple, agenda. You would be in some often disagreeable, sometimes dangerous place before you discovered what he wanted. Later, back in civilisation, you might find out what he was really up to.

It started off in the usual way. Would I please take a large case to Lisbon? I sat in his hotel room in London and watched him pack it. The suitcase was extraordinarily heavy, although I'm sure he didn't put in any guns this time. In Lisbon Al explained that he was particularly interested in Christianborg castle in Ghana. I knew it was a wonderful building, but I also knew it was the heavily guarded home of a rather paranoid generalissimo, Flight-Lieutenant Jerry Rawlings. He definitely didn't like unexpected guests.

'Dogs of war again, is it Al?'

He gave me one of his sly laughs. 'No, this is a straight film.'

He showed me the dummy of a big picture book on African forts. The one printed chapter had some tremendous photos. He wanted the book to tie in with a twelve-part TV series which he hoped to sell worldwide. I was to produce the pilot. As most of the castles were located in nasty dictatorships, no permission had been sought to film in any of the countries he wanted me to visit. We would do it with a small video-8 camera which we had to smuggle in.

Here we go again, I thought.

Normally Al was noticeable by his absence in any of the places he asked me to visit. That suited me fine. He had an overbearing presence, despite his great charm. Most cameramen could take him only in small doses if he tried to play the great director. On this trip Al played the great white hunter *and* movie mogul. Two-man teams work well in war zones or tin-pot dictatorships. When we arrived in Abidjan, the capital of the Ivory Coast, I discovered Al was bringing his wife and two friends on our jaunt. He was paying so I couldn't really complain. But the cameraman, Tommy Doig, and I did our best to escape on our own. Tommy, in his early fifties, cynical, tough, and experienced, was a veteran African film-maker whose work I admired. He was an old friend of Al's, and unlikely to be intimidated by his famous temper and constant changes of mind and mood.

We went to a restaurant in a seedy downtown area of Abidjan. Afterwards Al wanted to show his South African friends what a ghetto was like at night. Tommy and I knew better and went back to the hotel. Al's entourage arrived back a half an hour later.

'Have a nice time?' I asked politely.

Al did not know the meaning of sheepish grin, but he came as close as he could: 'Yeah, interesting. Brought the others back for security reasons.'

Tommy and I explored in daylight. Central Abidjan was swish, modern, very French. Many restaurants were expensive, as were the imported wines. It used to be an African success story.

'It's the one place on the continent where the numbers of whites increased after independence,' a French official told me.

Foreign aid poured in and the profits poured out. Ivory Coast, or Côte d'Ivoire, played along with Western rules in the Cold War. Like next-door Ghana, it listened to the IMF. Urged on by aid donors, both countries boosted their mainstay, cocoa. (Coffee was also produced, but it was the awful instant stuff sold in big tins.) Then prices collapsed. The French settlers, originally 40,000 strong, began to drift away.

The wily and benevolent despot of the Ivory Coast, Félix Houphouët-Boigny – whom Tommy dubbed 'Humphrey Bogart' – started losing his grip, despite the presence of immaculately dressed French troops. The French were growing tired of propping up their client states in Africa; paras were now sent into francophone Africa sparingly and reluctantly. Instead they advocated 'Paristroika' – usually French blueprints to conjure up 'national conferences' to end endemic dictatorships and establish multi-party democracies.

There were one or two half-successes – a few more or less free elections – before some sergeant or other grew bored in barracks on half-pay. In remote states such as the Central African Republic and Burkina Faso the military paid mere lip service to reform. In many countries the national conferences had set southern, more urbanised tribes (who often had more to gain from 'democracy') against traditionally nomadic, often Muslim, northern tribes who tended to dominate the militaries. Some West African states resisted foreign demands for multi-party systems. In French West Africa, however, relying on France had become a habit.

The French had been more successful colonists than the British in the region because, as one journalist put it, 'All the colonisers stuffed up the locals, but at least the French called them "monsieur" while they did it.'

Paris, as usual, was playing a double game. Despite Paristroika, France still sent troops and weapons to bolster autocrats. Cameroon was a recent example. The excuse was that Paris didn't want to support 'anarchy disguised as democracy' as Roland Dumas, the French foreign minister, declared. I don't think Brezhnev could have put it better.

West Africa was an important indicator of the continent's health. The European connection with black Africa was here old and complex. I wondered whether the 500-year connection had helped or hindered West Africa. The area was notorious for its virulent corruption: an indigenous trait or bad habits learned from centuries of encounters with the most rapacious of European traders and slavers? Whatever the cause many West African states were simply sinking into a morass of their own graft and venality. In February 1992 Nigeria's election commission revealed the existence of some twenty million 'ghosts' – fictitious people who had dutifully registered to vote. The whole mess used to be blamed on greedy colonialists. But they had left decades before and the economies had deteriorated rapidly, with a few exceptions such as the Ivory Coast. Nigeria could have become an African superpower but it was heading for chaos.

The West was bored with Africa. Besides regular catastrophes only the occasional media circus grabbed attention. John Paul II and Michael Jackson had recently made (separate) papal tours of West Africa, for example. The West still officially showed some interest in 'good government' in Africa but it was a fleeting diplomatic flourish, for the simple reason that free-market economics and free politics do not necessarily go hand in hand, especially in Africa.

Ghana had frightened off investors but its slight economic recovery was praised by the World Bank and donors. Everyone ignored the strong-arm tactics of Flight-Lieutenant Rawlings, perhaps because he was not as obviously bonkers as some of his fellow dictators in uniform, or because he was practically the only African leader who deliberately avoided a personality cult. The fundamental question remained: can embryonic democracies take really tough economic decisions without slipping back into dictatorship? In West Africa the answer had usually been no.

Al gave me three days to fly to Ghana alone and get permission to film in Rawlings's castle. He and Tommy would drive down the coast and cross into Ghana by road, filming some of the coastal forts en route. But all the flights to Accra, Ghana's capital, were fully booked. I tried my luck with the manager of Ghana Airways, a large formidable woman. For once in West Africa a bribe just wouldn't work. I tried to pull rank, showing her a letter Al had received from the presidential palace about his book project.

'You are not Al J. Venter and this letter is six months old.'

I decided to try the emotional approach. I had never been to Ghana before but I did have a female friend in Accra. I was looking forward to seeing her, although our relationship had been no more than the occasional lunch while she was studying in the UK. I apologised to the manager for trying to bribe and pressurise her. Everything I said was true, but I was trying to get to Accra quickly for personal reasons as well. I wanted to visit my friend, Mercy, for her birthday.

'Is she Ghanaian?'

'Yes.'

'That is good. Come back in ten minutes.'

She bumped an obnoxiously pompous white businessman off the plane. He made an awful fuss. I felt a bit guilty until he started racially abusing my benefactor. She gave him short shrift, summoned the airport security, and winked at me. I liked her so I sent her a postcard from Ghana.

I hate lying, but a successful journalist has to refuse to take no for an answer, especially in the third world. It contradicts all the rules of comfy Western journalism schools, but real life is different. Ethics are important in that you also say no, equally determinedly, when anyone tries to influence what you say. How you get the story is your business; what you say may be everybody's concern.

Accra airport was seedy, corrupt, and chaotic: anglophone West Africa, unlike the sleek, efficient, French-style airport at Abidjan. In this region I soon learned that baggage is treated as a hostage to be ransomed in big bucks, so I fought my way, literally, through a host of would-be porters and crooks trying to grab my bag and ran for a car shared with a French businessman I had met on the plane. I wanted to find Mercy as soon as possible, so he dropped me at the hospital where she worked – the only address I had. They gave me her home address.

I booked into a hotel and got a taxi to find her ramshackle house, at the back of an obscure market in a remote suburb. Her large family, intrigued by the white visitor from Britain, entertained me with beer. Mercy seemed vaguely pleased to see me and reluctantly accepted my dinner invitation. My conscience demanded that I dine her as if it were really her birthday. I asked her advice on how to get into the dictator's castle, although I didn't put it that bluntly. After she had told me – with cautious glances around the restaurant – about the political situation, and her father's imprisonment for political opposition, I felt I could trouble her no more with my quest.

I had another angle: the dictator's brother-in-law, David, was a journalist I had met in Britain. David had also been imprisoned but his wife and Rawlings's spouse were sisters. His imprisonment had been brief. I arranged to meet Mercy again after contacting David.

The next day I left a message for David and explored Accra: wonderful, if you like cities where the traffic is one big stock-car race and the streets have open sewers. I spent the day looking for bookshops. Ghana once had an excellent educational system and a very high literacy rate, but I was curious as to what they read. It couldn't have been books. Even the university bookshop was rather like the Monty Python cheese emporium. After a day's hunt I found a book on Ghana's sixty-odd castles and forts.

I also managed to contact the top civil servant in Christianborg castle. Al had written to him, and received a polite if wary reply. The fact that there had been a reply at all was very surprising and encouraging. More than half of government spending was on the civil service. One estimate put the number of civil servants as twenty-two times larger than the armed forces. That seemed a little unlikely in a state ruled by the military, so I didn't sully that piece of information with any hard research. The castle official agreed to see me the next day, again such an unusual experience in Africa that I was extremely suspicious. I began to think of bills I hadn't paid, letters I hadn't written, friends I hadn't seen, the future of my dog without a master ...I even tried to ring my mother-in-law.

David's jovial arrival pulled me out of my gloom. He was one of the most intelligent and energetic men I knew. David couldn't help me officially, but said if I hung around for a while he might be able to fix up a social drink with Jerry. I said thank you but knew that I was lousy at small talk with dictators. David left early, but not before arranging for some of his friends to take me on a tour of the world's seediest bars and whorehouses, although they may have been the best on offer. Accra was full of very friendly women and a very high rate of AIDS. Besides, I was boringly obsessed with castles, especially Christianborg. I had one more day before Al arrived, and unless I had fixed things up the noise of Al's temper tantrum might conceal the gunfire from any number of local coups. I talked politics and castles with the well-educated madam of a brothel with good beer. Really.

The next day I donned a suit, passed endless security checks, and waited around for two hours after the appointed time. I relaxed; this was the Africa I knew and loved. And I had wormed my way into the castle. I studied the architecture and worked out what to say.

'Have you seen the film *The Dogs of War*, sir? I have some nice well-behaved mercenary friends who want to come in and take pictures. Is that OK?'

When the time came I was ushered into a small office full of papers and the smell of booze. Again I felt more at home. After I had shown the senior official copies of the correspondence he became seriously aggrieved that Al had not responded to his letter of six months previously. I tried every tack possible. I couldn't mention video cameras because we had no permits to film, and asked merely to be allowed to take still pictures for Al's book. I got nowhere. Then I mentioned my contact with David. That went down like a lead balloon.

On the point of giving up I tried the rustic touch. I started talking about Wales. The man's face lit up. By sheer coincidence he had been treated for a serious complaint in a hospital a mile from my home. The warmth and tenderness of the National Health Service in Cardiff had won his eternal affection. This might come as a surprise to sixty million Britons, but perhaps not many of them have been sick in Accra. He offered to see Al as soon as he arrived so I fixed up an appointment. I had been lucky.

Mercy's boss had lent me a car and driver to meet Al at Takoradi, a long way down the coast towards the Ivory Coast border. 'Uncle Boet', the driver, was late. He was a lovely old fellow so I didn't have the heart to tell him off. I would pay him handsomely and I knew the advantages of travelling in his government vehicle. We would sail through the roadblocks. The coast road was reasonable by African standards but the driving was genuinely terrifying. Cars drove straight for us, swerving away at the last minute. This was survivable in the day, perhaps, but suicidal at night. Many of the cars had religious inscriptions on them. I could understand why.

I was late. Al had endured endless harassment crossing roadblocks from the Ivory Coast border. (Since he was travelling in a car with Ivory Coast plates – Ghana and Ivory Coast were hostile to each other in the best Anglo-French colonial tradition – he should have expected hassles.) Al also had a hangover and an embarrassing abscess in his crotch, and Ghana was not the best place to have a needle stuck in your nether regions. He bawled me out before I had a chance to tell him I had arranged everything. Tommy was embarrassed, but we set off to film some castles with me doing stand-ups in front of them. I put Al's rudeness aside and concentrated on work.

St George's Castle, at Elmina, was built by the Portuguese in 1482 with dressed stone brought from Europe. It is perhaps the most important and certainly the oldest colonial edifice in sub-Saharan Africa. We approached it along a palm-fringed beach full of custom-painted, long-prowed pirogues. Decaying colonial buildings squatted around the castle. Parts of it were beginning to deteriorate but it was still imposing. In the morning mist it looked like an African Camelot.

In the courtyard the Portuguese had built a Catholic church, which the Protestant Dutch turned into a mess hall and slave market. From the castle ramparts we filmed across the lagoon with its spectacular display of fishing boats. On the hill opposite stood Fort St Jago, another colonial monument built in the fifteenth century. Like several other Ghanaian forts, it had been transformed into a rest-house. When open, accommodation in the forts was usually basic. Very.

The marauding Europeans had used these forts to seek ivory and pepper, as well as gold, before the coast became the centre for exporting over twenty million slaves to the Americas. Europeans bought the slaves, but local African chiefs sold them. By the end of the eighteenth century there were as many slaves inside Africa as outside. But that does not minimise the atrocious stain on European expansion. In African tradition slaves usually had some rights; in the hands of white Christians they had none. They had the same value as cattle and horses. The wealth that slaves brought caused many wars between the slaving posts and later the colonial governments which took them over. Private traders and government troops fought each other, the indigenous peoples, the weather, pirates, and disease. Malaria was the biggest killer. One sailor's warning went:

Beware and take care of the Bight of Benin,
There's one comes out for every ten that goes in.

The castles were redolent of suffering, of both black slaves and the white overlords. Besides Elmina, Cape Coast Castle was the most accessible and impressive. It was founded by the Swedes, taken by the

Danes, and eventually became the main base for British control of the Gold Coast, as Ghana was then known. It was extensively renovated in the nineteenth century. We walked and filmed through a maze of damp, claustrophobic dungeons where slaves were held before being transported. During the Ashanti wars of the nineteenth century three robust little forts were built on hills around the castle. For tourist income some attempt had been made to keep the castles at the level of maintenance insisted upon by the British before they left. It appeared to be a losing battle. Locals had built slums around the castles, creating a poignant counterpoint between the colonial period and independence. We usually paid a small amount for permission to take still and video pictures in the castles. The smallness of the video camera made it look like normal tourist kit, although our radio mike and other extras would have betrayed us to a professional. But there were always hustlers who tried to charge us for filming anywhere, especially around the castles. Added to this was an appalling stench of open sewers. At Cape Coast Castle Tommy had to stop filming while he retched.

Ghana offered much more inland away from the coast, especially in the Ashanti areas, but our job was to film coastal forts. We did travel twenty-five miles inland across dirt tracks to reach Gross Friedrichsburg, a fort at Princestown erected by the German Branderburgers in 1683 and restored since independence.

Back in Accra Al informed Tommy and me that we were to leave the next day for Senegal. I mentioned our appointment at Christianborg castle, for which I had sweated blood. But Al had changed his mind. It was his show. I did manage to leave a message for my new Welshophile friend that our appointment had been cancelled, and wrote a long apology to cover Al in case he changed his mind again. I am sure we could have taken at least still pics in the castle. The guy had seemed genuine. In nearly all other cases, the length of delays or prevarications by African bureaucrats usually signalled the size of bribe required. You learn to count the 'wells' or '*mais monsieur*'s or '*é impossivel*'s, get a mental calculator out, and make your offer.

Accra airport had become infamous for its corruption: bribes were demanded on a grand and highly organised scale. Al knew of a black American professor who'd been strip-searched and had his anus examined for gold. Apparently the poor professor had just been searching for his roots, but found Mother Africa was not quite so maternal to her long-lost sons. Instead customs had examined his roots.

All six of our party arrived at the airport more than two hours before the flight, which had been confirmed the previous night. First we were told the plane had left; a planeload of people was waiting, so this seemed dubious. Then we were told it had to leave early and we did not have time to board – unless a few little presents were arranged. Our baggage might get lost if we did not take out insurance at $100 each. These threats were from officials, not hustlers. Al had already thumped two alleged porters who tried to grab our bags. We needed six of us to keep our luggage from disappearing in the throng. Al offered the baggage handler $50 to escort us through customs, another minefield. Once we were through Al gave him half, although he was angry enough to sabotage our luggage before it got to the plane. A favourite tactic, endured by some of my Ghanaian friends, was the simple removal of passports by customs officials. You had to buy them back or miss the flight. I should imagine that few tourists ever returned willingly.

We flew to Dakar, the capital of Senegal. This ex-French colony sits in the middle of the belly of West Africa, swallowing the thin appendage of The Gambia (formerly British) like a greedy Pac-man. Dakar had touches of elegance, especially compared with run-down Ghana, and was almost Moroccan in flavour, a bit like Casablanca. To my ears the locals spoke excellent French. The main purpose of our trip was to visit Gorée Island, once a major slave entrepôt. The island was charming, full of eighteenth-century homes with wrought-iron balconies. It had a lovely beach with open-air cafés. The centrepiece was the sombre Maison des Esclaves, where slaves had been processed for three months or so while awaiting transport across the Atlantic. The curator told us how the slaves were stuffed into pens measuring six yards by ten, inspected, and valued as though they were cattle. Uppity slaves were chained to the walls and seawater piped into their cells to keep them partially submerged. The slaves fought for the scraps of food, the weaker ones died and were fed to the fish. Survivors were branded with the shipping company's insignia and packed like sardines into airless, rotten ship holds. American visitors, black and white, wept openly. Despite being on the *Roots* tour, Gorée was tragic and serene at the same time.

*

Al, Tommy and I left our fellow sightseers to continue with the more arduous part of our trip: trying to get into Guinea-Bissau, one of the world's most unwelcoming countries, not least to journalists. En route we stopped in The Gambia, where Al wanted us to film the main forts in a few hours the next morning. After arriving at Yundum airport we booked into a Butlins-type hotel in Banjul, the tiny capital.

The state is not only named after a river; it is the river. The Gambia existed because the British wanted to exclude French access to West Africa's finest waterway. Except for the sea, the country's 700,000 people were surrounded on all sides by former French territory. The narrow strip of land either side of the river was supposed to mark the maximum range of British naval guns. Everything was on a small scale; the capital's population was 50,000. This largely Islamic country was an exceptional (if temporary) paragon of political virtue in Africa: a democracy with no real army and no political prisoners. Even the minister of the interior had the friendly name of Mr M'Boob. The economy was based upon groundnuts and tourism.

The Gambia, to me, had lots of simple charm, but the recent rapid growth in the numbers of package tourists from Britain and Scandinavia (50,000 per annum in the late 1980s) disturbed me. Just like Germans on the Kenyan coast, Swedes were said to flock to The Gambia for sexual safaris. There wasn't much else to do after a day on the beach, it must be admitted. But I hated to see Africa turned into a giant bordello to work off European lusts, just as the sex industry has despoiled parts of south-east Asia. Perhaps it was always so. The historian Ronald Hyam postulated that the principal impetus behind the British empire was the export of surplus sexual energy, not of surplus capital.

I didn't have any surplus energy in The Gambia. Tommy and I rushed to catch a ferry and hire a scrapheap to get to Juffure, the tiny village Alex Haley claimed as his ancestral home. An old lady, Binta Kinte, who purported to be a direct descendant of the *Roots* hero, demanded a little bit of compensation from each visitor for all the historical wrongs. Since a boatload of Scandinavians, presumably full of surplus historical energy, was being led by the hand, and the nose, to Mrs Kinte we chose to ignore the rip-off. Haley was alleged to have written the Gambian bit of his book *before* he arrived in Africa. Since the names Juffure and Kinte are the region's equivalents of crossroads and Jones in the UK, geographical and demographic exactness could not be expected. But I couldn't blame the tourist board for making the most of a bit of fiction. The Gambia didn't have much else, except a fort.

Our taxi-driver helped us haggle for the hire of a very leaky longboat which took us upstream to Fort James, built originally by a German aristocrat, the Duke of Courland, in 1651. In 1661 it became the first permanent British settlement in Africa. James Island had been severely eroded by the river, and all that was left were romantic ruins and baobabs.

On the way back we took a quick look at the ruins of a French trading post established in 1681, just a few hundred yards from Kunte Kinte's alleged home. Poor old Kunte was surprised to find slavers in the area where he was caught and shipped off to American slavery. This showed either a singular lack of intelligence on his part or a serious deficiency in Haley's historical research. Still, it was a good story.

All this debunking made us late. I was glad about this because Al wanted us to fly to Guinea-Bissau on Air Mauritanie, which did not have the world's most impressive safety record. Al said our special visas for entering Guinea-Bissau were awaiting us at the capital's airport, and we now had to go by road. A taxi took us to the Gambian–Senegalese border, where hordes of Senegalese children demanded *cadeaux*, as did their parents. After some hard bargaining we persuaded a driver to take us south through the Casamance. Except for the occasional coastal resort, including one Club Med – which the locals called Club Merde – the region was largely untouched by tourism. The spluttering of a local separatist insurgency was most helpful in this respect. We were forced to be travellers rather than tourists: living the day-to-day life of the country, foraging where we could rather than hiding away in hotel restaurants to avoid stomach upsets. Strangely, most tourists I met imagined they were great travellers. The fact that I had got the shits in more places than they had should not have made me feel superior.

We found a real piece of France in a hotel in Zinguinchor, where I hugged the restaurant for its French cuisine and wines, and baguettes for breakfast. Before dinner Al and I set out to find the Guinea-Bissau consul to procure visas. Whenever I asked the way in West Africa I always found the village idiot. On this occasion he jumped in the taxi and gave us a guided tour of the town. We never did find the consul; we would have to bluff.

Al liked to think that he was an expert on all things African, which he was. But then he also fancied himself as a multilingual border expert, which he was not.

We left Senegal and entered no man's land before the Guinea-Bissau border. Suddenly, around a bend, we saw a rope across the road.

Al said, 'I'll sort this out,' meaning, 'Let me show you how to do it.'

He was very impressive for someone with only a few phrases in French and fewer words in Portuguese, although he did need to ask for one of the plastic half-bottles of whisky I kept for such occasions. It was a dramatic performance. After half an hour the man let down the rope, happily clutching his Scotch. Al seemed pleased with himself. I didn't like to tell him that, while he was giving a long speech about his personal friendship with the president of Guinea-Bissau, I had left the car to relieve myself in the bush and seen the border post half a mile down the road.

Al soon realised that the rope man was there just to slow down the one or two cars a day that passed through. Tommy was cruel enough to chuckle.

Disheartened, Al said to me: 'You can handle this border post.'

Guinea-Bissau was perhaps the least known and most closed state in Africa, run by a paranoid military officer who didn't like strangers even when they came from the World Bank. The place had opened up a little recently, it was true, but we still didn't have visas. Al had landed a tough one in my lap.

I spent forty-five minutes in reasonable French and broken Portuguese persuading the group of officials to let us in. I had finally reached the back office and was alone with the head honcho, about to seal the deal with a full bottle of whisky, when Al stormed in to ask why the fuck I was taking so long. He then left as abruptly as he came. I took a further fifteen minutes to persuade the now jittery official that we were not escaped convicts or lunatics; we were tourists who liked unusual places. I gave him the whisky and he gave me the visas.

Al said: 'Hell, I could have done it in half the time with just half a bottle of whisky.'

There was no point in arguing.

We took ferries, taxis, and buses, and eventually arrived in Bissau, the derelict capital. I couldn't believe the state of the harbour. Large ships had sunk at their moorings; some of the wrecks looked as though they had been stuck there since the Portuguese left in 1974. I wondered why they had stayed for the previous 500 years – there was nothing much there except peanuts. Yet the country was unspoiled and beautiful, not that locals had much to eat except beautiful nuts. The interior was a vast plateau covered in almost impenetrable forest. The coast was flat, swampy, and very unhealthy. Transportation was difficult because of the many rivers and few surviving bridges.

Tommy and I managed to hire a four-wheel drive, amazingly brand new. We drove for four hours through almost virgin Africa, sometimes along dirt roads with avenues of trees with pink blooms, to reach the fort at Cacheu. Sixty feet square and built in 1589, it contained a bizarre tableau of Africa's history. Statues of Portuguese colonial heroes such as Vasco da Gama, dumped there after independence, had recently been joined by dethroned Marxist gods – Lenin and Stalin. On the way back we found some diesel, dispensed from a hand-pump made in the 1920s. Tommy had insisted that I drove, even though we had to traverse broken bridges which necessitated balancing the jeep on two railway sleepers.

We got back to find Al in trouble with the police for refusing to pay a taxi fare. The manager of the hotel (a former Portuguese army barracks) eventually sorted it out, after Al agreed to pay half the 200,000 pesos demanded. The manager said his workers were paid only 150,000 pesos a month (roughly £30). In his arguments with the police Al went on about his special visit to the country to see the president, General João Vieira. This was partly true. Al had covered the colonial war in the country and wrote a book on the subject jointly dedicated to the generalissimo. He wanted to give him a copy in order to meet him. The little I knew of the leader suggested it was unwise dedicating even a limerick to him. In contrast, the founder of the revolution in Guinea-Bissau, Amilcar Cabral, was one of Africa's most influential thinkers . . . before he was assassinated.

After Al's cocktail do with the general we went straight to the airport. Although escorted by a presidential aide and the hotel manager, and although we had just left *el supremo*, we met a brick wall of red tape and aggressive demands for bribes from airport officials. We did have problems with visas: my efforts at the border had got us in but I had not secured a permit to leave. Once it was firmly established that Al had just been a guest of the president the officials finally relented. We marched out of the airport cattle-shed and waited on the apron, Tommy heading for Johannesburg, Al and I for Lisbon.

Al and I started work in Lisbon, where I hired another cameraman to do general views and stand-ups around historical buildings. On the final night Al took me to a *fado* restaurant. The evocatively sad songs almost had me in tears. I am not sure whether it was entirely the music. Nor did I hear any more about the film.

11. SOUTH AFRICA – THE NEW ORDER

I was bored teaching journalism at Deakin University in Australia. Oz is a great place to raise kids but I don't know about adults. The stunning outback is dull and empty compared with the African bush. And even the grandest European cities are grey and lifeless when contrasted with the chaos, colour and vitality of Africa. I had to be there: the first democratic South African elections drew me back from the comforts and safety of Australia.

The place, the people and, as a journalist, the story beckoned. Chris Munnion, the London *Telegraph* correspondent and doyen of old Africa hands, wrote: 'Every other bugger is trying to get out of here and into Oz and you want the reverse. Are you mad?'

Yes.

It was April 1994. In the Jan Smuts customs hall a fat, middle-aged Afrikaner was grumpy about my papers. Same old South Africa. Although a resident, I had to have a special journalist visa.

'Don't you tell lies about us,' she warned.

Once I explained that I was a returning resident, she spoke to me almost confidentially in Afrikaans: 'We're going to have a civil war here after the elections, you know.'

After hiring a car, which took ages, I drove into central Johannesburg. I had last been in South Africa six years before; the number of brash new buildings, especially in the largely white, élite areas, was astounding. So much for sanctions. Later I was told that many of the glass-palatial offices were empty.

I went straight to my old suburb, Melville, to pick up a few friends for lunch at Roma, a favourite haunt. Ornella and Enrico, the owners, refused to let me pay for the meal. 'It's great to have our best customer back.'

South Africa was warming up for me. The friends took me back to their house, where I asked why the kitchen was stacked with tins of baked beans and dog food. 'Strange mixture?'

'Yah, the dogs are gonna eat and the humans are gonna fart the siege away.'

The old defensiveness of white Johannesburgers. Living in Australia I had almost forgotten about security. I had stopped locking my car; now I was told not to stop at traffic lights at night. Car muggings had become an epidemic. 'Armed response time' – the speed with which private security firms reacted – was a main staple of conversation.

My white friends still seemed to live reasonably well, however. They had servants – 'domestic workers' now – although they were sometimes downright suspicious of them. Fewer workers now lived on the premises, partly on account of the cost and partly because of white insecurity. Even wealthier friends didn't have enough surplus rands to ask about doing a deal for US or Oz dollars. Maybe the black market had become more subtle.

Andy Gancewicz, my aggressive Polish friend, took me hunting on my second day back. After a year of political correctness at my university in Australia I was arming myself to go hunting defenceless animals. I hadn't held a gun since I was last in South Africa. It felt good. Driving through north-western Transvaal I noticed signs proclaiming a *Volkstaat* (Afrikaner people's state). In the shops of towns such as Ellisras, whites replied in Afrikaans when I addressed them in English. The old master–servant relationship between blacks and whites also seemed to persist.

We saw lots of game. The 350 hunting farms had brought tourists and animals to a bush which twenty years before was almost bereft of wildlife. My rifle skills had not improved, and I didn't shoot anything. I didn't really want to. I just walked in the sun and smelt the bush, and the familiar aroma of woodsmoke on the tracker's clothes. Sunny Boy, the tracker, didn't say much; he just glided through the bush with me clumping behind, trailed by a stubborn ostrich which had taken a shine to me and followed me all day. I felt alive again amid the serene sunsets and the perfume of the land when the first rains came.

Back in Johannesburg I did the round of obligatory dinner parties. I was not invited for my repartee, I suspected, but for my expertise on how to wheedle into Australia. I had missed these lively dinner parties, full of the soul of survival politics. And in Oz you had to wash up yourself.

I had missed the black humour, the cynical racism which infused white banter. 'There's good news and bad news about the new South

Africa. The bad news is that the shit is going to hit the fan. And the good? The fan ain't gonna be working.'

The whites I met in Johannesburg were distinctly jittery in the days before the election. It was not surprising. Hordes of hacks streaming into the city all expected, and some hoped for, a bloodbath. I sensed real fear in the white northern suburbs, huddled around shopping malls shifting ever northwards, away from the black town centre. The bombs didn't help, but I suppose they generated work for the ubiquitous security guards. The blacks I spoke to – especially those who lived in the townships – were also, frankly, shit-scared about the expected polling mayhem.

I was much more upbeat. When I had left, Mandela and the ANC were absolutely taboo. The secular saint now beamed at me from nearly every lamppost. After being unpersons, the names of key black leaders were tossed around by even the most unwashed of whites. This was a refreshing change; the whites had been shaken out of their 'dreadful calm'. Everybody talked politics. The whites seemed resigned, weary, a few hopeful, a tiny minority euphoric.

One white businessman said at a soirée: 'The whites have had an easy ride up until now. They must expect that the black man will have his day too. And the whites are going to pay. They shouldn't be surprised.'

South African television had changed. Some of the tongue-tied, brain-dead white presenters were still preserved in aspic but some lively new black faces had arrived. True, this might have been no more than tokenism, but TV was better. The end of the Equity union ban on British programmes had made a difference: Basil Fawlty's walk was much more entertaining than P. W. Botha's finger-wagging. But I couldn't understand why the 8 p.m. split between English and Afrikaans survived. I had never figured out why the Afrikaner overlords didn't allow at least English subtitles for the forced diet of Afrikaans. Some of the new experiments in bi- or tri-lingualism were laughable (especially as there were eleven language groups) but it was a stutter in the right direction, particularly in the inevitably brief interregnum of press freedom between Afrikaner and ANC authoritarianism. It was encouraging to see communist stalwarts such as Joe Slovo exchanging friendly televised banter with white Nazis.

Johannesburg's northern suburbs were always incestuous, a touch paranoid. I needed to get out. Buthelezi's impis were about to storm central Johannesburg; friends said I should stay for the action. It seemed more interesting to go to Zululand. So I was in Kwa-Zulu when the mercurial chief finally decided to hop on board the electoral train. The sense of relief was almost tangible in the province. Whatever Buthelezi was promised (a fixed election victory in the local parliament?) it made the vital difference between ballot and bullet.

I toasted the prospects of peace with Dave Willers, editor of the *Natal Witness*. Dave lived in Hilton, in the plummy white highlands. Here many whites prayed for the Zulu warrior's success, although Dave's white friends were ANC people. Dave and I celebrated till late, then I shared the euphoria by broadcasting on the radio to Australia. Switching from personal hopes for peace to detached observer, I had to do a live crossing by phone at 2 a.m. to fit in with the time difference.

In Durban I listened to a tired Zach de Beer, leader of the liberal Democratic Party, singing the same old songs. What was different was the invitation to three 'former freedom fighters' to come on to the stage. They were from, it was said, the military wings of the ANC, the black consciousness movement and Inkatha. Two were painfully embarrassed by this outpouring of white liberal sympathy. The third was obviously a psychotic megalomaniac, if there is such a condition. With eyes rolling insanely he shouted something about dying for the Democratic Party and 'Viva DP'. That was a bit like goose-stepping in a synagogue.

Natal and Transvaal were for politics, the Cape for wine and architecture. On the Twee Jonge Gezellen wine estate I was intrigued by the kibbutz-style living for the coloured workers. The white wines there were far superior, in my ignorant though extensively researched opinion, to their Australian equivalents. Staying in excellent farmhouse accommodation, I fell into drinking and talking with the local farmers. I didn't mention that I understood Afrikaans (although only just after years away).

In the most gentle of tones, one farmer admitted: 'I benefited from apartheid. I felt guilty but I made money. But I'm glad it's over.'

The contrition was tempered by a later outburst when he discovered some squatters had moved on to his land and were stealing his produce.

Tulbagh had one of the finest streets in South Africa. Each Cape Dutch building in Church Street was an architectural gem. It also had two excellent restaurants, where I drank with some sullen ex-Rhodesians who chided me about my reportage of their war. I nursed my hangover the next morning by chewing biltong, the thing I had missed most about South Africa. The dried meat strips are highly addictive.

In nearby Stellenbosch I enjoyed the bibulous hospitality of an ex-colonel who knew his way around *mampoer* as well as guns. He was an ardent admirer of General Constand Viljoen, leader of the right-wing Freedom Front, and told me the white call-up would have been 5 per cent without Viljoen, whose quiet intervention boosted the 'campers' (reservists) to about 65 per cent.

'He will save the election,' said the ex-colonel.

Mandela's lavish praise of Viljoen seemed to confirm this opinion.

In Cape Town's refurbished harbour area, I had lunch with the coloured ex-girlfriend who had taught me so much about art, and apartheid, when we flouted so many of the hated laws in the 1970s. Now an ANC organiser, she bemoaned the fact that so many of her people would vote for their former oppressors, the National Party. She was right: the Western Cape voted to keep in the Nats and keep out the ANC. The Afrikaners had begun in the Cape; now the regional parliament was the last redoubt where they held a majority of seats.

For sentimental reasons I wanted to vote in Melville. I toured the bomb damage in downtown Jo'burg, right outside my former office. Whites were muttering about Lebanon revisited – the comparison was laughable. Central Johannesburg and Hillbrow, the nightlife district, had changed dramatically. They had become African. It could have been West Africa, except more goods were on sale, the ghetto-blasters were marginally quieter, and the streets were cleaner. Whites talked about the changes with disdain, whereas I considered the noise and colour much better than the stark glass and treeless desert I remembered.

In tense Sandton I met up with Marie Bruyns, once the top producer for SATV. She still had the brains and looks which had once both irritated and charmed the dour *apparatchiks* in SATV headquarters. I told her that I – we – had been wrong to make programmes trying to side-swipe apartheid. I had thought I could work within the system; I had been wrong. We gave credibility to a propaganda monster. We had produced some powerful programmes that might have done some good but we were still wrong. She seemed more hurt than angry.

Came the first day of the elections, the queues were too long in Melville. But the multiracial community atmosphere boded well for the future. The bombs stopped, as did nearly all the killing. The voting process was chaotic but, except for Kwa-Zulu, the chaos was a result of cock-ups, not conspiracy, or so it seemed to me. There were no voting rolls and no real idea of the size of the electorate. Chaos was inevitable.

I voted on the second day when the queues had diminished, choosing the liberal Democratic Party nationally. I couldn't vote for the ANC simply because of its alliance with the communists. I had experienced the devastation in Eastern Europe. The Nats I could never forgive, no matter how much I might respect F. W. de Klerk's gutsiness. I never had much time for the upper-class twittery of the liberals, especially the Progs, but I admired Helen Suzman's courage. She might have been severely economical with her charm (at least to me) and had a voice like a dentist's drill, but she had stood alone in a racist parliament. I didn't agree with her anti-sanctions stance but whites like her, Helen Joseph, Bram Fischer and even Uncle Joe Slovo had done much to prevent black perceptions of a total racial chasm. That was vital for the future of all whites. I estimated that the DP would get about 5 per cent; I was slightly surprised by their poor showing but Zach was clearly yesterday's man. I voted, I guess, for Helen's bravery.

On the eve of the elections Sue Ollemans, who owned a gallery in Rosebank, Johannesburg, told me merchants were removing valuables from their display windows. On the first day of liberation everybody expected looting – or 'affirmative shopping' as cynics called it. Her black partner suggested they should put some Africana, especially fetishes, in the window to deter thieves. Must have been powerful *muti* (medicine/magic), for it worked on a grand scale, and I heard of very little looting.

Buthelezi called the elections he had almost derailed 'a miracle'. Many of the 5,000 hacks who poured in expecting a replay of the Gulf War were clearly disappointed by Mandela's relatively peaceful triumph. CNN dismantled its huge approximation of a NASA launch, and the correspondents drifted off to the genocide in Rwanda. I had seen enough tragedy in South Africa to hope fervently that the peace could lead to genuine reconstruction and reconciliation. It was a hope, not an expectation.

*

On the first day of the new order, I went back to the citadel of Afrikanerdom, Pretoria, and said farewell to the *Voortrekker* monument. The Afrikaner shrine was appropriately empty. The greater number of uniforms and fewer hawkers than in Jo'burg seemed to say: 'We Boers still run the show here.'

I spent my penultimate day at that ultimate metaphor of white society, the Lost City, two hours' drive north of Jo'burg. It was a spectacular piece of kitsch attached to the gambling and golf resort of Sun City. The Lost City was an almost surreal re-creation of an ancient complex, a mix of Alan Quartermain, a high-as-a-kite Salvador Dalí and a set for an Indiana Jones movie. Amusing myself on the near-empty waterslides, I wondered about the erstwhile emperor of the area, President Mangope, who ruled the former 'independent' homeland of Bophuthatswana. Nobody would or could tell where the dethroned and deranged Mangope was hiding.

Before I left I wanted to see a woman who had meant a great deal to me in Africa . . . Letitia. She was too beautiful in a too-conventional way, having been Miss South Africa, runner-up in Miss Universe and a successful international model. We had been good friends, more brother and sister, and I never told her I was in love with her. My return to the dark continent had stirred my dark soul but I still didn't talk frankly when we lingered over wine in an upmarket Sandton mall. She told me that she had queued for seven hours to vote: this, once the most apolitical of *meisies* (Afrikaner girls).

'I had been going to vote for the ANC but for seven hours the two guys in front for me said what they, the ANC, were going to do to us whites. In the end I voted Nat.'

I don't think she was joking. After too much good wine, I began to take my leave.

Sensing my unstated feelings, her last words were: 'Why did you always take the piss out of me?'

I was going to say: 'What did you expect, voting for the Nats like that?'

Instead I said lamely: 'You were always surrounded by adoring men, what else could I do?'

I wished goodbye to her and her new family for ever. She later went to live in Israel, then Australia, part of the growing white South African diaspora, though I heard she returned after her divorce. I chose not to look her up on my return trips to South Africa.

Friends saw me off at the airport and we talked politics, of course. I thought but didn't say that in a few years' time, as in Zimbabwe, local politics for whites would be like talking about the weather – interesting but nothing to be done about it.

South Africa was a much better place in 1994 than in 1990, a morally comfortable perspective for foreign observers. It was, until the elections, a much more dangerous place for locals. Nearly 14,000 political murders were committed after Mandela was released. The killings receded after the ANC victory but the already chronic crime rates increased. For a while tourism would grow too, now South Africa was a politically correct place to visit. Like Eastern Europe after the fall of the Berlin Wall, the republic was a novelty attraction. It had first-class hotels, roads, wines and game parks, often at third-world prices. Some Western investment would come in, if much was left over from bolstering Russia and its former empire. But there would never be enough to satisfy the 'liberation dividends' demanded by the feral youngsters in the townships.

For four years of the odd-couple tango of F. W. and Mandela, the suits and *tsotsis* had been ripping off the country. Monsters like Winnie Mandela could really jump on the gravy train before the wheels came off. The crisis of expectation – one person, one promise – was much more dangerous than the explosion of corruption. Whites would suffer reverse discrimination as blacks were 'artificially assisted' to top jobs. Whites with options, and even opinions, would leave. Maybe, ten or fifteen years on, affirmative action would insist that whites came back, like the Mozambicans begging their sleazy colonial masters to return and set up businesses again.

It had taken me two hours of inefficient assistants and milling, cursing crowds to get my long-ordered cheque book from a Jo'burg bank; it would take two minutes in Australia. Some Oz banks paid you $5 if you had to wait more than five minutes. But I had forgotten . . . I was in Africa. The sun shone. Nobody had been rude to me. I hadn't paid a bribe. I had stayed at world-class hotels at African prices (the Lost City excepted). Morally, I had committed myself by voting. Immorally, I wasn't staying. I was glad I had been there to witness it all. I did not know, however, when I would return. South Africa now had a chance, and I really did believe the election was a miracle.

I left, however, with a disgruntled white's comments ringing in my ears: 'South Africa was a first-world dictatorship, now it's a third-world democracy . . . for a while.'

Bill Clinton, Boris Yeltsin, and Nelson Mandela are engaged in a long conversation with Jehovah. Clinton asks how long it will take for his country to solve its problems.

'Not in your administration,' says the Lord, 'but in the next one.'

Yeltsin asks the same question.

'Not in your lifetime but in the lifetime of your children.'

When Mandela asks, God sighs and replies: 'Not in my lifetime.'

Nothing new out of Africa

In retrospect, I can pinpoint the moment that white Africa died. Large numbers of white right-wingers, particularly from the AWB, had been pouring into the tottering statelet of Bophuthatswana to back the apartheid puppet Lucas Mangope. On 17 March 1994 three neo-Nazis, travelling through the capital in a dilapidated green Mercedes, threw racial taunts at a group of blacks. A local black policeman fired at the car, fatally wounding the driver.

The two whites with him stumbled out of the car, their hands in the air, but they still used the term 'black bastards' to nearby journalists. Two minutes later both whites were killed, shot in the head by other black policemen. A picture flashed around the world: a black man in uniform stood pointing a rifle at the head of a white lying prostrate in the dirt. Such pictures had not been widely seen since the massacres of the Congo in the 1960s, and never in South Africa, still cocooned by the spluttering racism of apartheid's last days. The 'awe factor' – instinctive if often bitter respect for whites – had finally been eradicated as a political force in Africa. Whites in southern Africa were now fair game . . . both for criminals and for greedy politicians eager to seize back the white farmlands and take over businesses. That was soon to happen in Zimbabwe, and South Africa looked like it was going the same way. The miracle of the 1994 election faded fast.

I returned to work for the UK Ministry of Defence as a senior instructor at the new joint military staff college. I did go back to Africa on official business to research and lecture. It was June 1998 when I next found myself travelling through Johannesburg. I half felt that I was going home, although the South African Airways flight was now different. I didn't hear any Afrikaans announcements and the language had disappeared from the in-flight magazine. And Hugh Masekela had thankfully replaced *Boeremusiek*.

My first stop was again my favourite restaurant in Melville. Enrico, the owner, had just been shot at and robbed, but the food was still good. Razor wire had proliferated, while the rand had slumped. My old house looked like Fort Knox. Everywhere young blacks 'guarded' your car for a small fee. Crime was the dominant topic of conversation. Nevertheless, I attended the usual round of dinner parties, even though whites were much more careful about travelling at night.

At one soirée, a psychiatrist told me that his fiancée had recently been killed in a carjacking. 'They just shot her through the window,' he said. 'Didn't give her a chance to run away.'

It was the sixth such killing that day, he added. I later mentioned this to a former colleague who was still teaching at an Africanised Durban University.

'Six in a day,' I said on the phone.

He deliberately misunderstood: 'What? Six fiancées in one day. That really is bad luck.' Black humour was probably the best survival mechanism.

At the same party, I spoke to a former ANC guerrilla. He cheerfully told me about some of the bombs he had planted during the struggle. I said that I could understand black poverty driving people to steal cars, but why kill the drivers as well? The broken window and blood everywhere made no economic sense to a car thief.

'It's the general dehumanisation of apartheid,' he explained. 'Life is cheap in the townships.' He admitted that there were perhaps elements of political revenge, as well as drugs, drink and the 50 per cent unemployment rate.

I needed to be cheered up so I went to see some of the elegant women I had worked with. My favourite was still the TV producer, Marie Bruyns. I jokingly mentioned all the old magazine articles about her and noted that she had been a sexual icon.

She flashed back: 'I don't object to the term icon, but I do object to the verb tense.'

I visited Gill, an old flame, who now lived behind a fortress front to her suburban house, all festooned with wire and CCTV cameras. She said: 'I am paranoid about leaving my house now. I rarely go out at night.'

Dangerously, I quipped: 'Why don't you marry me and live in England?'

'Okay,' she said with alacrity and apparent sincerity. Things were obviously very desperate on the crime front.

My long-term collocutor, Denis Beckett, was in predictably upbeat mood, however. He outlined all the social progress the new government had made. 'And remember,' he said, 'the transition could have been much worse. There's been very little bloodshed.'

He was right. And Denis had also become a big TV star in the new South Africa.

I travelled to Pretoria to attend a military conference. I spotted the freshers, the black generals, but 95 per cent of the officers in the new South African National Defence Force were still white. The lean look of the old fighters I had known in Angola and Namibia had gone. Most now looked like content and portly farmers. Nor was there any sense of a vanquished army.

I also spent some time with British officers who had played such a key role in the political transition by training and integrating the former guerrillas into the unified national army. A small group of Brits had done a great deal to finesse a very difficult process, and on important occasions had shown outstanding individual bravery by quelling mutinous behaviour by sheer force of personality. This was a major British achievement, but it was largely unsung for obvious diplomatic reasons. Their role had irritated the hell out of the French and Americans – which was a nice bonus.

Some of the true Brit spirit must have accidentally rubbed off on me, because I found myself intervening in a knife fight the day after the conference. In the morning I had been bitten by a British colonel's dog (in the good old days of colonialism dogs knew better than to bite a white man coming up the driveway in broad daylight). I was also wearing a brand-new suit, a rare extravagance for someone who much preferred wearing old comfortable clothes. The ripped suit (for which the colonel compensated me) was less annoying than the hunt for a tetanus jab in a clinic.

Exiting the clinic around lunchtime, in a very bad mood, I bumped into a black who slumped bloodily at my feet; in hot pursuit were some drunken blacks wielding knives. I should have walked away, which I suspect I might have done if I had still lived in Jo'burg. I shielded the prone, probably also drunken, fellow, and probably deterred his pursuers. In dragging the man out of the road to avoid being run over, I ruined another new jacket, covering it in blood. I had not had a good morning.

I had come 'home' and realised that the past is a completely different country. I was also spooked by a sense of insecurity; maybe it was me, and maybe I was losing my nerve. Although I heard gunfire at night in the distance, nobody shot at me, but I was less comfortable than I had been in the recent mayhem of the Balkan wars. Perhaps I was disappointed. I had wanted South Africa to be different from the rest of the sub-Saharan states. As Mandela gave way to a much lesser man as president, all the familiar woes of corruption and incompetence looked as if they were rearing their heads.

If I was looking for an African success story, Zambia still wasn't on the list. A few months later I left London for Lusaka on the day Rhodesians used to celebrate their UDI (the eleventh hour of the eleventh day of the eleventh month – when the 1918 Armistice is commemorated). My resumed civil service status entitled me to a club-class flight. I couldn't quite master the fancy seats and kept jerking up and down like a dentist's chair in overdrive. Eventually I settled down to watch the film. It was *Armageddon*, all about space ships crashing on to asteroids, a strange choice for an in-flight movie. We stopped briefly at Harare airport. I didn't get off; I was still banned. Yet the sight of a single jacaranda tree in purple bloom was enough to overwhelm me with pleasant memories of the country I had once called Rhodesia.

In Lusaka I was whisked through customs by a British diplomat and then briefed at my hotel by a very pretty Foreign Office official. I was giving a key lecture at the Zambian staff college, but she asked me not to mention any Zambian connections with Unita – yes, the Angolan war still raged on. I was taken immediately to Kamwala base, the former Zimbabwean guerrilla camp which had been severely attacked by Rhodesians. Now it was tidy and properly whitewashed; the commandant, I later discovered, had been trained in Britain. I was ushered into a large hall, with steeply rising tiers of seats. No one could get the computer systems working so I had to jettison my carefully prepared Powerpoint presentation. I had some back-up slides.

Then I was put on a lonely seat in the middle of a large stage to face an audience of about 150 officers, while the generals sat behind me. The person introducing me spoke for about twenty minutes, outlining my life and times and mispronouncing my name in four different ways. At the end of the intro I was asked about my family, especially how many children I had. I explained that the previous exploits mentioned in detail – especially the guerrilla wars, which had earned me credits with a tough-looking audience – had meant that I'd had no time for children. To the African audience, even if I had been Lawrence of Arabia, my lack of offspring meant that I was not fully a man. Not a good start.

The first slide came up and it was the Zambian football team. Titters. I caught the mood and asked whether the blackouts on the windows still meant that the Rhodesians were coming. Laughter. After three hours of talking and questions they started treating me like Henry Kissinger. I presumed to talk about world politics and I watched the Foreign Office types shifting uncomfortably in their back-row seats. Good.

The commandant gave me a plaque inscribed with my name and then I was driven off to meet the British diplomatic corps. Over dinner at the polo club, after talk of their grooms and horses, I asked why so much taxpayers' money was being spent on the Zambian basket-case, which had zero economic prospects and a large diplomatic mission, yet we had only one diplomat in Tajikistan, for example. There was oil there, and lots of problems with Islamic extremists. Perversely enough, I was invited back to give another lecture, though I never found the time.

I took a day off to visit Glenda, with whom I had shared a home during the tumultuous final years of white rule in Salisbury. Her husband was farming sugar in Mazabuka. I enjoyed the 'when-we' dinner with a few other expats, but the conversations confirmed my dismal view of Zambia's economic prospects, and the social apartheid: I was told blacks rarely came to dinner in the ex-pat community.

Nevertheless, the brief stint in rural Africa – especially the scent of frangipani and jasmine in Glenda's garden and the final farewell from the red flamboyant at the airport – raised my spirits.

A week later in London the Foreign Office included me in their guest list during the official visit of Afonso Dhlakama, the Renamo boss. He had eventually secured some of the recognition he had yearned for, and finally been invited to London. Britain had played a constructive role in the peace process in Mozambique, the country had joined the

Commonwealth, and Dhlakama had become leader of the opposition. A parliamentary opposition was rather rare in Africa, and Renamo had transformed itself into an effective political party. He might even have won a fair election. The London trip was his reward. It was strange to meet the Renamo chief in the Park Lane Hotel and not in the bush. He remembered our earlier meetings and treated me with some affection, inviting me to visit soon.

Since he was in with a fighting chance of winning the next elections, despite the inevitable Frelimo rigging, I decided to take him up on his offer. In January 1999 I flew to Durban to stay with Professor Sandy Johnston, who taught politics at Durban University. I visited some of my old haunts, and observed that little of the hedonism of the whites had changed. It was much more relaxed than Johannesburg, perhaps because of the (relatively) lower crime rates.

At the airport I sat in a waiting room for a small plane to take me to Maputo, the capital of Mozambique. A woman of about thirty-eight with an air of tired sensuality and big eyes sat down next to me. Her eyes grew larger and larger. Becoming obviously agitated she finally spoke: 'I've never flown before. I'm *dying* with fear.'

I explained it was a very short flight.

A well-dressed young man wearing a plain white shirt came in and sat on the other side of her. He looked very much in command of himself and so the young woman fixed on him for support.

'Do you fly much?' she asked.

'I hope so,' he said. 'I'm the pilot.'

The plane flew low over the lush rolling hills of Zululand and followed the coastline. After an hour it swung inland, across a river with rusting and sunk hulks and dilapidated oil storage tanks. The airport seemed deserted except for some old Soviet-era military aircraft. The five passengers entered a large empty hall, which complied with the regulation that it should smell of urine. A Renamo official speeded my entry, although we had to wait forty-five minutes for his driver to pitch up.

We proceeded into the city through bone-breaking potholes, passing astoundingly garish socialist-realist murals of Frelimo heroes. As we drove along the city foreshore, the pastel-coloured colonial-era villas looked as if they had not been painted or repaired since their white owners fled in 1974. Residents seemed to be camping rather than living in the buildings.

My hotel, the Cardosa, was good, but the asking price of US$170 a night was very steep for a developing country. I renegotiated the price downwards. Almost immediately I was taken to see Dhlakama. We met in a dark room in his house, which was guarded by young men with AKs. The Renamo leader looked tired but greeted me warmly and called for a beer, which I accidentally knocked over his shiny new table.

His aide eased my embarrassment by saying: 'It is customary to spill a little beer for the spirits.' Nice bit of diplomacy, I thought. We chatted for about two hours about his prospects of winning the presidency (he didn't win). We also chatted about religion. He said he was still a practising Roman Catholic but he didn't go to church very often. We reminisced about his years as a guerrilla leader. I asked him what he would have done if he could have chosen a different path.

'I would have been an economist.'

A strange choice for someone who had been accused of being a mass murderer.

I succumbed to sightseeing; it was good not to be encumbered with all the paraphernalia of TV journalism. The grand colonial station was resplendent on the outside in its striking green and white paint. Inside, though, the passenger coaches were more like cattle wagons. Long queues had formed for the slow journey to Jo'burg. Obviously Mozambique had learned from Britain's rail privatisation.

Nearby was a teeming indoor market, with an impressive array of fish. The car Renamo had provided kept breaking down but we made it to the old Portuguese fort, where I wandered around admiring cannons and remnants of colonial exploits. Another memory of colonial days was the charming disused bullring. The hawkers were far more laidback than in West Africa; and I actually felt like shopping for carvings. I was going soft in my old age.

A Renamo official, Chico, took me outside the capital to see new economic developments, including a dam. We talked politics, especially the hopes for democracy in Africa.

'There are not many good precedents,' he admitted, 'but maybe Mozambique can show the way. We are making democracy work. Things are improving here, despite Frelimo's faults . . . and ours. But we need investment.'

I suggested that investors had little faith in Africa. Some strategists had argued that even UN military intervention on the continent should be a thing of the past. Perhaps African wars should be fought to a conclusion. International intervention merely prolonged many conflicts. Victory by one side was perhaps a better closure.

'Maybe Africa must look after itself, if it is to have a real renaissance,' I said.

'What of globalisation?' Chico said. 'A disaster in one area of humanity is bound to affect another.'

The political debate continued when I went to meet the British High Commissioner in the building where Churchill had sought help after his famous escape during the Boer War. A plaque commemorated the event. The High Commission was adjacent to V. I. Lenin Street, and the road running past the US Information Service office was named after Kim Il Sung. The Museum of the Revolution, however, was run down, the curtains tattered and ripped, the lights broken and the attendants asleep. Revolutionary ardour was apparently on the wane. Maybe, after so long a war, the new Commonwealth member had a chance to develop capitalism and democracy. The prime requisite of Africa – peace – had been accomplished here.

I left Maputo in a tropical rainstorm. The taxi just managed to get to the airport. Even the immigration official handed back my passport with very little fuss. Only then did he ask me politely for 'something for the weekend'. I wondered exactly what he wanted for a second, but he was so nice about it that I gave him $2.

The advent of the new millennium had not been kind to Africa. Man-made disasters had been compounded by natural disasters of drought (Kenya and the Horn of Africa) and floods (as in Mozambique).The two superpowers of the continent had not shown real leadership.

President Thabo Mbeki of South Africa promised an African renaissance, but then lost credibility by suggesting that AIDS was not caused by the HIV virus. He also failed to rein in Mugabe's long march to economic suicide in Zimbabwe. In fact all the dire predictions of Ian Smith came true – much of the white expertise and capital had been forced to flee, leaving behind a starving black population.

True, Nigeria had shown some leadership in West Africa with its peacekeeping forces, but at home the imposition of Islamic law in some states of the north led to riots and reciprocal violence in the south. Anarchy and warlordism had spread through much of West

Africa. In Angola, Savimbi remained (for a while) as the classic warlord. His struggle was not ideological, but commercial. War was his way of doing business.

Diamonds had also fuelled warlordism in Liberia and Sierra Leone. Even without diamonds Somalia also became a warlord state. A new generation of white mercenaries, many from South Africa and the UK, were called in as commercial counter-armies to defeat the warlords and regain access to the mines. Much of the war in the Congo – sometimes dubbed 'Africa's first world war' – had been about grabbing minerals.

With the exception of Botswana, all the countries which had been held up by Western economists and politicians as models of development had instead developed serious problems, although chronic misgovernance and war had not been the sole factors. Higher oil charges and the collapse in the world price of commodities from Ghana and Uganda also contributed to the downward spiral. It was not all bleak, however. The UN helped to end the totally unnecessary war between former allies Eritrea and Ethiopia. There were even elections in Senegal and Ghana in which ruling politicians accepted defeat more or less gracefully, a rarity in Africa.

Africa could no longer blame outsiders, especially former imperialists, although the tyrannical Mugabe had tried roasting that old chestnut. More often, African governments would scapegoat other tribes or foreign workers (as in the Ivory Coast). Emigration – increasingly difficult now to Western countries – was often the sole recourse. In sub-Saharan Africa nearly all the colonists had left, and so too had many of the investors. It was time for Africa to set its own house in order. And South Africa was simply too busy with its own troubles to take a robust lead.

EUROPE

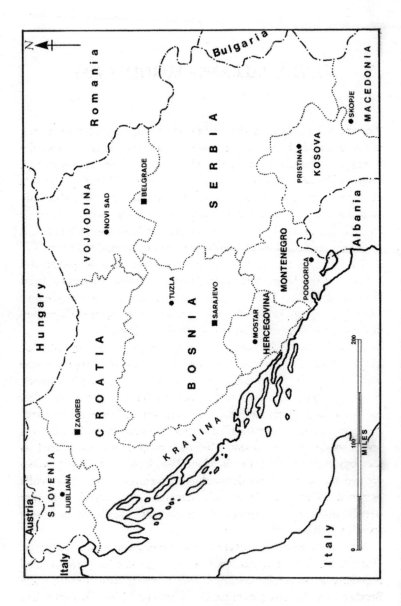

Yugoslavia

12. THE BALKANS – EUROPE'S WAR

'For those who stand in the way of unity, a spit in the face, a sock in the jaw, and, if necessary, a bullet in the head.' Enver Hoxha, the Albanian communist leader, didn't like anybody disagreeing with him. That's what Marxism was about in the Eastern bloc: if the people didn't like the government, change the people. A trip to Romania made me think hard about the implosion of communism in Europe. Nicolae Ceausescu had been one of the maddest and baddest of a very bad bunch. Once, the Cold War was in the centre of Europe – in Berlin. For most of my reporting life it had shifted to the peripheries – wars in Asia, Africa, and South America, proxy conventional wars in the Middle East. Pan-European history had frozen in the *glacis* of East–West confrontation. But, with *glasnost*, wars were springing up in the heart of Europe, most notably in the Balkans.

The collapse of the Soviet Union spelled the death of orthodox Marxist parties in Europe. A world mission was the original *raison d'être* of Bolshevism. Destroying belief in the inevitable triumph of international socialism was bound to have a knock-on effect on electoral support for designer socialism in Western European democracies. Marxism had failed as a means of economic development and a model of government. Moscow's propaganda proclaimed its ideology would conquer the decadent West. Instead, the Soviet system created the starving and demoralised proletariat it was specifically designed to prevent. Above all, Marxism was judged a disaster because of the (now) obvious and extraordinary fragility of the former socialist regimes.

Marxism's downfall brought many changes, not least in language. From A to Z, from *apparatchik* to Zhivago, the 'evil empire' had popularised numerous concepts and phrases; now Orwell's Big Brother and the gulag became less fearsome terms. Novelists had to invent alternatives to James Bond, moles and KGB honey-traps. The biggest change was that Marxists no longer set the intellectual agenda. John Torode, a British journalist, called Marxism 'a millennial cult disguised as the ultimate scientific philosophy'. It was a secular religion, but history had pronounced its god dead. Scientific socialism was proved as bogus as Nazi race theories.

Marxism had seduced generations of leading Western academics, writers, artists and poets. These fellow travellers, dubbed 'useful idiots' by Lenin, never missed the chance to blame all evil on the USA while giving the USSR the benefit of every doubt. The murder of many millions by Stalin was deemed impossible in a 'workers' paradise'. In the social science faculties of Western universities it was a brave person who publicly defied the Marxist consensus. The intellectual frame of reference often began and ended with Bob Dylan's first album. Yet after years of defending Marxist lies, very few, if any, dons recanted or apologised for misleading their students. Instead, a deafening silence ensued.

The year 1989 was one of political wonders. At the beginning the Cold War seemed almost in its prime. By its end the Berlin Wall had crashed, and so had the Russian empire. And the Communist Party in China had to slaughter its young in Tiananmen Square to cling on to power. The last European dictator to survive the Russian collapse was Ceausescu. On Christmas Day he was executed by his own military – exactly ten years to the day after the Soviets appeared to be at the height of their imperial hubris when they invaded Afghanistan. Soviet imperial pretensions were proved hollow, but so were Western predictions about the 'End of History' (the Darwinian acceptance of liberal democracy as the final form of human government). Many of the Western dons had also swallowed that tosh.

Initially, the re-emergence of Eastern Europe seemed such a simple matter. Once the Wall was down, light would flood in. The Reds were gone or were going, and everyone would be free. Accustomed to seeing those behind the Wall as somehow uniform, uniformed, regimented, homogenous, an assumption was made that they would become uniformly free as well. But they didn't. Difference became the antidote to the old failed ideology. Monolithic communism was easy to understand, hate, fear and fight. After the Fall, it became necessary to wade through a fog of quasi-democrats, good old-fashioned fascists, born-again communists, bandoleered nationalists, mafiosi and Ruritanian warlords – stirring stuff for hacks, except that most of them liked taking pot-shots at journalists.

Romania

A friend of mine, Peter, was involved in sending aid to Romanian orphanages. In July 1991 he invited me to see what he was doing. We travelled to Bucharest on the same day. He was a charity worker so he flew classy Swissair; I risked economy class on TAROM, the Romanian airline, which made even Pakistan's 'Inshallah Airways' look upmarket. The only good part was the absence of cameras. Travelling the world with video gear is like running a marathon attached to a bulky vacuum cleaner.

The aircraft, of obscure origins and past its sell-by date, looked likely to fall from the sky. When I met the passengers, a planeload of Scottish football fans, I almost began to hope that it would. The airline food was seriously unrecognisable, with chunks of what I could see was vaguely meat but didn't risk tasting; normally, I will eat anything. Bucharest international airport was on a par with the style of cuisine: poorly lit, seedy, officious and studiously unwelcoming. It was a fair reflection of the whole country – post-revolutionary Romania was in the grip of a post-Orwellian nightmare.

After queuing for an hour for my baggage, I was swamped by taxi-drivers drooling for payment in real currency. I found a man who looked and sounded like the idiot in Eco's *The Name of the Rose*. He spoke a smattering of all European languages in a way that suggested he had no native tongue. In a torrential downpour he had to retrieve and then attach his windscreen-wipers – such capitalist trimmings were far too valuable to be left on a car. On our way through the flooded streets to the city centre I could see remnants, a few villas here and there, of the old grandeur of the 1930s. Bucharest once called itself the 'Paris of the East'. Unfortunately most of it had been demolished by Ceausescu and replaced by appalling concrete towers dedicated to the socialist utopia.

The late Romanian messiah had decided to pull down much of the old picturesque Romania. I suppose he was also the sort of person who checked his desktop for bits of fluff. Ceausescu destroyed villages wholesale, sometimes giving the peasants forty-eight hours to quit their homes. He levelled historic districts of his cowed capital to build egomaniacal monstrosities. In the very centre was a great citadel, the Casa Republicii, where he wanted to be buried. It dwarfed anything even Hitler or Franco had attempted. Dictators too often try to mask their personal insecurities by building massively ugly monuments.

Ceausescu had spared the old hotel I stayed in, but it had seen better days . . . maybe better centuries. My room was a decayed masterpiece of Art Deco, but many of the important bits, such as the shower head and light bulbs, were missing. Peter and his Romanian girlfriend, Diana, arrived to help me negotiate room service. Prices were cheap. The £700 monthly rent on my house in Britain could have bought Diana's flat outright. She paid less than a pound a month in rent.

I asked her about local politics, life and booze, but I could never get a straight answer on anything. She was like a chameleon on a tartan rug. Most Romanians were evasive on most topics . . . except the possibility of getting out of Romania. Perhaps it was because they had spent a lifetime being threatened with jail for unauthorised conversations with foreigners. Bucharest reflected a weird, shabby, sad, disorganised society. Take the lift in the hotel. In the day it was manned by an old woman who must have been in the Olympic wrestling team in her youth. At night it was driven by a striking peroxide blonde in very tight blue ski-pants. She spoke to me in broken Italian, although I never discovered whether she provided any extra night-time services.

I spent the next few days driving around Bucharest in a white coat in a brand-new ambulance donated by a British charity. It was sticky hot and we stopped to buy drinks from a roadside vendor. We wanted to take the bottles away with us. This was impossible, explained Diana. To do so we had to give the vendor the equivalent number of empty bottles of the same size. But how do you start off your bottle collection if you are new to the country? We offered to pay extra for the privilege of taking a drink plus bottle; but no, we needed our own bottles. I began to understand why Romania had one of the world's highest suicide rates.

I was also beginning to comprehend Eastern Europe's transition to capitalism. The first advertising billboards had just appeared in the city, praising Panasonic and Xerox. You could get Coke in a few hotels. Even imported beer could be secured if you paid in foreign currency. Diana led me into dark alleyways to meet shady characters who swapped me money at three times the official rate. The city had a currency black market but very little in the shops. Once Eastern Europe had socialism without social justice, now it had capitalism with very little capital. I wondered which came first, political reform or economic development. In Romania the question seemed irrelevant: it had no chicken and no egg.

Romania was something of an odd man out in the Soviet empire. Romanians liked to think they were Latins, the French of Eastern Europe. During the Cold War the country reinforced the prejudices of both sides. To the East, its apparently enormous growth rate proved that communism worked. To the West, the fact that it was still one of Europe's least developed countries proved that it didn't. Ceausescu tried to be the de Gaulle of the Warsaw Pact. He was friendly with China, spoke to Israel, and condemned the invasion of Czechoslovakia. For this he was fêted in the West. Actually, it was a clever bit of Moscow manipulation, but that didn't stop even the House of Windsor showering royal accolades upon him. On their trips to the West, the Ceausescus would strip every hotel room or noble house they stayed in and send all their loot back home.

Only in Romania was military force used extensively in an attempt to save the regime from the revolutionary fervour that swept Eastern Europe. The entirely out-of-touch Ceausescu was overthrown by a combination of popular insurrection and a local communist party coup, encouraged by Moscow. The National Salvation Front, led by Ion Iliescu, won handsomely in the subsequent polls, elections judged 'flawed but not fraudulent' by international observers. Iliescu was seen as the Saint George who slew the Ceausescu dragon. Romanians had a disturbing history of flocking to support all-powerful leaders. Unfortunately the leadership of the National Salvation Front was largely made up of former communists, merely parading on the stage of democracy for the benefit of Western aid. Romania was an unfinished revolution.

The Salvation Front played upon traditional Romanian xenophobia, in particular discrimination against the large Hungarian minority in Transylvania. As one journalist put it, this had been the 'real bloodsucker of democracy' since the apparent revolution. Perhaps the best way to judge a country is by how it treats minorities. The government had not tried to stamp out lingering anti-Semitism, even though only 18,000 Jews had survived Nazism and communism. Defenders of the new government told me Romania was part of the typical Balkan culture where bouts of head-bashing and corruption were inevitable, pointing out the horrendous legacy bequeathed by the worst dictatorship in the Soviet bloc.

Romania was the most backward state in Europe, except for Albania. The economy was pitiful. The workers and the population in general seemed utterly demoralised. Little foreign investment ventured in – and for good reasons. Elements in the government were paranoid about Romania being 'taken over' by foreigners. There had been 300 per cent price increases in key items such as petrol. Escalating unemployment prompted numerous wildcat strikes, but the general inertia made it difficult to judge whether Romanians were striking or working. They exemplified the classic Russian workers' joke: they pretend to pay us and we pretend to work.

As one foreign expert put it: 'Romanians will be happy to make do with half a capitalist loaf after having been denied the communist one.' Maybe. Life had been very hard under Ceausescu: a seven-day working week, with lighting, hot water, and heating severely rationed. He denuded the country in his (largely successful) attempt to pay off all foreign debt. I heard variations of other Russian jokes.

'What is five miles long and eats only potatoes? . . . A Russian meat queue.'

Few Romanians I met wanted the return of dictatorship, but the complaint 'at least things were cheaper under Ceausescu' was very common. Romanians, desperate to find out about the outside world, could now risk chatting to foreigners. Previously the dreaded secret police, the *Securitate*, monitored nearly all contacts with outsiders, deploying a ruthless intelligence system: one in four Romanians was said to be an informer. On an individual basis Romanians, I found, could be very charming to foreigners, but they still looked over their shoulders and talked cautiously until they got to know you. The government had reformed but not disbanded the *Securitate*.

The atmosphere of fear and deprivation created a society with degraded values. Misha Glenny, when he was the BBC's Central European correspondent, used the phrase 'psychotic proletariat'. Hence the horror tales of dumping and trading in babies. Ceausescu's rundown of the medical services meant that Romania accounted for half of Europe's child AIDS victims, according to official figures. But Romania was also milking the AIDS and orphanage stories for all they were worth. I wanted to find out whether Western aid was getting to the sick and abandoned children, or simply being siphoned off by desperate and greedy officials. After years of bumbling around the third world – in which I definitely included Romania – I had become rather jaundiced about aid. I had met some saintly aid workers, but my general impression was negative. In

Africa it destroyed local initiative, enriched the élites and created armies of aid junkies. I was predisposed to expect the same in Romania, and I was not to be surprised.

I saw some aid enterprises in Bucharest but I wanted to get out into the country, away from PR exercises – not that Romanians were capable of understanding modern PR, but they'd had decades of training in public lying. Peter drove me to Slatina, about three and a half hours from the capital. I had heard of massive industrial pollution in Romania but I didn't see much evidence of it, just drab peasant country with ribbon developments of roadside shacks. One or two shacks were elaborately decorated in the Eastern style; most were breezeblocks, wooden or occasionally square mud huts. Donkey-carts were everywhere. So were soldiers. I wondered where the war was.

Slatina seemed more cheerful than grey, ill-lit Bucharest. It had a main street with recognisable shops. The orphanage had been given a few hours' notice of our visit. The children's home, in a normal apartment block, was also a home for senile adults. It stank of must and urine. Peopled with staring-eyed cripples and toothless dribbling crones, it was straight out of Dickens. We sat for a few hours in various offices where pot-bellied, unshaven admin types did nothing. Absolutely nothing.

Then we had an inspection. Toys donated by British charities were taken out of a large box; the kids obviously hadn't seen them for a long time, if ever. The children went mad for a while, but soon seemed more interested in the attention that Peter, Diana and I were giving them. They appeared utterly starved of affection. Although they didn't look unfed and were vaguely clean, they lived in stark, primitive surroundings. Their rooms – with open windows on the fourth floor – had just a few playpens and dirty mattresses. There were no pictures and nothing else, once the toys were returned to the big box. All the children were mentally handicapped. One had just pulled his own eye out. As they clambered all over us, I had to leave with tears streaming down my face.

When I recovered, I asked Diana why unskilled volunteers had to come all the way from England. Peter had brought four sixth-form volunteers to spend their summer helping in the orphanage. Why couldn't some of the many unemployed locals, who spoke the language, help out? I was treated to a classic piece of Romanian evasiveness in response.

Diana negotiated a hotel in Slatina for our volunteer do-gooders. It took less than half an hour. The place didn't have working toilets but it did have some food. The cabbage was OK and the rye bread and tomatoes were excellent. Tomatoes, I noticed, were always available in Romania. Even beer and Coke were on sale. In the bar a group played a terrible mix of folk music and Turkish rock 'n' roll. The male singer sang in falsetto; the most moving thing about his performance was his hairpiece. It sounded like Nana Mouskouri played at very high speed.

Peter commented: 'You've got me into some bad things, but this is the worst.'

Then and there I decided to nip over the border to Yugoslavia. 'I'd prefer to get shot at than listen to this. I'm going to Yugoslavia tomorrow. At least it'll be quieter there.'

Peter laughed. He understood my impulsiveness.

The next morning Diana took me to the railway station, where she spent an hour talking in Romanian. It seemed like a complicated deal to rent the place. She eventually emerged with a ticket, and spent an hour explaining how I would get to Serbia. So many possible vagaries were offered that I just climbed on the next west-bound train. It was heading for Transylvania; that seemed interesting enough. The train was out of some Second World War movie, with carriage exteriors painted in metal grey like *Wehrmacht* trains in the early 1940s. I thought it would be an adventure to travel in an old Nazi caboose.

Clearly, nobody had done anything to the carriages since the Germans retreated. A peasant woman boarded with a basket full of day-old chicks. People took their shoes off and lounged around. A young man opposite kept staring at me while he munched sunflower seeds. He picked bits out of his teeth with his tongue and blew them on to the floor. Various swarthy men with droopy moustaches and 1940s clothes glowered at the obvious foreign intruder. Lots of gypsies, real ones, boarded. It was rather like London's Northern Line. Again I felt at home.

The Sunflower Kid kept staring, and I began to wonder whether he was among the one in four Romanians moonlighting as informers. He stared, almost without blinking, for half an hour. I was determined not to be the first to break. I ignored him or gave him an occasional half-smile, one of those English specialities cultivated for the workplace. Eventually the starer spoke to me in very broken English. He wanted to live in England. I didn't meet a single Romanian in a country of fervent nationalists who wanted to stay at home. Luckily the Sunflower Kid had a reasonable mastery of the train timetable. He advised me to proceed via Craiova to Timisoara, the largely Hungarian-speaking town where the revolution had begun. Since Romanian long-distance trains did not have buffets I ate enough sunflower seeds to germinate the whole of Wales.

Craiova station was like a large mausoleum, lit with a single bulb in the high domed roof. I found someone who I thought might sell me a ticket. She was operating a large machine which was at least fifty years old. I spent fifteen minutes trying to buy a ticket. I knew no Romanian but I did understand fifteen minutes of no. Eventually a very beautiful young woman came to my rescue. She explained in French that if I gave her a wad of lei – just a few pounds – she would sort out my tickets. A train was due in four hours to the Serbian border via Timisoara. She said she would meet me later in the station bar. As I am always a sucker for a pretty face, I gave her the money and went in search of a beer.

The bar was in a large dowdy room. In the dim light I tried to attract the waiter. He skirted around me just once but thereafter ignored me. I had missed my chance: the only way I would get that much attention again was to marry his sister, or at least give him some cigarettes. I didn't smoke, but I always carried some good foreign cigarettes for such occasions. After I offered him one he rushed to bring me a beer. Soon my table was crowded with extras from the set of a 1930s Chicago gangster movie. Two self-proclaimed poets joined in the fray. To be fair, although I flashed the cigarettes, they were happy to buy me beers.

After an hour or so I remembered my promised ticket. I didn't expect to see the raven-haired beauty again and at about 10 p.m. I started asking about accommodation. I was offered various private homes, whorehouses, and possible hotels, but was saved from the agony of decision by the arrival of my ticket.

She shooed the Crazy Gang from the table and sat down to share a coffee. The train would be leaving in two hours, she said, handing me a ticket worth the exact amount of money I had given her. I cautiously offered her a few dollars for her trouble but she refused. She would be happy to sit and talk until my train left. That suited me fine.

Adela had worked for the railways for five years but was very frustrated with her menial job. She had worked in France and was very eager to return. Since my French was fairly basic she asked me basic questions.

'Are you married?'

For the only time in my (brief) married life I almost said: '*Quelquefois*,' but refrained.

She asked me to come back to visit her while I was in Romania. I told her I would write and that she was welcome to stay with me and my wife. After two hours of charming conversation with a striking 26-year-old woman I was beginning to change my mind about Romania, even about going to Yugoslavia, but she put her arm in mine and led me to the train. She gave me a farewell which easily outclassed any kind of hospitality offered by any other railway official in the world. It was a pity I was standing on a platform with both hands full of luggage. I wasn't stupid enough to think my boyish charm had won her over so quickly. That such a stunning female should be so desperate to get out of Romania was a tragic comment on her country.

Adela had organised the very best Romanian railways could offer, which wasn't much. I was booked into a 'first-class luxury sleeper', which translated as a doss-house on wheels. I shared a small compartment with an upper-class Romanian family. We endured constant rude interruptions by ticket inspectors and customs officials who had forgotten nothing that the Gestapo had taught their old Romanian allies.

The Serb officials also combined the very best of Nazi and communist bureaucracy. I was glad to arrive in Belgrade's Hotel Moscow. Since the outbreak of the Yugoslav war tourists were thin on the ground and I haggled successfully for a half-price room. There I sat down to enjoy the intermittent electricity and read a tourist booklet describing Yugoslavia as 'a land of contrasts'. For contrasts I had come to the right place at the right time.

Former Yugoslavia

Until the break-up of the Yugoslav federation newspaper editors tended to avoid political stories on the country because it was so bloody complicated. But the world's media began to fill up with little lectures on, and maps of, Yugoslavia's six republics and two autonomous regions, as well as its different languages, religions and various -isms. The contrasting cultures may have exacerbated the political strife but the great variety of language, cuisine, architecture, and scenery attracted me.

Straddling East and West, Yugoslavia once had everything, from picture-book Alpine villages, ancient Roman ruins and glorious coastline to reasonably efficient hotels, phones and transport. The abundance of splendid cathedrals, monasteries, and mosques echoed the fact that, although most Yugoslavs were Catholic or Orthodox Christians, the federation also had Europe's largest Muslim community. Scarcely larger than Britain, the country ranged in the north from Slovenia, a little Austria, to the Albanians in the south, one of the most backward regions of Europe. Many of the twenty-four million inhabitants spoke some English, especially in the main cities and on the hot, dry Adriatic.

In addition to the destruction of the package tourist industry, the war had done untold damage to the area. When I got there Slovenia had just seized independence in the Ten-Day War in the summer of 1991, which had cost the lives of only twenty people. Slovenia didn't matter much to the Serb communist politicians and generals who ran the old show. But Croatia was different. Lots of Serbs lived there. The fight to hold on to Croatia was just beginning. I had been involved in a number of Yugoslav-based war-games while at Sandhurst, and knew something of the passions and the number of guns. I anticipated a long series of wars throughout the Balkans. First Croatia, then Bosnia, then Macedonia, and, the most volatile of the lot, the Albanians in Kosovo province. I wanted to see something of the place before it all blew up in the faces of the smug Serb centralists trying to keep Tito's political corpse alive.

Belgrade was the federal capital and one of Europe's oldest cities. Because of its strategic position on the Danube it had been conquered and rebuilt thirty-eight times. I wandered up to the much-restored Kalemegdan fortress right in the centre of old Belgrade, which offered a wonderful view over the city and river. Just outside the fortress stood the neo-baroque Orthodox cathedral, full of icons. The newer sections of the city were bustling, efficient, Western, and expensive, but I had just left third-world Romania so perhaps my perspectives were a bit askew. By comparison Belgrade was a very cosmopolitan place where politicians wore dark suits and dark socks, often simultaneously.

I found the press club and made a few contacts, ending up in the Skadarlija district which my new friends likened to Montmartre in Paris. Like the Romanians, Serbs used France as their lodestone. I was happy to agree with their comparison. The cobbled streets, open-air restaurants, wandering musicians and hawkers were a pleasant backcloth to the excellent ethnic dishes. I spent most of the long meal being inducted into the arcane history of Greater Serbia. Each person carefully explained that he or she was 'a moderate', not to be numbered among the crazy Serb nationalists. They were middle-class intellectuals who could see the wider picture, they insisted. When I touched on basic issues, however, they were as chauvinist as the 'crazy nationalists' they purported to despise.

I asked: 'How can you expect to hold on to Kosovo, which is 10 per cent Serb and 90 per cent Albanian, especially when you treat the majority like scum?' (My actual phraseology was slightly more diplomatic.)

This prompted a long history lesson of battles in the Middle Ages. When I mentioned Croatia I got a blow-by-blow account of Croats bending over backwards to outdo the genocidal Germans during the Second World War, which seemed to tally with my own reading of recent Croat history. Nonetheless, despite the veneer of rationality, most Serbs I encountered glowed with an inner fire of intolerance. Everyone I met felt that full-scale civil war was inevitable. Fighting talk was the rule, not the exception. Above all, the ancient hostilities between Serb and Croat fed off one another. For all their hatreds the Serbs and Croats spoke essentially the same language, albeit Serbs used Cyrillic script and Croats used Roman.

The EC was trying to maintain a ceasefire between Croatia and Serbia when I was there, but no one was listening to Brussels. In central Belgrade numerous armed policemen relaxed in the summer heat. The federal army had called up its reserves. Were they preparing to fight for the dead federation or the new Greater Serbia? About ten million of the old federation were Serbs. Despite the apparent prosperity of the city, Serbs complained about economic decline, massive hidden unemployment and inflation. Until recently inflation had been 2,500 per cent, but then it had dropped considerably. The more prosperous Croats and Slovenians claimed that the taxes they paid were being wasted by the bungling, bullying communist *apparatchiki* in Belgrade.

I asked a Serb lawyer why he wanted to fight when further conflict would destroy the fragile economy. 'The English insist on hanging on to Northern Ireland. We feel the same about our people in Croatia.'

About 600,000 Serbs lived in Croatia; some of the Serb-dominated areas had just declared themselves autonomous republics.

I caught a train from Belgrade to Zagreb, the capital of Croatia. The Serbs in my compartment warned me to stop talking politics when we reached the Croatian border. They were visibly angry but also tense when Croatia's new defence force stopped the train and demanded identity documents.

An old Croat woman, dressed all in black, started to cry. 'All my family was killed in the fighting between Serbs and Croats during the Hitler war. I don't want it to happen all over again.'

Once the Croat soldiers had left, a young Serb said: 'Those fascist Croats killed tens of thousands of Serbs in camps during the last war.'

The bitterness ran deep . . . and the new war was only just beginning.

In Zagreb independence flags were as commonplace as the rumours that federal tanks were about to seize the city centre. Croatia seemed more efficient but not necessarily more democratic than Serbia. The country was ruled by a single party, the Croatian Democratic Union, which owed more than a few debts to its fascist predecessor. The break-up of Yugoslavia was not simply a question of brave little democracies challenging a communist centralism.

Inevitably the Balkans was unravelling the treaties imposed after the First World War. It was no coincidence that the two extremities of the old Ottoman empire, Slovenia and Kurdistan, should be demanding freedom at the same time. The general collapse of communism was another factor. Yugoslavia was more like the Soviet Union than the recently freed states of Eastern Europe. Both enforced federations were on the point of economic as well as political disintegration. That was why the EC was so reluctant to recognise the independence of Slovenia and Croatia, for fear of encouraging the premature collapse of the Soviet Union as well as separatist demands in other European countries, such as Czechoslovakia.

Germany, Croatia's old ally, was pushing for recognition; France, Serbia's traditional friend, was hostile. Political warfare embroiled the EC. In eastern Croatia real fighting between Serbian and Croatian irregulars was intensified by the intervention of regular Croatian and Serb forces. Hundreds had already been killed in this region. Because the overt invasion of Slovenia seemed to have failed, hard-line communist generals in Serbia appeared to be adopting a policy of creeping annexation of parts of Croatia. Serbs already controlled about a third of Croat territory.

If Serb tanks were going to rumble into Zagreb – which the local papers insisted they would – I wanted a good vantage point. I booked myself into a room with a view, the top floor of the Hotel Dubrovnik overlooking the main square. I was excited; it was what I imagined Warsaw felt like in the early autumn of 1939.

I had often done voice reports for BBC Wales news, phoning Cardiff reverse charge and doing ad lib three-minute pieces live or recorded for later use. Looking out over the square I rang up the Beeb, but none of my usual contacts was around. Some inane woman asked me whether Yugoslavia was an important story. She had the news sense of a butterfly. I tried to explain but she said she had to break off because an office party was going on. It was some time before I bothered to report again for BBC Wales. Besides, they paid a pittance. (While in Cardiff I had actually been asked to talk about the Middle East, but arrived in the studio to find that I was expected to talk about golf not the Gulf. A later typographical error demanded that I talk about bonsai, not Bosnia.)

Since no tanks had appeared I decided to explore Zagreb. It seemed a wonderful city, a little Vienna, clean and quiet except for the immaculate trams. In the plush piano bar of the best hotel in town I fell in with some foreign journalists. I wanted to go to Osijek, the scene of fierce fighting, so I needed some instant knowledge. If I had been filming I would have felt obliged to leave immediately for the front. But I was half on holiday, so I decided to roam around Zagreb persuading myself that the tanks would come any minute. Frankly I didn't care. Without seeing it via the lens of a video camera, it would not have seemed real to me.

The medieval part of town was dominated by the twin towers of the cathedral, first consecrated in 1217. Two other churches interested me: St Mark's, the roof of which displayed the coats of arms of Croatia and Zagreb in enamel tiles; and St Catherine's, built by Jesuits in the seventeenth century. I was entranced by the baroque detail. Outside the main government building multi-coloured Toytown soldiers paraded up and down in an amazing march, part goose-step and part ballet. Zagreb took its cultural role seriously, with numerous theatres and museums. The most famous museum was Muzej Mimara, which housed one of the world's great art collections. The town's classical architecture was well proportioned, Austro-Hungarian style, rococo in parts but not over-dressy.

Zagreb was not all art, architecture and piety. I would argue that it was perhaps the best place in Europe to sample outdoor café life. Winding through the old town were streets full of open-air restaurants buzzing with vitality. Perhaps because visitors were thin on the ground, people came up to talk to me. An attractive art student asked if she could join my table; within five minutes she had volunteered to take me on a sightseeing expedition. She was about to move to Vienna, and was savouring Zagreb's delights before what she knew would be a long separation.

I hired a car to drive to Ljubljana, the capital of Slovenia, normally an hour's journey. It took me considerably longer as some main roads were blocked or damaged by recent fighting. This was my good fortune because the side roads yielded scenery which was idyllic in its rustic charm: utterly tidy villages with spotless Alpine-style houses, perfect little guesthouses, and everywhere little churches with onion-domed spires. War in Europe seemed even more preposterous in this setting.

Slovenia was the most advanced area of Yugoslavia, in economic terms the Sweden of the Balkans. Indeed, Slovenians always thought of themselves as European rather than Balkan. The prosperity of the little state of two million people seemed to justify their traditional smugness. They were also tense. In the capital, queues had formed outside a shop selling old Russian gas masks at exorbitant prices. The adjacent restaurants were full, however. With more hope than conviction Slovenians told me that perhaps Austrian or even Italian armies would help them if they were invaded again. This was the kind of talk which fuelled Serbian propaganda claims that Germany was trying to establish a 'Fourth Reich' by making Slovenia and Croatia economic satellites. But diplomatic recognition of Slovenia and Croatia was inevitable. After federal Yugoslav planes launched air raids on Slovenian cities – the first such incident in Europe since 1945 – Western support was bound to swing towards Slovenia.

I had seen the occasional burnt-out tank and armoured vehicle on the way into Ljubljana but the city itself seemed unscathed. The River Ljubljana ambled peacefully beneath an array of over-decorous little bridges. The small city was dominated by a twelfth-century castle and, below it, the cathedral next to a daily open market full of produce, flowers and people.

In spite of the war, I really liked ex-Yugoslavia. The occasional bursts of old-style communist bureaucracy aside, the mood of Oriental decadence, Balkan intrigue, ubiquitous courtesy and European sanitation was very appealing. In early 1991 it was obvious even to me that nobody could put Yugoslavia's Humpty Dumpty together again. I wrote at the time that the problems of dividing up that Rubik's Cube of mini-nationalities would probably be accompanied by major population movements. I had not anticipated the future horrors of ethnic cleansing, and naively believed that the EC could be a peace-broker. Brussels had immense clout: 53 per cent of federal Yugoslav trade was with the Community. I never accepted that Europe's borders were sacrosanct, preferring Balkanisation to Lebanonisation. Instead, the EC proved to be totally inept; after years of slaughter it was left to the blue berets and NATO planes.

I was right on Austria's border; I could board a train to Paris. That was my first inclination, but I had promised to take Peter out for dinner in Bucharest and had left some of my kit there. Reluctantly, I would have to go back. I dreaded returning to Romania. On one of the last trains to run from Zagreb to Belgrade before Croats and Serbs started a major war which killed over 7,000 people, I found myself next to an apostle of peace: an Australian mystic called Marga. For the first hour he did not speak, meditating in the lotus position like some frozen Buddha with the occasional audible mantra. Since no one else was in the carriage I became bored and disrupted his trance. This was a mistake – for the next five hours I suffered a detailed description of his diet and bowel movements. He was a self-centred, health-obsessive neurotic who would drive anyone to murder not karma.

When I gratefully left him at Belgrade station I offered him my hand. Instead he cupped his hands together and gave an Oriental bow. 'You're a nice bloke but I don't shake hands. Catch too many diseases.'

I wondered what Mother Teresa would make of that, and prayed for divine help to inspire a Croat sniper or Montenegrin bandit or Bosnian fundamentalist to zap this phoney Buddhist. I trusted that Saint Peter would extend his hand only to those who arrived at the pearly gates free of all -isms.

Near Belgrade station I ate two meals on the trot and bought supplies for the desert of Romanian railways. As the train started off a young blonde medical student came into my compartment. She spoke excellent English – the long ride to Bucharest might not be so bad. After five minutes of animated conversation she abruptly walked out of the compartment. Did I have some dreadful disease of which the Buddhist and the medical student had observed subtle symptoms?

Hours later she came back to apologise, explaining she had to negotiate a money deal in foreign currency, the only way to survive in Romania. I would have given her extravagant rates just for her company. In the interim, her place had been taken by a suspicious-looking Algerian with whom I chatted in French; he seemed a good sort. The notoriously xenophobic Romanians detested Arabs as well as gypsies, Jews, Hungarians and, I presume, Welshmen . . . well, they didn't seem to like anyone except the French. I knew in my bones that the border would be trouble.

A very large Romanian customs official entered the compartment and demanded my passport. He looked at it and asked for what seemed a large amount of Romanian money. I am always confused by numbers in foreign languages. '*Je voudrais expliquer, monsieur. . .*'

He told me to shut up in very precise French and walked off with my passport. I had a second valid passport secreted in my bag, but I wasn't going to let him bulldoze me. A soldier came into the compartment and pointed his rifle at me. It took me a while to realise that I was to get off the train. He indicated that he would guard my luggage. Two other soldiers frog-marched me into a room where the US dollar price of a visa (which I already had) kept escalating. I was torn between my desire to haggle and the possibility of the train going off with my gear. I could see other passengers being yanked off, including my new Algerian friend.

I was taken to another room to be interrogated, this time by a young woman who spoke good French and reasonable English. She asked me what I was doing in Romania. I explained the orphanage bit with heavy emphasis on the foreign donations and no mention of any journalism. I've never yet met an immigration or customs official who has shown me the slightest bit of warmth once they find out I am a hack. She noticed the 'Dr' on my passport and told the other security men in Romanian that I was engaged in vital medical work in Bucharest. I think that's what she said. It was the only time I have ever pretended my D.Litt was an MD. But I paid a small fee and decided that silence was the better part of ethics.

The Algerian and I jumped on the train as it started to move. He could hardly comment on Romanian racism, having seen me given a hard time, and just said: 'All socialist states are the same . . . too much bureaucracy.'

At Timisoara the compartment filled up with ethnic Hungarians. One nodded discreetly that I should follow him into the corridor. Always curious, I did so. He pulled out a bottle of Romania's famous plum brandy and shared it with me, along with his life story, explaining that he wouldn't talk to me in front of the other people in the compartment. A schoolteacher, he made me his instant friend and pupil. He acted as guide and mentor during the constant surprise attacks by jack-booted ticket collectors. The whole compartment would be asleep with the lights out when officials would burst in, flicking on the lights to see if we had been digging escape tunnels. Waiting an hour for everyone to fall asleep again, they would launch another raid. Perhaps the Romanian tourist authorities ran a special charm school for them.

Back in my Bucharest hotel I had prepared a few Italian phrases for the voluptuous blonde lift-operator. Unfortunately the all-in wrestler was doing night duty, undermining my theory about earlier approaches from the blonde. In a very short time in Romania I had received a surprisingly large number of offers from attractive young women. Ceausescu had a lot to answer for.

After seeing Peter and debriefing the volunteers about their orphanage experiences, I flew out from Bucharest. Diana had spent the best part of a week preparing the paperwork for my flight so none of the usual Romanian hassles impeded me. A young Romanian physics teacher sat next to me, on her way to Britain, and the West, for the first time. She was obviously intelligent and spoke good English. 'I do not want communism in Romania but nor do I want capitalism.'

She described modern Britain to me: Dickensian conditions which formed standard Eastern bloc propaganda. She had never heard of the National Health Service or free education. I didn't argue. If Russia was Upper Volta with rockets, Romania was just Upper Volta. Her first trip outside her own country would open her eyes.

I told her a little about my bad impressions of Romania. Like the society, much of the environment was ravaged. But how could ancient, mass-polluting industries close when already serious unemployment was multiplying? Economic reform would mean ending government subsidies and even more price increases. Above all, it meant dealing with diabolical foreigners. Despite and because of its strong-arm methods, Iliescu's government still feared another popular insurrection. The physics teacher supported the return of the king. Diana had said the same thing. Increasingly Romanians were hoping that King Michael, deposed in 1947, would return from exile. Perhaps they yearned once more for another 'great man' to save them. The futile royalist reverie was interrupted by our touchdown.

I felt glad to be back in Heathrow. Things worked. Even the passport official smiled this time.

Bosnia

I felt ashamed to call myself a European after the genocide in Bosnia. I had lived too long in the shadow of Auschwitz to believe it could ever have happened again. But it did. Forty-four per cent of Bosnia's former population – before the mass exodus and killings – were Muslim. Saddam Hussein rather cheekily complained about human rights abuses in Los Angeles and, with more justice, of the Muslim plight in Bosnia.

If it was morally right to attack Iraq to remove Saddam's occupying forces in Kuwait, why shouldn't foreign Islamic forces help liberate Bosnia after Serbia's (and Croatia's) invasion? Iran offered to send troops to do precisely this. Bosnia was recognised by the EC and the USA. Then the country was subjected to foreign occupation, torture of civilians, *de facto* annexation of territory by force, and contempt and harassment of neutral representatives of the EC, UN and Red Cross. From the Bosnian Muslim perspective the question was clear: why didn't the overwhelmingly powerful Western European armies launch a Balkan version of Desert Storm? They didn't need massive airlifts; they could drive in from next door.

It could never be that simple in the Balkans. In the mid-1990s the battlefield status quo looked like being the basis of new permanent frontiers. The Bosnian Muslims were left with a tiny state. The fighting in Sarajevo was the heaviest in any European capital since 1945. To an outsider it seemed so senseless, not least because the various communities there had lived together peacefully for decades. The peace movement was much stronger in Sarajevo than in jingoistic

Zagreb and Belgrade. The genocide in Bosnia would continue to have major repercussions on minorities throughout Europe and Central Asia, not least among the Hungarians in Romania and the volatile Russian minorities on the fringes of the former Soviet empire. The Serbs and Croats originally denied that religion should define nationality. The Muslims were fellow Slavs who spoke Serbo-Croat. But Muslim Bosnians argued that since religion was their main definition of nationhood, it was that much more important to them.

It could have been argued that it was in Western Europe's interest to see Bosnia carved up between Catholic Croats and Orthodox Serbs. What Western government wanted a unified Muslim-dominated Bosnia, led by a 'mad mullah', right in the centre of Europe? There was already disquiet at the march of Islam in the Asian successor states of the Soviet Union, as well as the growing influence of Turkey. Bosnia threatened to be the first fully fledged Islamic state in Europe. True, Albania was a country with a Muslim majority, but the trend there was towards a secular nationalism. In Bosnia, Muslims did not usually distinguish themselves by any factor other than their religion.

Many Bosnian Muslims sympathised with Saddam Hussein in the Gulf War. Arab states provided money and weapons for the Bosnian army. Although the Bosnian president, Alija Izetbegovic, was a deeply religious man, Bosnian Muslims did not form a mullah-ridden society. The scenario of a militant Muslim state in Europe was not a likely one. But the Austrian, Italian and especially German outcry over the Serb treatment of Slovenia and Croatia took a long time to be extended to Bosnia, and only when the death toll reached fantastic proportions. Scores died in Slovenia; hundreds of thousands died or were injured in Bosnia. Why? The sheer complexity of Balkan politics? Western compassion fatigue? Or innate racism in a Europe increasingly fearful of being 'swamped' by immigrants, especially from Muslim states?

The crisis in the Balkans would continue to fester. In 1914 violence in Sarajevo led to the First World War. The massacres in modern Sarajevo were not likely to cause a pan-European conflict. But if the killings had continued the continent's major political problem – minorities threatening violent revision of state boundaries – could have dashed all hopes of European peace, let alone unity. After all, Bosnia's Muslims were also Europeans.

*

In Europe you don't expect to find people foraging for grass to eat. That's what it looked like in Sarajevo, although I was told the locals were hunting for 'wild lettuce'. Passers-by in smart-looking clothes ignored the scavengers. I sat drinking a cappuccino in an open-air café while snipers were blazing away a few hundred yards from the relaxed coffee set. It was September 1994. I needed to remind myself why one of the most cosmopolitan cities in southern Europe was tearing itself apart.

I had travelled from Zagreb. Apart from the barely visible presence of tens of thousands of refugees, the Croatian capital appeared untouched by war. The cleaned-up Austro-Hungarian buildings and the green-domed churches were at their best in the late-summer sunshine. The good company of a friend, Slavka, added to the holiday mood. She had spent most of her twenty-eight years in Australia but spoke fluent Serbo-Croat. As journalists, we both had UN accreditation and could have flown, with our flak jackets and tin helmets, in a UN plane to Sarajevo . . . war permitting. Instead, we decided to go overland by bus. Before the war, the trip might have taken six or seven hours.

After twenty-seven hours of roadblocks in a bus crammed with Bosnian peasants, refugees and food parcels, my holiday mood had dissipated. The shelled ruins of Mostar had depressed me. The sticky heat and pungent body odour were a minor problem compared with my concern at driving at night, without lights, in a large bus along hairpin bends on the tracks of Mount Igman, the only road access to the far outskirts of the Bosnian capital. The Serbs had largely stopped their shelling, but had tightened the siege by blocking all roads to the Bosnian government-held parts of the city.

Six miles short of Sarajevo, the bus was hit by cannon shells from a Serbian anti-aircraft position firing in a suppressed trajectory. The bus was overcrowded with mainly women and children. The first burst went through the windscreen. The bus stopped, a sitting target for the directional tracer bullets which kept up an intermittent fusillade for fifteen minutes in a flow of molten white hyphens against the night sky. In the confined space, the smell of shit, cordite, fear and sweat was overwhelming. There was little screaming or panic.

I tried to impress upon Slavka, who had her leg jammed under a seat, the need to translate loudly: 'Get the bloody door open.'

I had been prepared enough to sit by the central door, with a quick 'grab bag' containing my basics, passport and bribes.

Eventually the door opened. I pulled Slavka out across the live, prone bodies jamming the aisle. After crawling on all fours through some undergrowth, we hid for a while as the anti-aircraft gun kept pounding away. Then came the crack of small arms and some shouting and what appeared to be torches. It looked as though Serb patrols were moving in for the kill.

I took off my light-coloured shirt; although bare-chested, I certainly didn't feel like Rambo. Bunny-hopping under fire, bizarrely leading Slavka, an old woman, and a young Bosnian woman in a game of follow-my-leader, we found an old trench. The granny prayed, the Bosnian girl was in deep shock and I was trying to remember the Serbo-Croat word for minefield. I told the young woman to take off her white top and dirty her white slacks with mud, because she was sticking out like a beacon.

It took an hour to sneak to the bottom of the mountain into a Muslim area. I traded some whisky for a Bosnian army unit's agreement to allow us to join their forceful attempt to get into the city. That failed, and we were left with the only other route, a tunnel under the main minefield. Only one Western journalist had managed to get through the tunnel and I was keen to try, even though it was just three feet high and airless.

It took twelve hours to queue and get permission; the locals were not keen on journalists using their precious tunnel. We were all crowded into a small courtyard. In it were some seriously deranged people, many straight out of central casting for Fagin's den in *Oliver Twist*; actually, some looked ready to star in *The Canterbury Tales*. An old crone asked for a sip from my water bottle: she drank some and then ran off with the rest, cackling loudly. Children were trampled and injured, but this went ignored.

A well-dressed woman said to me: 'We are behaving like animals; look what the war has done to us.'

By this stage the Bosnian girl, Vedrana, was in extreme shock and turning blue. I gave her some chocolate and Slavka and I tried to comfort her. The tunnel would be almost impossible for Vedrana, even if Slavka and I tried to carry her.

It was time to use 'connections', the Bosnian way of doing business. A passing French armoured vehicle refused to take a local, no matter what state she was in, even though I climbed on top of it and implied that President Mitterrand was my close relative. I tried to get them to radio Brigadier Vere Hayes, the British commander in the area. He had been at Sandhurst with me. The French were at their obstinate best, however.

I finally persuaded a chivalrous British warrant officer to break all the rules (and risk his career) by taking the three of us on board his UN vehicle and negotiate the French roadblocks, arguably more touchy than their Serb counterparts.

Slavka and I stayed at the ravaged Holiday Inn and joined the other hacks feeling their way around the pitch-black corridors. There was intermittent cold water and even occasional electricity. Vedrana's father, a local bigwig, insisted that we stay at his house on the snipers' front line. He wanted to thank us for getting his daughter into town. He insisted on giving me long candlelit lectures on the division of the Roman empire into East and West accompanied by endless maps. We never got beyond twelfth-century Bosnian history. I found his broken German, and the distinctly twentieth-century rattle of constant small-arms fire in the street outside, rather distracting.

Many in the Balkans, especially Bosnia, seemed addicted to cartography. Journalist Ed Vulliamy, in his book *Seasons in Hell*, observed: 'The answer to a question to a Serb about a Serbian artillery attack yesterday will begin in the year 925 and is invariably illustrated with maps.'

Their memories were indeed long, like those of the Irish. I listened to a variety of Bosnian raves about a Serb crime in the dark medieval past. And I would have to say something along the lines of: 'But that was in the fourteenth century.'

'Yes,' the Muslim soldier would say, 'but I heard about it only last week.'

I needed a bath and a drink. Water was scarce, but the Sarajevo brewery was intact. Vedrana was a Slovenian; her boyfriend Tomo a Serb, and their friends Muslims. After the rudeness of our initial welcome, I was treated to the most magnificent hospitality available in the old Muslim quarter of town. Because of the 10 p.m. curfew, the drinking started very early and very earnestly. I could see why the Balkan tragedy was dubbed the 'slivovitz war'.

Over a few drinks I asked Tomo what would happen if he – a Serb – was caught while fighting for the Sarajevo government. 'They would treat me as a traitor,' he replied. 'I would be tortured and then torn apart.'

Most of our conversations were punctuated by sniper fire, sometimes as close as from 300 yards away. Previous artillery shelling had deliberately targeted the city's famous historic buildings. Every Sarajevan I met wanted to know why the world had betrayed them.

'All your Western armies defended the dictatorship in Kuwait. You could have just driven in and saved our democracy,' said one Muslim officer.

'Ah, but we have no oil,' said his friend. 'All the EC talks about is cantonisation. That's just a classy name for carving us up,' he added. 'Look at how we all get on – we're Serbs, Croats and Muslims drinking here together. It's the peasants in the countryside and outside propaganda that are destroying our city.'

Everyone I had ever encountered in the Balkans accused the other sides' leaders of being bedwetting psychopaths. Long ago I had come to the conclusion that Serbs and Croats were right about their politicians. The Muslims, the cement of Bosnia, were caught in the middle, and the shortest-lived state in modern Europe had been almost destroyed. Like rape victims, the Bosnian Muslims were obviously asking for trouble. Maybe it was because the Balkan names were too difficult for Western foreign ministries. To adapt P. J. O'Rourke, the unspellables were shooting the unpronounceables and committing unspeakable atrocities. UNPROFOR, the UN Protection Force, 'monitored' some of the wholesale rapes and massacres, but their mandate allowed them precious little room to do anything about them.

'This hell of a crazy war,' said Tomo in broken English. 'I commute front line in a tram. I think I have a nervous fall-down.'

His Muslim friends were even crazier: they wanted to fight their only (unreliable) allies, the Croats, while the Serbs were strangling the city. This was *Ruritania* with lunacy and guns.

Like Romania, some of the besieged citizens asked me how to get out of their urban Hades, but most were surprisingly resigned to the day-to-day hazards.

'How do you cope with the drama?' I asked one resident.

'Drama gets lost when you live it.'

I talked to the assistant editor of the main newspaper, *Oslobodjenje*, who had somehow kept his paper alive throughout the two years of constant shelling. The children, he told me, had lost an average of over one and a half stones in weight. One youngster explained how he had tried to prise open a fifteen-day-old loaf of bread with a hammer. Aid, a substitute for effective Western intervention, was now being flown regularly into the city. Water supplies and electricity started working a little better. Even the Pope was coming. When he didn't, the largely Muslim city felt let down once more by the world. Cynics said food aid just fattened them up to make easier targets for the snipers. It was a tough war for hacks, too. Nearly forty had been killed by the end of 1994.

Almost innocently, I said to Slavka: 'I don't know whether you've noticed, but it's bloody dangerous around here.'

She laughed. Slavka was more concerned with the lack of shower facilities than the presence of gunfire. It was time to leave, however. I had run out of whisky and cigarettes. Avid foreign members of the anti-tobacco lobby became 'Sarajevo smokers' because of the strain, and cigarettes were an almost compulsory ice-breaker at roadblocks. It's hard for a man to kill you when you are doing your best to give him a Marlboro. I had salvaged my luggage from the shot-up bus. It contained some food and two small bags of coffee, traditional presents to a good host. We gave them to Vedrana's family.

I did not intend to return by bus. Instead Slavka and I flew out on an RAF Hercules, the UN route dubbed 'Maybe Airlines'. Maybe it flew, maybe it didn't. Forced to wear tin hats and flak jackets, we had to run to the waiting plane with its engines revving. The plane, however, took us not to Split, where we had intended to go, but to Ancona in Italy. We were in no position to argue with a crew flying mercy missions.

After a pizza and wonderful wine we took a ferry across the Adriatic. The ferry broke down, which inspired an unplanned exploration of Dugi Otok island. It was charming, except that we had run out of cash, Deutschmarks, and our credit cards were not accepted. We had to scrimp like ageing hippies for a few days until the next ferry came.

On the mainland, at Zadar, our credit cards were accepted at a hotel full of refugees. Zadar, once the ancient capital of Dalmatia, boasted a long – and torrid – imperial history dating back to the time when the Romans enforced their strict town-planning rules: a rigid grid of streets around the forum. The city changed hands thirty times between the eighth and sixteenth centuries, and was bombed on seventy-two occasions during the Second World War.

We fled the refugees for the fleshpots of the Croatian capital. I tarried for a week or so in Zagreb, partly because of its architecture and partly because Slavka's fluency in the language helped me get to grips with the Croat mentality. I tried to find out why they were so constantly bloody-minded.

Slavka, herself a Croat, said: 'They will lie to your face, even when *they* know *you* know they are lying. They enjoy being perverse.'

Yet *she* is the most honest person I know, and a fine journalist.

I decamped to Vienna by train and then flew to London. The most difficult part of my journey back from Sarajevo was yet to come: my luggage was (temporarily) lost by British Airways, and strike-bound British Rail marooned me, at midnight, fifty miles from the advertised destination. But at least the BR official to whom I complained didn't bother lying to me.

And the wars went on. . .

Slobodan Milosevic died and went straight to Heaven. But St Peter was wise and insisted that the Butcher of the Balkans be sent down to Hell. A few hours later, thousands of demons started queuing up outside the pearly gates. St Peter asked what they were doing.

'We're the first wave of refugees,' they said.

Milosevic's drive for Greater Serbia was a root cause of the turmoil in the Balkans, but for too long Western leaders saw him as the solution, not the problem. Journalists, however, tended to blame the Serbs, justifiably, for most of the warmongering and atrocities. The more literate hacks referred to Serbia as the Land of Mordor. This of course served only to reinforce the deeply ingrained sense of Serb victimhood. 'Ancient tribal rivalries' became the handy, if incorrect, media shorthand for the opposing factions. In fact, most of the antagonism was recent and artificial, stoked up by firebrand politicians and the indigenous media in the new republics.

Europe could have prevented the Bosnian war; NATO could have ended it much sooner once it had started. For 970 days the alliance kept its fighters in the air over former Yugoslavia, but it was only on 10 April 1994 that NATO fired its first shots in anger against the Bosnian Serbs. After the first round of alliance strikes and the resolute Serb response, the UN and NATO, their reputations severely tarnished by the failed cosmetic device of 'safe havens' – over 7,000 Muslims were massacred by Serbs in Srebrenica – backed down in Bosnia. NATO suspended air operations in September 1995. Russian pressure on Belgrade, Slobodan Milosevic's desire to end sanctions on Serbia and the sweeping advances of Croat and Bosnian government forces in Bosnia in the summer of 1995 all brought the war to a stalemated conclusion. Within a few months the Bosnian peace agreement was signed at Dayton and Milosevic was hailed as a peacemaker. This was Munich revisited, and a prelude to more wars.

The Serbs had pretty much held on to their original territories in Bosnia, although they had been driven out of Croatia. Dayton had effectively cantonised Bosnia, even though this was the opposite of what NATO had intended. I wanted to see what was happening on the Serb side; maybe I had gained the wrong impression by being at the wrong end of their guns.

It was early February 1998 when I found myself in a spartan single room at RAF Brize Norton. A squawking tannoy in the room woke me up at 4.30 a.m. Many hours later an RAF Tristar, full of squaddies, landed at Split airport.

No customs formalities intruded. At the temporary British base nearby, however, we were forced to undergo a lengthy briefing on VD. A sergeant said that sixty-five men out of a unit of 410 had caught the clap. This was a staggering figure bearing in mind that troops were issued with numerous condoms, many of the local communities were very conservative, especially the Muslims, and, except for patrols and other duties, troops were not allowed out of barracks – and even inside they were not supposed to consume more than two cans of beer a day. Clearly, British troops must have been very resourceful – and stupid – when it came to sexual adventures. We were also warned about the crazy Balkan driving and the numerous land-mines.

Buses, I decided, were definitely out. I hitched a ride in a Lynx helicopter to Banja Luka, a city in the Bosnian Serb heartland. Flying in the semi-darkness, helped by night-flying goggles, I took in the rugged mountains, some sprinkled with snow. A machine-gun straddled the door, and the pilot explained how he could lock on to missiles. We landed on a helipad in a disused metal factory on the outskirts of the city.

Accommodation was in a warehouse, in an edifice comprised of shipping containers, each packed one on top of another like a vast Lego kit. I donned military camo, although I noticed that my companion, a fellow civilian instructor at the Joint Services Command and Staff College, had put on slippers, a dressing gown and pyjamas. He looked (and talked) like Noël Coward.

I went to the officers' mess and rapidly consumed the allotted two cans of beer. I was invited by the towering Major-General Andrew Pringle to join him for a dinner with a small number of guests. As we sat down, I had to sneeze and reached urgently into my camo jacket to find a tissue or handkerchief. Instead I pulled out a pair of heavily scented scarlet lace knickers which a girlfriend had playfully secreted in my kit. The general harrumphed slightly and moved his briefly startled stare from one to the other of his two guests, both relatively senior MoD civil servants, but refrained from comment. Perhaps using the lingerie as his cue, he urbanely dissected the misdemeanours of journalists he had met, although he praised Martin Bell's reporting in the Balkans. I refrained from arguing, and drinking, any more because the general had given me permission to accompany a night patrol of the city with the military police.

The MPs were relaxed, wearing only side-arms. This allowed time and opportunity to stop at one or two coffee bars to chat with the local Serbs (assisted by a young Serb woman translator working with the police). I was told that the unemployment rate was 85 per cent, so I wondered – as I had in Lebanon – how people could drink, drive cars, and wear (relatively) trendy clothes.

The translator summarised our discussion over coffee with some youths: 'It's the black market,' she said. 'People manage somehow.'

'Are the young people optimistic?'

'No, they all want to emigrate – like me – to the USA.'

We stopped outside a shop, and she pointed out a pair of shoes in a sale. 'Those shoes', she said, 'would cost the average monthly wage.'

The next day a friendly US Marine took me to Prijedor, in the far north-west of the zone run by British forces. The small town had been the site of extreme ethnic cleansing; now only mines populated the houses. The Marine was glad to be in the British zone, as he could relax without body armour and a phalanx of heavily armed companions. The USA could never do the British sort of hearts-and-minds stuff because they arrived in villages looking like an invasion of *Star Wars* troopers. Not risking casualties was paramount; the body-bag syndrome dominated everything. The British took more risks and engaged much more with the locals.

*

I rejoined British forces at Gornji Vakuf, way to the south. This town had witnessed heavy fighting between Croats and Muslims. The Brits had the job of persuading refugees to return to their houses, but this would have created a monstrous housing chain throughout the country. If you moved people back, then the squatting family had to move, and so on. The official policy was to re-create the Rubik's Cube, but that would only have exacerbated the original tensions. Maybe ethnic apartheid was the only workable solution.

Joining a patrol by Sabre light tanks, I could see that the Brits were keeping the lid on things, and in a later foot patrol to an isolated Muslim village it was clear that in this village at least the British elements of SFOR (the Stabilisation Force) had won the gratitude of the locals. If SFOR left, however, few doubted that the inhabitants of the various Balkan statelets would regress to shaking each other warmly by the throat.

In Split, I had to wait for a ride in an RAF Hercules. RAF passenger flights are notoriously late, but journalists can't complain because they are often free and frequently the only flights available in war zones. Instead of staying in a barracks, I opted for a hotel on the island of Trogir, which is connected to the mainland by a handy bridge. The Venetians ran the place for nearly 400 years and it showed: the splendid medieval architecture enticed me into a web of narrow streets. You can explore the whole island in a day, although a more discerning visitor than a jaded hack could spend a whole day in St Lawrence's cathedral.

Kosovo

In the Yugoslav war-games played in Western military colleges during the 1970s and 1980s, Kosovo was nearly always the first country to blow up; I was surprised that the province, which contained roughly 90 per cent ethnic Albanians and just 10 per cent Serbs, remained relatively aloof when Yugoslavia actually fell apart. The crunch came in the summer of 1999. Finally, Serb atrocities in the province forced NATO to bomb Milosevic into submission. The professed goal of NATO's nineteen democratic nations was to stop the eviction of the Albanian Kosovars. This failed. Approximately half of them – over 800,000 – were forced out or fled. Many thousands became internal refugees.

The Kosovo war had other aims, notably stabilising the Balkans and, by default, the preservation of NATO's credibility. Gradually, the alliance's war aims expanded. Unlike the case of Saddam Hussein in the 1991 Gulf War, some Western politicians said that the Serb regime had to be toppled. Also, unlike the Gulf, there was no exit strategy in Kosovo. The war against Saddam had been about oil, but the Kosovo war was partly fuelled by genuine humanitarian impulses. One British newspaper columnist even described Prime Minister Tony Blair as 'the high priest of the secular religion of human rights'. Britain was certainly the most hawkish NATO member; the government hinted that it might have been willing to commit 50,000 troops if a ground invasion had been required, although where they would have found that many was a different question.

The allies thought that a short, sharp air war would topple the Belgrade strongman – maybe even in seventy-two hours. 'Air power', as Eliot Cohen noted in the *Foreign Affairs* journal, 'is an unusually seductive form of military strength because, like modern courtship, it appears to offer gratification without commitment.' In Kosovo it was to be *Blitzkrieg* Lite. It took NATO twelve days to launch the same number of combat operations that it had ordered in the first twelve *hours* of the 1991 Gulf War. The alliance dithered because it became clear that combat troops on the ground – American casualties – would be required; or at least the credible threat of sending in the infantry was needed. President Bill Clinton's luck held – again. Moscow leaned heavily on Belgrade; Milosevic realised he was largely on his own, except for a little bit of technical help from China and Baghdad.

The Serbs capitulated without a single combat fatality on the allied side. American troops had been prepared to kill, but not to be killed. But, to be fair, most of European public opinion was pretty wobbly about casualties as well; Milosevic had gambled on this to stay in power. The Serbs cleverly used propaganda to trumpet the dichotomy between the failure of NATO's humanitarian mission on the ground and the extra casualties caused by the air bombardment. The Serbs penetrated the psychology of NATO's decision-making cycle with the aim of confusing and paralysing it. NATO – just – managed to maintain its cohesion.

Milosevic survived long enough to finesse a deal: an international force was sent into Kosovo to maintain a protectorate, which was autonomous but not independent. In fact, international peacekeeping troops – including Russians – were dumped with the task of curbing the unruly Kosovo Liberation Army and its bandit allies in Albania proper. When Milosevic's regime started to totter, the allies also had to cough up billions of dollars to pay for the repair of the bomb damage in Serbia. Perhaps a smaller bribe before the war might have worked better.

NATO's aims were to get the Serbs out, NATO forces in, and all the Kosovars back. Most of the ethnic Albanian refugees did go home. Without NATO's war, their camps might have assumed the festering resentment of Gaza. With the Balkans in turmoil, Greece and Turkey might have come dangerously close to outright war. A long war may well have destroyed NATO, and even the European Union.

I wanted to be there if only to see German armoured vehicles rolling into the Balkans again. With my usual immaculate timing, I missed the first wave of Operation Joint Guardian, as the influx of peacekeepers was called. The RAF plane touched down at an airport recently and audaciously seized by Russian troops. In a flashback to Afghanistan, the Mi-24 gunships gave me the jitters.

I chatted to the Russians in their primitive armoured troop carriers, now parked at the side of the airport. Their kit was poor and they had to scrounge food. Their dash to grab Pristina airport was perhaps the last campaign of the Cold War. The British general, Mike Jackson, had been ordered to send in his troops by helicopter to confront the Russians, but Jackson refused to obey his NATO commander, US General Wesley Clark.

'I'm not going to start World War Three for you,' the Brit famously declared.

When the matter was referred to London and Washington, Jackson – sensibly – got his way.

Yet, despite the very recent slaughter, the capital city, Pristina, seemed full of life. Except for the few destroyed military targets, it was difficult to differentiate between war damage and the standard run-down and half-finished buildings. Little red tractors hogged the country roads as they tried to save the harvest. Pristina's streets were crammed with cars that bore German and Swiss nationality stickers but rarely any number plates. Many were allegedly stolen. Traffic lights worked occasionally, and no traffic policemen were to be seen.

'Dog-fight driving – that's the only way to survive,' my British military driver told me.

Restaurants bustled with life. Some draped British flags or were renamed 'Kfor Café' in honour of their liberators. Very pretty girls paraded up the main street in micro-skirts. Not even Cat Stevens, aka Yusuf Islam, who was visiting as a born-again Muslim missionary, could have persuaded them to dump their provocative garb. Muslim men drank alcohol freely; except for the dwindling Serb minority, Kosovo's population was only nominally Islamic.

I mentioned the astoundingly beautiful Muslim women to a sergeant whose patrol I had joined, adding that on TV many of the females had looked like toothless crones.

'Aye, that suits me fine,' he replied, 'otherwise my missus back home will get really upset.'

Fraternisation with the locals was strongly discouraged, however. Whereas, in a disused bottle-top factory, I was sharing a tent, *inter alia*, with a very attractive female army captain. This was my kind of war.

The British controlled a large swathe of territory around Pristina, although Kosovo itself is only the size of Hampshire. British law was enforced, but it made no impact on the dodgem-style driving. As in Ulster – in the beginning – army patrols were greeted by friendly children. The kids all spoke some basic English, despite the lack of schooling, due to the boycott of enforced Serbian education. 'They watch a lot of American satellite TV; that's how they learn so quickly,' a local teacher told me.

The reputation of NATO, however, depended not on Albanian gratitude and the initial joy at liberation, but on the survival of the remaining 35,000–40,000 Serbs. I visited a British field hospital in Pristina where doctors were treating Serbs who had been victims of reverse ethnic cleansing.

I also accompanied night shifts with the Royal Irish Regiment, which despatched troops on 'reassurance patrols'. They said they understood discrimination because of their front-line duties in Ulster, and boasted of their house-to-house search experience 'back home'. One tough sergeant, a Catholic, was very forceful with a family of Kosovo Albanians who had illegally occupied a Serb-owned flat.

'We are the law here,' he shouted, sounding like Judge Dredd. His patrol had surrounded the ground-floor flat. 'C'mon out,' the sergeant shouted, 'or I'll kick the door down.' *Sotto voce* to me, he said again that he was used to this in Northern Ireland.

'They must have different doors in Belfast,' I said equally *sotto voce*. 'That one is reinforced steel.'

Without a comment, or hesitation, the sergeant sent his squad around the back to enter via the windows.

Serbs saw the 'men in black' as the main threat. The Kosovo Liberation Army had been forbidden to wear uniform or, except in special cases, to bear arms. But they wore black civilian clothes to display their allegiance. One Serb woman I met had been permanently evicted from her home with just the summer dress she was wearing. Another young teenager told me how she had been threatened with gang rape unless she left for Serbia.

A highly intelligent young Serb student explained that she could not even go to the market for food, because her accent would betray her. 'I can't stay here and I can't go to Serbia,' she said, 'because I can't get an education there. I'm in the middle of nowhere.'

The Irish regiment had set up an elaborate system to identify where isolated Serb families lived, and arranged for Serb interpreters to call them regularly as well as providing a telephone hotline. British soldiers frequently hid in tenements to catch the Albanian thugs, but the troops could not guard every Serb family. The regiment distributed food parcels, especially to elderly Serbs who were imprisoned by fear in their own homes. One corporal used much of his precious free time playing chess with a frightened Serb pensioner.

All I met put themselves into the category of good Serbs; maybe it was like Germany in the summer of 1945, when no one admitted to being a Nazi. In Cikatovo I walked along a steep ditch where dozens of murdered Albanians had been hastily buried. A child's shoe here, feet protruding there, abandoned spectacles . . . The thick, gagging smell of death permeated the tents where Belgian forensic experts were methodically examining the exhumed Albanian victims of Serb atrocities. Linda, my translator, came from the area and she knew some of the victims. She appeared matter-of-fact about it all. Indeed, Linda was more an interrupter than an interpreter that day; she wanted to talk about other things, in particular that I should not delay her shopping expedition in Pristina. Maybe this was her way of coping with tragedy.

In a decade of Balkan-bashing I hardly met any native who did not display a very relaxed attitude to sanity. As a bonus, every local I met in Kosovo seemed to have a character, and name, which complemented Tolkien rather than Tolstoy. I slipped into fantasy mode myself. My regulation army camo had been so frequently modified that a major asked me whether I was going fishing or fighting.

Wearing a British uniform of sorts was useful in getting around the country. It also allowed me to join in military functions, especially a 'liberation ball' in the main municipal buildings which the Brits had occupied in Pristina. I was treated to the unusual sight of German officers dressed as French maids, wearing not leather but costumes made of bin-liners. Rommel would have turned in his grave.

'This is just like JFK,' said one German captain.

I looked quizzical.

'Ich bin ein Bin-liner.'

I danced with my pretty tent-mate and took in the surreal atmosphere. It was, however, hardly a romantic return to our dwelling. Two (male) sergeants snored between our camp-beds (which had been made in China for much smaller people and so were prone to collapsing).

The army food was excellent, the loos were overstretched, and the cold-water showers even more so. All were shared with the females, except the showers. As to be expected, the female officers behaved with entirely appropriate dignity, and even refrained from laughing when, inside the large tent, I insisted on dressing inside a large towel. A few of the young ladies serving in the ranks, however, were not so much interested in finding Mr Right, but Mr Right Now, at every opportunity. These louche cannons caused friction with some of the married male soldiers, especially as communications with the UK were poor. Borrowed mobile phones were not so much used in war-fighting roles, but rather in battling with the missus at home.

Morale was high, however, despite having waited for months in Macedonia to get on with the job. The British experiences in Ulster – Europe's longest terrorist war – helped to make it the most effective force in Kosovo. The army's honeymoon period with the Albanians, I thought at the time, was going to be as short-lived as it was with the Catholics in Northern Ireland, especially as the Brits tended to be tougher with the KLA than other NATO forces.

It was a short war but it would be a long peacekeeping operation, not least because of the deep political divisions among the Kosovars. The amorphous KLA had a semi-fascist wing and another which was steeped in old-style Marxism, while the leading moderate, Ibrahim Rugova, a long-time advocate of passive resistance, had been sidelined by the military men in the armed resistance.

On the positive side, NATO had, almost by accident, refashioned an alliance which had lost its rationale. Above all, the Kosovo war had shown that Europe had to unite to define its response to a pressing European – or world – threat. True, American resources had to be committed as well. But gone were the days of NATO's European members affording themselves the luxury of squabbling and then waiting for Washington to bang heads together. America would have other concerns. In future the USA might respond only to a united European appeal; it would not take the weight of European differences on its shoulder to wage a war that was much more Europe's concern than America's. From the time of Philip of Macedon to that of Bismarck and Hitler a quick-fix solution to the Balkans had never been on offer.

Western troops had to stay for more than a decade in Kosovo. It declared independence, challenged by some states, in 2008. Elsewhere in the former Yugoslavia Slovenia joined the EU, and Montenegro gained its independence peacefully. Ethnic tensions continued in Bosnia, but few predicted a return to civil war, though it was estimated that it would take at least seventy-five years to clear all the minefields. The savagery that ravaged the Balkans in the 1990s had not, so far, been revisited; soon the NATO powers were to be busy fighting major wars elsewhere.

SUDAN

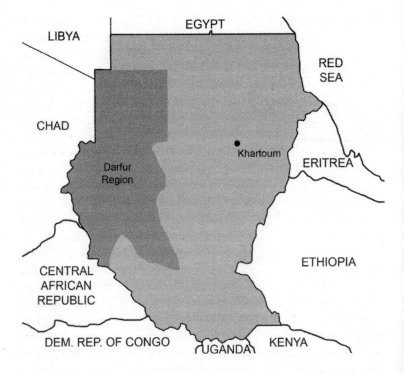

Sudan

13. SUDAN – LOOKING FOR OSAMA BIN LADEN

Bin Laden wasn't so infamous in the mid-1990s when I set out to follow his trail. I wasn't too keen to find him in Afghanistan, but he was hanging out in Sudan. With the exception of 1885, when Islamic warriors speared and decapitated the British governor, General Charles 'Chinese' Gordon – played in the film *Khartoum* by Charlton Heston, of course – Sudan had been a media backwater. Despite being the largest country in Africa and the most tribally complex, as well as enduring the continent's longest civil war, Sudan's travails were largely unreported. The 1983 alcohol ban, reimposed after the 1989 Islamist revolution, was unlikely to entice foreign correspondents. Nor did Sudan encourage even the most ardently teetotal hack. No film crew had covered the war there for a few years, at least from the northern side. Reporting from the south entailed long walks in malarial swamps. Besides, the man I wanted was in the government-controlled northern part of Sudan.

In 1996 Sudan suddenly became newsworthy; I could sell a TV documentary or two in advance to fund my latest adventure. The country had been accused of harbouring and training Islamist terrorists. The Egyptian government claimed that 15,000 Muslim militants – including members of Hamas and Hezbollah – were undergoing training in thirty camps in northern Sudan. The Sudanese armed forces were overstretched, so who was providing the expertise? The CIA said that Osama bin Laden, the multi-millionaire Saudi warlord, was a possible mastermind behind an international terror network based in Khartoum.

From the US perspective, the real problem with Islamist Sudan was the threat it posed to Egypt and Saudi Arabia, pillars of Western influence in the Middle East. The US government accused Sudan in general and bin Laden in person of complicity not only in the 1993 bombing of the World Trade Center (later proved to be untrue) but also the 1995 assassination attempt on the Egyptian president. The Khartoum government denied these claims, and insisted that the USA was waging a terror war on its territory. Washington, it said, had underwritten neighbouring Uganda, Ethiopia and Eritrea's support for guerrillas who were fighting Khartoum.

The war in the non-Muslim south had raged on and off since 1955, its origins a complex mix of tribal and religious animosities, as well as chronic neglect and secessionism. Khartoum was anxious to end the southern war, not least to secure access to the large oil reserves there. An insurgency in the north-east had also just broken out. The Beja guerrillas operating there included the Hadendawa clans who 'broke the British square', once the British infantry's standard defensive tactic, and who were immortalised by Rudyard Kipling as the 'Fuzzy Wuzzies'. Sudan was obviously a rather interesting country for an occasional war correspondent.

The West was also using other sticks to beat Khartoum, especially the allegations that it practised slavery and forcibly converted Christians to Islam. The government view was that Western critics were exaggerating human rights abuses to isolate the Islamic revolutionaries. Washington did regard it as a rogue state, and had inflicted a number of economic sanctions. Sudan had retreated into its shell and kept out external busybodies, especially hacks. I spent months trying to get in. I chatted up Sudanese military men who occasionally came to London. I suggested that I was practically a holy warrior after my experiences in Afghanistan and elsewhere. I talked to exiled opponents and Christian lobby groups, who implied that Sudan was not so much a country as a near-death experience.

I also needed a cameraman crazy enough to come with me. The usual suspects were tied up. Irwin Armstrong, a veteran of Northern Ireland, wanted a sunny break from his own province. Visas were eventually obtained in London, and a nearly empty Sudanese Airways aircraft soon deposited us in Khartoum. The Hilton Hotel and its bar were also empty. Luckily, I was fond of Coca-Cola.

Khartoum was very run down and dusty, although touches of imperial grandeur clung to the former governor's palace overlooking the Nile, where, after I had arranged our press permits, we went to see Dr Abubaker al-Shingieti, the director of political affairs at the Presidency. Climbing up the very steps where General Gordon had probably taken his last breath (at least in the film), I wondered how our two-man team would fare, especially in the southern war zones . . . if we got that far.

The director of political affairs said, in a pronounced American drawl: 'You are free to film in Sudan.' Back at the hotel, we had an hour to wait for our guide – minder – so we took Dr al-Shingieti at his word. Hiring a taxi, we went to film in the nearby bazaar, just to get a little local colour in the can. We filmed very camera-shy traders, males only and with their permission. Within one minute a low-ranking policeman had stopped us to investigate our brand-new permits. Grudgingly he let us proceed but followed us.

Within two minutes a higher-ranking policeman repeated the exercise and let us continue, provided we did not film any females. A crowd had gathered around us.

Within five minutes a very angry official in a safari suit accompanied by some heavies accosted us. We were shoved into two large BMWs and the safari suit declared we were under arrest. I heard a rather English voice adopt an imperial tone. 'Under whose authority are you arresting us?' It took a few seconds to realise it was mine.

The safari suit eventually deigned to reply: 'Under *my* authority.'

'And who might you be?' said the echo of the Raj.

'I am the Minister of Justice.'

Fair cop, I thought. Arrested within four hours of arrival on my first day in the country, and by the Minister of Justice himself. This might be a record I could wave in front of envious hacks.

The minister was spitting venom.

'I saw a German film last night which defamed our country,' he said in excellent English. A perfect product of this former British colony, I thought, and almost asked whether we had been to the same college. He continued his tirade: 'I am absolutely sure you were filming southern people and you'll say they are slaves.'

I was pissed off now. Arresting us was one thing, but telling us what we were trying to film when I didn't have the slightest idea what I was doing was definitely insulting. But I was sufficiently diplomatic to avoid mentioning bin Laden.

'We've been in your country for only a few hours – our first visit, by the way. I wouldn't know whether they were from north, east, south, or west – or from Mars for that matter.'

The Minister of Justice ignored me. Then I threw in what I thought was my ace card. I mentioned that we had just been to the presidential palace to see Dr Abubaker al-Shingieti. Our arresting officer blew his top. I had managed to mention the one person in the government whom the Minister of Justice truly loathed. Bad call. Silence then fell.

In continuing silence we were taken to police headquarters; that definitely was not on my film schedule. They wanted to seize the film. On principle I refused, but did say they could view the two or three minutes of very jerky shots of male traders that we had managed to take; the sequence was mainly of a man operating a foot-powered sewing machine, hardly top secret. That meant their hunting for a video machine capable of viewing our type of tape. That would take hours or days. Eventually we were rescued – not without some courtesy.

We had been let into the country only, I presumed, to show how democratic the Islamic revolutionary government was. Dr Abubaker al-Shingieti tried to resume his PR offensive by taking us to dinner. In very reasonable, even philosophical, terms he outlined his dislike of the Saudi monarchy, and particularly the hostility to US troops on holy soil. It was an affront to all Muslims everywhere, he said. He also explained how Sudan was misrepresented in the West.

I grabbed my chance: 'The trouble in the West is that you have been harbouring Osama bin Laden and allowing him to train Islamic fighters.'

Dr al-Shingieti was aghast at my statement. 'Mr bin Laden has just left our country. And there are no training camps.'

I eventually ascertained that the bird had indeed flown, but I was still keen to visit some of his camps. I thought I knew that a number were positioned around the capital, although they had large local militia training camps placed near them, presumably as an explanation for satellite surveillance pictures that the CIA were touting around. So I wasn't going to get an interview with bin Laden. I had missed my first chance when I was working almost next door to his *muj* in Afghanistan. Second chance, in Sudan, lost by a few days. To make up for this, I wanted to film his training camps, apparently for Jihadists. I also wanted to travel to Juba, the long-besieged capital of the south, where no one had filmed for at least two years.

This would require time and permits and schmoozing of the generals and the spiritual leader of the revolution, Hassan al-Turabi. Sudan was run by a military regime, but real influence was also wielded by civilian Islamist intellectuals such as al-Turabi. The two sides were in conflict, however. Also a division festered between those who wanted to appease the West and the hardline Islamist isolationists. Meanwhile, my friend the justice minister had bent a few ministerial ears and I gathered we were about to be kicked out. A general I had befriended promised he would take us out of the capital to the war zone in the south, to keep us out of trouble. We trooped off to the military airfield, but the general was countermanded and we had to slink back to the capital to await our fate.

The best course of action was to speak to the boss: Turabi. He seemed highly unavailable, so – against strict Islamic norms – I contrived to interview Mrs Wasil Turabi, who was active as head of various women's organisations. I had also promised a colleague in London that I would try to help him with his documentary on female circumcision, a subject apparently dear to Mrs Turabi's heart. We chatted on the flat roof of her house, surrounded by guards with AKs. Under the circumstances, I refrained from asking about her direct personal experiences of the subject, and we got on rather well.

I asked her whether she influenced her husband's thinking.

'Yes, I talk to him about politics.'

'Does he listen?'

'Yes, sometimes.'

'Would he listen if you asked him to give me an interview?'

She smiled sweetly. 'I will try.'

It was unsubtle but it might work, I hoped.

Subsequently, Mrs Turabi invited me to dinner. I had assumed the great man would be present for dinner in his own house, but I was to be disappointed. Wasil Turabi treated Irwin and myself with great kindness and we left bearing gifts, but alas no interview with the country's spiritual leader.

Now that we had established some rapport with the pre-eminent family we were unlikely to be deported, but we did want to be transported to the war zone. We tried to film around Khartoum, although the presence of minders discouraged much interaction with the locals. We filmed a Catholic service; the singing was very moving, until we were moved along by our minders. Then we joined a lecture at a girls' college. All the women were veiled, and some were completely covered in the Afghan fashion; a few further protected their modesty by wearing black gloves. I did manage to talk privately to a group of economics graduates. Although covered from head to toe, they loudly proclaimed, in good English, that they were fervent feminists. One boldly declared: 'I can choose my husband for love, not because my family chooses a husband for me.' I almost offered her a subscription to *The Guardian*.

At a Koranic school for young boys the poor fellows had to study five days a week, sixteen hours a day, learning the Koran by rote. A colleague had filmed at similar schools in Sudan some years before and had seen youngsters in chains because they had tried to run away from the harsh regime. The school I visited had no chains, but the masters did prowl with big sticks. They had almost no proper facilities, and the food was indistinguishable from the local mud. I didn't bother to consult a rep from the teachers' union.

I always try to visit British war graves, especially in far-flung former colonies, although Sudan was technically an Anglo-Egyptian condominium until 1956. At a small War Graves Commission site in the capital I met an Englishman from Hull who was teaching two Sudanese to manage the small cemetery. The well-tended graveyard contained graves from the 1880s to the Second World War. I commented on the heavy price of empire.

'All the costs of tending UK military war graves around the world are less than one fighter jet,' he said curtly; then he asked me for permits from the British embassy before I could film.

I decided to call in on the embassy, not for permits, but to talk to the resident spook. I was indulged with a typically cynical, if useful, Oxbridge-style Foreign Office briefing. Bin Laden's departure was confirmed, and I was told to be cautious of how I should interpret any training camps I was allowed to visit. Slavery was not a major issue, I was informed, although people, especially children, were captured, and sometimes ransomed, during tribal clashes. I asked about the so-called 'ghost houses', where opponents of the regime were tortured. These were constantly moved, I was told. Finally, I was briefed on the various peace initiatives to end the war with the Sudan People's Liberation Army in the south. The war, I was told, had been partly inspired by the alleged forcible conversion of the Christians (a minority) and the animists in the largely 'black', non-Arab, population.

I did the rounds of often highly articulate government ministers, some educated in the USA and UK; I also managed to speak to opposition people, one of whom, a Christian leader, went on camera to talk about being tortured. The government boasted an Anglican bishop as a foreign minister, although many Sudanese Christians regarded him as a stooge. I found him unconvincing when I interviewed him. Christians were technically exempt from the tough Islamic Sharia code, especially in the south, but other clergymen complained of constant discrimination in housing, schooling and employment.

Technically, as a non-Muslim, I could drink alcohol, but none was to be had, although moonshine was available in the south. So I pressed the authorities to speed our permits to go into the war zone. Also, as a non-Muslim, in theory I was not subject to the harsh Sharia codes.

When I accidentally purloined someone's lighter, Irwin joked: 'Have you decided which hand you want chopped off?'

We filmed in the sprawling refugee camps around the capital; two million southerners had taken refuge in them. Food and health care, I was told, had been manipulated as subtle means of conversion by both Christian and Muslim charities. Most charities appeared to be Islamic, however. I spoke to a highly independent American UN representative in the capital, after I had slipped my minders.

He said that he had questioned a Dinka tribesman (from the south) who was wearing a cross but standing in line at a Muslim feeding centre. The man laughed: 'I might be a Muslim in the morning, a Christian in the afternoon, but at night I pray to my own [Dinka] god.'

To give some balance, we attended a mosque, and then filmed the famous whirling dervishes, adherents of the mystical Sufi tradition, who say they can achieve a higher state by constantly spinning around. It produced great TV footage but little personal enlightenment.

After two weeks in the capital, our military contacts finally turned up trumps. We scrambled into a Russian Ilyushin cargo plane with no seats. We had waited on the tarmac for what seemed like hours before taking off, in a baking tin can, and we were all drenched with sweat – which then froze when we reached our cruising altitude.

We were accompanying the transitional Speaker of Parliament, Colonel Mohamed al-Amin Khalifa, one of the original officers involved in the 1989 coup, and the very tall Riek Machar, an SPLA rebel who had recently signed a peace deal with Khartoum. The SPLA had split into various ethnic factions, and Machar led a Nuer group of fighters. Machar was a man of many parts, including doctoral study in the UK, and later courtship of an English rose, Emma. She died in a car crash along with her unborn child, and her brief polygamous marriage to a guerrilla leader inspired a book

313

and film. Machar soon rejoined the rebels, and later became vice-president of the Government of South Sudan.

The war in the south

The plane took us to the deep south-west, to a town called Wau. After the deserts of the north, this seemed green and fertile, more like tropical Africa. We were escorted in four-wheel-drive vehicles to the governor's 'palace' in a crumbling former British cantonment. A bizarrely dressed and astoundingly out-of-tune military band greeted our arrival, not just two hacks, but the accompanying government generals and Riek Machar. I tried to imagine how it must have been in its orderly imperial heyday. A list of British governors and district commissioners still adorned the panelled entrance hall. The last civilian administrator was a J. E. C. Mackrell, who was 'Sudanised' in 1954.

We stayed in a guesthouse with few comforts. Irwin, despite his magisterial inexperience of Africa, exhibited a taciturn Ulster toughness, so I risked a little teasing about the genuine problems of tropical diseases, in particular Ebola, which was prevalent in the south. I also invented a few animals such as the brown-spotted buttock viper that could be found coiled at the bottom of latrines waiting for a target of convenience. Taking it all in good humour, he was destined to have the last laugh.

Since we were finally in the south, where Christians allegedly could drink booze, I decided to apply what we dubbed the 'Guinness test'. I asked our hosts if I could have a drink. A convoluted series of night manoeuvres followed. A group of Christian soldiers had to be persuaded to volunteer to drive me to a nearby shanty town. I expected a cheerful African shebeen. Instead I was left outside, under guard in the army vehicle. Eventually, after four hours, I found that I had paid for a plastic bag of clear liquid. It looked – and tasted – like jet fuel, but I had to sip it publicly.

Afterwards, I poured it down the non-flushing loo at the guesthouse. An hour later, I settled down for a cigar. Just as I was absent-mindedly about to throw the match down the loo, Irwin shouted a warning: 'You'll certainly get bombed if you do that.'

The Irishman might have been a fresher in the bush but he certainly possessed a highly developed nose for dangerous incendiary devices.

Wau was uninteresting; it was made worse by sitting in stifling hot

314

halls for hours during long political sessions conducted in Arabic. Riek Machar did address a subdued outdoor crowd in the local vernacular, where a translator helped. Machar told the assembly that the government had promised a federation for southerners and that a referendum would be held for them to decide their own fate. The crowd looked as if they had heard it all before. I passed much of the time reading Robert Harris's *Enigma*, which I found as tedious and complex as Sudanese politics.

We flew on to Juba, the capital of the south, which had been under close siege by the SPLA rebels. Two large Russian transport planes had been abandoned on the end of the runway. A sense of despair and dereliction hung over the town like a cloud. We passed gutted petrol stations, and fleets of vehicles mounted on bricks littered the lush equatorial landscape. We ended up in the Salaam Hotel – Hotel of Peace. Certainly we were not disturbed by any service or amenities. But nobody was shooting at us, because the rebels had been pushed up to sixty miles from the city. Or so the Khartoum generals told us.

Irwin and I were now 'guarded' by four military policemen. The officer in charge, I discovered, was a Catholic called Patrick. At night, during a heavy tropical storm, I persuaded him to take us to see the Roman Catholic archbishop of Juba, Paulino Loro, who was under house arrest. He told us in private conversation that the guerrillas were all around the town, and indeed in it. The priest lashed out at the forced Arabisation of the south, and the many attempts to undermine the Christian faith. His frankness and bravery, despite many death threats, were impressive. When the camera started rolling he was distinctly unimpressive. It was partly, no doubt, sensible caution. But it was also the habit many Africans have of believing 'I have told you once, now you know it'. If you start too early with the camera, people sometimes freeze and, besides, in much of black Africa you have to parley for hours, even days, to reach the rich seam of rapport which makes for a good interview. If you leave it too late people get talked out, or the interview may be interrupted by hostile elements. I got it wrong with the archbishop. I couldn't use the hard-won interview in the London edit suite when I tried to weave it into the TV documentaries we later produced.

By luck, however, the next day the government forces put on a televisual display of mounted troops and marching bands during a 'peace rally' to discourage local resistance to Khartoum's war machine. Our luck held when Irwin and I scrounged a lift in a Puma helicopter to Torit, eighty miles from Juba. It had once been the SPLA headquarters of General John Garang, the American-sponsored hardliner who refused to go along with Khartoum's blandishments. Irwin managed to film the aerial shots he needed. We also shot some wonderfully sensual sequences of traditional African dancing, with tribesmen with chalk-painted limbs and faces, and women in skin loincloths. The town was almost in ruins. A clutch of serviceable colonial-era stone buildings with reasonably intact tin roofs stood empty, while people lived next door in grass huts.

We choppered back to Juba, and the Saalam Hotel. Although I had lived in African swampland before, I took extra precautions against malaria. For the first time I used insect-repellent cream, burnt coils and even deployed netting over my bed, but I did get bitten a few times. I thought nothing of it. I felt fine when we flew back to Khartoum in a Boeing cargo plane, with former rebel soldiers chatting amiably to government troops. Back in the Khartoum Hilton, I concentrated on securing an interview with the elusive Turabi. I also attempted to talk to opposition politicians who were under house arrest in the capital.

Taxi-drivers are often government informers under authoritarian regimes, but sometimes front-lobby porters can play a shifty game too. One porter whom I had befriended explained that he was a Christian from the south who supported the former communist party. He said he would fix me up with some contacts. Then the head waiter left me notes about contacting a disgraced former prime minister, after a lengthy tirade on world politics served with a rather sad steak. One evening the laundry manager sidled up to me in a very furtive manner and whispered his opposition to the current government, and then apologised for losing my shirt. I came to expect an exegesis on Nietzsche from the pastry chef. Some of the approaches might even have been genuine. They perhaps showed distrust and dislike of the Islamic revolution, but in a real climate of fear no one would have risked approaching a foreign journalist in a public place. Sudanese have a reputation for friendliness and hospitality; it seemed true, despite the authoritarian nature of the revolutionary administration. Khartoum's inhabitants didn't appear to be too cowed by the regime's muscular piety; Turabi and his military allies were not ruling by sheer terror. The Organisation of African Unity had recognised the (non-party) elections earlier in 1996, but many OAU officials probably wouldn't have recognised a fair election if one jumped up and bit them.

Despite the recent protests in the capital over food prices, the Islamic government looked fairly sturdy; this had less to do with its toughness and more to do with the ineffectiveness and fractiousness of the (illegal) opposition parties. The revolution's fervour, such as it was, centred on one man: Dr Turabi.

Finally, he let me interview him. I had been warned that he had the verbal dexterity of a snake-oil salesman. This proved true, but he was also bright and charming. Apparently at ease in both tie and turban, he claimed to know America well; after education in Britain and France, he had spent the summer of 1961 on a US government-sponsored tour for student leaders. He was utterly convinced that the USA was in decline, but he employed sophisticated dissimulation, in excellent English, to avoid provoking Washington into adding military reprisals to the list of economic and diplomatic sanctions that were being served up. He maintained that the Americans were using the slavery and terrorism issues in Sudan to undermine Islam.

'The Americans know that the African-Americans are very sympathetic to Sudan,' he claimed. 'They want to persuade the African-Americans that US policy towards Sudan is all right because Sudan is involved in slavery. There is absolutely no slavery in Sudan.'

When I tackled him on his friendship with bin Laden, he claimed that as a good Muslim he had offered him hospitality. The Saudi warlord had been involved in proper business and charity work. No military training was involved, he said.

'Can I see these alleged training camps, then?'

The shambles I was shown made Dad's Army look like the SAS. We filmed the world's worst (barefoot) marching, and women stripping rifles who probably thought they were rolling pins. My minders said these were people's militia camps, the Popular Defence Force, a sort of Territorial Army for unemployables. I did not doubt that, but I suspected that the CIA's claims that some of these were fronts for real training camps may have been true.

Bin Laden had gone, and I had no evidence on film of his camps. But I had some interesting footage, especially of the south, which nobody else had managed for some years. I could make something of it – provided Irwin and I could leave.

It may have been the bureaucratic torpor or my old friend the justice minister's machinations, but departing Sudan was a problem. We had already registered at the Hilton on arrival but, on returning from the south, there had been a glitch in re-registering. Apparently because of pressure from Washington to monitor international terrorists, Sudan had introduced the three-day registration process, presumably because the international community believed that Mr bin Laden and his associates would stay at the Hilton and register their passports. Eventually, the hotel manager was blamed, and I had to accompany the police to arrest him.

Meanwhile, for the first time in over twenty years of travelling in Africa, I was struck down by malaria. Somehow, we eventually reached London, edited the film, and sold it successfully before I collapsed with a rare double dose of intestinal and cerebral malaria. I'd suspected malaria; but assumed I'd contracted an ordinary version. Unpleasant, but I had seen a lot of friends deal with it in southern Africa. What I didn't know was that I had the acute version of cerebral malaria. I was told that a person can survive without proper medication for thirty days. It was on the twenty-sixth day that I admitted myself, in a terrible state, to hospital. Barely able to stand or speak, and vomiting heartily, I did not want to spend four hours in a queue. I told the reception that I had just been on the Congo border, where Ebola was rife, which was true.

'I suggest you put me on my own in a quarantined room.'

Which they did with alacrity.

The Royal Surrey County Hospital in Guildford worked hard to save my life. An eminent Indian specialist, an expert on malaria, knew exactly what he was doing. Thank you. And, as in all bad war movies, I later managed to date the junior nurse who looked after me.

I made a fuss when I wasn't allowed visitors. 'You asked for quarantine, so you got it,' said a feisty ward sister.

I checked myself out immediately, with the connivance of said junior nurse. And I was lucky, suffering only one repeat bout of the disease.

At the time, despite my general interest in and, I hope, understanding of Islamic movements, I just couldn't bring myself to like the Turabi regime. The concerns of Western Christian groups were valid, but there was less freedom of religion in Saudi Arabia and the West was pretty pally with the Saudis. I had some sympathy with the southern rebels, and planned to try filming with them in the future, provided I didn't have to walk too far. The rebel army, however, had never represented all southerners and had a pretty brutal history as well. The Israelis had helped out earlier, and then the CIA took over. The US State Department later gave $3 million to the southern opposition alliance to improve its logistics. But when the oil began flowing from the south in 1999, even the Canadians (briefly) ignored US pressure in order to make a quick buck or two.

In August 1998 the Clinton administration launched a cruise missile attack on the al-Shifa medicine factory in Khartoum (as well as on Afghanistan) in retaliation against bin Laden's involvement in bombing two US embassies in East Africa. I seriously doubted whether the al-Shifa factory had anything to do with bin Laden's chemical weapons' potential. Irwin had recently filmed inside the place, and we arranged to sell the footage of the factory which, *inter alia*, produced anti-malaria pills. My instinct was borne out. It is now widely accepted that this was a monumental American intelligence fiasco, the result of politicised intelligence about 'weapons of mass destruction'.

The Sudanese Islamist movement subsequently split. Turabi himself was eventually put under house arrest. Khartoum, while continuing to depopulate the south, especially around the oil fields and pipelines, tried to improve its international image in order to get sanctions lifted. When bin Laden became Public Enemy No. 1 in the West, the Sudanese insisted that he had been under their tight control until March 1996. He had not been involved in terrorist acts before that date, and was not guilty of the World Trade Center bombing of 1993. Further, they *said* that he had often declared – in the strongest terms – that the use of suicide missions was totally un-Islamic. Khartoum officials *said* that they had told the USA they would keep bin Laden in Sudan under their watchful eye, but the Americans had bullied Sudan into forcing him to leave. It was Washington's fault that he went to Afghanistan and put himself beyond any control, they said. They also reminded me that bin Laden had been trained and funded by the CIA during the war against the Russians in the 1980s. The Sudanese had a point, maybe, but fear of further US bombings was an inducement for such apologias. The Sudanese also made a bad mistake in appearing to condone Saddam Hussein's invasion of Kuwait.

Elements in the US State Department who remembered the American humiliations accompanying the fall of the Shah sometimes portrayed Sudan as Iran Mark 2. Iran was a largely Shia Muslim (non-Arab) state, whereas Sudan was the first militant Sunni Arab state. Other big differences were manifest, not least that Sudan was an intriguing – if dangerous – mix of Arabia and Africa. But as long as Khartoum was seen to be emulating, in Africa, Iran's revolutionary role in the Middle East, it would continue to get a bad press – alienating the USA and even the more conservative Muslim states. And perhaps Khartoum should have been a bit more choosy with its house guests.

THE LONG WAR

Iraq

14. THE CLASH OF CIVILISATIONS?

'Buildings collapsed. Democracy stands' ran the leader of the *Los Angeles Times*, a few hours after the 9/11 al-Qaeda attacks. That abomination changed the world dramatically, as did the events that flowed from it – especially the subsequent invasions of Afghanistan and Iraq.

And yet . . . 9/11 may also have crystallised long-existing currents in world politics. The optimism generated by the so-called end of history and the 'new world order' after the Berlin Wall fell had already faded. Jihadism had long been a threat, as evidenced in a previous attack on the same World Trade Center in 1993. The 2001 onslaughts were a serious intelligence failure in the same way that Pearl Harbor was; in both cases the writing was already on the wall. The attacks also provided an opportunity for the George W. Bush administration to implement pre-existing plans, especially the removal of Saddam Hussein, as part of a neo-conservative vision to transform the regimes of the oil-rich Middle East. Removal of Saddam was the key to unlock the whole region and to magic it into a patchwork quilt of pro-Western democracies. Instead, the invasion of Iraq was to alienate friends in NATO and in the Islamic world, and to fire up Jihadism worldwide. In the Cold War, the West eventually won the battle of ideas. In the long saga that followed from 9/11, the West soon lost the media war and the moral high ground. In the Cold War people merely feared a Third World War; after 9/11 the West was engulfed in real third-world wars.

On the day of the attacks on the US, I was comfortably ensconced in Whitehall. I had just spent three largely frustrating years lecturing at the Joint Services Command and Staff College, but was happy commuting to the heart of the Ministry of Defence in Whitehall, working in communications, with a licence to roam almost at will. I was supposed to leave the civil service for the second time the day after 9/11. I was flattered when the MoD rang up my future employers to say that I was needed in Whitehall. Not only the Americans, but also the Brits were caught out by al-Qaeda. Even my stale and very limited knowledge of Afghanistan was in demand.

I'd learned more about strategic security issues in Whitehall than I did in decades at university and in numerous war zones. Yes, I had seen some of the truth of *Yes, Minister* mandarins running circles around hapless politicians, but I was also truly impressed by the dedication of senior MoD officials, especially as they rallied around in the 9/11 crisis. And I never ceased to be amazed by the calibre of the British armed forces. The 'lions-led-by-donkeys' cliché is usually based on politicians portrayed as terrible and MoD civil servants seen at best as a nuisance, while the brave soldiers in the field have to survive both groups. And this had more than a grain of truth. In this regard the MoD was often its own worst enemy, crippled by its petty paranoia and the tendency always to keep things quiet, and rarely for sound national security reasons. Defence lies in a unique category but, like most organisations, the ministry displayed the workings of a natural law that as an organisation grows larger than, say, a thousand people, it no longer seems to need the outside world.

I soon returned to journalism. That gave me the freedom to travel in the various war zones that now opened up across the world, and it gave me licence to talk to many of the key players, for and against, in the so-called global war on terror. First, however, I broke a stern promise to myself: I returned, albeit briefly, to Afghanistan, courtesy of my old employers.

Afghanistan revisited

The Islamic world displayed some sympathy for, or at least toleration of, Washington's invasion of Taliban-ruled Afghanistan, the sanctuary for al-Qaeda. The 2001 war, from a Western perspective, was successful and rapid. US special forces, the use of proxy armies (the Northern Alliance) and that old war-horse, the B-52 bomber, soon forced the Taliban out of Kabul. Another old war-horse, the BBC's John Simpson, was the first journalist to 'liberate' the Afghan capital. The BBC did not have a good war, however. It had been scooped by Al-Jazeera, which had a bureau in Kabul and a monopoly of coverage from the Taliban side.

Except for the failure to catch Osama bin Laden – a big exception – the initial war in Afghanistan was a victory for the American military, especially over the hacks. The coalition had relied on air power, which was impossible for the media to cover in any detail, and special forces' operations, which are always off-limits to journalists. And many Afghans associated with the Northern Alliance simply viewed journalists cooped up in the northern enclave as a means to extort US dollars by fair or foul means.

The US-led alliance had defeated the Taliban, now it had the unenviable task of trying to rebuild the country by propping up a pro-Western administration in Kabul. And, for the fourth time in its military history, British troops returned to Afghanistan, though it was a moot point whether London had learned anything from the previous Anglo-Afghan wars.

That morning was very cold in Kabul on 29 April 2002. It was 2.30 a.m. and the sergeant's voice boomed in the airport tent as he briefed fresh troops and tired correspondents.

'There are eleven million mines in this country – almost one for each person living here,' said the sergeant. He also warned of the endemic diseases, including anthrax and cholera.

'Afghanistan has eleven types of venomous snakes and there are scorpions everywhere.' He then went into painful detail about a scorpion found hiding in an Italian officer's trousers.

'The driving is terrible,' he added. 'And, by the way, prostitutes are available, but it's illegal. And, remember, the police are heavily armed. They use RPGs [rocket-propelled grenades] for traffic control.'

A British major-general, John McColl, was commanding a nearly 5,000-strong force from nineteen nations – the International Security Assistance Force (ISAF). Its job was to police Kabul. Elsewhere, however, tribal leaders and warlords held sway. Thousands of insurgents still gave allegiance to al-Qaeda, the Taliban and the famous warlord Gulbuddin Hekmatyar – and they all regarded Western troops as fair game. ISAF was called a peacekeeping operation, intended to be distinct from the war-fighting missions of US troops and UK Royal Marines to the south and east of Kabul.

The heavily mined Kabul airport had been attacked by rockets three hours before my giant RAF C-17 had touched down. A broken-backed Russian cargo plane slumped near the entrance of the terminal buildings, a relic of previous civil wars, not a victim of recent assaults.

At 4.00 a.m. I was summoned to another, higher-level, briefing.

'Kabul is like Berlin during the Cold War,' said Colonel Richard Barrons. A good comparison: four different parties, of varying tribal and political allegiances, made up the interim government, headed by President Hamid Karzai, but the Northern Alliance controlled the key ministries because they had the guns and tanks in Kabul. ISAF's mission was to hold the ring in the capital until a national convention – the *Loya Jirga* – organised a more permanent, and ideally more democratic, government. Meanwhile, coalition troops would train a new national army. The first element was the First Battalion of the Afghan National Guard, helpfully abbreviated as Bang.

The Karzai government directly controlled about 10 per cent of the country. It had to negotiate with the rest. Negotiation was usually about force or money. And lots of the promised Western aid money was needed quickly if Karzai was to survive. Reconstruction could happen only if there were security – that was the continuous conundrum facing the Western allies. And the country had been insecure for decades.

The Brits, in the jargon, were into 'quick-impact CIMIC' (Civil–Military Cooperation) – using the little spare money to achieve noticeable improvements in the community. The British-led forces had stabilised Kabul. Crime had dropped though not to the level enforced by the draconian Taliban regime. Many schools, including classes for girls, had reopened. Commercial life – at a basic level – had resumed. Kabul's streets were bustling with cars and market stalls, often accompanied by long-forbidden music. Kites were being flown again. And beards were no longer compulsory.

Kabul, however, offered few attractions to Westerners. The locals enjoyed outings to the zoo, despite the almost complete lack of animals. The most arresting species on my visit were the two UK female officers who constituted my security escort. *Burqa*-clad ladies were astounded (as far as I could see) by two blonde uniformed women sporting weapons, driving and commanding armed men. This was a culture shock with a vengeance. The British responded by naming their mess tent the 'Burqa Bar'.

I attempted to deploy this novelty factor by asking the two officers to help me with my shopping. I thought that they, plus their heavily armed infantrymen, would provide a suitable distraction while I haggled for a silk carpet. I completely failed to capitalise on their shock and awe presence to get the price I wanted.

The British troops were seriously engaged in hearts and minds. I visited schools and orphanages where the soldiers handed out pens and writing paper, although female soldiers were tasked with donations to the girls. Later, a foot patrol with the Royal Anglians was transformed into a Pied Piper parade, as children flocked around the troops. This was no PR fix: the soldiers were obviously welcome. But for how long was the question I kept asking myself. Over the previous 160 years British troops had often gone into the country in large numbers – sometimes even by invitation of one Afghan leader or other – and it had nearly always ended in mayhem and massacre, including the Victorian empire's most humiliating defeat.

British troops were not taking any chances in an isolated observation point on the top of a large hill overlooking the southern access from Kandahar. It was a former Russian gun emplacement. The latest occupants were being harassed by occasional artillery and small-arms fire. A squaddie from the Royal Anglians told me: 'When I arrived I was told to look out for armed men, but – bugger me – all the men around here are armed.'

Much of the capital was still in ruins, particularly the grand old buildings such as the Royal Palace, the damage done by the civil war of the early 1990s. Nevertheless, I found Kabul a relatively pleasant town to visit if you liked people who hadn't heard of David Beckham, and Manchester United shirts were not in vogue (though you could buy fakes in the bazaar for $50). Football was being played again in the national stadium, where – just a few months before – the Taliban were beheading their victims, or, if they were in a good mood, just amputating the odd limb.

I didn't join the trips organised for the other hacks nor did I share their accommodation. Normally I am one for solidarity, but I decided that a single room in the officers' mess was better than a camp-bed in a tent. Nevertheless the hacks, as reward or punishment, delegated me – as 'the senior journalist' – to give a brief talk on the role of the media in places such as Afghanistan, as well as the formal thanks to our hosts. I had never before considered myself a senior anything; maybe I *was* getting too old for war zones.

But moving around solo – on patrols and visiting police stations and schools etc., as well as mooching around the bazaar – gave me a chance to talk to the locals. I had forgotten much of the little language skill I had picked up in the 1980s, so it might have been translation problems. Nevertheless, even after six months' occupation, some of the residents thought that the Russians had come back. It was either astounding political illiteracy or the international forces were not quite as touchy-feely as I had been led to believe. More probably, it was simply that to Afghans all infidels looked, and perhaps behaved, alike.

The base I stayed in was a former Afghan officers' college, and before that had been used by British officers during the Raj. Clearly it had not seen much paint since Queen Victoria's days. The most stylish aspect of the location was the panache with which the Italians modelled their uniforms, and especially their sunglasses and silk cravats. They had also airlifted in an excellent restaurant-size coffee machine. It was as if all the nationalities were deliberately confirming their stereotypes. The French moodily kept themselves to themselves, the Dutch hoarded their beer supplies, while the Germans were generous with alcohol. I must admit to being somewhat transfixed by their armoured vehicles with the modified German army cross on the side, and I took endless pictures of them. It must have satisfied this schoolboy collector of panzer models.

A number of former MoD colleagues and officers who had been my students at Staff College insisted on giving me VIP treatment and access. I was allowed the run of briefings and operational planning at the ISAF HQ. It was a nice change for a hack to feel trusted. And it was the first time I had ever been kissed by a lieutenant-colonel, one of the charming female officers who had so patiently shown me around town.

Overall, ISAF had achieved a near-miracle in a very short time – in the capital. Elsewhere, banditry, warlordism and drug-running were rampant. Many Afghans realised that this brief breathing space might be their last to chance to settle their internal differences peacefully before a major resumption of hostilities. Coalition forces had imposed peace, partly because Washington managed temporarily to end the war by bribing and cajoling nearly all the neighbouring states into acquiescing in the American design. It was obvious to me, however, that America's legions would soon be called away for duty in the Middle East, especially Iraq.

Back again in the Holy Land

A series of Palestinian uprisings, known collectively as the *intifada*, which literally means 'a shaking off', began to undermine both Israel's political system and the deterrence effect of its powerful military. The first *intifada* began in 1987 and lasted six years. Both the first and the more aggressive second *intifada*, which began in 2000, were born of a deep-seated and bitter frustration with both the Israeli occupation and the ineffectual Arab leadership, locally and in the neighbouring states.

The war to remove Saddam Hussein from Kuwait had improved Israel's military position. Its enemy Syria had lost its Soviet patron, and Iraq had been humbled. America had become the linchpin of the Middle East. The Arabs, cowed by US technical wizardry in the Gulf, had lost immediate interest in fighting Israel. In one sense, however, Saddam had won an accidental victory: he had placed the Palestinian uprising back at the centre of the world stage.

After 1993 the Palestinian Authority had been established in parts of the occupied territories. Its leader, Yasser Arafat, appeared unable to contain the endemic corruption or the rise of Islamist fundamentalist groups such as Hamas. Hamas had won popular support not necessarily because of its Islamist stance, but because it was perceived as leading the resistance. And Hamas activists, largely free of corruption, had created a mini-welfare state for their followers.

The Israelis withdrew from southern Lebanon (and later from Gaza) but found no peace. So the Israeli Defence Force (IDF) reacted with reprisal raids, as the zealots sent suicide bombers into Jewish civilian areas.

This time the media coverage was different. Al-Jazeera, founded in Qatar in 1995, had created a revolution: for the first time reportage was going from East to West, instead of the reverse. The dramatic pictures from the occupied territories created a sense of immediacy and support in the 'Arab Street'. Israel could no longer claim to be using reasonable force to contain the Palestinians, when Al-Jazeera showed otherwise, daily and hourly. Israel and Jewish lobbies worldwide, realising the media-savvy Palestinians and Al-Jazeera had outflanked them, fought back. They accused Al-Jazeera of bias, although it had been the first Arab channel regularly to feature interviews with Israelis.

Above all, it was the one-sided backing of Israel, with Washington's blind eye to UN resolutions critical of the Jewish state, that continued to rankle in the Arab world. The security barrier that Israel was building to keep out suicide bombers appeared as *de facto* new borders in the West Bank, and especially around Jerusalem. The IDF also re-occupied West Bank towns, most notoriously Jenin. Prime Minister Ariel Sharon said he was determined to 'uproot terrorists'.

Staying in empty hotels in Jerusalem was a little like emulating Jack Nicholson in *The Shining*. I was bemused by the lift which had worked previously, then – of its own volition – started stopping at every floor, even though no one else was round to press anything. I complained to the manager about the lift. He insisted it was working fine. It took me some time to appreciate that, on the Jewish Sabbath, the lifts were programmed to stop at all floors, to avoid a devout Jew having to work on the day of rest by pressing a button.

I was practically alone in a charming Jewish-owned small hotel in East Jerusalem, except for an Arab-Israeli businessman who confided: 'Both Sharon and Arafat are crazy old men. They hate each other – this is personal. They are stuck in history. They both must go before we can move on.'

Did Sharon commit in Jenin a major war crime, on a par with the massacre of Palestinians in the refugee camps of Beirut twenty years before? Or was the devastation in the northern West Bank town an inevitable consequence of a pitched battle against entrenched terrorists in a crowded urban setting? What was the truth amid the storm of conflicting propaganda claims?

The IDF invaded the town on 3 April 2002. For eight days Israeli Merkava tanks, armoured personnel carriers and Cobra helicopters, firing wire-guided missiles, waged war on Jenin's inhabitants. On 9 April, thirteen part-time Israeli soldiers were killed in an ambush in the narrow winding streets. Ten other Israeli soldiers also fell in the battle. This triggered fear and anger in the besieging forces; bulldozers – giant armoured vehicles the size of a double-decker London bus – were summoned to demolish the centres of resistance. Some of the houses were destroyed with civilians inside. About 25 per cent of the camp was flattened.

Palestinians recounted tales of a last-stand replay of the Alamo. I was told that thirty-five fighters were holding out. Three came out, with their hands up, it was said – but they were shot. The International Red Cross finally negotiated the surrender of the others, I was told. So many stories were circulating about the siege and the media reports were largely relying on partisan sources. The hacks needed to get in to see for themselves.

Israeli armour encircled the refugee camp, abutting the main town. During the five-day curfew, bodies were left to rot in the streets. On 14 April a trickle of international aid was allowed in, but journalists were still barred. With great difficulty, travelling partly across country in an armoured Land Rover, courtesy of Channel 4 TV, and guided by friendly Palestinians, field by field in the end, we reached the edge of Jenin's camp. I accompanied Tim Lambon and Lindsey Hilsum of Channel 4 News and Marie Colvin, working for the *Sunday Times*. We finally entered the town, chased by a large Israeli tank, which menacingly waved its barrel. We turned quickly into a narrow alleyway, and managed to elude the much larger vehicle. I was reminded of the sequence in the Clint Eastwood film, *Kelly's Heroes*, when Clint's tank similarly tried to evade the much bigger German Tiger tank.

On 18 and 19 April, amid the awful choking stench of decaying flesh, I spoke to scores of survivors. The landscape was more like an earthquake zone. Indeed, Palestinians claimed this was their Ground Zero, in a reference to the site of the razed Twin Towers in New York.

The Arab world had been calling Jenin a massacre site. Casualties had clearly been inflated by the Palestinians and minimised by the Israelis. I counted twenty-one bodies being buried amid nearby Israeli machine-gun fire, although it was not aimed at the burial party. Elsewhere I saw remnants of six people, small pulped lumps, with bits of clothing and the odd bone – the result of pulverisation by tons of debris. Lost children wailed on mounds of crushed stone which were once their homes. People were digging with their bare hands to find survivors or to recover possessions.

'This is Sharon's fault. And Bush's,' lamented one Palestinian woman who had lost most of her immediate family.

A few inhabitants, upon realising I was British, harangued me, blaming Foreign Secretary Arthur Balfour for his pro-Zionist declaration in 1917. The Palestinians had long memories. My half-hearted attempts to blame the English and to explain that I was Welsh were completely lost in translation or in my atrocious Arabic.

One young boy, aged about eleven, told me his mother and brother had been killed by the soldiers. 'When I grow up I want to be a suicide bomber too,' he said firmly.

Over a thousand men of 5 Infantry Brigade had entered Jenin's refugee camp from four directions. Few of the Israeli reservists, unlike the regulars deployed, had received training in urban guerrilla warfare.

To avoid an international outcry, the Israeli cabinet had decided not to use F-16 war planes or artillery, even though this would mean heavier IDF casualties. According to Israeli intelligence, the camp contained approximately 200 fighters, drawn from Hamas, Islamic Jihad and Al-Aqsa militias, as well as Palestinian police and security forces, who had constructed very intricate defensive positions.

Palestinian propaganda initially claimed 500 of their people had been killed. Final estimates had fifty-two Palestinians, and twenty-three Israeli soldiers, killed. Over 200 on both sides were treated for wounds.

Because of the originally very high numbers of claimed deaths, I was surprised by the lack of wounded. I visited the three nearest hospitals and encountered only a few men with minor war wounds. In such wars, the figures are usually three wounded for every fatality. Perhaps many of the wounded Palestinians were taken into custody along with other captured fighters.

In my opinion, this was no planned massacre to avenge the hundreds of Israeli civilians killed by suicide bombers. The evidence did show that Palestinians were used as human shields, and families were taken hostage as the IDF secured individual houses as their bases within the camp – in fact an elaborate maze of large brick and breezeblock structures. Such actions were violations of international law and the Geneva Convention.

On doors and in alleys the Israelis faced numerous booby traps – many of which I saw still intact. And so the soldiers used civilians to knock on their neighbours' doors, or they detonated or hammered their way through basement walls of houses to avoid street-level booby traps or ambush.

The bulldozers had been used as new and terrifying weapons of war and clearly some women and children had been trapped in the buildings, too fearful to come out when Israeli troops used megaphones to tell them to escape.

'The fighting was the fiercest urban house-to-house fighting Israel has seen in thirty years,' Major Rafi Laderman told me later in Jerusalem. This part-time officer – a marketing consultant in civilian life – explained how he personally had led hundreds of women and children out of the camp at the height of the fighting. 'Jenin was a capital of terror – 50 per cent of the suicide bombers came from there. We cleared out this nest of terrorism.'

Inside the camp, I saw numerous posters – extolling heroes who died in battle or in suicide explosions – along with vengeful graffiti written in Hebrew. I also witnessed Palestinian fighters removing light machine-guns from ruined houses. Jenin's Hamas and Islamic Jihad armed insurgents were a justified target for Israeli retaliation, but the court of world opinion would damn the excessive use of force against civilians. Nevertheless, in urban warfare – especially where women volunteered for suicide missions – separating combatants from the innocent was often impossible.

The IDF was often very sophisticated in dealing with Western journalists. This time, trigger-happy – or plain nervous – troops treated the press aggressively. One Italian journalist had just been killed by an Israeli sniper.

We were detained twice, but we had entered Jenin illegally.

It was too dangerous, let alone uncomfortable, to stay in Jenin. Our Land Rover left, intending to overnight just over the border in Israel. It was stopped by a no-nonsense tank and infantry group. The gun barrel, trained on us, moved back and forth to further intimidate us. The two females were well treated, but the four male occupants were pulled out of the Land Rover and told to strip off their shirts.

Fair enough, my beer gut could have been a pretty bulky suicide belt. I managed to joke, in poor Hebrew, then good English, with the Israeli sergeant about my stomach posing as a war machine. Luckily he had a sense of humour and this defused the tension. I could see Tim's anguished face – he no doubt recalled twenty years of my irritating habit of making bad jokes in dangerous situations.

The soldiers started to search the vehicle. Tim said laconically: 'We're journalists here – there are no guns, just toothbrushes.' The sergeant smiled again. The soldiers politely let us leave Jenin, but told us not to come back.

We stayed at a guesthouse in a kibbutz. It was friendly and clean and the food was good. I recalled my days as a student living on kibbutzim and the endless debates about the collective system, where all was owned in common. Earnest kibbutzniks claimed it was the only place in the world where communism worked, because it was voluntary. You could leave and change your lifestyle. But what I had just seen in Jenin seemed a long way from the early ideals of Zionism.

I had a good chat with Marie Colvin, first about the IDF tactics, and then I asked about how she had lost an eye while reporting with the Tamil Tigers. I meant it when I said her eye-patch made her look even more elegantly exotic.

We returned to Jenin the next day and managed to sneak in again, with some difficulty. On the way out, however, we were arrested a second time, by a much more serious army unit. The colonel angrily arranged our detention for the night and deportation the next day. I took him aside and tried to win him over by talking about my previous experience with the British army and my research on the IDF, name-dropping that the current prime minister, then merely a General Sharon, had personally assisted my earlier work. My charm, logic and general brown-nosing failed completely. The tough colonel was hell-bent on making an example of us. He had corralled not only me, Channel 4 News and the *Sunday Times*, but also CNN and the *Financial Times*.

The colonel's temper had cooled a little, and I tried a second time to reason with him, one to one, in his office. I said that deporting such high-profile correspondents would be bad publicity for an already beleaguered country facing a hurricane of international condemnation about the alleged massacre in Jenin.

He looked me straight in the eye and said: 'Good PR doesn't stop a single suicide bomber.'

He kept us at his roadblock. For a while we were stuck in the boiling heat in the tin can of the Land Rover. Everybody's mood was grim after what we had witnessed in Jenin and we were frustrated by the hours of arrest. Tim suggested, foolishly, that 'I should entertain the troops.'

The only way to deal with adversity, we both knew, was humour. Besides, we had been in far worse situations. Being unceremoniously dumped on a plane out of Israel was not the end of the world, and the Israeli troops had been restrained towards us.

Sitting uncomfortably on the jerry cans in the back, I started up an impromptu DJ session: pretending to put on records and then doing impersonations of various sixties and seventies songs. Lindsey even sent in some requests. After doing Elvis especially for her, Lindsey suggested I dedicate a song to Marie. She knew I had a soft spot for the famous war correspondent.

I said brightly: 'I am going to play Cliff Richard's "The Day I Met Marie".' Just as I launched into the song, I realised that the next line, after the title, was 'With the laughing *eyes*. . .'

Plural.

I simulated a bad scratch on the record, and immediately switched to 'The Young Ones'. Marie didn't notice that I just managed to avoid a possibly hurtful reference to a beautiful woman's recent injury. It showed how deranged we had all become that I was encouraged – I repeat, *encouraged* – to croon for some *hours* after that.

Eventually, after some American diplomatic intercession inspired by the CNN guy, I suspected, we were released by a none-too-happy Israeli colonel. As soon as we crossed into Israel, we were flashed by a speed-camera – it seemed a paradoxical return to mundane law-and-order problems after our two days in the Jenin butchery.

Back in London I did phone to offer Marie dinner, and a sing-song, but funnily enough she never took me up on my more than generous offer.

Build-up to the 2003 war in Iraq

The deliberate and constant drip-feeding of anti-Saddam demonisation by intelligence leaks to the media created a vicious circle. Journalists stood accused of 'mainlining uncut propaganda' and reporting 'faith-based intelligence'. The combination of hyped newspaper stories and the highly selective use of intelligence data by politicians powerfully influenced policy and public opinion. This chain of Chinese whispers soon took on its own mangled truth. London and Washington, however, were about to face reality in what Winston Churchill had called the 'the thankless deserts of Mesopotamia'. Or, as Jon Stewart of America's tongue-in-check newscast *The Daily Show* would dub it, 'Mess-o-potamia'.

The neo-cons in Washington needed little persuasion to go to war against Iraq; the House of Commons required a lot more. The case for war depended on a series of propositions about the nature of the Saddam regime: its secret obsession with weapons of mass destruction, its ability to deceive UN weapons inspectors, and above all the consequences of his removal for the whole region. Although George Bush's new pre-emptive war strategies were supposed to be founded on sound intelligence, Western intelligence agencies were wrong on all the above propositions. The White House and Number 10 generally sexed up the intelligence to suit their pre-existing prejudices and plans. So, in essence, Tony Blair and George Bush stand accused of hoodwinking both national and international opinion.

This, however, is the advantage of hindsight. At the time, Britain was divided about the war in a way not seen since the Suez crisis of 1956. I tried to report on this wide gulf in British politics by talking to the key Anglo-American voices in the new wars of the West. In 2002 I spoke to nearly everyone who would speak to me. In a very rare interview, Lord Guthrie, the former SAS commander and chief of the defence staff, was miffed by my suggestion that he had perhaps mellowed. He then went into some detail about his throat-cutting exploits in the jungle. He jokingly said at the end of the long interview, 'I wasn't going to cut *your* throat' – which provided a punchy headline.

I tackled the Americans as well. I enjoyed a lengthy, very early 'power breakfast' with America's so-called 'prince of darkness', Richard Perle. He was very smart and, unusually for a public intellectual, was prepared to listen as well as talk. With John Jumper, then the Chief of Staff, US Air Force, I talked about the arcane logistics of teaching dog-fighting to unmanned aircraft. Richard Lee Armitage, the former tough marine who became US Deputy Secretary for State, lived up to his image. He was forthright and honest, and honestly lost his temper to a deliberately incendiary question. It was thankfully a phone interview. I back-tracked and we continued. It would, however, have made a great TV interview. It is an art, which I had not fully mastered, of knowing when to drop the killer question into the discussion: too early, and you might get nothing else, too late and the interviewee might have to rush off or just lose interest or patience.

I also tracked opinion in the anti-war camp. I wanted to hear what the new archbishop-designate of Canterbury, Dr Rowan Williams, had to say. His PR advisers had kept him in purdah for a few months, because of the heated arguments in the Church of England about gay priests and female bishops. Stepping into the anti-war furore was definitely out. Disingenuously, I asked for an interview strictly on religious issues, namely the 'just war' doctrine.

His press secretary gave me an off-the-cuff negative: 'Until he becomes archbishop, Dr Williams will give interviews only in his native tongue.'

'You're on: I'll do it in Welsh,' I heard myself saying, without much thought.

The offer had to be honoured on both sides. My poor 'Valleys Welsh' and pub vocabulary had seriously to be beefed up with new phrases such as '*Arfau difa anferthol*' – weapons of mass destruction. I arrived in Oxford – in of all places a Jesuit college – to conduct the interview, with a very carefully prepared Welsh text and two tape recorders to help with the later translation.

As it happened, Rowan Williams, one of the leading Welsh-language scholars, took pity on me as I started my very faltering questions in the language of heaven; he switched kindly to the idiom of our English oppressors. It was a flawless interview. He constructed a flow of perfect sentences. And the substance was important too. As I had intended, we drifted into the politics of the coming war. He warned presciently that the plight of Christians in Iraq, and the wider Middle East, would become far, far worse if the invasion went ahead.

I also spoke to George Galloway, probably the best speaker in the House of Commons. I disagreed with much of what he said, but – my God! – he said it so persuasively and powerfully. I disliked his thinly disguised anti-Semitism, though I did not share many of his fellow MPs' disdain of his involvement in Iraq – the 'Member for Baghdad South', as he was called. George, however, lived up to his other nickname of 'Gorgeous George': his Commons office was staffed by the most alluring of young Palestinian female interns. He smoked cigars and was down-to-earth and I enjoyed his company. (I later thought he made a complete prat of himself on the *Big Brother* TV programme, which was only partially redeemed by his brave and brilliant testimony to the US Congress on the Iraq war.)

He gave me an eminently quotable interview; at the end, in a throwaway line, I said: 'George, next time you go to see Saddam, please take me with you.'

He nodded in polite agreement, and I thought no more about it.

The journey to Baghdad through the desert from the Jordanian capital of Amman used to take about twelve to sixteen hours, depending on the mood of the men with the moustaches at the Iraqi border control. Nearly every adult Iraqi male sported the Saddam bristle. The border post was also festooned with pictures and statues of the 'Great Leader'. Iraq was in the grip of a leadership cult as intrusive as those of North Korea, Stalinist Russia or Nazi Germany.

In September 2002, a small group of journalists, courtesy of George Galloway, was on its way to see the Saddam regime close up. Despite George's real influence – he had been dubbed locally the 'Scottish Prince of Arabia' – we still had major headaches with the customs people, especially about the sat-phones. Our kit was searched carefully in front of everyone else. This was embarrassing for the *Independent* correspondent. After a fuss about his communications kit, the Iraqis pulled out a big stash of loose condoms.

'You must think Baghdad will be very lively,' said one hack.

'We might all write about this,' I added.

'So long as you say they were Jumbo-size,' the *Independent* man said defensively.

He immediately earned the nickname of 'Jumbo'.

It took us just under five hours to reach Baghdad. The greatest danger was the madcap motoring – so many graduates of the martyrs' school of driving. I saw little sign of military activity, although the well-maintained motorways could have doubled in places as emergency airstrips. On the outskirts of Baghdad, one rather slack group of troops manned a roadblock; nearby stood an ancient anti-aircraft gun.

Accommodation was in the famous Al-Rashid hotel, long a watering-hole for foreign correspondents lucky enough to blag a visa. The hotel entrance was adorned with the infamous floor mosaic of George Bush Sr, with broken teeth and fixed grin. The in-laid caption announced: 'Bush is criminal.' A British journalist danced a jig on the face of the former president. An Arab delegation, wearing traditional dress, stood bemused in the foyer, but soon started to laugh and cheer at the political jig.

I immediately bumped into my old pals Tim Lambon and Lindsey Hilsum. I had a discreet chat with Tim about how ill-prepared the Iraqi military appeared to be. I knew little after a few hours in town but that didn't stop me doing a BBC Radio Wales commentary that first day. This was common: regular BBC reporters often had to cite 'local sources' – that is, the taxi-driver from the airport – when they had to do an instant report. At least I had made some observations en route and had Tim's expert military insight.

The Al-Rashid hotel was hosting two consecutive conferences, one advocating peace and then one to boost tourism. Both seemed unlikely prospects. A massive poster of Saddam posing jauntily at an historical site quoted one of his great sayings: 'Tourism is a river of gold.' Daily newspapers, full of his activities, also carried headline panels of the leader's words. Even in Arabic his musings seemed trite or so confusing as to compare unfavourably with the philosophical cant of the great Eric Cantona.

So far, however, Saddam had proved a genius – in the art of survival. He had led his turbulent and talented nation for over twenty-three years. His methods were ruthlessly direct. He didn't need tanks on the streets: his secret police had the country wrapped up. My room was bugged, but in a cack-handed way – the bathroom light tripped the phone bug. The regime's PR style was equally ham-fisted. Their plan for us, presumably, was to boost anti-war opinion in the UK.

Tariq Aziz, a Christian who acted as the external face of the regime, told a concurrent peace conference that journalists could visit any WMD site they chose. We did choose and monumental foot-dragging ensued. Despite its PR smiles, this looked like a regime with a lot to hide.

George Galloway gave a rousing speech to the conference, with no notes. He insisted that Iraq had no WMDs. At the top of his voice he shouted: 'Are you listening, Tony Blair?'

I argued on a number of occasions with George about Iraq's WMD. I was convinced, for good reason, not least from friends who had been UN weapons inspectors, and senior Whitehall sources, that Saddam at the very least had low-grade chemical weapons, and would use them, as he had done before. I certainly did *not* buy the tabloid junk about nukes with the range to hit British bases in Cyprus or any al-Qaeda connection with Saddam. The devious behaviour of our hosts – and I met many top people – all gave me the impression that they were seriously up to no good.

That's why I told George I would eat my hat if WMD were not found. This promise would come back to haunt me.

Ordinary Iraqis were hospitable, I found, on the occasions when I could give our minders the slip. I roamed around the alleyways of the souks in search of information and, if truth be told, of Saddam paraphernalia: watches, clocks, plates, radios and lighters as souvenirs – my *Guardian*-reading intellectual friends always scooped up any such gewgaws and militaria I brought home. The Iraqis seemed relaxed, playing backgammon and smoking hookah pipes. I was asked to play and smoke with them.

I was sometimes accompanied by Mark Seddon, the editor of the left-wing *Tribune,* who was not only charming company, but also had a keen eye for antique silverware. I bought a silver snuff-box which, Mark explained from the markings, came from the Marsh Arabs, whom Wilfred Thesiger had lionised. Obviously the sanctioned economy had forced people to sell their family heirlooms; I felt guilty buying an antique at a tenth of the price it would have cost in London.

I also purchased a wonderful blood-red kelim for my little cottage in the Surrey hills; the more exotic or dangerous my assignments, the more I tended to do long-distance nesting, and to feel homesick, though sometimes I was disoriented about its exact location, especially when I woke up in the morning. I was never sufficiently cosmopolitan, however, to forget which constituted my first language.

Many of the shopkeepers were professional men, though graduate salaries could be as low as £10–15 a month, and they were keen to speak English when it was clear we had no minders and we were in a secluded area of the shop. It was still difficult though, even then, to get them to talk freely. Often they parroted the official line.

'September 11 was a Mossad and CIA plot,' one teacher earnestly informed me. 'Look at those 3,000 Jews who called in sick to avoid going to their offices in the World Trade Center.'

How often had I heard identical conspiracy theories in the bazaars of the Middle East? Many dictatorships internalised their own international propaganda.

Others insisted that the UN weapons inspectors were spies. 'Why should we let them in? They will only tell the Americans exactly where they should target their bombs,' said another shopkeeper. This was a more valid point.

The markets bustled with life. Conditions had improved, I was told, in the previous year or so in Baghdad, despite sanctions. The restaurants were certainly full and the food abundant, if dull. One evening along with the doughty representatives of *The Guardian*, *Sunday Telegraph* and *Independent*, I visited a former caravanserai, tastefully restored as a restaurant. It had a capacity of 500, but besides our small group only two others sat at the tables. We were surprised by this, as we had paid a small extra sum for the privilege of being entertained by 'Arabic dancing girls'. After a nondescript meal, the man from *The Guardian* offered to raise the absence of dancing girls with the management.

'What would Polly Toynbee say, if we told her, especially if you put this on expenses?' was the kind comment from *The Telegraph*.

No ladies appeared and the shimmying *Telegraph* hack made a poor substitute.

Even late at night, smart shops were selling smuggled or fake Western designer clothes. Life was good for some, especially the élite, who had benefited from an economy which survived on contraband. Eking out a living was harder in the poorer districts, such as Saddam City, and in the countryside, where malnutrition lurked, especially among the children.

Government spokesmen played down the imminence of war, but there was evidence of stockpiling of food by ordinary citizens and hospitals. The general mood displayed both a truculent determination to resist 'American imperialism and Zionist aggression' as well as a general war-weary lassitude. As in most wars, more civilians than soldiers were likely to be killed.

The Amiriyia bunker was a reminder of this. On 14 February 1991 two American bombs had killed 408 civilians, mainly women and children. A small group of us were taken to the bunker and we talked to a survivor. I spent a long time looking at the photographs of those killed. Whole families were burnt or blasted to death. Long lines of haunting portraits of children reminded me of similar photographs in the Yad Vashem Holocaust museum in Israel.

I visited Baghdad's imposing 'Mother of All Battles' mosque which was begun in 1998 and was still not fully completed. The minarets were modelled on Scud missiles and their launchers, future targets perhaps for an American general with a sense of irony. The imam was in full flow. From the distorted tone of the blaring external loudspeakers, he sounded as if were launching a personal *jihad*. I went inside to listen and discovered he was preaching about good relations within marriage.

Our small clutch of hacks was really there to get an interview with the top dog himself; instead we were promised access to Tariz Aziz, the deputy prime minister. We waited around all day at the hotel.

At least Iraq was a Muslim country with a taste for beer, not least in the Al-Rashid. I spent a long time talking to Yvonne Ridley, the journalist who had famously gone from captive to convert after she was briefly imprisoned by the Taliban in 2001. She had not yet actually converted so we drank and smoked together. Like St Augustine, presumably she had said: 'Lord, make me chaste, but not yet.' She told me about her good treatment in Afghan captivity, and that she had promised her captors that she would read the Koran on her release – which she did. She also recounted her time in the Territorial Army and her three husbands. One had been in the British police, the second worked for PLO intelligence, and the third in Mossad. She said she had no idea that the last two were spooks until after she'd split up with them.

'C'mon, Yvonne, you must have had some idea.'

'No, absolutely none at all.'

'Then it shows what an ace investigative journalist you are.'

She laughed generously and she gave me a signed copy of her book on the Afghan saga. I reciprocated with one of my books, and inscribed it, adding 'Major, Free Wales Army Intelligence Corps, in case you hadn't worked it out'. (Yvonne later converted and married a Muslim; she hosted a number of TV programmes on various Islamic channels. She was gracious enough to forgive my jibe and invited me regularly on to her shows.)

After a number of false starts, finally we were ushered into a fleet of Mercedes to journey to a palatial building owned by the ruling Ba'ath party.

I asked Saddam's deputy about Israel; the Iraqis called it 'the Zionist entity'. 'Would Iraq hit Israel again if war comes?'

'We will fight only in our homeland,' he said.

Tariq Aziz explained that, just before the 1991 Gulf War, US Secretary of State James Baker had warned him that America would reduce Iraq to a pre-industrial state, and it would get rid of its leadership. 'Then Baker asked me if I would attack Israel. I said: "Absolutely, yes."'

'And this time?' I asked.

'That's a meaningless question. Now we don't have long-range missiles.'

Actually, I thought it a vital question, because a number of Israeli generals had told me personally that if Iraq were to hit them with WMD, they would retaliate in kind . . .'even if there wasn't a single Israeli casualty'.

Aziz then appealed to Britain to restore normal relations. 'We had a dispute in 1972, but this was settled peacefully . . . I personally met

Mrs Thatcher in the 1980s. Why should Mr Blair want war with Iraq?' Saddam's deputy again insisted that Iraq did not have any WMD. 'The Americans know that. They are only using this as a pretext.'

I was convinced he was lying. I was soon to be proved wrong.

The Iraq war

In early 2003, a coalition of the willing was assembled to fight Iraq. Veteran correspondent Martin Bell was succinct: 'To call them a coalition was a supine use of language.' Active members comprised the US, Britain, Australia and Poland. Unlike 1991, no Arab states contributed, and no clear-cut UN resolution authorised the invasion. The US-led onslaught was a military masterpiece. The *Blitzkrieg Lite* worked, the *Occupation Lite* did not. If the big mistake in Afghanistan was to target the opium crop, the glue of the economy, then the equivalent in Iraq was to demobilise the Iraqi army. Throwing tens of thousands of angry armed young men out of a job was a surefire recipe for insurrection.

The Brits knew that, so did the US State Department, but the Pentagon wasn't listening. I had been doing quite a bit of media punditry during the lead-up to the war, and my old ministry had occasionally briefed me. The Brits seemed to think that the Iraqi top brass would depose Saddam at the start of the war, and so the army, instead of melting away or being demobilised by the US, would keep order. Instead, a security vacuum was created, and years of nasty sectarian civil war and terrorism soon filled it.

I had wanted to be 'embedded' with the military as a correspondent; instead, an MoD mandarin – by chance a member of the Whitehall Taffia – asked me, 'Would you like to return to the colours?' I had not planned on again rejoining the ministry but my alleged expertise in 'media ops' was deemed useful. Besides, the magazine company I worked for had just gone bust, after bouncing my pay cheques. I could serve my country and my bank balance, as well as get close to the action. So I said yes.

It was strange to be back at my old desk in Whitehall, and with the same phone number. I was greeted warmly by former colleagues as a repentant sinner returning to the fold. I could, however, no longer write or broadcast on what was happening around me. That was a fair exchange for being at the centre of war planning. Nevertheless, I became frustrated with flying a desk, and was soon agitating to be sent to Iraq.

I did the compulsory pre-operation training. This included rapid donning of a chemical and biological (CBW) suit. The sergeant had despaired at my clumsy, and dangerously slow, cross-dressing from scruffy civvie to smart nuclear-age combatant. And we also had to be briefed by ex-special force instructors in how to resist interrogation, should we be captured.

I had originally been posted to too-safe Doha, but I wangled my way into Kuwait. Since I was now no longer a free agent, I could genuinely blame Whitehall for my missing the first push into Iraq.

It was now early May, and I spent my last weekend at home. I told a virulently anti-war girlfriend that I was working in my riverside garden.

'You are more likely to find WMD there than in Iraq,' she said tartly. 'Besides,' she added, 'I'm sure six months or so in Iraq will provide a healthy break in our relationship.'

No warrior-off-to-war empathy from her then.

I staggered off to war, barely able to carry my Bergen which was two-thirds full of CBW kit, and not in the best of spirits.

I flew from RAF Brize Norton in a venerable VC-10: 'one of the newest in the fleet', I was told. After the inevitable RAF delays, I reached Kuwait for an induction session, and then drove across the desert to Basra.

I received an excellent breakfast in the British base at Basra International Airport. It was well organised, even palatial. Again, a charming female officer took me under her wing. 'I've been in theatre three months,' she said. 'As far as accommodation is concerned, I've gone from sand, to gravel and to marble here in Basra.' Another Brit base was literally all marble – Saddam's riverside palace. The general squalor in Basra contrasted with the luxury of Saddam's lifestyle.

I moved from the airport to a small outpost twenty miles away at Az Zubayr and stayed in the Duke of Wellington Regiment's mess. Needless to say the 'Dukes' were much taller than me. I had a device similar to a domestic hot-water bottle which you left in the sun, and which heated up solar panels to provide hot water. The problem was I couldn't reach the rail in the makeshift shower to hang my bottle over. And the shower itself was next to an open sewer. I tried using a broom handle to hoist my bottle, but in the darkness I almost tipped into the sewer. The batteries in the torch attached to my head, like a small miner's lamp, had run down.

I despaired of showering, and instead used my small amount of water to try to clean my teeth. In my wash bag, I had two tubes, one of Euthymol toothpaste and the other containing a tube of Preparation H, pile cream which was commonly used in the extreme heat and sand-in-the-arse-and-everywhere environment.

In the dark, I mixed them up.

And then rushed to the mess to scrounge a soft drink to get rid of the acrid taste.

The colonel commented thus on my predicament: 'Your teeth may not have stopped itching, but at least your arse should be gleaming white.'

That night I slept very badly after trying to set up my mosquito net properly, and then realising that a scorpion the size of a small rat had occupied my small camp-bed. Without my light I had trouble finding it. I banged around in mild panic, waking my MoD photographer colleague, Allan, who'd had the good sense to have installed fresh batteries in his torch. The scorpion scuttled off like the creature in *Alien*.

I was not at my best when I jumped on the open Land Rover to go on patrol early the next morning, though my widely disseminated Preparation H story did pep up the squaddies' morale. I was hardly living up to the leadership qualities I had tried to engender when I was a Sandhurst instructor so many years before.

The Dukes had served recently in Northern Ireland and Kosovo and were swiftly adapting to their peacekeeping roles. A lieutenant on my patrol pointed out the pressing issues: 'No water, no electricity, no schools, no sanitation, and widespread looting'.

The lieutenant said that, despite the local shortages, some of the villagers had offered food to his patrols, especially fresh fruit. 'They saw us eating our army rations and assumed we were starving. Maybe they did have a point.' He also explained that everyone had weapons. 'It's the Arab gun culture.'

The Brits were trying to introduce gun permits, a rather thankless task. They would confiscate weapons unless the owner had a 'weapons authorisation card'. They had used the same system in Kosovo, another gun-happy culture.

As I had recently witnessed in Afghanistan, here too British troops were busy trying to get schools functioning. 'The Ba'athists', I was told, 'had lots of caches of weapons in the schools. A little girl had been playing with an Iraqi bomblet and had been killed. Unexploded ordnance is a major issue.'

Presumably a lot of it also had been stamped 'Made in US'.

The Brits were endeavouring to get the local councils up and running. The Arab elders' constant complaint was lack of jobs. The British army, now controlling an area in southern Iraq half the size of England, did not have much money for nation-building. The Americans did, but getting money from their HQ in Baghdad was difficult. In short, the British were trying to do a great deal in Iraq with little money and far too few troops. The best analysis of this dilemma can be found in Rory Stewart's tragi-comic memoir *Occupational Hazards*. Stewart looked like a naughty public schoolboy, but he ran a small empire. The resourceful ex-officer-turned-diplomat struggled to manage the political side of the occupation of Maysan province and later Dhi Qar. It was the Raj revisited.

I was constantly told by the Dukes' officers that their earlier experience, especially in the Balkans, had enabled them to do far more than the Americans with precious few resources. But their 'quick-impact' projects were mere 'band-aids'.

Nevertheless, optimism was the official line. They expected to stay for just a year, or perhaps two. One officer told me: 'People think Iraq is broken. It's not. It just needs a bloody good service.'

Relations with the locals were good. The troops patrolled in soft hats and no Ray-Bans. Wandering around markets in Basra – though this time I had to be self-disciplined enough not to sneak off on my own – the natives responded mostly in a hospitable and generous manner. Some moaned about the lack of electricity and water, and a few deliberately pointed to posters of Iranian-backed Shia clerics. I sensed, however, that sectarian fervour rather than fluffy-bunny hearts and minds would shape the occupation as it soon outstayed its welcome.

I also spent time with the Royal Military Police, who were trying to curb the looting, and impounding all the many stolen vehicles. Cars were plentiful in a land where petrol was cheaper than water. 'We need a proper penal system and a judiciary,' I was frequently told. 'Where do we put all the criminals that we arrest? Saddam had released all the prisoners.' The RMP were busy reopening police stations and training the woefully equipped local police.

In the Dukes' mess I fell into conversation with an impressive army chaplain, Patrick Aldred. I heard a familiar refrain: 'The younger guys come out as teenagers and return to the UK as men.'

Compared with sparse church attendance at bases in Germany or England, he was overstretched providing communion and services to packed congregations. 'Where there's hurt and pain, that's where you find Christ,' the Methodist minister explained to me. 'If Christ were anywhere he would be on the battlefield.'

Pat Aldred was not much taken by my argument that God shouldn't take sides in wars.

'Much of my work is pastoral . . . They like the idea that God's looking after them.' The padre took charge of lots of farewell letters and weddings rings. 'That hasn't changed since the First World War.'

He added: 'Despite the high-tech battlefield, the guys want you to pray with them, and to say the Lord's Prayer.'

I kept asking officers if they had got wind of any WMD. I always received politely evasive answers. Perhaps to shut me up, I was taken to various sites of probable mass graves of Saddam's Shia opponents, and also to vast hangars where the remains of the dead from the Iran–Iraq war were housed. No doubt Saddam was a very nasty bastard, but had he possessed WMD?

I met a senior officer who had been on a military visit I made to the Ukraine in 2000. He reminded me of a small diplomatic function I had attended with the British ambassador in Kiev. I was not used to large slugs of vodka to accompany toasts, and so became a trifle disruptive. I was sitting opposite a member of the British Royal family, and we light-heartedly discussed music. Naturally I mentioned my minor obsession with Del Shannon, a 1960s rock singer. There was a polite response so I immediately offered to voice a short medley of Shannon's hits.

The Royal was in full dress uniform, but did not stand on ceremony. He said simply: "Can you sing Have You Got a Light, Boy?"

'I can and will, if you join in the chorus.'

I immediately stood up, tapped my glass with a spoon, and declared that I would sing by royal request. I shall never forget the ambassador's agonised expression. It was as though I had asked Dracula to sell his coffin.

I started to sing the song, in the dialect and lisp of the original ditty by the 'Singing Postman', Alan Smethurst. I was sober enough to realise that if the Royal did not join in the chorus, my little act would fall completely flat.

Luckily, he stood to attention and we sang the chorus together, loudly and lustily. I had been saved from obloquy, and made a new friend.

But the now commanding officer in my part of Iraq must have thought I had previous form as a troublemaker, confirmed by my current enquiries about WMD. I found myself transferred back to Basra airport.

Here I slept in one of the massed array of bunk beds, using the luggage carousel to stow my kit. I bumped into hacks from *The Times*, *Telegraph* and the affable and able Matthew Hickley, the *Mail*'s defence correspondent. They were having hassles with the media ops staff, which I tried to smooth over. Some of the correspondents wanted to leave the protective cover of the army facility and go off on their own, to investigate accusations of British war crimes. The general rule was: leave the facility and you don't come back.

I was inclined to hang around the airport because the canteen food was excellent, but I was tasked to visit Shaibah, the site of the 202 Field Hospital, and which had nothing to do with refuelling on Preparation H. Despite the searing wind and the sand, to my non-medical eye, the standard of treatment, for soldiers, local Iraqis and Iraqi POWs, was very impressive, and better than the often tawdry NHS experience at home. I spent a lot of time recording the largely positive comments of the patients. Outside, the Americans had put up a mobile Pizza Hut – that also affirmed my good opinion of the tented hospital.

I moved to Iraq's main port, Um Qasr, the first objective of coalition troops in the initial invasion. The allies were busy getting the facilities to work to Western standards. I was surprised to see that the Brits, with US help, had managed to get some trains working, including an old-fashioned set of Orient Express-type passenger carriages.

I told the British army engineers that since they had got the war-ravaged Iraqi railways operating so quickly, they should turn their attention to the South-West network running into London's

Waterloo . . . but only after the RAF had bombed the hell out of the existing third-world infrastructure. I also fantasised about US electronic warfare equipment wiping out signals to those morons, in the so-called quiet carriages, who used mobiles – the ghetto-blasters of the middle class.

I visited the media ops team in the port, and was briefed by the TA Captain there, Emma Welch, a smart PR lady in civvie street who walked like a Paris model, even in her camo. She foolishly admitted to a weakness for Welshmen, because her previous boyfriend had been a scion of the Brains brewery family in Cardiff. Despite my being short, and certainly short of a brewery or two, Emma helped me with all sorts of useful introductions. Since I wasn't going to find any WMD, I wanted to chase up the next big issue – shortage of kit for the fighting men.

I was allowed into the container that housed the MoD logistics team. In the terrible heat of this tin can a small group of very ordinary civil servants from the Defence Logistics Organisation was doing a very extraordinary job, keeping a large army of troops, and their prisoners, supplied. Like the military, the civvies worked long hours seven days a week, with little or no booze and very little communication with their families at home.

The Brits, both in uniform and the MoD civilians, were showing true grit, endurance and ingenuity, but they were grossly under-resourced. Many troops still had heavy-duty black boots and camouflage designed for European winter warfare, not the Iraqi desert. The logistics people tried to procure locally, mainly from Kuwait, but they ended up as self-confessed characters in the 1992 TV movie *The Borrowers*.

One senior civil servant admitted: 'The Americans have everything. We are always scrounging. It shows we just don't have the proper resourcing.'

It required stamina to keep going day after day, week after week, in the heat, even if no one was shooting at you. For the umpteenth time, I admired the military, and came to despise the Treasury's tight-fisted treatment of the forces that the politicians, in their cosy Westminster cocoon, sent to war, without the tools to do the job. Brit soldiers were still lions, but resourced by dinosaurs.

I had been in theatre for a very short time, but I was completely knackered. Emma kindly drove me to the military airport in Kuwait. On the drive we talked about media ops, and I mentioned my problem with keeping some of my colleagues tied to their programme. One journalist had already been flown home on a ventilator machine, with a full medical team, suffering from heat exhaustion.

'Bad idea to lose a journalist on a trip,' Emma said. 'And the trouble is, Whitehall might then stop people coming out.'

'Some inexperienced hacks lack common sense,' I said, 'not least about constantly rehydrating with lots of water in the desert. Generally, the military supply sufficient water bottles to their guests.'

'You can't treat journalists like kids.'

'Ah,' I replied, 'Rule Number One in dealing with hacks: *don't* treat them like grown-ups.'

At the airport, I relished the chance to eat in the super-abundant American fast-food canteen. The departure tent, just before the X-ray machines, hosted the standard 'amnesty bin' for illegal military souvenirs. Next to the bin was a very long vet's glove beneath a sign stating: 'We do internals.' Though why anybody would want to stick a grenade or AK up their backside quite eluded me.

Back in Whitehall, I worked out my last month partly dealing with the fall-out from the suicide of Dr David Kelly. He was the weapons expert who had become embroiled in the alleged 'sexing up' of WMD intelligence to get Britain into the war. I felt that Kelly had been scapegoated by the MoD, though I did not buy into the allegations that he had been murdered by his own side. On the last day at MoD Main Building I worked late on a press release about Kelly. I left with a sour taste in my mouth about the scientist, who had served the ministry with distinction. I was returning to the world of free speech, but I decided that I would keep my views on the Kelly scandal to myself.

I spent much of the next year, 2003–2004, immersing myself in what the Americans had dubbed 'homeland security', partly because I became the founding editor of *Resilience* magazine. It didn't prove to be very resilient because it ceased publication after a few issues. Nevertheless, I got to speak to lots of people in the emergency services to see how prepared they were for al-Qaeda doing to London what it had done to New York and Washington.

One of my favourite writers, Rod Liddle, in one of my favourite mags, *The Spectator*, wrote a feature lambasting me and *Resilience*, saying it was all hot air. He lampooned particularly my concerns with

Islamist attacks on European trains. The day after his article was published, the Jihadists hit the trains in Madrid. *The Spectator* had the good grace to print my response the following week, outlining my frank views on one of the most egregious mistimings in modern journalism.

We published other more successful and more durable magazines, particularly a niche journal on CBRN (Chemical, Radiological, Biological, Nuclear), edited by my friend Gwyn Winfield. I hoped that our previous prescience would not materialise in a chemical or biological attack in the UK. After the 7 July 2005 bombings in London, the next threshold was a dirty bomb. It might not kill many people, but it would be a weapon of mass effect, the contamination doing untold economic damage to the City – even more than the bankers themselves would do later.

I continued to be a gadfly about a whole range of foreign security issues, including the question of coalition cluster bombs in Iraq, as well as human rights issues of the occupation. I also continued to question the other occupation in Afghanistan.

The main premise of the 2003 Iraq war was the presence of WMD; when it became clear, even in Washington, that none were going to be found, I rang up George Galloway, the sole Respect MP in Parliament.

'George, I apologise for arguing with you about WMD. I was wrong, and you were right. And I promised to eat my hat if there were no WMD. Would you give me a choice of custard or cream on it?'

'Paul, you are the only person who has rung up to admit they were wrong. I appreciate that.'

And I appreciated that he didn't press me for the penitential lunch.

I made two big mistakes in my journalism career. After my first long interview with him in 1980, I thought that Robert Mugabe was a genuine conciliator; instead he became an archetypal African dictator. Secondly, I believed that Saddam had WMD. I was glad that he had been toppled, but I spent a long time anguishing about the occupation fiasco.

Typically, Martin Bell put his finger on the 2003 war: 'The United States and Britain didn't make a coalition, but a gang of two, a latter-day Don Quixote and Sancho Panza, armed and dangerous and tilting at oil fields.'

Iraq had failed the reality test: it possessed no WMD and no link with al-Qaeda. Doing away with Saddam may have benefited Iraqis but it was also a major diversion in the fight against al-Qaeda. It had been a propaganda gift, and a syndicated training manual, for the Jihadists.

By the mid-noughties, all three components of the so-called Axis of Evil – Iraq, Iran and North Korea – were more dangerous than when the phrase was coined in 2002. Worse, the US, and the West, had lost the war of ideas, and the high moral ground after Abu Ghraib, which were the most potent weapons in the face of the nihilism of Islamic extremism. It was not until Barack Obama replaced George Bush that Washington began to relearn the lessons of the Cold War: the need for alliances, not least in Europe; economic and cultural engagement; and subtle diplomacy, especially with Iran and Syria, keys to a semblance of an orderly withdrawal from Iraq. Luckily, Britain declared victory and extricated nearly all its troops in early 2009. Exiting Afghanistan would be much tougher.

AFRICA IV

15. MORE AFRICAN TURMOIL

Return to Sudan

After 9/11, and the war in Afghanistan, Sudan thought it was next in line. The US had, after all, been providing aid to the southern rebels for years. American hostility had reached a climax in 1998 when President Bill Clinton authorised a cruise missile attack on the al-Shifa pharmaceutical plant in Khartoum. Washington soon realised that this was a massive intelligence error, but it didn't bother to apologise.

Sudan launched a successful PR blitz in the West to avoid being another victim of the war on terror. Critics of the Islamic regime, however, insisted that this was not so much a charm offensive as a form of diplomatic deterrence by a very manipulative government in Khartoum. Whatever it was, it worked. The Sudanese attempts to hand bin Laden over to the Clinton administration, and its repeated attempts from 1996 onwards to cooperate with Washington on counter-terrorism issues and warnings about al-Qaeda, were leaked to a British newspaper and then became the subject of a devastating article in *Vanity Fair*, a magazine read by Congressmen, their wives and mistresses. This article, which appeared in late 2001, was ruthlessly exploited by the Bush administration and its supporters to deflect any criticism regarding 9/11 on to the Clinton crew. They had a point and Sudan was probably off the 'who's next after Afghanistan?' list.

Khartoum desperately wanted peace with the US, and with the southern insurgents, who were still waging the longest-running war on the continent. Khartoum needed stability to exploit its new oil bonanza. UN and EU sanctions were dropped; America kept its restrictions in place. Behind the scenes, the US – supported by the British and the Norwegians – had backed a series of peace talks in Kenya, to end the north–south civil war in Sudan. The principles of the agreement were that the south could have autonomy for six years to be followed by a referendum on secession. Oil wealth and the jobs this created were to be shared equitably. Sharia law, though, was to remain in the north. Its imposition in the south had been a major factor in firing up the rebellion among the Christian and animist communities.

Khartoum also upped the volume of intelligence cooperation with Washington, especially regarding al-Qaeda. In the immediate aftermath of 9/11 Washington was understandably obsessed by Osama bin Laden, and his long connection with Sudan (he had lived there for five years before being kicked out in 1996). I also had a major interest in the Sudan connection and so went back to Khartoum in January 2002.

The Sudanese government line was that bin Laden was involved in purely civil engineering and charity projects. I talked to the al-Qaeda chief's friends and acquaintances to check this out. Nobody had a bad word to say about him. Even his travel agent bemoaned his departure: 'He used to pay promptly with his American Express gold card; lost good business there.'

I visited his former houses, had a look at his damaged private jet, and enquired further with those who worked on his engineering projects. Bin Laden was fascinated by heavy plant, one engineer told me. 'And he always asked after my children. He was very polite and kind.'

I suppose even Saddam Hussein had his good days.

According to one Sudanese government minister who knew him well, bin Laden was 'very angry'. 'The Saudis and the US didn't even pay you – you are throwing me out for nothing,' the warlord said.

The embittered bin Laden returned to Afghanistan. Denied an opportunity to engage in more constructive enterprises, he turned to terrorism. Again this is the official Sudanese line. Western intelligence sources indicated, however, that bin Laden was politically active in Sudan, coordinating what became the al-Qaeda network.

I had learned the hard way, over many years, that to secure real access and to get anything done in authoritarian states you had to deal directly with intelligence, often military intelligence, because the military was often the only national organisation that vaguely worked.

My first visit was to Major General Yahia Hussein Babiker, whose role was equivalent to the deputy head of the British MI6. In the intelligence HQ, sitting in a deep grey-green leather seat, he speculated that the probability of another US attack was 'low', but 'suitable preparations' had been made. As the very articulate intelligence boss was conducting his personal briefing, a TV screen to his side was displaying an American NBC news programme with a prominent map of the world's counter-terror targets, which included Sudan.

I paid a call to the overall head of the powerful *Mukhabarat*, Sudanese intelligence. Lieutenant General Gutbi al-Mahdi said this: 'When bin Laden was here he was under surveillance. We were watching him. He was busy. He was preoccupied with his business. Kicking him out [because of US pressure] was a mistake.' Bin Laden was also being monitored in Sudan by Western intelligence agencies. In Afghanistan nobody could keep an eye on him. This miscalculation led directly to 9/11, argued the General.

The Sudanese head spook also insisted that Khartoum had offered in 1996 to hand bin Laden over to the Americans, just as Sudan had handed over Carlos the Jackal to the French. Later, some Western intelligence experts argued that Khartoum was too implicated in the embryonic al-Qaeda ever to donate the warlord to the CIA. Elements in the CIA were prepared to take Khartoum at its word, however. Others in the US State Department maintained that there was not sufficient evidence to convict bin Laden in US courts, and that the Sudanese offer was a bluff. Moreover, the intelligence dialogue would weaken the sanctions pressure on a rogue Islamist state that Washington was trying to isolate.

To me it seemed a very basic issue: if Khartoum was prepared to hand bin Laden on a platter to the US or UK agencies, then why bloody not take up the offer? I pressed this question later in Whitehall. One senior FCO man warned me that the Sudanese were not as open as they pretended. 'They have skeletons in the cupboard and they don't want us to get too close.'

A CIA official was more blunt. He told me: 'Do you really think we would turn down any information on bin Laden, especially from an organisation like the *Mukhabarat*? It just doesn't make sense to say no.'

The US ambassador to Sudan at the time, Tim Carney, described it as 'at best a fuck-up'. And I had to agree with him. Bill Clinton, after he left office, publicly confessed that the refusal to take up the bin Laden offer was the 'biggest mistake' of his presidency.

Whether the Sudanese government would have really handed over bin Laden in 1996 remains an open question. Khartoum would have been condemned by the Islamic world, but the Sudanese might just have done it in return for the lifting of its pariah status. At the very least, advance warning of bin Laden's ejection could have provided an opportunity for an American special operation.

The General kept patting four stacks of dusty files on his desk. 'These are some of the al-Qaeda files,' he said. 'You are welcome to examine them.' He gestured with an open right hand.

I felt obliged to take one from the top of the pile nearest me. I flicked through it with apparent concentration and returned the Arabic documents. I had a feeling that General al-Mahdi was not about to let me take some of the files home with me, not least to get a proper translation.

The General told me that the Americans were very slow in taking up the Sudanese offer, post-9/11, to examine the files, which had detailed CVs, and photographs, of many al-Qaeda operatives. Eventually, the CIA took copies and air-lifted them back to the US. That was a full month after 9/11.

The Brits were even more tardy. MI6 was very sniffy about dealing with Khartoum, but other UK intelligence agencies realised, in 2002, that they needed to beef up their resources to hunt for Islamic extremists based in England. Perhaps the unofficial Sudanese jibe to the Americans – 'if you want to bomb a country with Islamic terrorists you should try hitting London, or Saudi Arabia' – had finally found its mark.

While at the Khartoum Hilton, I happened to bump into Clare Short, the British Minister for International Development. She gave me a short interview, in which she was typically direct. But what impressed me about her was her good relationship with the civil servants accompanying her. Many ministers behave with hauteur even to senior Whitehall staff. Clare, in contrast, gave her press officer a friendly hug. The warmth was obviously reciprocated.

I also chased up a Canadian diplomat who was said to have detailed knowledge about bin Laden's long holiday in sunny Sudan. He did know a lot about the warlord. So I said: 'There have been sightings of Osama recently in Sudan.'

'Yes,' he said. 'I can confirm there have been a number of sightings – about the same number of claimed sightings of Elvis.'

*

President Omar al-Bashir's government remained a thinly veiled junta, though Khartoum was trying to modify its military and fundamentalist image. I was invited to meet the reclusive defence minister, General Bakri Hassan Saleh, a towering man sporting imposing sunglasses indoors. In his first ever media interview with a foreign journalist, he told me: 'Oil does allow us extra revenues which permits some modernisation, but if we modernise we are accused of militarism.' He explained how the US had at different times supported military incursions from a variety of the nine countries surrounding Sudan. And helicopters were needed to guard the pipelines, he added. It was true that some of Sudan's neighbours had provided brigade-level fully armoured forces to support the Sudan People's Liberation Army in the south.

Peace to exploit the oil and political reforms to counter its pariah status were the main pillars of Khartoum's image-building. This was the theme of the interview the Sudanese president gave to me and Dr Bob Arnot. Bob was a medical doctor who had become a nationwide TV presenter in the US, subsequently perhaps best-known for his *Doctor Danger* series. Bob had gigantic charm and intellect, but the attention span of a gnat; he was very instructive company if you could manage to distract him for more than a few minutes. Bob did focus on Bashir, deploying his linguistic skills in Arabic, while I felt I had to rely on a translator, always less effective. The presidential interview was amiable, but inconsequential. Still, a presidential audience was always useful in opening doors elsewhere.

The President talked of the economic advances. Government statistics – although Sudan was usually a twilight zone for hard facts – claimed that the country was enjoying an 8 per cent rise in its GDP. Khartoum's streets had been almost deserted on my first visit, now traffic jams were common. The boom in luxury cars, mobile phones, property and construction was evidence of the new prosperity, at least in the capital. US sanctions remained in place, but now Sudan was cosying up to China. Sudan provided the oil and in turn China supplied all sorts of nice things in exchange, not least of which were arms.

Domestic American lobby groups often influenced US policy rather more than Sudanese realities, as Washington vacillated between constructive engagement and imposing isolation, between military assault and wanting to share in the oil bonanza. Washington, however, did play a vital role in organising a ceasefire in the war in the south, and helped to defuse disputes with Sudan's neighbours. Diplomats and intelligence agencies were focused on the north–south peace deal which was eventually signed in Naivasha, Kenya, in early 2005. This was one of the untrumpeted achievements of the Bush administration – bringing the north and south together. After decades of broken agreements, both sides instinctively distrusted each other. The two regions were very different: in terrain, culture, religion and ethnicity. 'How can those with turbans on their heads have peace with those who wear ostrich feathers,' joked President Yoweri Museveni of Uganda, in a lively breach of political correctness.

Good news, for once, was breaking out in Sudan. Peace came to the south, at last, although the settlement could easily be derailed. Tragically, a major insurrection had been launched in western Sudan, in Darfur. Like the proverbial moth to the flame, I would soon become a regular visitor to this inhospitable area, the size of France, or, for American readers, Texas.

Darfur

The British conquered the Sultanate of Darfur during the First World War. A senior Khartoum minister once told me: 'Actually you British caused the problem – you separated north and south when you ruled Sudan; and you, by accident, sowed the seeds of conflict in Darfur when you didn't give the settled land-rights to some of the nomadic herders when you took over in 1916.'

Funny that, wherever I travelled in the world, the Brits, and therefore me, would get it in the neck for imperial misdeeds – even more funny given that I'm from England's first colony, Wales, first in and yet to leave.

Intermittent fighting had broken out in Darfur since 1916, mainly caused by drought and inter-tribal disputes. In February 2003, however, full-scale modern warfare disrupted the optimism engendered by the increasingly successful north–south peace talks in Kenya. The complex war in Darfur was distinct from but also related to the war in the south. The first 2,000 Darfur rebels were trained by the SPLA, who clearly wished to see more pressure applied to the Khartoum authorities even as they negotiated with them. The Darfur conflict was tribal and political, but it was not racial. It was not Arab versus African, not Omar Sharif versus Kunta Kinte, the hero of *Roots*. Intermarriage usually made it impossible to physically differentiate 'African' from 'Arab' among the thirty-five tribes and ethnic groups, which could also be roughly categorised as either nomadic herders or sedentary farming communities.

Alex de Waal, a critic of Khartoum and probably the leading Western expert on the region, wrote: 'Characterizing the Darfur war as "Arabs" versus "Africans" obscures the reality. Darfur's Arabs are black, indigenous, African Muslims – just like Darfur's non-Arabs.'

I ended up travelling in various parts of Darfur and frequently challenged the locals as to whether they could identify a Darfurian stranger as 'Arab' or 'African'. They nearly always got it wrong. Often darker-skinned Darfurians turned out to be Arabs, while the lighter locals often claimed to be African. The only difference I could see was that some 'Africans' could speak an African language as well as Arabic.

While the historical conflict between Arabs versus Africans has been a recurring theme of Sudanese history, it would be wrong to assume that the Arabs were always the victors and the Africans the victims, especially in Darfur.

Ten years after the Rwandan massacres, the US State Department dubbed the tragedy in Darfur a 'genocide'. Figures varied dramatically, but hundreds of thousands were killed and millions displaced; both sides committed atrocities. Kofi Annan, then UN Secretary General, contradicted US claims when he said: 'I cannot call the killing a genocide even though there have been massive violations of international humanitarian law.'

It is true that Africans – if that term can be used – were in a majority among the displaced, and most of them would say they had fled attacks by the *Janjaweed*, a generic term for bandits, but often also applied to pro-government militias. But there were also displaced 'Arab' communities who were attacked by 'African' groups. Besides inter-'African' ethnic fighting, in parts of South Darfur, for example, the World Food Programme could not work because of highly charged traditional conflicts between rival 'Arab' groups.

I did say that Darfur was complicated.

Darfur's catastrophe also was caused by factors associated with climate change: the desertification of the Sahel. In this sense, it became perhaps the first environmental war of the twenty-first century. The crisis also had roots in old-fashioned warfare. A government scorched-earth policy had destroyed many 'African' villages, thus draining the Maoist-style sea, to prevent the rebels from operating. Soon after February 2003, following surprise rebel attacks, Sudan's intelligence services initially had free rein to operate in Darfur, and the military and their various militias went in very hard.

The rebels – and by 2009 there were at least twenty groups, although the Justice and Equality Movement (JEM) was the most cohesive – claimed that Khartoum had marginalised the three Darfur states (despite recent improvements in transport, education and physical infrastructure). Factions in Chad, often tribally linked, also meddled across the border; equally, Khartoum stirred the pot in Chad. A fratricidal factor was the intimate civil war within the Islamist revolutionaries in Khartoum. Elements loyal to Hasan al-Turabi had formed JEM. Although US intelligence was rightly concerned about the growth of *jihad* in the Sahel – a soft underbelly of both pro-Western North African states and Europe itself – the alleged al-Qaeda connections with JEM had been overdone.

In essence, the Darfur insurgents had seen what was on offer to the southerners – especially oil dividends, jobs and autonomy – and they wanted some of the same goodies too. When the emergency feeding programmes had reached a reasonable level of stabilisation, the rebels – by attacking aid convoys – sought to use famine as a means of concentrating more international pressure on Khartoum. The African Union sent in a small number of peacekeepers, backed by a handful of EU observers, but the rebels wanted to provoke a much larger foreign military intervention.

Historically, Sudanese government forces would intervene to settle the tribal and nomad-versus-pastoralist battles. Formerly, Khartoum was seen as a referee, but now the government had become a prime, and sometimes brutal, antagonist. While the rebels called for more African Union and then UN intervention, Khartoum said no, arguing that Western intervention in another oil-rich Islamic state could create chaos, drawing in Jihadist crazies from A–Z, Algeria to Zanzibar. Sudan was often portrayed as a tough authoritarian state, but the continuous warfare in the south, then the west and also in the east, threatened state implosion, possibly replicating Somalia.

*

My first visit to Darfur was in late 2004. After much permit-chasing in Khartoum, I caught an internal flight to El Fasher, capital of North Darfur. If I had moaned about no beer in the Hilton, run-down El Fasher had no hotel, not much at all in fact, except lots of donkeys, and plastic bags adorning urban scrubland. I was travelling with my old mate Irwin Armstrong, but we soon fell in with other friends: Sam Dealey, a young correspondent from Washington, Pieter Tesch, a small Dutchman with a big beard who wrote for Irish papers, and David Hoile, also half-Dutch. I had first come across David in Mozambique. He was now a public affairs consultant specialising in Sudan, working for corporate clients and the Khartoum government. He had made a name for himself as a deconstructionist of media coverage of Darfur. Together we managed to find a sleazy couple of spare rooms in an Arab household. Facilities were minimal, although running water was available.

Irwin, David, Pieter and I managed to forage for some basics in the market, buying bread and tinned cheese, and we had some jam hijacked from the Hilton. Sam didn't seem interested in shopping for food. We soon discovered why. He had brought commercial camping food based originally on US army ration packs. They were clever – all you had to do was rip the top off and tilt the package and it would heat up, giving off delicious aromas. The recipes were pretty fancy too. Sam enthused about US ingenuity, and his foresight in bringing these packs. Worse, he sat there eating his packs every evening, while savouring, and commenting, on their delights. He even offered a spoonful so that we could agree with him. We politely declined of course, despite our rumbling stomachs.

We all thought that this was a damn poor performance. I would have shared the packs, equally, and without hesitation. Sam was an extremely charming, properly brought-up and well-mannered Texan, but he didn't seem to pick up on our annoyance. I put it down to his relative inexperience in war zones; here you share your food as though it were your last meal, because it damn well might be.

When we got back to Europe, and after we had become good friends, I told Sam about his error of protocol.

'You were all old Africa hands, so you should have come better prepared,' he said with conviction.

Food and footwear are two compelling issues in war reporting, but so is transport. We hired a white 4x4 and driver the first day.

Luckily the van was similar to the vehicles used by the African Union peacekeepers. I found out from a friendly South African soldier what time the convoy was leaving the next day for the rebel-held areas. On time, it left the AU base, and we tucked in to the end of it. Except for the lack of a big AU sign we looked official. So we sped through the government roadblocks and then through the Sudan Liberation Army (SLA) blockades to enter rebel territory.

After much rough cross-country travel, we reached Debed, the site of a recent air attack by government forces. I managed to find a villager who was a former English teacher; he recounted the details and deaths. Irwin filmed the burnt-out huts. And then I interviewed a loquacious Swedish army major, acting as an EU observer. We also filmed the SLA fighters, with dashing turbans and sunglasses, and all festooned in amulets which they believed made enemy bullets turn to water. Enduring various rough rides, and punctures, we made various forays into the unforgiving desert scrub around El Fasher. We filmed government-held villages such as Tawila, and later the camps for the IDPs (Internally Displaced Persons) squatting around the dusty capital. Sam was busy digging out accounts of rape by the *Janjaweed*, the theme of his story for *Time* magazine.

We also talked to NGOs. I found the most illuminating official to be Neils Scott, of the UN Office for the Coordination of Humanitarian Affairs. At his HQ he told us about the *Janjaweed* – literally the devils on horseback. 'The *Janjaweed* is historical,' he said. 'It's been around for years. What we're seeing now is, to a great extent, criminality . . .We're in a bandaging situation. What we need here is a political solution.'

That soon become my dominant impression too.

Most of our time was taken up with politics and the tragedy of the refugees. Irwin and I went into the big camps around El Fasher and filmed detailed life stories about the disruption of old traditional ways, of murder and rape. The camps were taking on a dispiritingly permanent air. The NGOs were doing a noble job, though the Darfurian political activists in the camps sometimes ensured that discipline was maintained by a reign of terror.

We took one break from filming to visit the camel market. This was one of the most genuinely traditional assemblies of tin-and-wood emporia I had ever visited. Sam bought camel bags and Irwin and I indulged in basketware. Not much else was available which suited our war-tourist tastes.

Getting back to Khartoum proved difficult; no flights were available for days, but somehow we eventually secured seats on an 'unscheduled scheduled' plane. Getting through customs was also irksome. We were made to put our film kit through the scanning machine, even though it wasn't working. For some reason the camel bags caused major confusion. They couldn't understand why Westerners needed camel bags as we didn't have camels.

Eventually we got back to Khartoum, and then travelled to London. My cab from Woking station was driven by a charming old man, who questioned me in detail about Darfur, after I had exchanged Muslim greetings with him. He invited me to the local Woking mosque and for tea at his house afterwards. I politely declined. It was a pleasant ideological change. Perhaps 90 per cent of the cabbies at Woking were Pakistanis from the North West Frontier or Kashmir. Many times on the twenty-minute trips to my home in the Surrey Hills, by pinpoint questioning, I would get a wave of more or less violent Jihadist opinions. I recalled the defensive Sudanese comments on the US need to bomb terrorist training camps in England.

I worked hard to edit the film in the ITN building in London. Irwin's photography was, as usual, excellent, despite the harsh desert conditions. It was shown on Channel 4 News not long before Christmas. After our package was aired, Chris Mullins, then Minister of State at the FCO, was interviewed live. He said that our film was 'the first one to acknowledge there are actually two sides in this dispute'. I had to agree: most TV commentaries were terribly one-sided, often ignoring the atrocities committed by the rebels, especially against employees of NGOs, who were doing their utmost to help Darfurians in need.

I started to visit Sudan and Darfur regularly, often with Irwin. But the reception one received was never predictable. The first visit had led to a rapid arrest; on the second we had VIP treatment, especially at the airport, maybe because we had a presidential interview on the schedule. This time, in June 2005, we had to fill in lots of forms and pay a large deposit to enjoy the privilege of keeping our film camera. We then had to get the usual police permit to stay more than three days in a hotel, and press accreditation, and apply for permission to fly to Darfur – something which involved five separate agencies and which took up to a week. Securing the initial entry visa in London could be another saga.

I kept asking Sudanese friends about these rituals, many of which they had to endure as well. Sudanese are famed for their hospitality, and on a one-to-one basis I found this to be justified. The exception of course was anyone in uniform and any bureaucrat.

I asked a European Sudanese expert: 'Do they like humiliating foreigners because we are white, because we are infidels or because they are xenophobic?'

'Probably all three,' he replied. 'But I can't help loving the Sudanese.'

Irwin and I booked into the Hilton with our wad of US dollars. Sanctions meant that credit cards were out and cash was king. The Hilton manager, another amiable Dutchman called Pieter, but a big man with a big heart, was always very welcoming, not least because, in the strict privacy of his own flat, we could share a beer or two. He was also a fund of local gossip.

Irwin and I were planning to shoot a long documentary on Sudan, to include the historical conflicts as well as the current wars. We managed to secure access to the archives of Sudan TV, as well as the military correspondents' film library. Sudanese military cameramen had taken some daring shots and nearly thirty had paid with their lives. We had shot a lot of material in the south on a previous visit; now we needed to look at the insurgency in the east, as well as return to Darfur.

The Beja people on the borders with Eritrea and Ethiopia had long proved reluctant to bend to Khartoum's will; sporadic insurgency, often supported by Eritrea and the SPLA, had destabilised the region. It was a long journey on broken roads, clogged with juggernauts on their way to and from the country's main harbour, Port Sudan. Eventually getting through police roadblocks, we stayed in a slum of an hotel in Kassala. We managed to film in a refugee camp, full of Eritreans escaping the extensive conscription imposed by the militaristic regime in Asmara. Our local police minders made it almost impossible to shoot anything else, although Irwin did get some shots of the charming, almost medieval, life around the souk. The silver jewellery, traditionally made by the veiled women of the Rashaida tribe, would certainly impress female war tourists. We caught sight of what Kipling once called the Fuzzy-Wuzzies, brave warriors who broke the British square. The few we saw still had big Afro hairstyles, walked tall and proud, and carried their swords. Kassala used to be famous for its fruit and its jebels, or hills. The strangely shaped jebels did, I suppose, add a certain mystical beauty to the place – from a distance. It was also considered a honeymoon resort, but any man who took his new wife there should expect an instant divorce. For our film, it was a gruelling waste of time.

Back in Khartoum, at a reception at the British embassy, I met the charming and elegant Reem. She was in the company of her uncle, Saddiq al-Mahdi, the prime minister deposed by the Islamist coup in 1989. I explained that I needed some help, particularly to find and record authentic Sudanese music. Reem was most accommodating, while always maintaining correct Islamic distance in the company of unrelated males. She took us to a music school and we filmed some impressive local musicians rehearsing. It also meant we did not have to pay performance royalties when the film was aired abroad.

Reem also guided us around the historical sites of the Mahdi period. She showed us the mud walls, with gun apertures, which defended Omdurman, Khartoum's sister city, against the Anglo-Egyptian forces when they returned to avenge the death of General Gordon. The Mahdi, played by Laurence Olivier in the film *Khartoum*, died less than six months after Gordon was beheaded. The tomb and mosque of the Mahdi, originally destroyed by the British, were rebuilt in 1947. Sometimes entry to the tomb was a problem; as Reem was a member of the Mahdi family, she finessed our easy access.

We also revisited the Omdurman market. Ten years before, it was possible to find the occasional genuine imperial relic, especially medals. Now it had been visited by too many diplomats and NGOistas. Nevertheless, it was still a fascinating glimpse into a world gone by. With effort and knowledge, you could haggle for hours and perhaps secure a genuine sword from the Mahdi period, as my occasional colleague, Richard Miniter, the veteran US correspondent and expert on terrorism, discovered. Richard was a consciously Hemingwayesque character; even when he wasn't trying, his cigar-chomping stories, always told with gusto, and exaggeration, reminded me of a cross between Winston Churchill and London Mayor Boris Johnson.

*

We set out again for Darfur, having secured all our various governmental and military permissions. This time we stayed in the guest quarters of the Wali, or Governor, a kindness sometimes granted to visiting journalists. The most that could be said was that it had a loo. Still, we were treated with kindness and hospitality. I needed the Wali's backing to persuade the army to let us accompany them on patrols against the rebels. The colonel assigned to mind us had no idea at all of what filming involved. Our explanations were met with blankness. He kept putting his hand in front of the camera, even before we left his base. In the end, we managed to secure dramatic pictures of government counter-insurgency, although it was a training exercise not real bang-bang.

As usual, we did the rounds of the NGOs and refugee camps, but the frequent presence of minders made reporting difficult. The only break in the monotony of the effects of war was to be a visit to the former Sultan's palace. Sadly, it was closed.

I remedied that on a visit to El Fasher a few months later with my friend Pieter Tesch, he of the short stature and big beard. Despite looking like a lost hobbit, he was an archaeologist with a real enthusiast's interest in Darfurian history. He took me around the run-down palace of the last Sultan, Ali Dinar, and explained in exquisite detail all the artefacts. The palace had been designated a museum, sadly not well cared for, despite the efforts of its underfunded curator.

El Fasher had been one the starting points for one of Africa's most famous caravan routes, the 'forty-day road'. Big camel trains, loaded with ivory, ebony and slaves, made the long trip through the desert to Aswan and Asyut in Egypt. There the young male slaves who had survived the journey were usually castrated.

The British infantry ambushed and killed the last Sultan in November 1916, and promptly made Ali Dinar a martyr. Technically, the operations in Darfur were designated a local colonial conflict, which irritated the British officers involved in the Darfur campaigns, who could not claim World War One medals for their actions. The reason was financial: the bill could be sent to Cairo, not the War Office in London. The introduction of modern weapons, and the arming of local militias, caused endless problems for the French and British imperial authorities long after 1918. I pondered on the many comparisons with the influx of new guns to Darfur in the early twenty-first century, and the impact on the successor states of the foreign empires in Chad and

Sudan. It is also ironic that the first use of armed, mounted Arab and African militias in Darfur was by the British army in its 1916 campaign. Were we perhaps responsible for the genesis of the *Janjaweed*?

Leaving El Fasher was again complicated by lack of planes. Just like the mercenaries in the *Wild Geese* film, we ended up having to run into the back of a lowered cargo flap of a UN troop plane, just as it was about to taxi on to the runway. Thank God, no health and safety busybodies plagued that airport.

Irwin and I wanted to complete our film in Khartoum with an interview with First Vice President Ali Osman Taha, an astute politician who had played a very useful part in the north–south peace process. Despite arrangements made weeks before, we waited for a week in the Hilton, then a whole day sitting in the VP's home. I had decided that we had to leave at 11.45 p.m. to catch our flight. I had already, at some cost, rescheduled our flights out. After various false alarms, switching off and on the camera lights, and putting off the air conditioner, I said to the head minder that we had to leave for the airport.

'That would show great disrespect for the Vice President.'

'Not as much as waiting around for eight days shows for us.'

We started to pack up our kit and leave.

'You will be arrested if you try to leave without permission.'

'Fine, that will add some spice to the conclusion of our film.'

As it happened, we were given a blue-light police escort to the airport's VIP room and ushered quickly on to the Lufthansa jet. It was lucky that we had business-class tickets. And it transpired that the Vice President didn't even know we were sitting in his house waiting for him. I hope that his diary secretary got the sack.

I worked on the film with Irwin in his editing suite in his offices in Belfast. It was always a pleasure to visit Irwin and his partner, Maggie, not just because of their expansive hospitality but also because I had covered some of the previous Troubles in the province. To see Belfast transformed was a heartening experience – gone were the searches and security gates and sense of dread; though, even at the height of the thirty-year war, I was always amazed by the friendliness of the natives, including traffic wardens, whether they were Catholic or Protestant. I had so often thought in the Middle East that the Shia–Sunni divisions were so like the inter-Christian feuds in Ireland. I had studied Ulster, during my Sandhurst and Staff College days, because it offered a classic example of protracted war in a liberal democracy.

The civil war in Northern Ireland was often treated as a form of psychosis. Tabloid headlines screamed variations on 'murdering mad bastards'. The army, in the beginning, bungled operationally in media and military terms. On occasion, the government behaved, particularly under Margaret Thatcher, as though the English media were in cahoots with the IRA. The media often took the path of least resistance, even censoring itself.

The Irish were totally unpredictable in so many ways. Some parts of the province were lyrically peaceful, but a few square miles of Belfast were like conventional war zones, where young street-wise kids would ask cheekily, 'Would you be needing a sound-bite, sir?' and then criticise the journalist's choice of shutter speed on his Nikon. Even in South Armagh, amid the serene countryside that constituted the majority of the province, stood the army observation towers, gangling, soaring contraptions of guy wire and pipe that looked as if Heath Robinson building scaffolds had cross-bred with the Martian war machines of H. G. Wells.

Underneath the superficial charm of the IRA and Loyalist spokespeople lurked intense emotions: the passionate anger of the IRA men who could starve themselves to death in prison protests, and the deep allegiance of the ultra-loyalists who would fight anyone, including the British, to remain British. Except for a few Fleet Street veterans of the Troubles, the English media were often bamboozled by the Irish people, as much as by their own government and army. In London it was easier to adopt the Basil Fawlty mantra: 'Don't mention the war.'

Of course I did, regularly, in Belfast. The debate was always lively, as were the restaurants and pubs, but no one wanted a return to the civil war (despite the spate of killings in 2008–9). As I often ended up in Belfast to edit my films, after touring so many war zones, it was comforting to work in a place which seemed to have overcome decades, even generations, of conflict. It gave me hope.

Ethiopia

A country which intrigued me was Ethiopia, which I had never visited. It had endured a long war with Eritrea, once a part of Ethiopia, and it played an important role in regional conflicts, not least in Sudan and

Somalia. On a recent visit to Khartoum I had contrived to be invited to a press conference for the closed-door symposium for nearly all Africa's intelligence chiefs, with some observers from agencies in the US and Europe. I had a press card for the one small area that was open to the media. I simply put my card in the pocket of a relatively smart suit, which was worn with my staff college tie. I kept out of the way of the MI6 people and, without a single word of duplicity, chatted to various delegates, who presumably thought I was a British spook.

I made it my business to talk to agency director-generals whom I admired or where I wanted to travel. The Ethiopian boss passed on both counts. So I arranged to see him in January 2006. I was greeted by the boss when I arrived at the Sheraton in Addis Ababa; we had a quick beer and he said he would organise meetings on the following Monday. That meant I had the weekend to myself.

In the hotel bar, I fell in with some German diplomats, and most usefully the military attaché. I soon got up to speed with local political and military gossip, particularly regarding the tenuous ceasefire between Eritrea and Ethiopia. In 1998 they had fought a major war over 150 square miles of pretty useless desert. The conflict dragged on until 2000, with mass casualties comparable to the Iran–Iraq war. The fighting, involving jet fighters, tanks and half a million troops, in some areas replicated the trench battles of the Great War. When I was in Addis six years later, despite the UN monitoring force, tensions seethed on the heavily land-mined 1,000-kilometre frontier.

I had also studied the 1930s war in Abyssinia (now Ethiopia). Evelyn Waugh's famous novel *Scoop* aptly summarised the tragi-comic nature of the times. One Boot-style account by a journalist held that the 'Abyssinians would conduct a brilliant guerrilla campaign, trapping the advancing Italians in lion pits and, if given guns, would, according to a widely held view in the United States, be able to fire them both with hands and feet'. The Italians bombed and gassed their way to colonial victory, but the Abyssinians rarely took prisoners, and frequently abused the Red Cross flag (which also happened to be a local symbol for a brothel).

During my spare weekend I also reread my friend Dick Snailham's story of his 1968 Ethiopian expedition to explore the Blue Nile. Dick and I had been friends at Sandhurst, and he had occasionally advised me on any dicey trips I was planning. I was busy gearing up to talk vaguely intelligently to Ethiopian officials on Monday.

Meanwhile, I indulged in some sightseeing. Addis seemed more rustic, open and friendly than tightly buttoned Khartoum. Five million people lived in Addis but it was a perplexing mix of modern and rural. Goats, donkeys and shabby shanties and village-style mud huts mixed in with high-rise buildings. The streets were relatively clean, attended by old women sweeping away in big straw hats. The fact that I could have a beer or two in the hotel also helped.

I went to the famous Mercato. It had the layout of traditional Muslim souks with spices in one area, tailors etc. in others. It was big and managed to hold my very limited interest in shopping for an hour or so. I also avoided the pickpockets.

I was more eager to visit the relics of ancient Orthodox Christianity in the mixed Muslim–Christian country. St George's cathedral, where Emperor Haile Selassie was crowned in 1930, was closed, but I could take in from the outside the rather severe Neoclassical style of the octagonal building. The museum next door was open. It contained a fine collection of religious paraphernalia, including holy scrolls, robes and ceremonial umbrellas – until then I hadn't realised why umbrellas were so significant locally. I also discovered a few reasonably good bookshops.

I returned to the Sheraton to be told that I had to leave because the hotel was full. I found myself in the downmarket Leopold hotel, where I was soon surrounded by some of the most beautiful women I had ever seen. Ethiopian women usually possessed the most graceful features with sensually large eyes. I had coffee with a few of the more eager ladies. Self-deceptive as ever, I put this down to my late-flowering Celtic charm, but had to accept, reluctantly, that I had moved into a knocking-shop. Age and concerns for my health kept me on the straight and narrow, however. But I enjoyed lively conversations in good English with women who in the West would have had good careers. Poverty and unemployment had forced them into prostitution. I was fortunate in that the beautiful young receptionist, in a smart airline-style uniform, took it upon herself to safeguard my honour. And she still sends me Christmas cards.

In the Leopold bar I met by chance a former British officer, Warwick, whose father had served in the Selous Scouts in Rhodesia, and with whom I was vaguely acquainted. The ex-officer, despite his service in the British army, could not get British citizenship, until the *Telegraph* took up his case. We talked about the war his father had served in, and

Warwick in turn briefed me on the country in which he was setting up a new business.

I was now ready to talk sensibly to Ethiopian ministers. The intelligence boss gave me his own briefing and I couldn't help but like him. He was small, modest and able; he reminded me so much of the West's longest-serving spy chief, Ken Flower, a good friend during my various travails in southern Africa.

I had various meetings in the Ministry of Foreign Affairs, and achieved little, not even permission to visit the border with Eritrea: mission unaccomplished.

I met the Ethiopian boss at another African intelligence summit a few years later. I jokingly told him off for invading Somalia (with Washington's encouragement) without bothering to inform me. We kept in touch, not least because I was about to dabble in Somalia – but that's another story.

Saving Darfur?

I continued to visit Darfur regularly, but enjoyed less freedom to roam around, unlike my early trips. The tempo of the war declined, after the dramatic fighting in 2003–4, but the suffering of the locals continued. I prevailed upon my old aquaintance David Hoile to assist me with my efforts in Darfur. To the opponents of Khartoum, he was a prince of darkness, because he was a very effective lobbyist for the Bashir government. It was a difficult place to work in, and David's influence was vital in getting permits and access. He also had a lively, sometimes macabre, sense of humour, indulging in practical jokes including placing large plastic spiders in the beds of often arachnophobic first-time visitors to Africa or Sudan. He apparently had a very high IQ, and was a member of Mensa. He often suggested I should seek membership of its sister organisation, Densa.

Even in my restricted visits to Darfur, it became abundantly clear that no military solution could be achieved. The African Union–UN hybrid monitoring force could achieve little. It was understaffed, lacking in proper intelligence and kit, especially helicopters. Only a political solution, along the lines of the north–south agreement, could end the war. Despite past brutality, it was clear that the new government of national unity in Khartoum (including Islamists and the SPLA) was trying to bring peace. The Darfur rebels, ever fractious, were holding out for more and more. What was needed was the kind of Western political investment (and now China) – banging heads together – that secured the north–south deal.

The Centre for Foreign Policy Analysis, a small independent think tank I had run since 2004, had very limited resources but we did our utmost to aid the peace process. I held, for example, a series of conferences in Whitehall, where the belligerents, enemies on the battlefield, renewed old friendships, many forged in school and university, over polite cups of tea – such an English way of doing things. At the Oxford Union, in a debate chaired by Channel 4's Jon Snow, I talked about peace, but the students felt that the route to salvation lay in Beijing. That prompted various trips to China to organise conferences with the new power-brokers in Africa, and especially in Sudan.

I travelled to Paris and Dubai to speak to Chadian opposition leaders, because the civil war in Chad was being ramped up by the fighting in Darfur.

In addition, I flew back to Turkey to speak at a Darfur conference at the University of Istanbul. Turkey's political balancing act had always intrigued me. Uniquely, this powerful member of NATO had good relations with the West, Israel and fellow Islamic countries in the Middle East. The EU's patronising attitude towards Turkey's accession soured Ankara's enthusiasm for the Western alliance architecture. Brussels sniped at the Turkish military's frequent intervention in domestic politics, in the name of securing the secular tradition, but the EU also fretted about the increasingly Islamic tone of the government. You could understand why the Turks felt they were in a no-win situation.

I continued to be fascinated by the Chinese influence on the Middle East and Africa, and went to Damascus to attend a China–Arab summit, partly because the Syrians were emerging blinking into the daylight as energised players in the Western diplomatic game. When I had lived and studied in Israel, Syrians were always portrayed as mad, bad and dangerous. I found every Syrian I met extremely friendly, however. I had finagled a diplomatic entry to the airport, so that erased my usual grumpiness about access to countries. I was whisked off to the excellent Cham Palace Hotel in the centre of Damascus. Since the conference I was attending was in Chinese and Arabic, with no English translation, I could concentrate on vaguely interpreting the Arabic for no more than an hour.

I decided to visit Krak des Chevaliers instead. I must confess that my trainspotter interest in old castles was also one of the enticements to visit Syria. This magnificent Crusader fortress, a few hours' drive north from the capital, is one of the most important preserved military castles in the world. It was the headquarters of the Knights Hospitallers. First captured in 1099, it fell in 1271. At its lowest point it was garrisoned by under 100 knights; I wondered how they managed to hold on for so long. The castle was very imposing, and conjured up many ghosts materialised by my reading on the Crusades. Yet the conservation was poor; on the other hand, little commercialisation intruded.

The fortress had been damaged on a number of occasions by the Israeli air force, according to local guides. On the drive back I couldn't help notice over 200 Soviet-era tanks, formed up, attended by ancient tank transporters and army vehicles. It was near the northern Lebanese border. The Syrians said they were trying to control smuggling, although US intelligence also indicated the presence of Syrian special forces – must have been very well-armed smugglers.

Back in Damascus I succumbed to sightseeing. The Al-Hamidieh Souk is said to be one of the most attractive markets in the world, and for once I had to agree with the guide books. The souk leads in to the magnificent Omayyad Mosque, which dates back to the early Islamic period. Adjacent are Roman ruins (a temple of Jupiter) and the tomb of Saladin. I also visited Christian sites, such as the Hanania Chapel, famous because of its connection with the conversion of St Paul. Damascus, my guide told me, welcomed all faiths, though he had no answer to my question as to why Jews who decided to leave Syria could never return.

The Americans chose to conduct their first major raid into Syria when I was there. Washington said they were chasing al-Qaeda; Damascus insisted that the victims were criminals, people smugglers, not Jihadists. I was privately informed that Syria had deployed crack troops on the border to control Jihadist movements into Iraq. They held, they said, over 2,000 al-Qaeda people in prison. Without this support, the American surge would not have worked so well. They were keen to reach out to the West, diplomats told me. They argued, *sotto voce*, that Syria and Israel were the two main buffers against Jihadism in the Middle East. That was an intriguing angle on an old problem. Still, Syria had to show a public response to the attack. The American school in Damascus was closed immediately, which annoyed

Syrian ministers and all the Arab delegations who sent their children to the best school in the capital.

Because my entry was so smooth I said I did not need a diplomatic official to get me out of the country. Big mistake. I spent nearly three hours in a chaotic throng of highly skilled, but manic, Arab queue-jumpers. The Iranians, however, outdid even the Arab masters. When I finally reached the check-in desk, I asked, very politely: 'Is it always like this?'

'Oh, no, it is usually chaotic.'

It was difficult to gauge what good I achieved from all this time on the road, although I think my conversations in Beijing did help to persuade China to put more pressure on Khartoum to accept the UN complement to the existing African Union forces. Yet this was just buying time. I became convinced that a political deal could and should be done. The various peace talks had been so close, down to a few million extra US dollars for the hold-outs' personal bank accounts in some cases, if I may be entirely cynical.

By March 2009 the talks between the Justice and Equality Movement and Khartoum were doing well in Doha. Then came the International Criminal Court's decision to issue arrest warrants for the Sudanese President, for his alleged crimes in Darfur. In theory, I was more than happy for monsters such as Mugabe to be dragged off to The Hague (where I also spent a lot of time). In the case of Sudan I thought it would be a disaster. In the north–south talks in which President Bashir paid a paramount role, no mention was made of punishing the many war crimes on both sides. What the ICC decision meant was the Darfur rebels would drag their heels indefinitely, waiting for regime change in Khartoum. They would have had to wait a long time, because the ICC action was taken as an insult to nearly all Sudanese, regardless of whether they hated or loved Bashir. The ICC entrenched Bashir, rather than destabilising him. Moreover, most southern leaders I spoke to were terrified that the north–south deal might collapse and war return.

My Centre organised a major London conference on the ICC, and I made myself very unpopular with the liberal chattering classes by insisting the peace must come before justice. Specialists such as Richard Dowden, the director of the Royal African Society, backed my view. As Richard put it, 'The ICC cannot hand out justice in Sudan as if it were Surrey.' Other experts, even the *Guardian* columnist Jonathan Steele, also supported my view, which leaned towards African modes of justice such as the Truth and Reconciliation process in South Africa. The AU, the Arab League and many African leaders, even those who detested Bashir, saw the ICC action – along with other indictments of only African leaders – as a form of neo-colonialism. I wanted international law to develop fully in Africa, but not if it meant delaying peace, prompting wars which killed many thousands, as had happened with the previous ICC intervention in Uganda.

The US, China and India, as well as 75 per cent of the world, chose not to join the ICC, partly because they feared its politicisation. The ICC's intentions, however, may well have been noble, aimed at securing peace in Darfur. Instead they made peace less likely. And my tiny part in the peace process much more frustrating. The ICC had once more proved the law of unintended consequences: Bashir had been made another African president for life. Like Mugabe, he could not retire for fear of international legal retribution. Another unintended consequence was the booming Sudanese economy. It was little troubled by the international crash of 2008, not least because of US sanctions, which – along with China's largesse – had quarantined Sudan from the worst repercussions of the collapse of the American financial markets.

Southern African safaris

I hadn't been back to South Africa for a while, so I accepted a last-minute invitation to attend the 'African dialogue' organised by the Oppenheimer family via their Brenthurst Trust. It was April 2006, and it was last minute because the Ugandan President had dropped out two days before. I did say that I didn't look like nor think like Yoweri Museveni, but I would do my best as a substitute. My BA flight was severely delayed by a riot in the first-class lounge caused by the rapper Snoop Dogg (aka Snoop Doggy Dogg) and his bodyguards. I hate rap music so I was pleased that they were all hauled off to police cells.

The Anglo-American lounge in Johannesburg was excellent and I was pleased to meet friends from South Africa and London. My 1960s college tutor, Professor Jack Spence, greeted me like a long-lost brother. A new friend was Brigadier Paula Thornhill, from the Pentagon, and it was fun at first sight. In the Gulfstream G5 I had never experienced such acceleration in a passenger jet, with first-class champagne and even classier air hostesses. The G5 took our small group to Tswalu lodge in the Kalahari.

Because I was not a proper VIP guest, I had to share a room in the luxurious rondavel lodge. Just my luck it was a senior Indian diplomat, who asked if I didn't mind his chanting. I did, but was too 'English' to say so. I drank late into the night with senior South African officers, especially Admiral Steve Stead, with whom I shared many past adventures and comrades. I returned the worse for wear with the Indian still chanting. I feel asleep eventually and told him in the morning that I had caught him levitating in the night – that's why I had tied his leg to the bed, to stop him floating out the window. He took the hint and moved, leaving me to my own room.

I spent much of the three-day session arguing privately with President Mbeki's foreign affairs adviser. I explained that Mbeki's indulgence towards Mugabe was ruining southern Africa. The implosion in Zimbabwe would infect the whole of the region, especially the flow of refugees. He managed to be loyal to his president, while genuinely agreeing with my position – clearly a better diplomat than his boss.

I enjoyed some hours in detailed private conversation with Jonathan Oppenheimer, who seemed very open and bright. I mentioned that I had once sat next to his famous grandfather, Harry, in the Jo'burg city hall, and I repeated my comment to Harry that I was surprised that the region's richest man could wander around on his own.

Jonathan said: 'I don't use bodyguards but I have them for my kids.'

The most fascinating person at Tswalu was Nicholas Stern, Lord Stern. He was perhaps the most famous eco-economist in the UK, but we talked pop music and sport. He seemed to enjoy (I think) my low-brow diversion at such a highly charged intellectual event.

It wasn't all talk. I thoroughly embraced the wet smell of Africa on the chilly night game drives, enjoying the sight of white rhinos.

Despite my long absence from South Africa, I found I could soon get into the arcane nuances of the local politics. It had moved on so much from the stark racism of the old republic. Criticism of the reverse racism reared its head, even among the polite white liberals who dominated the event.

After Tswalu, I returned to my old haunt of Melville and stayed at writer Heidi Holland's guesthouse. After doing the rounds of old pals which Heidi kindly organised, I got an impression of a defensive white society, animated by fear of crime. Denis Beckett, as a pathological optimist, was an exception. My close friends in Melville had been robbed at gunpoint three times in as many years. Not surprisingly each of the pretty little homes had been reinforced into razor-wire and electric-fenced fortresses. The streets were dirty, graffiti seared the once pristine white walls, and the roads and pavements were potholed. The restaurants and bars were multiracial and much more lively and welcoming, however.

I mentioned the crime problem to Heidi, who was busy completing her acclaimed book, *Dinner with Mugabe*. She said: 'Complaining about crime is merely a cover for white racism.'

'But Heidi,' I objected, 'you have a guard on your front door at night. That wasn't needed when I lived here. Crime is surely an objective fact.'

Heidi, like Denis, was resolutely upbeat about the rainbow nation. They were the exceptions. A number of my friends had witnessed savage and often fatal attacks on close family members. The power cuts were more indicative, I thought, of the creeping Zimbabweanisation of South Africa. 'Black-outs' was not an acceptable term, so 'power rationing' and the like were the preferred verbal currency.

Zimbabwe

I had been banned in 1986, and had slipped in once afterwards, a year later. In June 2008, I wanted to see what had happened to my favourite African country. Had Robert Mugabe truly destroyed it? I had just published a new book on the history of the Rhodesian war so my mind was attuned to what it had been; it was hard to take in what it had become.

I had taken some precautions by advance contact with the dreaded Central Intelligence Organisation. A brigadier met me at the airport, and smoothed my entry, though my luggage had disappeared en route from the brief transit in Johannesburg. The new airport was impressive, all glass and modern compared with the cosy old-fashioned building I remembered.

I stayed at the former Sheraton, renamed Rainbow Tower, the haunt of the ruling ZANU-PF party, and next to its HQ. I thought it best to keep my potential enemies close. Beer and food were in limited supply. If the party bosses were running out of booze, things must have been bad. The Japanese restaurant did not contain a trace of anything

Japanese. The money foxed me too. I bought some cigarettes on my first night and they cost just under five billion Zimbabwe dollars (Z$); the next morning they had gone up to Z$22.5 billion. That kind of inflation encouraged nicotine abstinence.

I knew how the black market operated but in the name of research I tried the formal route, standing nearly all day in endless bank queues. In the end I jumped into a cab and used my US dollars to reach Sam Whaley's house near the now closed university where I had once worked. Sam had been a close friend of Ian Smith and a generous host when I had lived in the country in the 1970s. I knew his daughter, Gill, was visiting, to look after Sam in his terminal illness. Gill welcomed me, and agreed to lend me some clothes – because of my lost luggage. I also spoke at length to Sam about the former Rhodesia.

Despite his illness and his ninety-three years, Sam was keen to reminisce.

'What would you have done differently?'

'We should have encouraged African participation more rapidly.'

'Would Nkomo or Muzorewa, in power earlier, have pre-empted the destruction wrought by Mugabe?'

'Perhaps.'

'But, Sam, that was the lesson everywhere of the long colonial recessional: too little, too late.'

And then we talked about Ian Smith. I suggested that all Smith's prophecies had come true: Mugabe, Smith warned in the late 1970s, would destroy the Ndebele, and then turn on white farmers. I also pointed out that even those to the far right of the Rhodesian Front had never imagined what a nightmare would descend on the most efficient country on the continent.

I saw Sam a few times and thanked him for his many kindnesses. I knew it would be the last time we would talk. He passed on a few months later, but his way of life, his code of integrity and his country had died many years before.

Gill took me to an Asian money-changer and I got a good deal for US dollars. Thereafter, I tried to buy some clothes, especially underwear. I was practically the only white person in Harare town centre, but I felt no threat at all. It was not like the tension in downtown Jo'burg which made me more nervous than Baghdad or Kabul. I eventually secured some Chinese underwear which cost me Z$30 billion. And they were far too small. As it happened the CIO then delivered my luggage to the hotel. I don't know if they found anything of interest inside, except my colourful boxer shorts.

The next day I went to Avondale, in northern Harare, to the shopping centre which once housed the police station I had served in. The supermarket was almost empty. Nor were the tills working. The Italian bakery coffee shop was still there and I met friends I had not seen for over twenty years, including Marda, the daughter of the former CIO boss, Ken Flower. Some of my white friends appeared to have had all their juices squeezed out of them – foraging for food and fuel was almost a full-time job. In the flea market in Avondale I found numerous second-hand book stalls, full of settler memorabilia, including copies of my early books – those that had not been banned in Zimbabwe.

My favourite book shop in Harare used to be Kingston's. It was once a bustling two-storey business. This time, in the reduced single storey, a handful of cheap locally produced books were on sale. I bought a book by the former President, Canaan Banana, a clergyman who had been imprisoned for homosexuality by the rabidly homophobic Mugabe. For me, this very poorly produced book by a shamed President symbolised the tragic decline of a once prosperous country. And it took an elaborate ritual involving three people to buy the damn thing. One man took the money; although there were not enough zeroes on the till to issue me a formal receipt, a woman gave me a hand-written one, and a guard took the receipt and recorded something in his book; job creation with a vengeance.

I went to my favourite haunt, the Reps theatre bar, which had not seen a lick of paint since I was last there, nor had it seen much beer in recent months. I enjoyed chatting about old times with chain-smoking grizzled regulars, and was amazed to hear the same mindlessly optimistic clichés of the Rhodesian war period.

'Things will come right.'

'We can always find a way of coping.'

Most had given up – I couldn't get an exact figure but the white Zimbabwean population was about 20,000 after reaching a peak of 270,000 in the 1970s. Meanwhile, more than three million blacks had fled to neighbouring states, mainly South Africa.

The deputy director-general of the CIO came to see me at my hotel, and baldly stated: 'The boss wants to see you.'

For a moment, I thought he meant Mugabe. Instead, I was escorted to Milton Buildings, a place I had not visited since the last days of white rule. I was led into the DG's office, which looked cosy but run down from when I had last met Ken Flower there.

The DG greeted me like a great friend.

I pretended to do the same.

Over tea and biscuits, he asked all about myself, though it was clear that he'd just been given a detailed CV. I wasn't going to admit that I didn't know him, because I knew he would break first. Eventually, he said: 'Paul, I remember you well from Staff College and the RCDS [Royal College of Defence Studies]. You taught me. And your *Chimurenga* book is one of our basic reference books for teaching our senior staff. Welcome back to Zimbabwe.'

I wasn't going to mention the fact that I was still banned, but I did think, very quietly, 'So we taught these bastards.'

He asked me about politics in the UK, and I asked him whether he had rigged the recent elections in Zimbabwe.

'Hardly, our man lost. But His Excellency Robert Mugabe will win next time.'

I bet.

He then came to the point. The CIO boss wanted me to pass on a message to the FCO in London. He went on about trusting me because I had worked in the MoD. I explained that I'd had a relatively junior position, and did not work in government any more.

'What's wrong with the British ambassador?'

Clearly a lot by his frown. He said: 'No. I want it to go direct.'

(I was not in a position to refuse, and did pass on the message to the relevant desk in the FCO. The Welshman in charge was rather sceptical about me as a courier and the contents of the message. I could hardly blame him.)

The CIO DG provided me with a car and an impressive escort of three senior officers to take me through the VIP airport lounge. My luggage and I had a very smooth exit.

I had a brief 24-hour stopover in Johannesburg. I stayed with Sarah Hudleston, who had recently completed a biography of Mugabe's main opponent, Morgan Tsvangirai. She arranged a small party so I could say farewell to friends who were just about to emigrate. I wondered again whether, in the longer term, there was a place for white Africans on the continent they tried so hard to call home. One friend, who refused to leave, said simply: 'Africa is not a place for sissies.' I now could call myself a sissy.

I had been nervous during my stay in Zimbabwe because I had written a series of blistering articles about Mugabe, which had been published just prior to my arrival in Harare, and not just in the US and Britain but also South Africa, in my fairly regular spot in Johannesburg's *Business Day*. The Mugabe propaganda machine had rebutted them with equally ad hominem toughness on various blogs. I had been lucky this time.

I decided I would not return until Mugabe was out of power. Short of dying in the job, who would get rid of him? His lieutenants had made it clear that he was terrified of being dragged to The Hague so he was likely to hang on to power for as long as he could. South Africa, which had all the levers, would do little. Western intervention was unlikely (although the MoD ramped up various muscular versions of their evacuation plans for Brit passport holders) and for a while it looked as though President Obama had flirted with an aggressive humanitarian intervention during Zimbabwe's cholera crisis.

No other country since 1945 had suffered such inflation or a meltdown of the economy (though Britain, under Gordon Brown, would soon start printing money as eagerly as Mugabe had done). AIDS was rampant, life expectancy had halved, the water supplies were polluted and electricity was rare. Foreign aid trickled in, but massive economic support would not materialise while Mugabe and his generals still ran the show. The opposition Movement for Democratic Change (MDC), led by Morgan Tsvangirai, formed a national unity government in early 2009, but this was likely to be a replay of Mugabe's absorption and neutering of his old nationalist opponent, Joshua Nkomo, in the 1980s. And even if the MDC somehow managed to take the lead, did they have the ability and honesty to reform a train wreck of an economy? It would take decades to rebuild the economy's three main pillars: agriculture, tourism and mining.

It was his mincing manner that surprised me most. When I first interviewed Mugabe in January 1980, it seemed jarring in a tough guerrilla chieftain. So did his dapper dress style. His English was slightly contrived, almost perfect BBC. His intelligence impressed me the most, however. For four years I had interviewed many black and white political leaders in the dying Rhodesia. Mugabe was head and shoulders above them all. Rhodesian propaganda had portrayed this Catholic-trained Marxist as a bloodthirsty latter-day Hitler. I initially believed, however, in his call for racial reconciliation.

Mugabe had been so full of promise when he started, but he ended up, as Desmond Tutu said, as the very caricature of an African despot. If he had left after his first term of office he could have secured a Mandela-like legacy. So far, however, he has hung on for thirty years, something of a record even in Africa. The manner of his departure might yet disgrace the whole continent.

ASIA

16. CHINA – THE NEW SUPERPOWER

Asian sideshows

My interest in Sudan propelled me to spend some time in China. I had 'done' most of the Asian cities on the tourist routes to break my long flights when I was based in Australia and, later, New Zealand. I had taught at Waikato University in Hamilton in the north island. I liked Kiwis: they appeared more refined and more laidback than Aussies, just as Canadians are often perceived as sedated Americans. I had mooched around Cambodia when I had the foolish notion of trying to interview Pol Pot, and I had crawled around the Viet Cong tunnels in Vietnam, but after the communists had won. Irwin and I had made a film about the civil war in Nepal. We were given unique access by the royalist army and had visited far-flung outposts in the mountains, and in lowland nature reserves. We had taken some exquisite footage from the back of elephants while on elephant patrols with the army. In fact, it was technically the best-quality footage we had ever shot, and with a fancy new HD camera. Ironically, it was the only documentary that I failed to sell.

I also tempted Irwin with a series of trips to the Maldives. People went there normally to explore each other, not the country. Few upmarket honeymooners noticed that it was led by the longest-ruling dictator in Asia. We made a number of films about the frequently jailed and tortured opposition leader, Mohamed Nasheed. I had so often been promised the first interview in the presidential palace by a whole rogues' gallery of warlords, exiled politicians and guerrilla leaders. But Mohamed honoured his word when he won the first democratic election in 2008. He kept a gaggle of high commissioners and ambassadors waiting while he talked to me on his first day in office. He also kept his word, the next day, when I asked him to send the country's police chief to escort me to Mohamed's former island prison, before he sacked him.

*

Beijing busybody

I had always wanted to see the Great Wall of China, and fulfilled my ambition in December 2006. I had not visited the People's Republic before, but I had spent a lot of time investigating and writing on China's role in Africa. Presumably someone in the influential Chinese Academy of Social Sciences (CASS) had taken notice, even though one article was cheekily entitled 'Africa: the big Chinese takeaway?' I was asked to lecture at a conference on Sino-African relations.

'The Chinese are rapidly developing a successful capitalist economy – it would be a shame if the Commies took over.' New visitors to Beijing might be tempted to utter that paradox, especially at Christmas when the shops and tourist hotels were decked out in Western festive paraphernalia. The most upmarket shops boasted European manikins, predominantly English signs and Western fashions. Senior Communist Party officials were rather embarrassed when Westerners asked about the great revolutionary leaders of the past – Mao was as long dead as Marx. What Chinese youngsters perhaps wanted most was Western culture, not necessarily capitalist democracy. The same could be said of many other authoritarian states, not least Iran.

At the Beijing conference, senior party cadres and professors politely applauded my lecture on why China was doing better in Africa than the West. Nevertheless, except perhaps for South Africa, no African state was strong enough to deal equally with China. On a divided, demoralised continent, Beijing could cherry-pick almost at will.

Beijing was cold, way below freezing and polluted, five times worse than London when I checked on a pollution scale for the December average. I wondered how the government would sort that out for the 2008 Olympics. David Hoile had also been invited to speak at the conference so on the first evening David, a champion shopaholic who had clearly been to China before, wanted to show me local markets. On the street, I was stopped by a pretty Mongolian woman and her friend, who said they were studying English at Ulan Bator University.

'Could we please practise our English?' they asked very sweetly.

Being a stranger in town, I tarried to politely converse. David kept on walking. I made my excuses and rushed to catch up with him. I told him off for his rudeness.

'They were whores,' he said sharply.

Ever ready to explain such frequent encounters as simply the power of my native charm, I told him he was wrong. Whenever obvious ladies of the night came up, David would say: 'Here's your chance to give an English lesson.'

And my stubborn insistence that the first encounter was innocent made me the butt of various jokes among my professorial colleagues at the conference. Even Admiral Steve Stead, with whom I had enjoyed many companionable hours recently in Tswalu in the Kalahari, politely said I was being naive.

I was probably also being naive when a very attractive Chinese woman sat next to me at the conference. She had a PhD from an English university, but I am not sure whether she'd fully imbibed the English sense of humour. Over lunch she congratulated me on my speech, after explaining that she was a senior member of the Communist Party dealing with foreign affairs.

I asked her: 'Do you have an application form?'

'Application for what?'

'I want to join the Chinese Communist Party.'

She looked bemused. 'I don't think that's possible.'

Presumably she was too polite to say that I wasn't Chinese, couldn't speak the language and probably wasn't a communist.

I persisted. 'Well, then, perhaps I can set up a branch of the party in London? Then I can join that.'

Her politeness was beginning to fade, I suspected. Slightly exasperated, she said: 'You can make a donation to the party here, if you are sincere.'

I changed the subject. She was not amused.

I needed the few stiff drinks at the British embassy reception, and then retired to the hotel to carry on drinking with Admiral Stead and Lucy, a captivating young student from Stellenbosch, who spoke Mandarin. I immediately dragooned her into organising a shopping expedition the next day. Speaking the language fluently, and distracting the locals with her long blond hair, we managed to get a few bargains. I was mildly irritated by people tugging at my clothes and I asked Lucy why the hawkers and single traders were so damned determined – desperation, saving face or pride in getting a deal? Poverty, probably, she opined. Like checking out at the hotel, the Chinese had not got a handle on modern accounting. In shops, receipts had to be obtained at each counter, then we had to queue to pay a designated cashier. It was very time-consuming, and a job-creation scheme – every small counter was staffed by a small mob of salespeople.

We stopped at a sort of antique shop. It was full of busts of all sizes of Marx and Mao. They were gathering dust and no sales. It seemed an apt comment on the obvious decline of revolutionary ardour. China was a communist state in name only; it was led by a tough authoritarian élite in which access to consumerism, not socialism, was the guiding principle.

We walked around the concrete desert which was Tiananmen Square, all forty hectares of it. It was a modern creation, as traditional Chinese town planning avoided squares, and disliked places where hostile crowds could gather. Not much change there then. The Forbidden City (the former imperial palace) was, however, enchanting, and not just because it summoned images of *The Last Emperor*. For five centuries ordinary Chinese were not allowed to enter, or even approach, the walls. From within the palace, with its 800 buildings, the emperors, the Sons of Heaven, ruled with absolute power – when they found time to take a break from their thousands of concubines. That was perhaps at least one of the reasons why the emperors rarely left the gilded cage of palace life. Moreover, the palace was considered the centre of the universe. It still resounded with references to the personal symbols of imperial power such as the dragon and phoenix (emperor and empress) as well as the crane and turtle (longevity of reign). We walked until we dropped. It was a magnificent place, now much restored, not least after the British had looted it on more than one occasion, as my Communist Party guide delighted in telling me. (The Japanese and retreating Chinese Nationalist troops had also been heavily into plunder.)

If Tiananmen smacked of traditional Chinese paranoia, so of course did the Great Wall. Wall building began in the fifth century BC and continued till the sixteenth. The peasants hated the wall because their bones and blood had nourished its construction. And the seven-metre-high, seven-metre-thick wall, with its 25,000 battlements, failed to do its job. A series of invaders got around or over it, Genghis Khan famously by bribing sentries; and it was of little use against the naval power of modern imperial states such as Britain and Japan.

Time permitted me the chance to visit only the touristy bit of the wall at Badaling, seventy kilometres north-west of Beijing. It was a cold December day so it was not too infested with visitors. I walked up to the much restored section, amid splendid hills. It had been almost rebuilt rather than restored, a modern reconstruction on ancient foundations, supervised – I was told – by German engineers with German funding. Another irony: the Germans were also great builders of futile walls, in France and in Berlin. (I wondered what the German taxpayer thought about all this, just as I had taxed the DfID boss in Beijing and asked why the Brits were funding aid projects in an emerging superpower rival.) Still, I was trying for once not to think about politics, and enjoyed the walk along the wall, if only the mile or so southern route to the cable car, taking the lazy route down.

On the way back to the hotel, I got to see a little bit of the countryside, so different from the urban malls and high rises of central Beijing. I stopped at the conventional tourist trap of a chinoiserie porcelain factory. The conditions of production were primitive and dangerous. You'd have thought that the various revolutions might have created a useful trade union or two.

One of my main purposes in coming to Beijing was to lay the groundwork for an international conference on Darfur, since China was so influential in Sudan. I had made some useful contacts among academicians, some who ranked as senior party members and ministers. I had difficulty in working out who stood where in the rather opaque pecking order of Chinese rule. I asked my old friend Lindsey Hilsum, then Channel 4 News bureau chief in Beijing, whether she had worked out the correct order of battle, as it were. She did her best to brief me. And she kindly allowed her driver to take me to the airport. Thick fog was about to close Heathrow. After many hours' delay in my stopover in Stockholm, I made it in, the last plane to land before Heathrow was closed. Sleeping bodies were strewn around the airport because of the delays. I was bound to compare London's third-world nightmare of an airport with the more efficient and ultra-modern Beijing one. Britain certainly could do with a Great Leap Forward, I concluded.

Perceptions of China

It was very arrogant of me to try to decipher China after just one visit, though many years in Africa had allowed a more thorough analysis of what Beijing was doing there. Beijing's economic, military and diplomatic growth had been so striking that it often caused knee-jerk reactions in Europe and America. Two main schools of thought dominated.

The first was the peaceful China: its new strategic cosmopolitanism was geared to expanding its national interest – not ideology – primarily to secure energy sources and to improve its trading patterns with the European Union and USA. Africa was merely a proving ground.

The difficult China: Beijing's outreach was part of an exclusionary policy, working with illiberal and rogue states. North Korea was a prime example. It developed trade patterns which ignored all human rights issues. This undermined Western conditionality strategies which aimed to improve conditions in autocratic states, especially in Africa. China could manipulate its dollar surpluses to bring down the US economy, though that would not be in Beijing's interest, particularly at a time when it was stealing Western intellectual property worth tens of billions of dollars annually. I'd noticed that pirated DVDs of the new James Bond film, at less than a dollar, were on sale even before it reached Western cinemas.

Chinese foreign policy was sufficiently nuanced to allow a variety of interpretations. Washington's policy towards Beijing contained elements of mutual economic cooperation but also strategies, especially with Japan, which could counter perceived Chinese military threats.

As far as Africa was concerned, the Western threat perception was based on economic penetration and a concern that long-established Western principles of conditionality – aid and trade in exchange for good governance – were being destabilised.

China's trade with Africa had risen four-fold in the previous four years. It was said to be $40 billion, and rising fast, by late 2006. China had overtaken the UK to become Africa's third most important trading partner, after the US and France. Because its oil needs were expected to double in fifteen years, China had invested in particular in Sudan, Angola and Nigeria. It was also investing in forestry in Equatorial Guinea, mining in Zambia and construction in Botswana, for example.

China had involved itself in Africa for ideological reasons in the 1960s and 1970s and helped with large-scale projects, the Tan-Zam railway perhaps the best example. This time the motivation was primarily about business, not politics. Some Western experts argued that the Chinese were now 'voracious capitalists' who were generating a new scramble for Africa.

This was a two-way street. China may have been pushing its Africa policy hard, but African leaders, increasingly scornful of Western conditionality, were welcoming the far less judgemental Chinese way of doing of business.

I thought: forget about Western campaigns about 'making poverty history'; instead 'make lecturing African leaders history'. Western aid hadn't worked, especially when it was accompanied by pious and ineffective lectures and double-counting (for example, including debt relief as part of aid budgets). Giving more aid to Africa was like telling an alcoholic he needed a stiff drink to help kick his addiction. The continent had been going backwards for many years until the 5 per cent growth rate of 2003–6. Chinese trade may well have played a role in that achievement. Rock singers' alliances with Tony Blair's messianic vision may perhaps have stirred the soul of voters in the UK, but they were unlikely to benefit Africa's poor. Opening Western markets would have been a more effective strategy.

What Africa needed was not liberal kindness but investment by business. But only very big Western companies – and the Chinese – tended to take the risk. The oil majors had shown that Africa need not be stable to make a profit. Nigeria and Equatorial Guinea demonstrated that oil brought in money, but it rarely benefited the 'masses'. Nigerian leaders in forty years ripped off $400 billion (from oil and aid money) – that was six times the amount the US Marshall Plan spent on successfully rebuilding Western Europe after the Second World War.

After more than $1 trillion of Western aid, many African citizens were poorer than ever. Western governments tried to impose good governance by lending or giving money with strings attached. Donors needed to recognise, however, that they could not 'buy' policies with their own money and expect African governments to 'own' these same policies which were imposed on them, and which often didn't work (although it could – sometimes – at the very local, African-'owned' level).

Simply no correlation existed between aid and economic growth. Africans didn't need to be told that aid merely saps initiative. Africa, like any other region, wanted to finance its recovery though its own resources and through direct foreign investment. Annual capital flight roughly equalled aid inflows; every year Africa's brightest talents left, while tens of thousands of foreign 'experts' briefly, and often clumsily, replaced them. This was the economics of the madhouse.

For the African worker, there was one thing worse than being exploited by Western capitalism (or Chinese neo-capitalism) and that was *not* being exploited – that is, no work. Foreign business investment in Africa was nakedly self-interested, but it should have been extended beyond extractive and agricultural industries. Yes, debt relief would help (though it also made African governments less credit-worthy), but more important was the curtailment of European and American domestic protectionism – even though the West preached free trade to Africa.

Direct Western military intervention, like the billions of aid dollars, was usually equally counter-productive. The first priority was to keep out the guns and aid gurus, and let more businesses in (and African governments could have started by dumping the red tape which deterred economic development). Western governments could help by encouraging the African diaspora to return; Western banks should also have played a role in repatriating more of the billions that corrupt dictators had stolen from their people.

Lindsey Hilsum had produced a number of powerful reports on China and Africa. The essence of her critique, during the visit of forty African heads of state to Beijing in November 2006, was this: African leaders, she said, 'are just thrilled that China wants to talk about trade, investment and brotherhood rather than pesky subjects Western leaders like to bring up like human rights, good governance, corruption, genocide and all that'.

Yes, China's support for Sudan and for Robert Mugabe's regime had been criticised in the Western media. And China had supplied large arms shipments to Sudan and Zimbabwe, including fighter aircraft – though it still lagged behind the Western arms deals on the continent. China had also been criticised for dumping cheap goods on Africa. This was particularly true of textiles and clothing. In a replay of trade structures imposed by European imperialism, South Africa exported raw materials to China while importing Chinese products which competed with, and undercut, local industries. South African trade unions had called for restrictions on Chinese imports. Following its experience in Latin America, China had responded to these concerns and agreed to limit exports of some garments and textiles to South Africa. China had also been criticised for bringing its own workers and displacing African employment on major construction projects. Chinese purchase of retail outlets had also caused resentment in Botswana and in Zambia, for example.

African leaders were generally much happier to deal with the

Chinese (despite the complaints from trade unions). President Festus Mogae of Botswana admitted: 'I find that the Chinese treat us as equals. The West treats us as former subjects.'

Because the Chinese were not imposing any ideology, it was willing buyer, willing seller. Above all, the phenomenal growth rates in China and the fact that hundreds of millions had been lifted out of poverty was an attractive model for Africans, and not just the elderly leadership. Young, intelligent, well-educated Africans were attracted to the Chinese example, even though Beijing was not trying to spread democracy (unlike the disastrous American policy in Iraq).

China was effectively building on its soft-power model. Over 900 Chinese doctors worked in Africa. Educational support was also extensively provided. Instead of aid that was often diverted into élite pockets, China had made a habit of providing iconic infrastructural projects, from new parliaments to football stadia.

Nor did China import an army of fat-cat 'expats' along with their families. Chinese workers usually lived in austere accommodation and worked hard for long hours and at salaries much lower than European or UN personnel. The Chinese were sometimes condemned for importing strict labour regimes, but their work ethic would be a useful inspiration in many African states.

China's one-party system necessarily precluded its proselytising for democracy. It stood by its economic record, an undoubtedly alluring model for many Africans. China's experience suggested that the removal of poverty should precede the introduction of democracy. Instead of considering a triangular zero-sum relationship of the West and China contending for African goodwill (and oil), there were many ways of cooperating, via the New Partnership for African Development and an array of other organisations. But first the West needed to escape from the instinctive notion that its policies were progressive in Africa while Chinese actions were negative and harmful.

Africa needed trade, not aid. And China, for all its self-interest, was providing just that. China wanted oil for its immediate needs, but it was also playing a long-term game. Its skilled diplomats knew that they required some stability and effective governance in its trading partners – even in Zimbabwe.

In 2006 more Chinese were living in Nigeria than Britons during the height of the empire. And in 2005 Angola's energy minister said that as many as three million Chinese could move to his country over the next five years. That figure seemed highly improbable. Even if it were quarter true, it would smack of a new imperialism.

If China's energy shortage and population surplus could help rebuild a largely derelict continent, then Beijing should have been applauded not castigated. While the EU viewed Africa as a burden, China saw a market.

The so-called African renaissance could come only when African leaders invested by preference in private capital growth in their own countries not in Swiss banks. China pulled itself up by its own bootstraps by relying largely on internal investment as well as smart foreign trade; Africa must not rely on external investment from China through selling its oil. Despite the dangers of a new imperialism, China might still provide an opportunity for Africa which Europe and the USA had simply failed to deliver.

Please excuse that rant. I believed passionately that aid had been disastrous in Africa. I had criss-crossed the continent and could list hundreds of examples of how Western development aid projects had been futile or plain destructive. Many Western agencies had developed a self-serving agenda, ruled over by bosses who had justly earned their titles of 'Lords of Poverty'. I had a different view of immediate humanitarian aid projects, such as in Darfur, or after natural disasters. But most of Africa's woes were man-made, and aid often made them worse.

After my first visit, I wanted to persuade the Chinese Academy of Social Sciences (CASS) to co-sponsor, with my Centre, a conference on Darfur. I had been back and forth to Washington for other projects in places such as Nepal, but for Darfur, it was Beijing which was most likely to influence Khartoum. I had to travel to The Hague to persuade Professor Yang Guang, head of the African section of CASS, to support my aim. Various other entreaties had failed. A mutual friend had kindly arranged for me 'bump into' the Chinese professor over a meal. Professor Yang knew what I was about, and it took us just five minutes to reach a deal, and shake hands, before we sat down for dinner. I could have my joint conference, provided no journalists came. I had attended numerous closed seminars and conferences in London with similar restrictions. I didn't like it, but I had no choice. Once the CASS boss had made the agreement, he stuck to it.

*

Beijing was hot in July 2007. I had arranged conferences in other Asian cities such as Bangkok, so I knew it would be even more difficult in a city like Beijing, especially getting speakers there from Europe and on time. Organising academics is like herding cats. I had fixed the flights and visas in London, so they had no excuse. Professor Stephen Chan, from the LSE/School of Oriental and African Studies, was no problem. Stephen was a polymath, with all the true poet's delicacy in build and diction, and surprisingly and pleasantly modest. I had often wondered how this former university vice-chancellor had got away with his long hair and sometimes colourful Alice bands. By chance, I discovered that, as a master in various martial arts, he trained special forces in unarmed combat. So I am glad I didn't ask about his hair band. Richard Dowden, director of the Royal African Society, had arrived early. His boyish enthusiasm and streetwise irreverence were always a bonus. He was staying with the Sky presenter, Peter Sharp; according to Richard's impish warning, Sharpie was still harbouring a faint grudge about my regular, and innocent, dancing sessions in Rhodesia – thirty years before – with a lady who eventually became his wife. Who said hacks don't have long memories? My old friend Professor Mohamed Salih, from The Hague, was a trouble-free and erudite complement to our efforts. Chinese scholars and other experts from Sudan also pitched up vaguely on time.

The conference was lively and, by local standards, quite outspoken, though the Chinese academics, even those who fancied themselves as intellectual dissidents, tended to sing off the same hymn sheet. Stephen Chan was his usual more than iconoclastic self: he suggested a precise Chinese contribution to Darfur peacekeeping, besides the engineering contingent. He said that China should send 100 helicopters with 1,000 support technicians – air mobility was the key deficiency in the current peace operations.

In the summary I took up a key point in Stephen's paper – China's insistence on non-interference. I said that I had been on the receiving end of Chinese alleged non-interference, for example, during China's support for Mugabe's guerrillas in the Zimbabwe liberation war. I also commented on my first-hand experiences of Beijing's very helpful non-interference – namely military support for the *mujahedin* in Afghanistan during the 1980s. The point of questioning the relativity of the Chinese principle of non-interference – which Stephen had said was outdated even by the AU standards – was to suggest that China did have a lot of leverage in Sudan, especially Darfur. China was, in effect, a 'reluctant superpower', which could do a lot of good in Africa in general and Sudan in particular. Although Stephen's suggestion about more helicopters was an interesting point, it was more important to concentrate on political solutions. There was a danger that increased military intervention, even under a UN banner, could radicalise the region and foment a *jihad* that would benefit only al-Qaeda. It was wrong, I said, to demonise US intentions, which, however misguided, were not evil. Washington could play a part in the political settlement, along with China. There was no peace to keep at present, so the UN mission was likely to be ill-fated. What was required was political leadership and political pressure, akin to the process at Naivasha. I concluded that, although the peace train did not run only through Beijing, China could and should play a more active role.

The cold logic of Stephen Chan and the high-voltage energy of Richard Dowden helped, I think, to encourage Beijing's pressure on Khartoum to moderate its hard line on Darfur, not least regarding allowing in the UN. That was the feedback we got later from various senior sources. I also had private conversations about the political dangers of China's continuing (though declining) support for Robert Mugabe. With a little help from my friends, perhaps my Centre had punched above its weight and managed to do some good.

Lindsey Hilsum – who prided herself on her 'Sudanorak' role – was irritated that journalists had been excluded, but I tried to assuage her by inviting her to the informal drinks party at the end of the conference. She had always been the most intellectual, and ethical, of journalists, so I was always surprised by her tolerance of my errant ways. She even put me up in her apartment and took me on a walking tour of the few remaining old parts of the city. After narrow streets, with little courtyards, and communal washrooms in the lanes, she led me to the Drum Tower (*Gulou*). From the vantage point of this fifteenth-century Ming creation, drums were beaten to mark the hours of day and night. I watched a troupe of drummers bang away on the giant drums inside. It was a sort of noisy medieval equivalent of Greenwich Mean Time.

After lunch at the excellent 'No name' restaurant, she took me shopping. The female assistants in a silk emporium, where she was well known, asked if we were married. I said in English that I was her twin brother. Lindsey replied in Chinese and they burst into helpless laughter. I later learned that she had simply said: 'He is rather simple.' Lindsey was always very honest and direct.

In the evening, we went to a very fancy restaurant for a party held for the movers and shakers in the arty set. I noticed that many white males were with beautiful Chinese women, but not vice versa. Lindsey explained that because so many Chinese men are short, European women tended to be 'heightist'. I countered that, despite being vertically challenged, I was not aware of any heightist antipathy.

Even if the Chinese had restrained Khartoum, the Darfur crisis continued. I organised a number of conferences in Whitehall, usually at RUSI, and talked at many more, ranging from the grandeur of the Oxford Union to run-down small theatres in north London. And I did a lot of punditry on radio and TV.

On one occasion I did a long interview live on Al-Jazeera (English) on China in Africa. I received a detailed email from a young woman in Hong Kong, thanking me profusely for defending her country. She said it was the first time she had responded to a TV programme. The pleasure of getting a rare fan-mail was tarnished by the footnote. She said her name was Bobo, and that she was, quote, a 'whore', adding a few of her specialities and her website. I checked that it was genuine by referring it to an IT specialist. I was often the victim of friends' practical jokes. And so I started wondering: was my TV style peculiarly attractive to the Chinese demi-monde, was Bobo into clever, if long-distance, marketing or perhaps just bright and bored, watching Al-Jazeera between turning tricks? I felt obliged to send a very short response thanking Bobo for her kind comments, and then got a longer list of more specialities, most of which I had genuinely never heard of. I was particularly confused by her mention of metal swings. I did not respond further. I forwarded Bobo's lurid email to a very old friend in Hong Kong, one of the city's most senior judges, asking if he knew Bobo. He did not respond further either.

CONCLUSION
A QUICK AND DIRTY GUIDE TO CONFLICT

Decline of the West?
The retreat of the Soviet army from Afghanistan and the revolt at Tiananmen Square were couched in implicit Cold War terms. How else could they be interpreted, after so many years of ideological conflict between capitalism and communism? Ever since the Russian revolution, most of the media, most of the time, took for granted this master pattern of good versus evil. The Cold War had conditioned the mind-set, morality and careers of nearly two generations of foreign correspondents. After the fall of the Berlin Wall, Washington, for the third time in the century, had the chance to step in and make a 'new world order', though it was not the 'end of history' as some had hoped. For a while the media generally reflected the US-inspired hopes for a 'peace dividend'.

The Soviet collapse brought knock-on effects around the world, for example in Cuba, Angola, Cambodia and the Horn of Africa. If Soviet withdrawal encouraged the old nationalisms in Eastern Europe, in the developing world it helped to display the fragility of the nation-state itself. Somalia was a classic example.

In its 'heroic' phase – the USSR in the 1930s and China in the 1950s and 1960s – communism had inflicted catastrophic damage on its own people, though little was reported to the outside world. Overall, journalism largely failed to report on the monstrous conditions in the Soviet Union and China during the Cold War, as well as their reflections in the numerous proxy wars elsewhere. The failure to cover the major tank battles in Angola was one egregious example.

At the beginning of the 1990s the US found itself in the unique position of being the sole hyper-power. America, however, could neither dominate the world nor withdraw from it. It found itself all-powerful and yet also vulnerable. Soon the country was about to enter another long ideological campaign, a substitute for the former capitalist–communist antagonism, where it would have to relearn the recent lessons of the Cold War: that military strength when misused could be highly counter-productive. Just as most media pundits failed to anticipate the imminent collapse of the Soviet Union, likewise few predicted the rise of religion as a key ingredient in modern warfare, though some would depict the rise of Islamic extremism as a crisis of modernisation, not faith.

How long would the new wars of the West continue? Years, decades, or another hundred years' war? Or would the wars of 2001–10, in the hindsight of an historian writing at the end of the twenty-first century, merely constitute a brief, if unruly, adjunct to the end of the long civil war in Europe (1914–1990)?

Many questions about the so-called war on terror remain. Why should the Anglo-Americans have bombed Iraq in the name of democracy but still support the fundamentalist dictatorship in Saudi Arabia? Secular Iraq, for example, was light years ahead in its treatment of women compared with the Saudis. Washington had stabilised autocracies in the Middle East, while preaching democracy to one and all. Professor Samuel Huntington was right in at least one sense: Islamic resurgence is mainstream, not extremist; pervasive, not isolated. The West must accommodate the Muslim 20 per cent of the world, but bolstering the dismal band of dictatorships will guarantee more floods of refugees and more terrorism from the region. The tactics of Jihadism must be fought by unified Western counter-terrorism, by hard military power on occasion, but more often by tough diplomacy and trade. Strategically it is not a war that can be won by military power alone.

So while there must be a place for muscular military responses to al-Qaeda and its various franchises, while Iraq and Afghanistan are battlegrounds many young Muslims will not want to listen to any appeals for compromise. The choice is stark. Either a deal must be struck with al-Qaeda and its adherents to withdraw all Western troops from the Middle East and Afghanistan and let Muslims decide if they really want a caliphate. Their religion, their countries, their decision – and meanwhile most will want to sell oil and trade with the West. Or a decision must be made: if this war is to going to last decades, it must be won, but by different means. A concerted Western ideological campaign must be waged akin to the strategy that won the Cold War. Soft power, now renamed 'smart power', might do a lot better than the (now retreating) occupations in Afghanistan and Iraq. The West's cultural and economic capacity might succeed where its tanks and gunships have failed, provided NATO and its allies show the patience, determination and, above all, unity which they failed to display in, for example, Afghanistan. The possible, even probable, future war with Iran may test the Western alliance to destruction.

A Western resurgence is predicated on a number of factors. It assumes the relative dominance of Western culture. This may prove relatively short-lived. Humanity is about the rise and fall of civilisations. My lawyer recently gave me a poster for my office which reads: 'Rome did not create an empire by having meetings – they did it by killing all those who opposed them.' Those days are long gone, not least for the old European empires and the new American one. The Chinese, for example, think of themselves as a dominant *civilisation* which temporarily was in abeyance. Far from Western universalism, the end of history, we are entering a new age of contested approaches to globalisation. Russia and China could become champions of a newly ascendant authoritarianism, while states such as India and Brazil challenge economically, if not ideologically.

The near-collapse of the Anglo-American financial system in 2008–9 is unlikely to prove fatal, but it will seriously hobble Western influence as it is challenged by the rise of countries such as China. The financial crash could be a culminating point when the balance of power tilts decisively towards a successful challenger. Financial crises often speed up the gradual shifting of the geopolitical tectonic plates: they are to history what earthquakes are to geology.

I'd had a privileged vantage point in examining these tectonic shifts, by working a little in China and a lot in the US. Like most Brits I found that America gave off a slightly acrid smell of brash power. Except for John Foster Dulles airport in Washington, I did not endure one bad experience in the US. The airport, however, was the turd in the punchbowl of the US–UK special relationship – though some Americans insisted that Heathrow was a mirror image of Dulles. I once attended, as the sole Brit delegate, an FBI/CIA conference with US Muslim leaders. Nearly all the males at the meeting – about sixty in all – had disturbingly elaborate slicked-down comb-overs. I was an exception with a normal haircut and a full head of hair (and my own teeth). And every Muslim, all US citizens, asked whether it was government policy for them to be searched, investigated and delayed, so that they missed their flights, even when they were supposed to be travelling abroad as missionaries to explain how wonderfully Muslims were treated in the home of the free. Dulles airport was the main target. I was last on the podium after this series of anti-airport diatribes, and I enjoyed myself hugely, and raised a few laughs (and hackles) by outlining numerous examples of extreme embuggeration at Dulles, even when I was on government business too.

My first visit to the US was many years ago to teach at Baylor University in Waco, Texas. The college – which had a good reputation for its journalism courses – was a strictly religious institution. Drinking, dancing, smoking and singing were all banned. I got away with them all, as 'English' eccentricity was considered a suitable waiver. I enjoyed the Texan charm, and even the slow-motion drawl, though in the end I could barely stop myself, as with dear friends who are chronic stutterers, from finishing everyone's sentences. I visited other southern states later, and was always impressed, 'you all', by the *Gone with the Wind* manners.

Even in California, and especially Los Angeles, when I was on a book tour, I found universal friendliness. When I was trying to flog a film script, I was initially enthralled by film people's over-enthusiasm for my project, until I realised that they were all priapically excited about everything, 24/7. I soon realised that my books and scripts were nothing special at all.

I did lots of more serious things in places such as the Pentagon, the State Department, Langley and Quantico, where my briefings once resulted in my being called 'the representative on earth of Donald Rumsfeld' (the then Secretary of State for Defense). It was strange to be attacked from the Democratic left in the inner sanctums of the US establishment. It was fascinating to discover how much opposition existed to George Bush's concept of the war on terror within the national security system as a whole.

The healthy and varied debates I witnessed within Washington were such a contrast to the stale and sinister single Washington–Zionist conspiracy so often depicted in the Middle East. I liked America, I liked Americans. In my experience they were nearly always well-meaning, earnest and diligent, while – and all Brits have to say this, playing sophisticated but weak Greeks to powerful but ignorant Rome and all that – they were often misguided. I shared the optimism at Barack Obama's victory (while irritating all my Democrat friends by pretending to claim that the Republican VP candidate, Sarah Palin, was the hottest thing since *Deep Throat*). Whether Obama could heal the military, economic and moral wounds and restore the lost American status in the Middle East was another matter.

The role of correspondents

Besides being a clumsy occasional war hack myself, I was also intellectually engaged in analysing the role of war correspondents, particularly their political impact. In 2008 I co-wrote, with Professor Phil M. Taylor of Leeds University, a major work on the subject – *Shooting the Messenger*. Phil added the academic rigour, and I chucked in a little humour and practical 'mud on my boots' experience.

Only 2 or 3 per cent of the small band of foreign correspondents become dedicated war correspondents. British TV journalist Andrew Marr defined foreign correspondents as the 'aristocracy' of the media: 'travel, excitement – and *meaning* as well; a certain sense of moral superiority, along with expense accounts'. Anthony Lloyd, a former army officer and hard-core war hack, described the 'affable clan of damaged children, a concentration of black sheep in the casino of war . . .they could fight and fuck one another with the abandon of delinquents in care, but they also looked after one another, linked by an altruistic camaraderie common to any pariah group'. From my experience, Lloyd, who worked for *The Times*, got it about right.

Journalists are rated alongside second-hand car salesmen, estate agents, and now bankers and politicians in public esteem, or lack of it, but war correspondents, especially if they secure a lot of TV 'face-time', tend to be an exception. Martin Bell was a classic British example of a highly respected and highly competent war reporter. It was Nicholas Tomalin, of the *Sunday Times*, killed in the Golan Heights in 1973, who famously remarked that all it takes is a certain way with words, a plausible manner and rat-like cunning. If only it were that easy. Just a handful survive long enough to get to the top of their profession.

In his excellent study of reporting conflict, *The Secret Life of War*, Peter Beaumont, of *The Observer* newspaper, commented on a medical assessment of his own traumas: '"The parts are wearing thin, but they haven't broken yet." Then he [the psychologist] offers the possible outcomes. "You get killed or otherwise messed up. You experience a breakdown you can't recover from. Or you get out of it. There are no other options."'

Given such odds, why do it at all? It is a mixture of professional pride, adrenalin, curiosity, maybe the lure of a Pulitzer Prize or perhaps a belief that they can have some effect in a disordered world. They probably don't do it for the money. The risk of death or losing a limb or two is too high for mere financial inducements. And freelance war hacks, the ones who most often get up close and dirty to the heart of war, often risk all for very little money indeed. The official BBC guidance is that 'no story is worth a life'. Hence all the recent survival courses and counselling for post-traumatic stress disorder.

Wars can be addictive for some; they experience the 'combat high' on which certain types of soldiers thrive. And often self-deception is involved. Death and injury always happen to the chap next to you. In the firing line, journalists, particularly the younger ones, believe they are immortal. Most soon learn the basic survival tactics, from distinguishing incoming to outgoing fire to hunches about when death is around the next corner. You learn to control and rationalise fear. Otherwise you could not function. Of course some hacks do stop functioning. But most emerge more or less unscathed psychologically. A sort of Darwinian process of self-selection operates, which ensures that most war hacks enjoy what they do, are good at it, and manage to dispel most of the ghosts which can haunt their waking hours. As with the military, war correspondents probably comprise a similar number of saints and sinners, with a minor sprinkling of barking eccentrics and the very occasional psychopath.

The 1990s idea of CNN, or now Al-Jazeera, dominating international relations is a myth. It is rare for even the most famous correspondent to be able to point to any real difference their reporting has made. Yet they can still be witnesses, recording the first draft of history, with all its flaws. I asked my friend Lindsey Hilsum for her comments. 'It is important', she said, 'that we as journalists tell the truth for its own sake, not because it's likely to change government policy.' For a North American perspective I asked Allen Pizzey, of CBS, who had shared some of my early African reporting: 'If we do our jobs properly, we negate the age-old excuse, "we didn't know", as a way to justify inaction or indifference in the face of brutality, suffering and injustice. "You did, because we told you."' Pizzey's and Hilsum's words constitute, I believe, the highest ideals of the profession.

A few brave 'soldiers of the press' who make up the 'little army of historians who are writing history from the cannon's mouth', to quote from Alfred Hitchcock's *Foreign Correspondent*, still maintain the legacy of William Howard Russell, the father of modern war reporting. In the final analysis, war reporting is not as glamorous as many Hollywood movies might suggest. It is not about victory or defeat, but death. It represents the total failure of the human spirit, and also the total failure of politicians to provide alternative solutions.

A personal note

I'd seen much of the world, and its wars, which bring out the best and worst in people. It had been a privilege but not always a pleasure, a bit like sleeping with a duchess perhaps. In both the allied terrains of sex and war, I had been more a detached observer rather than a combatant. I had embraced what maketh a man, especially a writer: war, love, poetry and poverty, the last almost a natural condition for a writer. I had become more cynical about humanity, though not all my earlier idealism had been displaced. John Humphrys, who also came from a humble background in Cardiff, and whom I got to know in Africa, became one of the most successful journalists of his generation. Yet he was always down to earth and helpful to his far less prominent colleagues, including me. He was not part of the small group of senior hacks who fancied themselves as famous media stars. As John Updike once wrote, 'Fame is a mask that eats into your face.'

John Humphrys, however, did capture something that I shared. 'I am a typical Welshman,' he said, 'who carries a little grey cloud around in my head.' On the other hand, I also learned that the worse the situation the more black humour was required, though it is up to my war-time companions to gauge whether my gallows humour always succeeded.

So why did I spend so much time trying to cover wars? I rarely did it for the money. I made very little, certainly not enough to compensate for the permanent damage I have done to my body (and perhaps my mind). I was always curious, and I hope I had a sense of adventure. That was partly satisfied, although I trust this is not yet my obituary. I doubt if I achieved anything on any major political scale. Perhaps, for example, my reporting on black taxis stalled or even prevented a piece of nasty racist legislation in apartheid South Africa. Maybe, along the way, I justifiably embarrassed one or two ministers or generals. I hope that I also developed a concept of searching after facts – truth is too grand a word – but I accept that sometimes my own prejudices got in the way. All I can say is that I did my best. Often I was on my own or with a few stout friends. I very rarely had any backing from a big organisation, although for a few years, and intermittently, the UK Ministry of Defence did provide some support for my travels. Luckily, I never needed that casualty evacuation helicopter which the military might have provided when I worked in government. For most of the decades described in this book, I would have had to make my own arrangements to walk or ride out of trouble.

I had also seen late-middle-aged hacks still addicted to war adrenalin, as sad as the alcoholism that often accompanied the condition. I have already noted that younger correspondents, and soldiers, believe they are immortal. Age and anecdotage, however, teach caution as well as endowing wisdom, often the same thing on the battlefield. I am now sixty-two, and less inclined to dash off to every war. After the removal of a brain tumour behind my right eye in 2009, I have lost most of my eyesight. I had suffered blindness in my right eye twice before, after two previous wounds; now both eyes are largely defunct. I continue to work, and trust I can still tap out the rhythms of the world with my white cane. Here, one legacy of journalism, touch-typing, helps.

War hacks are supposed to run *towards* the sound of gunfire, but sometimes you have to run *from* it, as well. And I have often felt past it, too tired, for all the hassles of getting in and out of war zones. And I worry about whether I still have the balls for it, especially if I am responsible for less experienced journalists accompanying me. To this day, I do not know whether courage is a finite capacity which can be exhausted, or whether it is like a muscle; the more often exercised the stronger it gets. I suspect it is the former.

I also grew accustomed to people saying 'just one more time', like an ageing boxer tempted into the ring. In March 2010, I led fifty volunteers to observe the elections in Sudan. It was tough going, especially in the war-ravaged south. I got everyone back safely, only to have them marooned by volcanic ash in Khartoum. It was perhaps a diplomatic success, but a personal financial disaster. Nevertheless, I wondered whether I might pioneer a niche market in blind observers for African elections.

*

A younger friend from Shere, Jean, took me to a club on a surprise night out. We had to purchase temporary membership cards. Over a drink later, Jean examined the back of the plastic membership card: 'It says the club has a strict age membership rule – thirty to sixty.' And she looked at me with mock accusation.

'Hell, Jean, I've been busted for many things, but never before for *over-age* drinking. That's almost like passive drinking.'

So my age had me seriously reflecting on my role as an occasional war correspondent. Yes, I did worry about being a voyeur, taking advantage of people *in extremis*. I believe, though, that in every case my intention was to highlight an injustice or wide-scale misery. The intention was good, although the results were usually insignificant. What did I learn personally? The experiences have changed me. Firstly, you go away for long periods and only your closest friends notice you have been away at all. It is an important ego purgative to realise how well the world functions without you. You come back from some bizarre place and all people say is: 'Why haven't you returned that book you borrowed ages ago?' Secondly, you notice how crowded the Western world is, how full of white people doing strange things. You look at your own country anew. For me, I was always fascinated by the unchanging rigmarole of the British class system. That's probably my own prejudice, my own chip on the shoulder.

In the end, what did so many years reporting or researching and lecturing on wars mean? Despite completing almost all my journalistic assignments and nearly always making at least a small profit, some of the grander schemes, such as interviewing Pol Pot or catching up with Osama bin Laden, ended in failure. That is the nature of journalism – you can't win 'em all. Here it might be apposite to quote Peter Cook and Dudley Moore.

> DUD: So would you say you've learned from your mistakes?
> PETE: Oh, yes, I'm certain I could repeat them exactly.

That would not be entirely true. So much travel, often in difficult circumstances, must have taught me something. It may be that making so many mistakes is the price I had to pay for leading such a full life. Thank you for reading about it.

INDEX